The Greening of the U.S. Military

The Greening of the U.S. Military

Environmental Policy, National Security, and Organizational Change

ROBERT F. DURANT

Georgetown University Press
WASHINGTON, D.C.

As of January 1, 2007, 13-digit ISBN numbers have replaced the 10-digit system.
13-digit   10-digit
Paperback: 978-1-58901-153-3   Paperback: 1-58901-153-8

Georgetown University Press, Washington, D.C.

Durant, Robert F., 1949–
    The greening of the U.S. military : environmental policy, national security, and organizational change / Robert F. Durant.
        p. cm. — (Public management and change series)
    Includes bibliographical references and index.
    ISBN-13: 978-1-58901-153-3 (alk. paper)
    ISBN-10: 1-58901-153-8 (alk. paper)
    1. United States—Armed Forces—Environmental aspects. 2. Military bases—Environmental aspects—United States. 3. Environmental responsibility—Government policy—United States. 4. Military privileges and immunities—United States.
    5. Environmental policy—United States. 6. Organizational change—United States. I. Title.
    TD195.A75D87 2007
    363.72'870973—dc22   2006031174

∞ This book is printed on acid-free paper meeting the requirements of the American National Standard for Permanence in Paper for Printed Library Materials.

14 13 12 11 10 09 08 07   9 8 7 6 5 4 3 2
First printing

Printed in the United States of America

To Rachel Leigh and Amy Lynn Durant,
and to the memory of Francis McLain Seely and
Jean Thompson Seely

Guide us, thy sons, aright,
Teach us by day, by night,
To keep thine honor bright,
For thee to fight.

—"Alma Mater," U.S. Military Academy, West Point

Contents

Preface

This book is a parable rife with practical lessons about the challenges, choices, and opportunities involved when contests over "principles and practicality" arise in the American political system. Moreover, it is a tale of a kind of reform that despite its implications for principles and practicality has garnered scant attention from scholars in the fields of public management, public administration, public policy, and political science. Specifically, the book's focus is on an epic and ongoing struggle to build a corporate sense of responsibility within the United States military for ensuring that its day-to-day operations promote national security without putting public health, safety, and the environment at risk. It is, in the process, a saga of the thrust-and-parry politics accompanying efforts to "green" the armed forces that began episodically during the Cold War, took on heightened salience and vigor during the Clinton years, and today competes during the George W. Bush presidency for attention and funding amid the War on Terror, insurgency wars in Iraq and Afghanistan, and a proposed and costly transformation of the military. It is also a cautionary tale showing how change is less about the power of ideas than about the protection and pursuit of political, organizational, and personal prerogatives. As such, this book is pregnant with implications for those interested in protecting national security in these challenging times without compromising public health, safety, and the environment in the process—and vice versa.

This book also is a story rife with implications for scholars concerning the adequacy of leading theories of large-scale organizational change when applied to public organizations. With a small but growing set of exceptions in the public management literature, most of what we think we know about large-scale organizational change is predicated on theoretical perspectives culled largely from research on private sector organizations. Moreover, even that literature is plagued by a variety of competing theoretical perspectives. Given this situation, the book discerns from the patterns of politics witnessed during efforts to green the U.S. military a polity-centered framework for understanding and studying large-scale change in public organizations in this and other policy domains.

I culled the data informing my analysis from documents afforded by the agencies and interest groups involved; congressional hearings; Government Accountability Office (formerly known as the General Accounting Office) and Congressional Budget Office testimony and reports; studies by the National Academy of Sciences and the National Research Council; and books, studies, and monographs by academic and military writers. In addition, I systematically reviewed all articles appearing between 1993 and 2005 in the leading industry newsletter on military affairs and the environment, the *Defense Environment Alert (DEA)*. The *DEA*'s reputation is unparalleled for its neutrality, accuracy, and commentary. Also informing the study are articles appearing in the *Washington Post*, the *New York Times*, local newspapers near military facilities where issues have arisen, a variety of law and military journals, and the *Federal Facilities Environmental Journal*.

I supplemented these data with interviews (and follow-up interviews) conducted between 1990 and 2006 with more than one hundred individuals in the public and private sectors either working in, or authorities on, the greening of the U.S. military. Interviewees included top-, mid-, and field-level officials in the Pentagon, in the military services, in regulatory agencies at the federal and state levels of government, in national and grassroots environmental organizations, and in academia. Confidentiality was offered to each of these interviewees, and most took advantage of that offer. I opted for this arrangement after realizing from initial interviews that this would be necessary in order to get candid assessments by insiders, especially from those with ties to the Pentagon. For those desiring anonymity, I typically cite organizational affiliation only. Those who waived this offer are cited by name in the book.

This said, readers should keep several points in mind. First, my occasional use of the terms "reform" or "reformers" does not connote support for any *particular* greening initiative. As public administrationists Sergio Fernandez and Hal Rainey argue, "Some ideas for change are simply ill conceived, unjustified, or pose harmful consequences for members of the organization."[1] Rather, the book assesses how well or ill suited the participants' actions are for discerning how best to ensure national security without compromising public health, safety, and the environment in the process. As such, I do not assume the military is wrong or right in resisting environmental protection issues in specific cases or that environmentalists have a monopoly on truth and virtue. Evaluations like these are context-dependent because of the complexities involved; sometimes resistance is warranted and other times it is not. What I do evaluate normatively is the extent to which the tactics used in resisting environmental and natural resources (ENR) regulations attenuate or foreclose probative deliberative processes. Absent clear-cut, willful, and substantial violations of ENR laws or indifferences to redressing them, which are noted, the key criterion in this book is the extent to which the actors involved exhibit behavior that either advances or retards a full, transparent, probative, participatory, data-driven, and results-based deliberative process regarding how best to advance both national defense and environmental protection.

Second, I break the total post–Cold War greening effort into discrete policy areas (e.g., cleanups and pollution prevention). All are part of an interrelated whole; none start from scratch. In fact, the patterns of politics witnessed in them are but the latest, strongest, and most sustained in a series of offensives since the late 1940s to try to green the military's operations in light of national security goals. Thus, the patterns of politics witnessed in these chapters were not only interrelated, in the sense that they were going on simultaneously during the post–Cold War era, but also were the latest iterations of an effort to maintain and defend any greening victories won during the Cold War and to build and expand on them by creating a beyond-compliance ethic. As such, the military was always on the counteroffensive to that historical greening offensive, an offensive given new energy by the end of the Cold War.

Third, I make frequent reference throughout the book to "the military" and "the services." As anyone familiar with the U.S. armed forces knows, significant cultural, attitudinal, and behavioral differences exist among the services. Moreover, there are significant differences in the ENR challenges faced, approaches taken, and progress made among the U.S. Air Force, Army, Marine Corps, and Navy. In fact, different services often are given lead responsibility for environmental issues depending on the extent to which they are affected by them. Although these factors historically have posed significant obstacles to joint operations, the Joint Chiefs of Staff (and through them, the Joint Staff—comprised of roughly eleven hundred officers from the U.S. Army, Navy, Marine Corps, and Air Force—which acts, among other things, as a long-term planning shop) do present collective advice to the secretary of defense. In addition, whereas the power of the military services' chiefs and secretaries has waned in the aftermath of the Goldwater–Nichols Act of 1986, the power of the chairman of the Joint Chiefs and of combatant commanders (known until 2002 as commanders in chief, or CINCs) to offer joint advice increased.[2] As such, and more for stylistic convenience throughout, I use the more conventional references to "the military" and "the services."

Fourth, I make repeated references to positions taken by the Pentagon (or, alternatively, the Department of Defense) and the military. This is not to suggest that the two positions always are taken unanimously or are synonymous. The literature on civil–military relations, for example, is replete with policy differences among political appointees in the Pentagon and the services, especially in the post–Cold War era.[3] Still, as I note in chapter 2, there is substantial evidence offered by former Pentagon officials, press observers, interviewees, and academics that the Clinton administration crafted a modus vivendi with the military: Don't push us too far and we won't push you too far. This also accounts, along with changes in circumstances, for Clinton ENR appointees occasionally taking positions that do not appear to advance greening. Here, they simply were outgunned by forces of inertia within the Pentagon. At other times, however, they agreed with the military's concerns and acted accordingly.

Even were this not the case, even some in the military contend that Goldwater–Nichols purposely decreased civilian control of the military. Typically citing no less an expert on the aims of the act than Senator Barry Goldwater, they argue that this happened in reaction to the marginalization of military expertise during the Korean and Vietnam conflicts.[4] Moreover, as public management scholars Michael Barzelay and Colin Campbell so compellingly demonstrate in their work, the Pentagon is "an organization dominated by career officials—in this case, the leaders of the armed forces."[5] Consequently, even where not noted in the text, Pentagon positions are, at a minimum, significantly informed by those held by military leaders in the services and, maximally, driven by them.

Fifth, and relatedly, I frequently use the terms "opposed to," "opponents of," or "greening opponents." Although pockets of resistance to greening per se existed in the Department of Defense, among service chiefs, and in Congress, to say that the Pentagon, the military services, or the Congress as a whole simply opposed greening is an overstatement. Consequently, when I refer to "opponents," I mean those who opposed greening on anything but the Pentagon or the military's terms (unless otherwise specified). The military services, as I will show, are adept at building leverage in Congress for pursuing what they want and stopping what they don't want. As military and intelligence affairs reporter Dana Priest writes, "The military . . . has a Capitol Hill staff of its own, the talents of which rival that of the renowned law and lobbying firms on Washington's K street."[6]

Finally, I use the term "post–Cold War" throughout the book. I am fully aware of (and sympathetic with) arguments that the tragic events of September 11, 2001, have placed the United States in a new era. Robert Kagan, for example, writes that the post–Cold War era ended on that date, calling it "the day the world for Americans changed utterly."[7] Former Secretary of State Colin Powell also has stated that those events "vaulted the U.S. past the post–Cold War period," ending the nearly ten-year interregnum wherein the nation's policy makers unsuccessfully sought a "center of gravity" or "new world order."[8] Keeping all this in mind, however, the shape of that era still remains in flux, as does support for the dominant paradigm both Kagan and Powell assumed would occur after September 11: the War on Terror.

Any project of this scope incurs substantial debt, especially to those interviewees who have been so generous with their time over the past decade and a half. Moreover, this book literally would not have happened without the support of my wife, Jennifer. Since 1993, she has compiled a nearly two-thousand-page computer database of biweekly summaries of articles (with important quotations and my commentary). Without her faith in and tireless devotion to this project, all would have been lost. Special thanks as well to Michael Maher of the University of Baltimore for his assistance in finding funding for this project. Finally, I wish to thank Gail Grella of Georgetown University Press, and series editor Beryl Radin of American University, for their valuable guidance, suggestions, and faith in this project. I also am especially indebted to the anonymous reviewers of my original manuscript. With the usual caveats applying, I hope they will agree that the final product has benefited enormously from their insights.

Notes

1. Sergio Fernandez and Hal G. Rainey, "Managing Successful Organizational Change in the Public Sector: An Agenda for Research and Practice," *Public Administration Review* 66, no. 2 (2006): 168–76.

2. During the Clinton years, there were nine commanders-in-chief, five organized on a regional basis (e.g., the U.S. Pacific Command) and four on a functional basis (e.g., the U.S. Transportation Command). A tenth unified combatant command, the U.S. Northern Command, was created after September 11, 2001. Secretary of Defense Donald Rumsfeld took umbrage at referring to any unified combatant commander as a "commander-in-chief," a title he felt reserved constitutionally to the president of the United States. He changed the title in 2002 to "combatant commander." Under the Goldwater–Nichols DoD Reorganization Act of 1986, the operational chain of command was specified to run from the president to the secretary of defense to the combatant commanders. The president can, however, direct that communications pass through the chairman of the Joint Chiefs of Staff, placing the chairman in the communications chain. Moreover, the secretary of defense can give the chairman broad oversight responsibilities concerning the activities of the combatant commanders. Still, the power of combatant commanders has grown appreciably.

3. Peter D. Feaver, *Armed Servants: Agency, Oversight, and Civil-Military Relations* (Cambridge: Harvard University Press, 2003), 2; Eliot A. Cohen, *Supreme Command: Soldiers, Statesmen, and Leadership in Wartime* (New York: Free Press, 2002); Peter D. Feaver and Christopher Gelpi, *Choosing Your Battles: American Civil-Military Relations and the Use of Force* (Princeton, NJ: Princeton University Press, 2005); Dale R. Herspring, *The Pentagon and the Presidency: Civil-Military Relations from FDR to George W. Bush* (Lawrence: University Press of Kansas, 2005).

4. See, for example, Christopher M. Bourne, "Unintended Consequences of the Goldwater–Nichols Act," *Joint Force Quarterly* (Spring 1998): 99–108.

5. Michael Barzelay and Colin Campbell, *Preparing for the Future: Strategic Planning in the U.S. Air Force* (Washington, DC: Brookings Institution Press, 2004), 129.

6. Dana Priest, *The Mission: Waging War and Keeping Peace with America's Military* (New York: W. W. Norton, 2003), 46.

7. Robert Kagan, "We Must Fight This War," *Washington Post*, September 12, 2001, A31.

8. Bill Keller, "The World According to Colin Powell," *New York Times Magazine*, November 25, 2001, http://nytimes.com/2001/11/25/magazine/25POWELL.html (November 25, 2001).

Acronyms

ACWA	Assembled Chemical Weapons Assessment
ARARs	applicable or relevant and appropriate requirements
ASTSWMO	Association of State and Territorial Solid Waste Management Officials
ATSDR	Agency for Toxic Substances and Disease Registry
BCT	BRAC Cleanup Team
BLM	Bureau of Land Management
BRAC	Base Realignment and Closure
C³P²	compliance, cleanup, conservation, pollution prevention (and technology)
CAA	Clean Air Act
Cal/EPA	California Environmental Protection Agency
CATT	Citizens Advisory Technical Team
CERCLA	Comprehensive Environmental Response, Compensation, and Liability Act
CERFA	Community Environmental Response Facilitation Act
CIA	Central Intelligence Agency
CMA	Chemical Materials Agency
CWA	Clean Water Act
CWC	Chemical Weapons Convention
CWWG	Chemical Weapons Working Group
DEC	Defense Environmental Council
DERA	Defense Environmental Restoration Account
DERP	Defense Environmental Restoration Program
DESB	Defense Explosives Safety Board
DoD	Department of Defense
DOE	Department of Energy
DOI	Department of the Interior
DOJ	Department of Justice
DRI	Defense Reform Initiative
DSB	Defense Science Board
DSMOA	Defense-State memorandum of agreement
DUSD(ES)	deputy under secretary of defense for environmental security
EIS	environmental impact statement
ENR	environmental and natural resources
EO	executive order
EPA	Environmental Protection Agency
EPCRA	Emergency Planning and Community Right-to-Know Act (Title III of SARA)

EPPs	environmentally preferred products
EPWC	Environment and Public Works Committee
ESA	Endangered Species Act
ESO	Environmental Security Office
ESPCs	energy savings performance contracts
ETI	Enhanced Training in Idaho
FEMA	Federal Emergency Management Agency
FFCA	Federal Facilities Compliance Act
FFPG	Federal Facilities Policy Group
FUDS	formerly used defense sites
FWS	Fish and Wildlife Service
FY	fiscal year
GAO	Government Accountability Office (formerly known as the General Accounting Office)
IAFWA	International Association of Fish and Wildlife Agencies
ICMA	International City Management Association
INRM	integrated natural resource management
ISO	International Organization for Standardization
ITAM	integrated training area management
JACADS	Johnston Atoll Chemical Agent Disposal System
JG-APP	Joint Group on Acquisition Pollution Prevention
LRAs	local reuse authorities (also known as local redevelopment authorities)
MHAFB	Mountain Home Air Force Base
milspecs	military specifications
MLWA	Military Lands Withdrawal Act
MMPA	Marine Mammal Protection Act
MTP	Military Toxics Project
NAAG	National Association of Attorneys General
NAS	National Academy of Sciences
NEPA	National Environmental Policy Act
NMFWA	National Military Fish and Wildlife Association
NPDES	National Pollutant Discharge Elimination System
NPL	National Priorities List
NPR	National Performance Review
NRA	National Rifle Association
NRC	National Research Council
NRM	Natural Resource Management
ODCs	ozone-depleting chemicals
OMB	Office of Management and Budget
OSD	Office of the Secretary of Defense
PAT	Process Action Team
PMCD	program manager for chemical demilitarization
R&D	research and development

R³	relative risk ranking
RAB	Restoration Advisory Board
RCRA	Resource Conservation and Recovery Act
RECs	regional environmental coordinators
RRPI	Readiness and Range Preservation Initiative
RRSEF	relative risk site evaluation framework
SAIA	Sikes Act Improvement Act
SARA	Superfund Amendments and Reauthorization Act
SERDP	Strategic Environmental Research and Development Program
TRCs	Technical Review Committees
TRI	Toxics Release Inventory
UXO	unexploded ordnance

CHAPTER ONE

A World Apart?

O n May 28, 1987, a "bombshell" launched from Western Europe flew by the windows of the Kremlin and landed near Moscow's Red Square. This bombshell was not an errant Soviet, U.S., or North Atlantic Treaty Organization test missile, but a young West German pilot named Mathias Rust flying a small Cessna airplane that had evaded the vaunted surveillance systems of the Soviet Air Defense Forces. Like the 1986 Chernobyl nuclear power plant disaster, however, the Rust incident further stoked perceptions that Soviet military might was hardly as invincible as claimed. As William Odom, former lieutenant general in the U.S. Army and director of the National Security Agency, writes, this bombshell "catalyzed a palpable change in public attitudes toward the military, replacing the services' iconlike status in the Soviet popular mind with a sense of betrayal for all the economic sacrifices made to it."[1] Adds Anatolii Chernyaev, special assistant to President Mikhail Gorbachev, the Rust incident symbolized a deeper, more enduring "moral rot" in the military stemming from the Communist Party's penchant for turning the armed forces into a "closed zone, beyond any criticism."[2]

Once the Cold War ended, all could see that the Soviet military's "warrior culture" left more than moral rot in its wake. Coining the term *ecocide* to convey the massive environmental and natural resources (ENR) devastation wrought by the Soviet military, two eminent observers write that "the armed forces' role as polluter was almost as secret as most of their weapons development program. Only a few officers were even assigned to monitor the army's treatment of nature." They add that the military had an "ingrained view of environmental protection as an unimportant, secondary business, and [were] convinced that shortcomings . . . would [only] be punished by a mild reprimand."[3]

Was this the logical consequence of an ossified, resource-strapped, and morally bankrupt totalitarian state? Hardly, if the experience of the Soviet Union's principal democratic adversary, the United States, is any guide. Wrought was a sorry toxic legacy from the Cold War that, depending on what cleanup standards are applied, will cost U.S. taxpayers between $330 and $430 billion to clean up between now and 2070.[4] Nor should anyone have been surprised. As the noted military historian, John Keegan, writes, "War is wholly unlike diplomacy or politics because it must be fought by men whose values and skills are not those of politicians or diplomats. They are those of a world apart, a very ancient world, which exists in parallel with the everyday world but does not belong to it. . . . The culture of the warrior can never be that of civilization itself."[5]

Until late in the Cold War, most U.S. citizens placed great faith in their own military's culture of the warrior. They wanted the services to do whatever it took to counteract Soviet aggression and ask questions later. When they did ask questions, however, they too came to appreciate Cicero's encomium, *Inter arma silent leges*: In a time of war, the law falls silent.[6] Apparent, too, was the source of the Pentagon's toxic legacy. Metastasizing within the U.S. military's own "closed zone, beyond any criticism" during the Cold War was a warrior culture of sovereignty, secrecy, and sinecure that thoroughly marginalized ENR values.

In terms of sovereignty, military leaders argued that they, not regulators, knew best how to reconcile environmental protection with military readiness. As such, the armed forces and their allies in Congress persistently challenged on national security and constitutional grounds the authority of federal and state regulators to hold the military accountable to ENR laws. In terms of secrecy, the military tenaciously tried to make its operations as opaque as possible to regulatory and citizen scrutiny. Among other things, the services decided what information about their activities should be released and adopted a "decide, announce, and defend" posture when taking actions affecting ENR protection. Finally, in terms of succor, the services treasured and protected their protean ties with defense contractors and subcontractors, members of Congress, and local communities near military bases, the epoxy of which was the political, financial, and psychic succor that President Eisenhower famously labeled the "military-industrial complex."

Prompted by these revelations, the first decade of the post–Cold War era (1991–2001) witnessed the most concerted, sustained, and persistent effort of the past half century to complete what several U.S. presidents, Congress, state regulators, and ENR activists tried sporadically to do during the Cold War: make the culture of the U.S. military more "like that of civilization" by fostering a corporate sense of responsibility within the armed forces for meshing ENR values with national security needs. Sought in particular was the creation of a "beyond-compliance" ENR ethic in the U.S. military. Minimally, this "green" ethic envisions the military as an exemplar showing all polluters (public and private) how to reconcile core organizational missions with ENR laws. Optimally, "greening" the military entails showing others not only how to meet existing ENR requirements but also how to exceed them proactively. Operationally, greening involves inculcating in military minds what Karl Weick refers to as "mental models" or "schema" that view ENR protection as central to national defense.[7]

The rub, of course, in the post–Cold War era was that greening meant the U.S. military had to abandon the Pentagon's Cold War ethic of sovereignty, secrecy, and sinecure in favor of a post–Cold War ethic of accountability, transparency, and resource reallocation. No easy task under the best of circumstances, this formidable effort at large-scale organizational change in the years since the end of the Cold War has been pursued amid military force restructuring, major budget cuts, and a rethinking of the services' strategic, tactical, and operational doctrines after the fall of the Soviet empire and in light of the War on Terror.[8] Nor has this task been rendered any easier during a considerable portion of this era by profound disagreements about how best to reconcile ENR values with those of national security.

Some view funding for ENR compliance, cleanup, pollution prevention, and environmental research and development projects as nondefense-related items that *divert* resources from military readiness and modernization. As such, they constitute a luxury affordable only in the best of financial times and best paid for by others (e.g., the Environmental Protection Agency, or EPA). Indeed, during the William J. Clinton and subsequent George W. Bush presidencies, the military referred negatively to its "encroachment problem." The Pentagon defines *encroachment* as anything that impinges on the military's ability to train "the way they fight," including ENR regulations, urban sprawl, and airspace conflicts with commercial airlines.

To others, greening investments are inherently defense-related expenditures that, if finessed in bad faith, actually threaten national security. Failing to anticipate the ecological, health, and safety "footprints" of military activities will cost more in the long run than averting them now. Moreover, the military will incur costly fines that divert funding from readiness and modernization coffers and risk shutdowns for violations at training grounds. These could also jeopardize the introduction of new fighting platforms that are not environmentally friendly and perpetuate costly adversarial relations with regulators.

How we reconcile these values is important in a practical sense for national defense, environmental protection, and civil–military relations, but the dilemma raises larger normative issues first addressed by James Q. Wilson and Patricia Rachal in a seminal article published nearly three decades ago. These scholars asked a provocative question: Can government regulate itself? They concluded that federal regulatory targets (like the U.S. military) were uniquely able to resist. Moreover, the consensus of the very limited amount of research conducted since is that public organizations are no more or less likely than private organizations to green themselves and to resist it strenuously by marshaling powerful allies in government.[9]

Notwithstanding the import of the issues raised by efforts to green the U.S. military in the post–Cold War era, scant empirical research exists on the topic in the public policy, public management, political science, and public administration literatures. To begin filling this vacuum, this book focuses on the patterns of politics accompanying greening efforts in seven ENR policy areas comprising the essence of a beyond-compliance ethic: (1) developing a corporate sense of ENR responsibility starting in the Office of the Secretary of Defense (OSD); (2) setting cleanup standards, priorities, and regulations to protect public health and safety; (3) transferring "clean" base properties for economic development;

(4) developing and implementing interrelated munitions and range rules under the Federal Facilities Compliance Act of 1992; (5) promoting integrated natural resource management planning on military training grounds; (6) preventing pollution, including minimizing waste, creating environmental management systems, and greening weapons systems; and (7) using nonincineration alternatives in the chemical weapons demilitarization process.

My purposes in this book are twofold. First, descriptively and analytically, I chronicle what happened and why as proponents of greening launched sustained, persistent, and multifaceted offensives to green the U.S. military during the Clinton years or to fight military counteroffensives to dull or roll back greening victories won during the Cold War era. I describe and analyze how, amid these challenges, the services and their allies adopted the ENR equivalent of the military's post–Cold War "shape, prepare, and respond" strategic doctrine to gain or regain as much stability, predictability, and security of operations as they could. As during the Cold War era, the military opposed greening on anything but the services' terms when it came to its substance, scope, and pace.[10] Produced, as a consequence, were not only mixed signals from the White House, Congress, and the Pentagon about the priority to be given greening but also a significant yet still halting, halfway, and patchwork record of progress in institutionalizing a green ethic in the U.S. military.

Second, and informed by the realpolitik revealed in this analysis, I distill the theoretical and normative implications of the greening experience in the post–Cold War era. Regarding empirical theory building, I cull from the patterns of politics accompanying the greening of the U.S. military an empirically grounded polity-centered framework for studying large-scale organizational change in the public sector, a framework suitable for elaborating and refining in future research in this and other policy domains and organizations. In terms of normative implications, I weigh competing views on the responsibilities of public organizations in general, and the U.S. military in particular, to comply with the nation's ENR laws and probe what the greening experience suggests about those obligations and their relation to U.S. national security.

I do *not* assume the military is wrong or right in resisting the substance of environmental protection issues in specific cases or that environmentalists have a monopoly on truth and virtue. Evaluations like these are context-dependent because of the complexities involved; sometimes resistance is warranted and other times it is not. My sole aim is to describe and draw lessons for practice and theory building from the behaviors witnessed across the chapters. In particular, I seek to see how well or ill suited the military's reactions were to fostering a full, fair, and open deliberative process in this important policy domain. Offered, nevertheless, is a cautionary tale about how large-scale organizational change was less about the power of ideas than about the protection and pursuit of the political, organizational, and personal prerogatives perceived by the combatants.

In the remainder of this chapter, I begin the analysis with an overview of the evidence typically offered to assess progress made in greening the U.S. military and why organizational commitment to a beyond-compliance ethic is better assessed by comparing the strategies and tactics of the military in the Cold War and post–Cold War era. I then afford a sense for the immense practical challenge involved in greening the military and in understanding the dynamics accompanying this effort theoretically by reviewing the complex, contradictory, and inconclusive nature of existing theories of organizational change in the public sector. The chapter next previews the five questions informing the analysis, the answers to which will inform the more empirically grounded and theoretically integrated polity-centered conceptual framework that I develop in this book. The chapter concludes with an overview of the remainder of the book.

Of Blind Men, Elephants, and the (Mis)Measurement of Progress

Any assessment of progress in the post–Cold War era first has to appreciate the magnitude of the challenge of greening the U.S. military. For starters, just the complex, often inconsistent, and ever-evolving nature of the eleven thousand–plus pages of codified and multimedia-based ENR federal regulations confronting the military has made realizing and charting progress difficult. Also inherently difficult is demonstrating progress in an organization as large, complex, and diversified as the Pentagon. As a 1996 study noted, the Department of Defense's (DoD) environmental restoration program is "large, diverse, decentralized, and complex," its policies and procedures are undergoing constant modification, and it must persistently respond to "many technical, political, and community-driven" challenges.[11] Still, the Pentagon repeatedly has stressed the amount of progress the services have made in the post–Cold War era in integrating environmental concerns with the nation's defense mission.

Toward a Kinder, Gentler DoD?

Sworn in as President George H. W. Bush's secretary of defense in 1989, Richard Cheney, former Republican congressman from Wyoming, White House chief of staff, and future vice president under George W. Bush, immediately began arguing that conditions were so bad at U.S. military bases that the Pentagon's mission "is no excuse for ignoring the environment."[12] He then followed up in 1990 with his vaunted "Defense and the Environment Initiative." In doing so, he noted that the Bush administration "wants the United States to be the world leader in addressing environmental problems, and I want the Department of Defense to be the Federal leader in agency environmental compliance and protection." Proclaiming the need for a corporate sense of responsibility for greening, Cheney argued that the "real choice is whether we are going to build a new environmental ethic into the daily business of defense—whether we will make good environmental actions a part of our working concerns from planning to acquisitions to management."[13]

Energized partially by Cheney's memorandum and by changes in law (e.g., the Base Realignment and Closure [BRAC] Act and the Pollution Prevention Act of 1990) and in objective circumstances (e.g., sizable cuts in the defense budget, shifting missions, and more married personnel with families on base), the DoD pointed to significant progress at its facilities by the time Bill Clinton was sworn in as the forty-second president of the United States. For example, between fiscal year (FY) 1992 and FY 1993 alone, the cumulative number of interim actions (1,015), remedial designs (524), and completed cleanups (571) at military sites increased by 49, 47, and 37 percent, respectively.

Granted, DoD expenditures for waste minimization and pollution prevention activities for FY 1992 and FY 1993 were still small (only 3 percent of all environmental expenditures). In contrast to the mid-1980s, however, they *were* on the military's radar screen. Indeed, officials reported in 1992 that their 1987 goal to reduce hazardous waste disposal by 50 percent was 80 percent completed.[14] Moreover, nearly 8 percent of that year's environmental budget went to ENR research and development, including waste minimization technologies. The Bush Pentagon also claimed that whereas the private sector's costs for hazardous waste disposal rose by 600 percent between 1987 and 1991, DoD's costs rose by only 100 percent as a result of pollution prevention. The services also had begun the process of identifying hazardous and toxic materials such as plastics and ozone-depleting chemicals (e.g., chlorofluorocarbons and halons).

Toward a Green Ethic?

The Pentagon also was not shy about reporting progressively more robust progress in greening the military during Clinton's eight years in office. By 1997, for example, William Cohen, former Republican senator from Maine and Clinton's third secretary of defense, boasted that U.S. military "forces today recognize that defense environmental protection is good management, good citizenship, good stewardship, and a good way to protect the health and welfare of our" men and women in the armed forces.[15] The next year, Sherri Wasserman Goodman—former Senate Defense Committee staffer and Clinton appointee as deputy under secretary of defense for environmental security—lauded progress made in the pollution prevention, environmental technology, and cleanup programs.[16] Also in 1998, Patricia Rivers, his appointee as DoD cleanup chief, argued that the program's efforts to involve citizens and rationalize the risk assessment process had "radically" and "positively" changed the public's and regulators' perceptions.[17] Later, in 1999, the navy's top career environmental official, Rear Adm. Andrew Granuzzo, proclaimed that the navy was "integrating environment into everything we do, not as an afterthought, but as part of the planning process."[18]

Offered to support these claims were a litany of administrative improvements in programs and processes as well as improvements in ENR outcomes. Notwithstanding the slow and daunting nature of cultural reorientation that its evaluators noted, for example, Clean Sites, Inc., a private contractor, reported in 1997 that the major component of the Pentagon's efforts—the Defense Environmental Restoration Program (DERP)—was doing well. Drawing funding resources from the Defense Environmental Restoration Account, DERP officials had established a number of "positive and encouraging [administrative reform] attributes" that were leading (as opposed to "lagging") indicators of progress in building a beyond-compliance ethic in the services. For example, DERP staff were not only "generally experienced, competent, and dedicated" but also were implementing a clear and consistent set of goals that set priorities and timetables for accomplishing them. These priorities were "consistently communicated to the ES [environmental security] staff," who in turn felt they were "well supported technically" by contractors and by the Centers of Expertise that the services had created to assist them.[19] Monitoring these efforts, moreover, was a quality assurance/quality control data system.

Similarly lauded by evaluators were the "significant improvements" made by environmental resource management personnel in areas related to the warrior culture's historical emphasis on sovereignty, secrecy, and sinecure. The services were doing better in emphasizing partnerships with regulators, improving public involvement in environmental resource management decisions, and recognizing environmental accomplishments by employees and installations. Likewise, the Pentagon pointed to administrative reforms that were speeding the transfer of closing military bases to communities for development during the first three rounds of BRAC (I, II, and III).[20]

In the process, the Pentagon claimed the services had reduced by nearly 80 percent the time needed for transfer and reuse of BRAC properties by cooperating with regulators and communities to accelerate cleanup schedules. Central to that effort, the Pentagon said, was the early involvement of stakeholders serving on Restoration Advisory Boards (RABs) at sixty-nine BRAC installations. Moreover, by 1999 even Lenny Siegel, a widely respected cleanup expert and sometimes Pentagon critic, was reporting that DoD had begun to appreciate the virtues of environmental stewardship.[21]

Military officials also marshaled statistical evidence at both the aggregate and base levels, as well as "best case" examples, to support their claims. The Pentagon even hired public relations firms to put these examples in the best light and to disseminate them as widely as possible. Consider energy conservation. Between 1985 and 1995, the DoD claimed to have reduced fuel usage by 20 percent and its average facility usage by 13.9 percent.[22] Or take pesticide use. In 1998 the EPA even awarded DoD an environmental excellence award for reducing pesticide use by 50 percent, with DoD meeting that target two years ahead of schedule.

The Pentagon also touted sizable reductions in toxic chemicals released into the environment during the Clinton years. Between 1994 and 1996, for example, the EPA's Toxics Release Inventory showed the military reducing on-site and off-site releases by over half (from 8.8 million to 4 million pounds of releases).[23] Indeed, by 1996 the services already had surpassed their goal to reduce emissions by 20 percent below 1995 levels.[24] By late 1999 the DoD's inspector general gave the department "high marks" for investing in twenty-two pollution prevention projects that produced annual returns on investment of $4.4 million and a one-time savings of $27.5 million. Indeed, the military reported in 1999 a 77 percent reduction of DoD's toxic chemical releases and off-site transfers from the original 1994 baseline. Also, in early 2000 the EPA credited the military with "significant decreases" in greenhouse gas emissions from domestic vehicles between 1990 and 1998, as well as lowered consumption of aviation fuel.[25]

Meanwhile, on the compliance and non-BRAC remediation (cleanup) sides, Pentagon officials pointed to longitudinal data that admittedly was mixed but nonetheless indicated progress in greening military operations. For instance, data collected by the EPA and published in its *State of Federal Facilities* series suggested that DoD's compliance rates with Resource Conservation and Recovery Act (RCRA) regulations improved consistently and significantly. In FY 1995, the percentage of inspected military treatment, storage, and disposal facilities *not cited* for Class I violations was 64.4 percent; by FY 1998, it was 87.5 percent; and by FY 2002, it was 96.9 percent. Likewise, military facilities increased their compliance rates with the Clean Water Act's (CWA) National Pollutant Discharge Elimination System (NPDES) permits by 21 percent between FY 2001 and FY 2002.[26]

Moreover, when Congress and environmentalists complained in the mid-1990s that too much money was going into studying DoD sites rather than cleaning them up, Clean Sites' analysis noted "reasonable progress." Using EPA's Comprehensive Environmental Response, Compensation, and Liability Information System database, their analysts concluded (with qualifications) that DoD's National Priorities List (NPL) sites were progressing toward remedy construction "at a solid pace," with the number of Superfund remedial actions completed doubling between 1992 and 1994. Furthermore, a selective marshaling of data on DoD's non–NPL Superfund sites showed a "slow, steady, upward cleanup trend over time, with the rate of increase accelerating after 1992."[27] Also, although only 30 percent of all cleanup funding went into actual cleanups in 1995, that figure spiked to over 70 percent by 1998.[28]

Finally, and more anecdotally, DoD cited examples at various facilities when claiming progress. Consider, for example, natural resource management. With DoD's 25 million acres of land containing more than three hundred threatened and endangered species and more than one hundred thousand archeological sites, Clinton appointees such as Goodman saw the institutionalization of a strong environmental stewardship ethic as critical for greening. So motivated, by 1995, DoD pointed to successes at various bases, including the Marine Corps's training base at Quantico, Virginia, and the U.S. Army National Guard's Orchard Train-ing Area in Idaho. In the former, the Pentagon argued that the corps was avoiding legal problems by protecting the dwarf wedge mussel under the Endangered Species Act. In the latter, the guard's monitoring of falcons and other protected birds permitted training schedules that avoided bird kills. Similar successes were cited at installations such as the U.S. Navy's Naval Air Systems Command test ranges, the Marine Corp's Camp Pendleton in California, and the U.S. Army's Pinon Canyon Training area at Fort Carson in Colorado.[29] Similarly, trend data collected by the Pentagon during the first term of Clinton's successor, George W. Bush, cited such advances as

- reducing the number of new notices of violation (federal and state) by 80 percent from a 1992 baseline;
- reducing hazardous waste disposal by 68 percent since 1992, with 41 percent of all solid wastes produced diverted from landfills to recycling;
- increasing the share of alternative fuel vehicles purchased to 77 percent of all non-tactical vehicles bought;
- providing drinking water to over two million persons worldwide, with less than 5 percent of that population receiving water that violated drinking water standards;
- having 83 percent of BRAC sites with cleanup remedies in place and 79 percent with cleanup actions completed in accordance with the Comprehensive Environ-mental Response, Compensation, and Liability Act (CERCLA);
- channeling over 60 percent of its ENR research and development efforts into proj-ects for sustaining ranges and range operations;
- becoming a "mentor" to other federal agencies implementing environmental man-agement systems; and
- reducing energy consumption by over 26 percent from a 1985 baseline.[30]

A Parallel Universe?

With statistics like these, the U.S. military is viewed accurately as a (if not *the*) leader among federal agencies in greening day-to-day operations. Yet evidence abounded throughout the Clinton and George W. Bush years that progress was nowhere near as broad, willingly pursued, or deeply ingrained as the Pentagon claimed. Consider, for example, a sampling of 1997–2000 headlines from the *Defense Environment Alert*. As we shall see with greater breadth, depth, and detail in subsequent chapters, these headlines exhibit the services' enduring pattern of confrontational politics:

- "Military Needs to Better Integrate Conservation and Mission Planning"
- "IG [Inspector General] Finds Funding, Training Deficient in Pollution Prevention Programs"
- "Environmental Group Pushing DoD to Release Community RAB Information"
- "Federal Court Considers Charges that Munitions Rule Is Not Protective"

- "Citizen's Group Will Fight Chemical Weapons Incineration through Defense Bills"
- "States Doubt Validity of Army Corps' Cleanup Assessments at FUDS [Formerly Used Defense Sites]"
- "Army Cited for Poor Financial Obligation Rates in BRAC Cleanups"
- "California, Navy Fight Over Latest Funding Levels for Cleanup Oversight"
- "National RAB Caucus Calls for Environmental Justice Ombudsman"
- "RAB Caucus Outlines Military Cleanup Problems, Suggests Solutions"
- "With Pollution Prevention Slashes, Army Centralizing Pollution Prevention Funding"
- "DoD Ponders Services' Slippage in Reaching Long-Term Cleanup Goals"
- "EPA Warns Defense Department of Urgent Need to Address Unexploded Ordnance Issues"
- "Senate Appropriators Criticize DoD's Cleanup Contracting Methods"
- "State Officials Blast Superfund Sovereign Immunity Report"
- "Army Warns Commands of Too Many Fines, Enforcement Actions"
- "Regulators Remain Concerned About Range Rule Risk Methodology"
- "RAB Caucus Calls for National Dialogue on Public Participation"[31]

Neither are the arguments of the Pentagon or its critics bolstered persuasively by the best practices or trend data noted earlier. For example, despite finding qualified progress, Clean Sites warned Goodman that "serious inaccuracies in data reporting and, more likely, changes in the definition of what constitutes a site investigation" made confident inferences from them problematic.[32] Nor were these problems confined to the DoD cleanup program by the end of the Clinton years.

Consider data on military facilities from four *State of Federal Facilities* reports published by the EPA between FY 1992 and FY 2000. No data on DoD compliance with any of the five statutes (the Clean Air Act [CAA], CERCLA, CWA, RCRA, and the Toxic Substances Control Act) are available for the first two fiscal years covered, making judgments problematic due to abbreviated trend lines. Moreover, compliance rates were sometimes stated in confusing double negatives (e.g., the percentage of facilities inspected that were not in significant noncompliance) that were inconsistently applied within statutes (e.g., the CWA and RCRA) or across them.

Compliance rates also ranged considerably across the statutes (from a low of 58.2 percent in FY 1998 for the CWA to 100 percent for the Toxic Substances Control Act) and within statutes over time, debunking facile generalizations about progress. For example, the up-and-down compliance rates with the CWA alone do not support the Pentagon's claims of persistent progress and inculcation of green values at all levels of the services. Yet, if DoD's persistently higher compliance levels with the CAA and RCRA since FY 1995 anchor the analysis, the claims of cynics indicting across-the-aboard problems lack credibility. Also posing significant interpretation problems were the EPA's absolute rather than standardized percentages for military facilities and its failure to break compliance rates down per service.[33]

Correcting for this latter problem in the data for the FY 2001 and FY 2002 reports (the last during the first term of the Bush administration), there was still considerable variation across the military services in compliance rates in certain areas.[34] For example, the U.S. Air Force by then was by far the most compliant with CWA/NPDES permit requirements (71.4 percent and 91.7 percent of inspected facilities in compliance in 2001 and 2002, respectively). In contrast, the U.S. Navy was the least compliant (31.8 percent and 52.2 percent of inspected facilities in compliance in 2001 and 2002, respectively). And whereas the Defense Logistics Agency reported a massive decrease of 79.1 percent in its release of Toxics Release Inventory contaminants between FY 2000 and FY 2001, the U.S. Army and U.S. Air Force reported increases of 37 percent and 45.8 percent, respectively.[35]

Even without these problems, however, the picture these data afford of ENR progress is not so much wrong as disastrously incomplete. For starters, evaluating progress on the basis of Toxics Release Inventory reporting is useful but can distort reality. These data are self-reported, do not distinguish between high and low risk pollutants, and fail to cover all types of emissions.[36] As one EPA careerist notes, "Full compliance becomes nearly impossible; most violations turn on paperwork or technical issues; [and] conformance with and interpretations of rules take precedence over environmental results."[37] Moreover, relying solely on outcome measures tells little about how much of the progress achieved, delayed, or squandered reflects attitudinal or behavioral changes by the military. As a draft EPA report notes, the "downsizing of the military is an obvious factor" driving significant reductions in greenhouse gas and toxic emissions.[38]

Further confounding assessments about cultural change is trend data relating to EPA and state inspections of federal facilities, two-thirds of which belong to the military.[39] Between FY 1993 and FY 2002, inspections for RCRA, CAA, and CWA/NPDES compliance decreased overall by 4 percent, a figure that masks RCRA and NPDES inspections going down by 18 percent and 36 percent, respectively, whereas CAA compliance inspections rose 59 percent. Even then, CAA inspections peaked in FY 1999 and decreased each year thereafter. Moreover, an EPA study published in 2000 indicates that environmental management reviews "vary greatly in thoroughness, formality and complexity, [and] . . . lack adequate environmental staff to assure adherence to environmental requirements."[40] Thus one thing is clear: You can't find compliance problems if you don't look for them or have skilled persons doing the looking.

Finally, generalizations about progress are inherently impossible from DoD's highlighting of "best practice" cases across the services. Success stories, by definition, indicate that variation exists and tell us little about the average or modal case, let alone average or modal progress. For example, the military boasted about community involvement at military sites like Fort Carson, Pendleton, Quantico, and the Sacramento Army Depot in California. Yet a 1999 national caucus of RAB community members noted that inadequate funding and restricted access to cleanup decision documents still hindered their input. Likewise, Bruce deGrazia, assistant deputy under secretary of defense for environmental quality and a Clinton appointee, testified in 1999 that the military "abides by the same standards and regulations as states, local governments and the private sector, and we have been complying for decades." Yet others vehemently took issue.[41] Ross Vincent, a leader of the Colorado chapter of the Sierra Club, for example, took the greening of the army's chemical weapons disposal program to task as a "relentless, decade-long, multi-million-dollar, taxpayer-funded, disingenuous spin campaign [that] hasn't worked. They might want to consider honesty and integrity in the future."[42] Added U.S. Senator George Voinovich (R-OH) regarding cleanups, "If a private [party] was doing what federal facilities [like military bases] are doing, people would be up in arms. Every federal agency would be on their back like a hawk and threatening to sue them."[43]

An Alternative Approach to Discerning Organizational Change

How, then, can one more confidently assess the progress made to date by the military in substituting a post–Cold War ethic of accountability, transparency, and resource reallocation for its Cold War ethic of sovereignty, secrecy, and sinecure? Arguably, a far better indicator of organizational change on this scale is to focus on whether or not the military's reactions to greening pressures in the post–Cold War era differed from those exhibited during the Cold War. To do this, any pretest-posttest assessment of comparative strategic or tactical behavior by the military has to address three interrelated questions.

First, in terms of accountability, are changes discernible in the substance, pace, and vigor of the strategies or tactics the military wielded to stymie greening on anything but these services' own terms during the Cold War? Progress in institutionalizing a green ethic would be indicated if, for example, the military seemed less prone in the post–Cold War era to challenge the expertise, authority, or constitutionality to act of federal and state regulators, to dispute and marginalize the benefits of greening relative to national defense, or to run to allies in Congress or the White House for regulatory relief.

Second, in terms of transparency and resource reallocation, are changes discernible in how open to external scrutiny the services were in the post–Cold War era and in how bent they were on preserving and using established relationships to stymie greening? Evidence of progress would include, for example, the military fighting less aggressively to keep its operations opaque to citizens, hide unflattering information from the public or state and federal regulators, and determine the timing, pace, and substance of information release. Indicative, too, would be less resistance by the military to doctrinal shifts, less predisposition by them to mobilize defense hawks in Congress to challenge greening initiatives, and less effort by Pentagon or service officials to circumvent ENR congressional committees when proposing changes to ENR laws.

Third, was the military more predisposed than during the Cold War to institutionalize a green ethic in its administrative, responsibility, and accounting structures?[44] A well-established principle in organization theory is that of alignment: Structure must follow strategy. Aligning strategy and structure "means examining virtually every facet of the organization to ensure each element [or business process or system] supports the achievement of" the organization's goals.[45] Thus, indicators of a more enduring commitment to greening than was exhibited during the Cold War would include clearer assignments of green responsibilities to units with sufficient expertise, resources, and political heft to move aggressively. Important also would be performance evaluation programs better suited to reward greening achievements and better information technology investments capable of getting information relevant to greening decisions to weapons, product, and service acquisition managers to inform their purchases.

Theoretical Perspectives on Large-Scale Change in Public Organizations

Once the extent of organizational change is ascertained, the why question immediately arises. The most parsimonious explanations, of course, should come from the theoretical literature on large-scale organizational change. As public management scholars Sergio Fernandez and Hal Rainey write, however, the organizational change literature is rife with complexities, multiple and conflicting theories, contradictory research findings, and, hence, inconclusivity.[46] What is more, with few notable and recent exceptions, this literature focuses largely on organizational change in private organizations.[47] As such, no widely accepted theory of organizational change in private or public organizations exists for one to turn for explanations and predictions.

The complexity, contradictions, and inconclusiveness of this literature notwithstanding, each of the dominant theoretical perspectives does offer a sense for how large-scale organizational change like greening the U.S. military is not a task for the meek, the impatient, or the politically unastute. Moreover, this "sense" becomes even more acute when one incorporates into conventional theoretical perspectives pertinent insights typically overlooked from other subfields, fields, and disciplines. Most salient are insights from the broader public policy, public management, public administration, comparative state building, civil–military relations, and corporate greening literatures. Each of these literatures deals in its own way with such key and traditional obstacles of organizational change as administrative conflict, displacement of existing goals, conflicting agendas, unsupportive organizational cultures, the resistance of central administrative units, and faulty or disruptive administrative reorganizations. Path dependency—the tendency for historical choices and experiences to limit change possibilities—is a formidable obstacle to success.

Rational adaptive theories (e.g., structural contingency, resource dependency, transaction cost economics, organizational learning, and common pool resources), for example, counsel organizational change agents to analyze their organization's environment.[48] They then must engage in the often daunting enterprise of aligning existing administrative structures with it in order to function effectively.[49] Moreover, although theorists see purposeful action by managers as driving change efforts like greening the military, they also see formidable environmental, political, cognitive, cultural, and resource constraints conditioning the amount of change possible.[50] This proactive perspective inheres also in the literature on the greening of business, with theorists emphasizing managerial commitment and "charismatic green leadership" or "transformational leadership." These are vital for coaxing and nurturing a beyond-compliance ethic like that envisioned for the U.S. military from reluctant employees, interest groups, and suborganizational units with conflicting organizational, policy, or personal goals.[51]

But like the sociological institutionalism literature (see below), research on corporate greening emphasizes how interaction between the firm, its leaders, and its immediate environment (i.e., its field of activity with its established goals, interest groups, and cognitive perceptual screens) is not one-way but multidirectional. Moreover, researchers taking this perspective see sense making, issue interpretation (or "issue imaging"), and enacting of the environment as vital components of an interactive leadership process.[52] Thus the environment is not so much a "given" to be coped with or that determines the behavior of actors as it is something that is malleable to change by them. Finally, like historical institutionalists (see below), corporate greening theorists also stress that sense making and interpretation by the actors involved or affected by change efforts help to explain variations in organizational evolution over time.

In turn, policy diffusion and innovation theories posit rationally strategic actors who purposively adopt new policies and programs. Those actors do so to improve their own political standing, to enhance their organization's effectiveness, to satisfy public demand for policies implemented in other jurisdictions, or to implement new ideas embraced by epistemic communities.[53] This perspective, too, has its counterpart in the corporate greening literature. There, for example, some scholars emphasize the role of information diffusion in efforts to move away from traditional top-down, command-and-control regulatory regimes and toward the adoption of environmental management systems.[54] Moreover, in both the policy diffusion and corporate greening literatures, familiar facilitators or obstacles to change arise. These include overhead administrative offices (e.g., central personnel offices), counterbureaucracies (e.g., inspectors general, the Internal Revenue Service, and the Congressional Budget Office), and competing agendas by other units in the organization(s) involved.

Meanwhile, dialectical and conflict theories of organizational change also portray strategically and tactically armed change agents, but they are seen as engaged in a sustained and formidable battle with those holding conflicting interests, ideas, agendas, and values. More precisely, the organizational world is pluralistic, marbled with conflicting interests, ideas, and values. Nor is this collision of interests inherently good or bad. Through confrontation and conflict, winning interests, ideas, and values emerge to challenge the status quo and ultimately, albeit painstakingly, displace it.[55] Similarly, recent research on corporate greening finds that social and regulatory "licenses"—that is, the intensity of public and regulatory scrutiny, along with local concerns and pressures—are critical predictors of success.[56] Recent scholarship finds increasing conflict in civil–military relations, with the services most likely to shirk change orders when they think they will not be caught or punished.[57]

Relatedly, some scholars in the rational choice literature on public agency design and evolution emphasize conflict. They suggest, moreover, that politics accompanying change may vary in domestic versus national defense policy arenas. Most researchers, for example, have found that domestic agencies change or evolve largely because of conflict among shifting interest groups and their legislative champions.[58] Yet others find that organizational evolution is largely determined in national security agencies by the efforts of presidents and bureaucrats pursuing their self-interests and "battling over agency structure far away from the Capitol steps."[59] Still others studying civil–military officers, however, assign a strong role to Congress in this domain.[60]

All this, in turn, leads to another possibility related to the dialectic-conflictual perspective: The dynamics of organizational change may be different in "hybrid" policy domains like that characterizing the greening of the U.S. military. Hybrid domains have elements of domestic and national defense policy animating them, which leads one logically to question whether change provoked by elements of both domestic ENR and national defense policy will spawn different patterns of politics from those occasioned by either domestic or national security concerns.

Meanwhile, seminal research conducted by Elinor Ostrom and her colleagues on the creation, maintenance, and change of self-regulatory institutions for common pool resources also has implications for large-scale organizational change efforts like these.[61] Her institutional analysis and development framework underscores the need for researchers to focus on the incentives for cooperation and conflict afforded by "nested" rule sets.[62] In her scheme, Ostrom identifies three primary types of rule sets: constitutional, collective choice, and operational. Respectively, these refer to foundational rules, norms, and values of a regulatory regime; policymaking, management, adjudication, and monitoring processes; and rules affecting day-to-day operational decisions in specific instances regarding the policy, management, adjudication, and monitoring or accounting processes. Logically, these rules, norms, and the incentives (material, purposive, and solidary) that they create are likely to be targets of change proponents and opponents because they help define, constrain, and facilitate what goes on in organizations.

In turn, three schools in the "new institutionalist" perspective (rational choice, historical, and sociological) offer disparate takes on path dependency and organizational change. Historical institutionalists, for example, disdain the focus of rational choice institutionalists on single organizations. They focus on the *"conjoint* impact of multiple institutions" on organizational and policy development.[63] "There is a tendency," Paul Pierson and Theda Skocpol write, "to doubt the power of many claims about institutional effects [and hence, organizational change] that rest solely on an analysis of that institution in isolation . . . [so] research . . . typically focuses on the interplay among multiple organizational actors in multiple institutional settings."[64] Also unlike rational choice institutionalists, sociological institutionalists avoid a focus on single organizations, instead stressing that organizational change depends on changes in *configurations* of policies, formal institutions, and organizational structures over time. In their most famous construct they posit change occurs through "mimisis": the adoption of changes made in "leading" organizations to gain legitimacy.

To this notion of configuration, one might infer from new institutionalist scholars such as Michael Cohen, James March, and Johan Olsen that change is constrained by the constellation of several internal and external forces.[65] Conceptually, these include decision structures, access structures, entry times, energy loads, and energy distributions. Respectively, these are defined as who has the authority to make decisions; the ability of other issues to be linked to change efforts; the timing of when issues arrive; the resources available to pursue the change; and the relative distribution of power, resources, and influence among proponents and opponents of change within an organization. Whether change is incremental, nonincremental, or totally stymied thus rests precariously on the difficult task of linking these factors together.

Relatedly, students of American political development working in this genre disagree with those in the more proactive conflictual model of organizational change. The latter typically see winning interests, ideas, and values challenging and replacing the status quo in the short term. Granting that change can occur on a scale even greater than greening the military, state-building theorists such as Stephen Skowronek contend that these frequently (or at least for very long periods of time) produce "halfway, halting, and patchworked" structures and outcomes. Akin to rational choice theorists, they also say this happens because combatants negotiate structures, processes, and procedures that allow all sides to continue pushing their claims and guard their interests in the future.[66]

Moreover, for Skowronek, particular rhythms of contestation exist to produce this result. These start with the recognition that existing structures are misaligned with new needs, a situation that scholars studying state building call a "historical-structural mismatch." Needed in this instance is the presence of leadership willing to tackle these misalignments after assessing the costs and benefits to themselves of acting. Once made, a decision to launch a reform effort then occasions offensives by proponents, counteroffensives by opponents, crises of authority about correct structures, and bargaining toward a resolution of the crisis. Bargaining in turn produces some progress toward reform but leaves the kind of halting, halfway, and patchworked structures, processes, and procedures noted above. Inadequate for meeting the new needs identified by reformers (or change agents), these misaligned structures become the grist for the next round of calls for reform.

At the same time, rational choice institutionalists offer much to think about regarding obstacles to large-scale organizational change efforts.[67] Winning legislative (or "enacting") coalitions, they aver, are uncertain about what the future may bring when creating an agency or program. In particular, they fear later efforts to change their original intent. These may come from legislators who hold different policy preferences from their own (i.e., "coalitional drift"), from bureaucrats implementing laws differently from their intent (i.e., "agency drift"), and from presidents unsympathetic with their aims. Consequently, when creating agencies, passing legislation, or reauthorizing statutes, legislators (and presidents) impose administrative structures, processes, and procedures that make significant organizational changes difficult. Meanwhile, opponents of a policy, program, or agency do the same, bent on increasing transaction costs for the winning coalition.

Coming from an even more reactive perspective to an extreme are theorists associated with organizational ecology theory. They see organizations as fitting within their environment, with only those "selected" by it surviving. Recently, however, some organizational ecologists have relaxed the assumption that organizational adaptation rarely occurs because of conscious intervention by change agents.[68] These researchers posit "intentional variations" in organizational structures, routines, and traditions, with change agents emulating only *successful* small-scale initiatives in similar organization. As such, large-scale change only comes in reaction to shocks to these systems (e.g., the end of the Cold War), because of large-scale forces beyond any organization's control and to which it must adapt or die, or because of similarly inspired shifts in what policy analysts call issue valence, salience, proximity, and boundary effects. Respectively, these refer to the amount of attention given to an issue by positive or negative perceptions of affected persons or policies, the import of the issue to citizens, how likely an issue is to affect given actors, and the linking of issues to other issues (e.g., linking environmental concerns to national security policy).[69]

Finally, life-cycle theorists emphasize natural rather than planned changes as organizations move through a linear aging or maturation process.[70] As Andrew Van de Ven and Scott Poole explain, "Change is inherent; the developing entity has within it an underlying form, logic, program, or code that regulates the process of change and moves the entity from a given point of departure toward a subsequent end that is prefigured in the present state."[71] These scholars are joined by some researchers studying corporate greening. They posit the existence of a naturally progressive set of stages through which corporations evolve on the way to a beyond-compliance ENR ethic. Greening is portrayed as gathering in momentum rather than moving in fits, starts, and reversals.[72] Also marbled throughout the literature on civil–military relations and the greening of corporations is an emphasis shared by sociological institutionalists and life-cycle theorists on the power of organizational cultures, power most likely to hinder if not halt organizational change unless deftly countered and recrafted by change agents.[73]

Toward a Polity-Centered Theoretical Perspective on Large-Scale Change in Public Organizations

Given the relative paucity of studies on public organizations, as well as the complexity, contradiction, and inconclusivity in the literature on private organizations, discerning a more empirically grounded conceptual framework for understanding large-scale change in public organizations is substantively, normatively, and theoretically overdue. This is especially true in policy areas such as the greening of the U.S. military that are vastly understudied, poorly understood, and yet can have life-and-death consequences for service members and civilians alike. As Edella Schlager contends, conceptual frameworks "direct the attention of the analyst to critical features of the social and physical landscape . . . provid[ing] a foundation for inquiry by specifying classes of variables and general relationships among them. . . . [As such,] frameworks attempt to identify the universal elements that any theory relevant to the same kind of phenomena would need to include."[74] Consequently, the aim of conceptual frameworks is less to test the validity of particular theories than to discern what each has to offer in explaining and predicting the phenomena under study and as a compass for future research.

With this aim in mind, scrutiny of the dynamics witnessed in greening the U.S. military in the post–Cold War era suggests that a polity-centered perspective of large-scale change in public organizations is promising. As offered by students of comparative state building, a polity-centered perspective portrays a nation's polity, especially its interest groups, politicians, and political parties, as the "primary locus of action" driving the evolution of national systems and policies.[75] Stressed also is how the "institutional configurations of governments"—that is, their structures, processes, and procedures—condition a nation's capacity to affect change.[76]

Critics, as well as the dynamics of the greening experience, however, suggest that existing polity-centered approaches inordinately privilege "high politics over bureaucratic politics."[77] As such, they must incorporate a more robust account of how policy, administrative, and political contexts influence change. The polity-centered framework developed in this book does this in unprecedented ways by integrating key aspects of and concepts from the organizational change, public policy, comparative state-building, public administration, public management, corporate greening, and civil–military relations literatures reviewed in the previous section. Rendered is a more complete understanding of how policy, administrative, and political factors interacted to affect large-scale change in building a beyond-compliance ethic in the U.S. military in the post–Cold War era, and how this framework might help inform future research on change in public organizations in general.

The details, relationships, and logic of this polity-centered theoretical perspective will be explained and linked more robustly to both competing sets of theories on organizational change and to the collective dynamics of the greening experience in the concluding chapter of this book. For now it suffices to say that the answers to five research questions afford the logic and concepts informing this perspective on large-scale organizational change. First, was there a discernible and consistent trajectory or rhythm to the patterns of politics animating the struggle to green the U.S. military? Second, what animated the behaviors of the participants in pursuing these patterns of politics? Third, what specifically did they fight over? Fourth, what tactics were used to fight these battles? Finally, what implications did these battles have for the substance, scope, pace, and durability of greening in the post-Clinton years?

Identified and hiked to conceptual levels informed by the various theoretical perspectives summarized in this chapter is a consistent trajectory of contestation. It is a trajectory animated by recurring motivational patterns among the actors involved, focused on the persistent targeting for change of particular sets of rules, and exhibiting a recurring set of strategies and tactics. In terms of practice, these patterns of politics left in their wake misaligned structures, processes, and procedures that sorely compromised the institutionalization of a beyond-compliance ethic in the U.S. military in the post–Cold War era. More theoretically, they offer the grist for developing not only a polity-centered theoretical perspective on large-scale organizational change in the U.S. military but also a theoretical perspective suitable for testing, refining, and elaborating in research on public organizations in general. Normatively, they beg attention to the responsibilities of public agencies when they become regulatory targets.

What Follows

With the preceding as background, and to afford overall context for the case analyses that follow, chapter 2 explores the broader challenges to the military's ethic of "sovereignty, secrecy, and sinecure" regarding environmental protection posed by the end of the Cold War. I discuss how the post–Cold War era brought new military threats that occasioned significant strategic, operational, and tactical choices. In the process, I review how these placed day-to-day military activities more squarely than ever within the crosshairs of ENR statutes and of more aggressive post–Cold War ENR regulators. I also show how the services' reluctance to move beyond a "Cold War lite" budget allowed opponents to portray costs for greening as compromising military readiness and weapons acquisitions.

In the next seven chapters I analyze the patterns of politics driving, and driven by, the conflicts over reconciling ENR and national security values which followed during the remainder of the Clinton era. Organizing the chapters are the relevant ENR questions that had to be resolved in each case. I also conclude each chapter with a discussion hiking to conceptual levels the answers to the five major research questions informing the polity-centered framework. Taken together, these chapters show substantively and conceptually how mixed signals, misalignments of structures with green strategies, and the political dynamics that spawned them made realizing a corporate sense of responsibility for a beyond-compliance ethic problematic in the post–Cold War era. They also show how the patterns of politics witnessed can most profitably be understood by integrating concepts from a variety of theoretical perspectives on organizational change, rather than from just one.

In chapter 3 I describe how despite the compromised ENR regulatory regime that was becoming more aggressive in its zeal toward the U.S. military, these shocks and minishocks catalyzed early, profound, and conflict-producing offensives and counteroffensives within the Pentagon. This happened as the Clinton administration tried to create a corporate ENR ethic in the E-Ring prior to when the Republicans became a majority in Congress in 1995.[76] They then continued in various guises in the Pentagon throughout the Clinton years. In chapters 4, 5, and 6 I deal with the patterns of politics involved in efforts, respectively, to define cleanup sites, set standards and priorities for cleaning them up, and transfer them for economic development amid the downsizing of the U.S. military. I then focus in chapter 7 on the dynamics of change efforts related to holding the armed forces accountable for natural resource management while ensuring that service members "train the way they fight." In the next two chapters I analyze battles accompanying efforts to destroy the nation's chemical warfare stockpile (chapter 8) and to introduce pollution prevention and energy conservation measures at U.S. military bases (chapter 9). Chapter 10 then offers a postscript chronicling the travails of greening during the first six years of the George W. Bush administration.

The book concludes in chapter 11 with a discussion of the practical and theoretical lessons learned from the analysis. After an extended discussion that cuts across the cases to reinforce and integrate the logic and concepts discerned from them, I offer a more concise rendition of a polity-centered framework on organizational change in the U.S. military. I offer it in the hope that others will test, elaborate, and refine it in future research on the military and in public organizations and policy arenas more broadly. I conclude the chapter with a discussion of the study's implications for the future of reconciling ENR and national security values in the post–September 11 era. I argue that a commitment to reconciling ENR and national security values is nowhere near as strong as it should be today in the Pentagon and the U.S. military. Bequeathed to the post-Clinton era was less a green ethic of accountability, transparency, and resource reallocation than an ethic to ensure stability, predictability, and security of operations until regulatory relief was possible. Consequently, proponents of a beyond-compliance ethic will have their work cut out for them regardless of who controls the White House or

Congress. Because of the complexity involved in ENR regulation, however, judging the performance of the military in the future should not be based on simplistic notions that resistance is inherently good or bad. Rather, it should be geared toward assessing the services' fidelity to democratic processes that they frequently have tried to breach in the post–Cold War era. Finally, I argue that reconciling ENR and national security values is a necessity, not an option, in the post–September 11 era.

Notes

1. William Odom, *The Collapse of the Soviet Military* (New Haven, CT: Yale University Press, 1998), 108.
2. Ibid. Mikhail Gorbachev felt that the military had staged the incident to embarrass him in retaliation for his efforts to end the Communist Party's open-ended funding of military budgets.
3. Murray Feshbach and Alfred Friendly Jr., *Ecocide in the USSR: Health and Nature Under Siege* (New York: Basic Books, 1992), 172.
4. Stephen I. Schwartz, ed., *Atomic Audit* (Washington, DC: Brookings Institution Press, 1998), 3. This includes cleanups at the departments of Defense and Energy facilities. The military's projected share of this total is approximately $30 billion. Moreover, between 1984 and 1997 the military had already spent $16 billion on cleanups at active bases alone (excluding DoD research facilities and formerly used defense sites). Predictions of future costs, however, have been notoriously underestimated in the past. For example, the DoD inspector general has found that average cleanup costs at closing bases are typically 60 percent higher than estimated originally.
5. John Keegan, *A History of Warfare* (New York: Alfred A. Knopf, 1993), xvi. Keegan is referring to a battlefield ethos or mindset, not to the perceptions of the military elites as to their role. This should not be confused with the evolution in civil–military relations that has taken place among military professionals over time, and that Samuel P. Huntington chronicled in his 1957 classic, *The Soldier and the State: The Theory and Politics of Civil-Military Relations* (Cambridge, MA: Harvard University Press).
6. Although it exaggerates to say that ENR laws were ignored, they clearly took a backseat to the military's production ethic during the Cold War.
7. Karl Weick, *Sense-making in Organizations* (Thousand Oaks, CA: Sage, 1995). As Kelman summarizes, these are also called "knowledge structures"; they "create a composite picture of what a situation is 'about,' which can then be used" to guide interpretation of appropriate behavior. See Steven Kelman, *Unleashing Change: A Study of Organizational Renewal in Government* (Washington, DC: Brookings Institution Press, 2005), 25–26.
8. Large-scale organizational change is also referred to in the literature as "organizational transformation." It is defined as "initiatives involving large-scale, planned, strategic, and administrative change." See Sergio Fernandez and Hal G. Rainey, "Managing Successful Organizational Change in the Public Sector: An Agenda for Research and Practice," *Public Administration Review* 66, no. 2 (2006): 168–76.
9. James Q. Wilson and Patricia Rachal, "Can the Government Regulate Itself?" *Public Interest* 46 (Winter 1977): 3–14. Similar findings are reported in Robert F. Durant, *When Government Regulates Itself: EPA, TVA, and Pollution Control in the 1970s* (Knoxville: University of Tennessee Press, 1985); Aseem Prakash, *Greening the Firm: The Politics of Corporate Environmentalism* (Cambridge: Cambridge University Press, 2000). Indeed, recent research by Terry Davies and Karen Probst has found that government agencies are responsible for 5 and 7 percent, respectively, of all nitrogen dioxide and sulfur dioxide emissions in the United States. Moreover, two-thirds of all facilities in significant noncompliance with the Clean Water Act are public entities. See Terry Davies and Kate Probst, *Regulating Government* (Washington, DC: Resources for the Future, 2001).

10. Although pockets of resistance to greening per se existed in the Department of Defense, the Pentagon, and in Congress, to say that the Pentagon, the military services, or Congress as a whole simply opposed greening is an overstatement. Consequently, when this book refers to "opponents" of greening, it refers to those who opposed it on anything but the Pentagon or military's terms (unless otherwise specified).

11. Clean Sites, Inc., "Independent Management Analysis of the Department of Defense Environmental Restoration Program: Summary Report for the Deputy Under Secretary of Defense (Environmental Security)," Alexandria, VA, 1996, http://www.dtic.mil/envirodod/brac/publish.html#CleanSites (January 5, 1997).

12. Seth Shulman, *The Threat at Home: Confronting the Toxic Legacy of the U.S. Military* (Boston: Beacon Press, 1992), 115, 118.

13. Ibid.,115–16, 118.

14. Thomas E. Baca, Deputy Assistant Secretary of Defense (Environment), testimony before the Senate Armed Services Committee, Committee on Appropriations, Subcommittee on Defense, Washington, DC, May 12, 1992.

15. "Cohen Defends Military Environmental Programs," *Defense Environment Alert (DEA)* 5, no. 10 (May 7, 1997): 23.

16. "Goodman Creates Board to Craft New Long-Term Environmental Strategy," *DEA* 6, no. 5 (March 10, 1998): 3, 21. Significantly, while Goodman (an attorney specializing in environmental litigation while in private practice) was working from 1987 to 1990 as a majority staff member for the chair of the Armed Services Committee, Senator Sam Nunn (D-GA). In that capacity, she had primary oversight of the Department of Energy's defense and environmental programs. Although the Department of Energy had ENR problems where her expertise was clear, Clinton appointed Goodman to the DoD, where she served during his entire presidency. As such, Goodman and her greening initiatives will be centrally featured in this book.

17. "Rivers Says Public Involvement, Risk Ranking Improved Military Cleanups," *DEA* 6, no. 8 (April 21, 1998): 22.

18. "Navy Official Sees Service 'Turn the Corner' on Environment," *DEA* 7, no. 25 (December 14, 1999): 16.

19. Clean Sites, Inc., "Independent Management Analysis of the Department of Defense Environmental Restoration Program."

20. Office of the Assistant Deputy Under Secretary of Defense for Environmental Cleanup, *Fast-Track Cleanup Successes and Challenges, 1993–1995* (Washington, DC: Department of Defense, January 1996), 2. Also available online at http://www.dtic.mil/envirodod/Policies/RAB/fast.htm. BRACs were approved in five rounds: BRAC I (1988), II (1991), III (1993), IV (1995), and V (2005).

21. "DoD Cleanup Tab to Exceed $50 Billion, Researchers Predict," *DEA* 3, no. 20 (October 4, 1995): 17–18.

22. "DoD Background Paper on a National Security Provision for the Proposed Climate Change Protocol," *DEA* 5, no. 20 (September 23, 1997): 4. This is measured in terms of BTUs consumed per gross square foot of floor area.

23. "DoD Reports Continuing Decrease in TRI Emissions for 1995–96,"*DEA* 6, no. 13 (June 30, 1998): 24.

24. "Services Reject Proposal to Centralize Dollars for Acquisition P2," *DEA* 6, no. 16 (August 11, 1998): 3–4.

25. "Inventory Indicates DoD Greenhouse Gas Emissions Lowered," *DEA* 8, no. 5 (March 7, 2000): 6.

26. Statistics for this paragraph are taken and collated from EPA, *The State of Federal Facilities: An Overview of Environmental Compliance at Federal Facilities, FY 1995–96* (Washington, DC: Office of Enforcement and Compliance Assurance, 1998); EPA, *The State of Federal Facilities: An Overview of Environmental Compliance at Federal Facilities, FY 1997–98* (Washington, DC: Office of Enforcement and Compliance Assurance, 2000); EPA, *The State of Federal Facilities: An Overview of Environmental Compliance at Federal Facilities, FY 2001–2002* (Washington, DC: Office of Enforcement and Compliance Assurance, 2004), 15.

27. Clean Sites, Inc., "Independent Review of the Department of Defense Environmental Restoration Program: Program Performance Report for the Deputy Under Secretary of Defense (Environmental Security)," Alexandria, VA, June 30, 1996, 23, 12.

28. "Goodman Creates Board to Craft New Long-Term Environmental Strategy," *DEA* 6, no. 5 (March 10, 1998): 3.

29. "Text: Navy Letter and Report on Environmental Planning," *DEA* 4, no. 6 (March 20, 1996): 8; "Environmental Security: Introduction," 1996, 5, http://www.dtic.mil/execsec/adr96/chapt _15.html.

30. Raymond F. DuBois, deputy undersecretary of defense (Installations and Environment), statement before the Subcommittee on Military Construction of the Senate Appropriations Committee, Washington, DC, March 30, 2004. Each year on Earth Day, the secretary of defense also issues environmental awards and celebrates previous year ENR accomplishments. In addition, each service issues awards each year recognizing ENR efforts and accomplishments in their respective branches.

31. *DEA* 4, no. 3 (February 7, 1996): 14–15; *DEA* 5, no. 22 (October 21, 1997): 6–7; *DEA* 6, no. 3 (February 10, 1998): 14; *DEA* 6, no. 7 (April 7, 1998): 14; *DEA* 6, no. 7 (April 7, 1998): 20; *DEA* 7, no. 2 (January 26, 1999): 10; *DEA* 7, no. 2 (January 26, 1999): 3; *DEA* 7, no. 2 (January 26, 1999): 4–5; *DEA* 7, no. 2 (January 26, 1999): 12–13; *DEA* 7, no. 2 (January 26, 1999): 13; *DEA* 7, no. 4 (February 23, 1999): 11; *DEA* 7, no. 8 (April 20, 1999): 3; *DEA* Special Report (May 6, 1999); *DEA* 7, no. 11 (June 1, 1999): 10; *DEA* 7, no. 21 (October 19, 1999): 15–16; *DEA* 7, no. 25 (December 14, 1999): 10–11; *DEA* 7, no. 13 (June 29, 1999): 3–4; *DEA* 7, no. 15 (July 27, 1999): 18–19.

32. Clean Sites, Inc., "Independent Management Analysis of the Department of Defense Environmental Restoration Program."

33. EPA, *The State of Federal Facilities: An Overview of Environmental Compliance at Federal Facilities, FY 1993–94* (Washington, DC: Office of Enforcement and Compliance Assurance, 1996).

34. EPA, *The State of Federal Facilities: An Overview of Environmental Compliance at Federal Facilities, FY 2001–2002.*

35. Ibid., 44. EPA issued its FY 2002 to FY 2004 report in November 2005. Overall, a slight increase in federal and state inspections occurred, but levels were still significantly below Clinton-era levels across all statutes and were falling for CWA inspections. The tendency for both under- and overreporting was stressed. Curiously, of those inspected, compliance rates involving significant violations went down (in some cases significantly) for all services, except when CWA/NPDES violations were involved. Moreover, variation in compliance rates was high among the services, with a nearly 40 percent gap for the CWA and a range of 88 to 94 percent for RCRA.

36. Rosemary O'Leary, Robert F. Durant, Daniel J. Fiorino, and Paul S. Weiland, *Managing for the Environment: Understanding the Legal, Organizational, and Policy Challenges* (San Francisco: Jossey-Bass, 1999), chap. 12.

37. Daniel J. Fiorino, *The New Environmental Regulation,* (Cambridge, MA: MIT Press, 2006), 194.

38. "Inventory Indicates DoD Greenhouse Gas Emissions Lowered," *DEA* 8, no. 5 (March 7, 2000): 6.

39. EPA, *The State of Federal Facilities: An Overview of Environmental Compliance at Federal Facilities, FY 2001–2002,* 22.

40. "EPA Releases Findings on Environmental Management Systems," *DEA* 8, no. 2 (January 25, 2000): 18.

41. "DoD Supports Waiver of Sovereign Immunity for Clean Water Act," *DEA* 7, no. 21 (October 19, 1999): 8.

42. "Colorado CAC Backs Alternative Chem Demil Technology," *DEA* 7, no. 21 (October 19, 1999): 6.

43. "DoD Supports Waiver of Sovereign Immunity for Clean Water Act."

44. Respectively, these refer to the following: Who does what? Who is responsible for what with what resources? Who holds them accountable in what ways? James D. Thompson, *Organizations in Action* (New York: McGraw-Hill, 1967). For an insightful example of the application of these

concepts to reform on the Pentagon, see Fred Thompson and Larry R. Jones, *Reinventing the Pentagon: How the New Public Management Can Bring Institutional Renewal* (San Francisco: Jossey-Bass, 1994).

45. John Kamensky, "Levers of Alignment," March 20, 2002, www.aspanet.org/publications/ COLUMNS/archives/2002/kamensky0320.html (April 25, 2002).

46. Fernandez and Rainey, "Managing Successful Organizational Change in the Public Sector." These authors note that over a million studies of organizational change have appeared in academic journals.

47. Exceptions include Daniel A. Mazmanian and Jeanne Nienaber, *Can Organizations Change? Environmental Protection, Citizen Participation, and the Corps of Engineers* (Washington, DC: Brookings Institution Press, 1979); Donald P. Warwick, *A Theory of Public Bureaucracy: Politics, Personality, and Organizational Change in the State Department* (Cambridge: Harvard University Press, 1975). More recent research on public sector change efforts stressing the role of leadership include Sanford F. Borins, *Innovating with Integrity: How Local Heroes are Transforming American Government* (Washington, DC: Georgetown University Press, 1998); Jameson W. Doig and Erwin C. Hargrove, eds., *Leadership and Innovation: Entrepreneurs in Government*, abridged ed. (Baltimore: Johns Hopkins University Press, 1990). Other noteworthy studies of planned organizational change in public organizations include John M. Bryson and Sharon R. Anderson, "Applying Large-Group Interaction Methods in the Planning and Implementation of Major Change Efforts," *Public Administration Review* 60 (2000): 143–62; Richard Chackerian and Paul Mavima, "Comprehensive Administrative Reform Implementation: Moving Beyond Single Issue Implementation Research," *Journal of Public Administration Research and Theory* 11 (2000): 353–77; Bonnie G. Mani, "Old Wine in New Bottles Tastes Better: A Case of TQM Implementation in the IRS," *Public Administration Review* 55 (1995): 147–58; Peter J. Robertson and Sonal J. Seneviratne, "Outcomes of Planned Organizational Change in the Public Sector: A Meta-Analytic Comparison to the Private Sector," *Public Administration Review* 55 (1995): 547–58; Lois R. Wise, "Public Management Reform: Competing Drivers of Change," *Public Administration Review* 62 (2002): 555–67. Two outstanding views of organizational evolution in ENR agencies are Jeanne Nienaber Clarke and Daniel C. McCool, *Staking Out the Terrain: Power and Performance among Natural Resource Agencies* (Albany: State University of New York Press, 1996); and Andrew J. Hoffman and Marc J. Ventresca, eds., *Organizations, Policy, and the Natural Environment: Institutional and Strategic Perspectives* (Stanford, CA: Stanford University Press, 2002).

48. This section incorporates this diverse literature into a framework articulated by Fernandez and Rainey that sorts traditional organizational change literature into six general categories: rational adaptive theories, institutional theories, life-cycle theories, ecological and evolutionary theories, policy diffusion and innovation models, and dialectical and conflict theories of change.

49. See, for example, Paul R. Lawrence and Jay W. Lorsch's contingency theory (*Organization and Environment: Managing Differentiation and Integration* [Boston: Graduate School of Business Administration, Harvard University, 1967]), the structural contingency framework developed by Thompson (*Organizations in Action*), resource dependence theory (Jeffrey Pfeffer and Gerald R. Salancik, *The External Control of Organizations* [New York: HarperCollins, 1978]), transaction cost economics (Oliver E. Williamson, "The Economics of Organization: The Transaction Cost Approach," *American Journal of Sociology* 87 [1981]: 548–77), a significant research project on organizational learning spawned by the work of Richard M. Cyert and James G. March (*A Behavioral Theory of the Firm* [Upper Saddle River, NJ: Prentice Hall, 1963]), and an important literature on common pool resource theory (Elinor Ostrom, *Governing the Commons: The Evolution of Institutions for Collective Action* [Cambridge: Cambridge University Press, 1990]).

50. Andrew H. Van de Ven and Marshall Scott Poole, "Explaining Development and Change in Organizations," *Academy of Management Review* 20 (1995): 510–40; Cyert and March, *Behavioral Theory of the Firm*; James G. March and Herbert A. Simon, *Organizations* (New York: John Wiley & Sons, 1958).

51. See Thomas Gladwin, "The Meaning of Greening: A Plea for Organizational Theory," in *Environmental Strategies for Industry*, ed. Kurt Fischer and Johan Schot (Washington, DC: Island Press, 1993); Richard Daft, *Organization Theory and Design* (St. Paul, MN: West Publishing, 1992); and Joel Hirschhorn and Kirsten Oldenburg, *Prosperity Without Pollution: The Prevention Strategy for Industry and Consumers* (New York: Van Nostrand Reinhold, 1991).

52. Neil Gunningham, Robert A. Kagan, and Dorothy Thornton, *Shades of Green: Business, Regulation, and the Environment* (Stanford, CA: Stanford University Press, 2003); Hoffman and Ventresca, *Organizations, Policy, and the Natural Environment*; Prakash, *Greening the Firm*; Peter T. Robbins, *Greening the Corporation: Management Strategy and the Environmental Challenge* (London: Earthscan Publications, 2001).

53. Jack L. Walker, "The Diffusion of Innovations Among the American States," *American Political Science Review* 63 (1969): 880–99; Frances S. Berry, "Sizing Up State Policy Innovation Research," *Policy Studies Journal* 22 (1994): 442–56; Frances S. Berry and William D. Berry, "Innovation and Diffusion Models in Policy Research," in *Theories of the Policy Process*, ed. Paul A. Sabatier (Boulder, CO: Westview Press, 1999).

54. See, for example, Jennifer Nash, "Factors that Shape EMS Outcomes in Firms," in *Regulating from the Inside: Can Environmental Management Systems Achieve Policy Goals?* ed. Gary Coglianese and Jennifer Nash (Washington, DC: Resources for the Future, 2001); Jan Mazurek, "Third-Party Auditing of Environmental Management Systems," in *Environmental Governance Reconsidered: Challenges, Choices, and Opportunities*, ed. Robert F. Durant, Daniel J. Fiorino, and Rosemary O'Leary, 455–81 (Cambridge, MA: MIT Press, 2004).

55. Van de Ven and Poole, "Explaining Development and Change in Organizations."

56. Gunningham, Kagan, and Thornton, *Shades of Green*. Social license refers to organizations pressured by interest groups in their environment to green their operations. Regulatory license refers to the centrality of combat between federal, state, and local regulators in bringing change in organizational behavior like that posited for military services.

57. The military services as "agents" engage in shirking (i.e., they are unresponsive to the desires of presidents as "principals") whenever they suspect that their behavior will not be detected and punished (also see Eliot A. Cohen, *Supreme Command: Soldiers, Statesmen, and Leadership in Wartime* (New York: Free Press, 2002), Peter D. Feaver, *Armed Servants: Agency, Oversight, and Civil-Military Relations* (Cambridge, MA: Harvard University Press, 2003); Peter D. Feaver and Christopher Gelpi, *Choosing Your Battles: American Civil-Military Relations and the Use of Force* (Princeton, NJ: Princeton University Press, 2005); Dale R. Herspring, *The Pentagon and the Presidency: Civil-Military Relations from FDR to George W. Bush* (Lawrence: University Press of Kansas, 2005).

58. Terry Moe, "The Politics of Bureaucratic Structure," in *Can the Government Govern?* ed. John E. Chubb and Paul E. Peterson (Washington, DC: Brookings Institution Press, 1989), 267–329; Terry Moe, "The Politics of Structural Choice: Toward a Theory of Public Bureaucracy," in *Organization Theory: From Chester Barnard to the Present and Beyond*, ed. Oliver E. Williamson (New York: Oxford University Press, 1990).

59. Amy Zegart, *Flawed by Design: The Evolution of the CIA, JCS, and NSC* (Stanford, CA: Stanford University Press, 1999), 7.

60. Cohen, *Supreme Command;* Feaver, *Armed Servants;* Feaver and Gelpi, *Choosing Your Battles;* Herspring, *The Pentagon and the Presidency.*

61. Elinor Ostrom, "Institutional Rational Choice: An Assessment of the Institutional Analysis and Development Framework," in *Theories of the Policy Process*, ed. Paul A. Sabatier (Boulder, CO: Westview Press, 1999), 50.

62. Ostrom, *Governing the Commons*, 51. Ostrom defines *rules* as "shared understandings among those involved that refer to enforced prescriptions about what actions (or states of the world) are required, prohibited, or permitted."

63. Paul Pierson and Theda Skocpol, "Historical Institutionalism in Contemporary Political Science," in *Political Science: State of the Discipline*, ed. Ira Katznelson and Helen V. Minor (Washington, DC: American Political Science Association, 2002), 707.

64. Ibid. Also see Walter W. Powell and Paul J. DiMaggio, eds., *The New Institutionalism in Organizational Analysis* (Chicago: The University of Chicago Press, 1991).

65. Michael Cohen, James March, and Johan Olsen, "A Garbage Can Model of Organizational Choice," *Administrative Science Quarterly* 17 (1972): 1–25.

66. Stephen Skowronek, *Building a New American State: The Expansion of National Administrative Capacities, 1877–1920* (Cambridge: Cambridge University Press, 1982).

67. See, for example, Jonathan Bender and Terry Moe, "An Adaptive Model of Bureaucratic Politics," *American Political Science Review* 79, no. 3 (1985): 755–74; Matthew D. McCubbins and Talbot Page, "A Theory of Congressional Delegation," in *Congress: Structure and Policy*, ed. Mathew D. McCubbins and Terry Sullivan (New York: Cambridge University Press, 1987); Moe, "Politics of Bureaucratic Structure"; David Epstein and Sharyn O'Halloran, *Delegating Powers: A Transaction Cost Politics Approach to Policy Making Under Separate Powers* (Cambridge: Cambridge University Press, 1999); Zegart, *Flawed by Design*; John D. Huber and Charles R. Shipan, *Deliberate Discretion? The Institutional Foundations of Bureaucratic Autonomy* (Cambridge: Cambridge University Press, 2002).

68. Howard Aldrich, *Organizations Evolving* (Thousand Oaks, CA: Sage, 1999), 45–46.

69. Frank Baumgartner and Bryan D. Jones, "Attention, Boundary Effects, and Large-Scale Policy Change in Air Transportation Policy," in *The Politics of Problem Definition: Shaping the Policy Agenda*, ed. David A. Rochefort and Roger W. Cobb (Lawrence: University Press of Kansas, 1994), 51.

70. John R. Kimberly, Robert H. Miles, and Associates, *The Organizational Life Cycle: Issues in the Creation, Transformation, and Decline of Organizations* (San Francisco: Jossey-Bass, 1980); Anthony Downs, *Inside Bureaucracy* (New York: Little, Brown, 1967); Robert E. Quinn and Kim Cameron, "Organizational Life Cycles and Shifting Criteria of Effectiveness: Some Preliminary Evidence," *Management Science* 29 (1983): 33–51.

71. Van de Ven and Poole, "Explaining Development and Change in Organizations," 515.

72. Expounding a stages theory, for example, are Nigel Roome, "Developing Environmental Management Strategies," *Business Strategy and the Environment* 1, no. 1 (1992): 11–23; and Paul Shrivastave and Howard I. Scott, "Corporate Self-Greenewal: Strategic Responses to Environmentalism," *Business Strategy and the Environment* 1, no. 3 (1992): 9–21. Among those finding no empirical support for a stages perspective, see Anja Schaefer and Brian Harvey, "Stage Models of Corporate 'Greening': A Critical Evaluation," *Business Strategy and the Environment* 7, no. 3 (1998): 109–23.

73. For an excellent summary of this literature, plus insights as to how to do this, see Anne M. Khademian, *Working with Culture: The Way the Job Gets Done in Public Programs* (Washington, DC: Congressional Quarterly Press, 2002). Also see Cohen, *Supreme Command;* Feaver, *Armed Servants;* Feaver and Gelpi, *Choosing Your Battles;* Herspring, *The Pentagon and the Presidency.*

74. Edella Schlager, "A Comparison of Frameworks, Theories, and Models of the Policy Process," in *Theories of the Policy Process*, ed. Paul A. Sabatier (Boulder, CO: Westview Press, 1999), 234.

75. See, for example, Peter Hall, "Policy Innovation and the Structure of the State: The Politics-Administration Nexus in France and Britain," *Annals of the American Academy of Political and Social Science* 466 (1983): 43–59; Martin Shefter, "The Emergency of the Political Machine: An Alternative View," in *Theoretical Perspectives in Urban Politics*, ed. Willis Hawley and Michael Lipsky (Englewood Cliffs, NJ: Prentice-Hall, 1976), 14–44; Theda Skocpol, *Protecting Soldiers and Mothers: The Political Origins of Social Policy in the United States* (Cambridge, MA: Belknap Press of Harvard University Press, 1992); and Skowronek, *Building a New American State.*

76. Skocpol, *Protecting Soldiers and Mothers*, 41.

77. Perri 6, "Joined-Up Government in the Western World in Comparative Perspective: A Preliminary Literature Review and Exploration," *Journal of Public Administration Research and Theory* 14, no. 1 (2004): 110.

78. The term "E-Ring" refers to the outer ring of the Pentagon where the secretary of defense, other high-ranking civilian leaders, and the chiefs of the services have their offices.

CHAPTER TWO

Greening, National Security, and the Postmodern Military

As international relations scholars James Rosenau and Paul Viotti so cogently put the dilemma facing military forces in the 1990s, "Enormous stresses and strains are rocking military establishments worldwide in the aftermath of the Cold War. . . . In a turbulent world of fragmenting polities, faltering economies, restless publics, refocused enmities, and vast international transformation, where do soldiers and military organizations fit?"[1] Among other factors animating and constraining these choices, according to Rosenau's turbulence model of world politics, are the emergence worldwide of such norms as human rights and such social ideologies as the peace, women's, and environmental movements. Each, Rosenau avers, tends to "narrow the freedom of action that armed forces have historically enjoyed."[2]

Perhaps. But prior research also suggests that the actual changes produced by environmental shocks to a system, such as the end of the Cold War, are neither easy nor predictable.[3] Scholars James March and Johan Olsen, for example, best state the profound instrumental dilemma that faces all reformers trying to seize upon these shocks to reconfigure organizational behaviors, attitudes, and cultures. "Institutions change, but the idea that they can be transformed to any arbitrary form is rare," they note. What is more, "it is easier to produce change through shock than it is to *control* what new combinations of institutions and practices will evolve from the shock."[4]

With the election of Democrat Bill Clinton as president in 1992, the planets seemed aligned for a fundamental perestroika in Pentagon thinking about greening the military in the post–Cold War era. The United States was the world's only remaining superpower, the Democratic Party held environmentally sympathetic majorities in Congress, and most expected Vice President Al Gore to be a strong, persistent, and effective advocate for ENR values within the White House. Meanwhile, court suits launched in the late 1980s against the military for alleged ENR transgressions had put the military on the defensive. Moreover, Congress had just passed the Federal Facilities Compliance Act (FFCA) of 1992, a statute designed, among other things, to address longstanding cleanup controversies regarding the extent to which Congress had waived the sovereign immunity of federal agencies from the procedural requirements, lawsuits, and fines afforded in U.S. hazardous waste laws. Likewise, the globalization of weaponry (because of interoperability needs among allies) combined with the international ENR

standards movement to make government contractors more amenable to greening weapons production lines for economy of scale purposes. Finally, with mar-
riage rates significantly higher for recruits than had been the case historically in
the military, internal pressures were building for greater care in handling, minimizing, and preventing health and safety problems for families living on bases.

Even under these propitious circumstances, however, proponents knew that
greening the U.S. military would not be easy. First, Clinton's behavior during the
Vietnam War struck many in the military as inappropriate for a commander-in-
chief, and for the Clintonites, the "culture of the military was foreign to them."[5]
Indeed, several seasoned observers of the Pentagon argue that President Clinton had virtually ceded control of the "building" (as the Pentagon is called) to
the military by the end of his first term and then abandoned partisan control to
the Republicans in his second term with the appointment of William Cohen as
secretary of defense.[6] Summarizing perceptions widely shared in Washington,
Dana Priest writes that an "unspoken pact" with the Pentagon was struck early
in the Clinton administration after brush-ups over gays in the military and embarrassing misadventures in Somalia and Haiti: "Don't push us and we won't
push you."[7] Second, fairly or unfairly, both President Clinton and Hillary Clinton
were associated with the countercultural movement of the 1960s, which many in
the military saw as denigrating the sense of duty, discipline, and patriotism that
was the essence of military life.[8] Lastly, some worried that resistance of military
traditionalists to greening might be exacerbated because of the ENR leadership
roles envisioned for women in the Pentagon under Clinton.

Against this cultural leitmotif, proponents of greening also knew that any
Clinton administration resolve could be deactivated further by the spiraling budget deficits projected as President Clinton took the oath of office in 1993. They
also knew well that the history of the "environmental presidency" in general,
and the regulation of federal facilities in particular, discouraged optimism.[9] Even
the most environmentally committed presidents abandon purity of philosophy
because they are held electorally responsible for a host of values more salient to
voters, such as the economy, balanced budgets, and military conflicts.[10]

As I chronicle in this book, optimism quickly and persistently ran pell-mell
into post–Cold War realism about the limits of large-scale organizational change
during the Clinton years. To place these dynamics in context, this chapter begins
the analysis by reviewing the dominant historical–structural mismatches driving
greening efforts. Covered in the process are the high stakes they occasioned for
the military and, hence, the sources of the patterns of politics witnessed in subsequent chapters. Discussed, first, is how the services' efforts to salvage as much
Cold War stability, predictability, and security as possible in the wake of downsizing and contingency operations stretched military budgets to their limit. This,
in turn, both prompted and facilitated efforts by greening opponents to portray
ENR spending disingenuously as a zero-sum tradeoff among environmental protection, military readiness, and weapons modernization. The chapter next re-

views how the post–Cold War revisions that did take place in military strategic, operational, and tactical doctrines further placed mission-critical operations in the crosshairs of federal and state ENR regulators. The chapter concludes by reviewing events at Mountain Home Air Force Base (MHAFB) in Idaho. This experience gives a flavor for how these shocks and minishocks interacted to force accommodations at the base level, as well as a sense for how the military moved to shape, prepare, and respond to the ENR battlefield to advance its aims.

The U.S. Military in the Post–Cold War Era

As Samuel Huntington has observed, the peculiar task of the military professional is "the direction, operation, and control of a human organization whose primary function is the application of violence."[11] Throughout most of the Cold War, the military, its congressional allies, contractors, and citizens saw little direct relationship between ENR protection and that peculiar task. Nor did this tunnel vision end in the immediate aftermath of the demise of the Soviet Union, much to the chagrin of critics seeking to green the military in the post–Cold War era.

Toward a New World Order?

Downsizing, realigning, and defunding the U.S. military were on many minds as the post–Cold War era dawned. Defense spending went from nearly half the federal budget in the 1960s as the United States fought the Vietnam War to under a quarter by the end of the 1970s. It then went back up to little more than a quarter of the federal budget after President Reagan's defense buildup hit a post–Vietnam War peak in 1989 ($338 billion). The Base Force Concept and the Bottom-Up Review cuts carried out successively by the Bush and Clinton administrations brought defense spending down dramatically to 16 percent of the budget by 1998 ($237 billion), a proportion that the Quadrennial Defense Review foresaw dropping to 15 percent by 2002.[12] This despite the Clinton administration's projection of massive budget surpluses over the next ten to fifteen years. Indeed, conventional wisdom was that the military would do well to keep pace with increases in inflation in the post-Clinton era.[13] Then came the War on Terror during the George W. Bush administration, further stretching resources absent a fundamental rethinking of military strategic, operational, and tactical doctrines.

In the early days of the post–Cold War era, however, talk of a "peace dividend" initially made the military wary that domestic agencies, the Democratic caucus in Congress, and a Democratic president would raid Pentagon budgets for their causes. Then, as downsizing, reduced funding, and realignment took place, the services grew particularly wary about expenditures for anything other than military readiness and weapons modernization. Lying at the heart of this debate was a presumed mismatch between Cold War force structures and the needs of the post–Cold War era.

What should be the funding priorities for the Pentagon in the wake of what Clinton's first secretary of state, Warren Christopher, called "a world transformed"? The answer to that question depended on defining what the major threats were to the United States in the post–Cold War era, when those threats would emerge, and how best to contend with them. These were high-stakes questions not only for national security but also for various actors within the military-industrial complex. Contested, for example, was how best to maintain the defense industrial base of contractors in the event of, first, the resurgence of the Soviet Union, and later, the rise of a mighty peer military competitor (most likely China). Likewise, within the military, funding for weapons systems dear to the hearts of various services lay in the balance, and careers could flourish or founder based on the answers to these questions.

As the Cold War wound down during the Reagan and George H. W. Bush administrations, some estimated that the force structure of the United States needed to be rethought to fight new kinds of threats. For instance, with the destruction of the Berlin Wall in 1989, most defense intellectuals contended that the military needed to prepare and train less for Soviet tanks thundering through the Fulda Gap in Europe, for using Navy attack submarines to "shadow" and sink Soviet nuclear submarines, and for using B-2 stealth bombers to evade air defenses deep within the Soviet Union.[14] Absent these needs, they argued, existing base infrastructure exceeded military needs by over 25 percent. Consequently, an infrastructure drawdown on that scale could safely occur without jeopardizing national security, and the remaining infrastructure could be realigned in light of new and emerging threats.

Some taking this view stressed an evolutionary path to modernization that updated existing weapons platforms to meet changing threat paradigms. Reinforced by military and political inertia, they pushed for slimming down the Cold War fighting machine but ensuring that it was still trained, equipped, and structured to dissuade and fight potential peer competitors with overwhelming firepower and attrition capabilities. Still others taking this incremental perspective looked at potential peer competitors like China and championed "leap-ahead technologies" that would shift the services "from mass warfare to mobility, from attrition warfare to agility, from overwhelming firepower to smart firepower."[15] Thus, for example, they urged an end to B-2 bomber acquisition and emphasized acquiring smaller, unmanned bombers guided by digital targeting systems.

Others, however, were more focused on immediate threats and saw "asymmetric" warfare (e.g., bioterrorism, cyberterrorism, and radiological terrorism) waged by stateless terrorists and financed by rogue states as the primary military challenge facing the United States for decades to come. As is now apparent in the wake of the War on Terror, these less militarily advantaged adversaries are capable of inflicting great pain on U.S. forces by investing in simple, low-cost, low-tech, and easy-to-use communications, surveillance, and weapons able to exploit vulnerabilities. To combat this new threat paradigm, the military had to prepare to fight a new kind of enemy, to deploy more rapidly and frequently against foes using civilians as shields, and to engage in "operations other than war" (e.g., peacekeeping or postconflict missions in failed nation states).[16]

Consequently, these strategists argued that each of the military services had to undergo a fundamental transformation predicated on what Pentagon planners saw as major theaters of battle for the U.S. military in the twenty-first century: urban warfare in the United States and abroad.[17] Put most directly by Maj. David Carstens of the U.S. Army, "Internal regional strife [occasioned by economic and environmental internationalism], not power-projecting challengers to US primacy [i.e., peer competitors], will likely spark the crises of the 21st century for which US strategy must be prepared."[18]

To these perspectives was added a third with deep roots in the strategic pluralism ethos of military professionalism: the doctrine of dynamic uncertainty.[19] Proponents argued that the only thing certain was uncertainty about the kind of future military threats the United States would have to confront. Consonant with strategic pluralism, proponents disdained "strategic monism, that is, primary reliance on a single strategic concept, weapons system, or military service" and urged the military "to 'play it safe' by covering all bets."[20] Their solution was straightforward, perhaps prudent, yet costly: Pursue both incremental and leap-ahead doctrines and weapons strategies simultaneously.

Finally, a fourth nascent perspective with few advocates or supporters initially among careerists in the Pentagon or the military services was called "environmental security." As defined conventionally, a national security issue is "any trend or event that threatens the very survival of the nation and/or threatens to drastically reduce the welfare of the nation in a fashion that requires a centrally coordinated national mobilization of resources to mitigate or reverse."[21] As the Cold War wound down, however, proponents of environmental security began arguing that national security planners also had to anticipate and find ways to mitigate resource, environmental, and demographic stress on societies worldwide.[22] Their logic was straightforward: Environmental resources are exhaustible, population growth diminishes them relentlessly, and ecological destruction (e.g., deforestation, malaria, AIDs, and unsanitary water supplies) leads to intra- and intersocietal conflict that may call for the intervention of U.S. troops.

Ships Passing in the Night

The strategic prudence of these approaches aside, through the first six years of the George W. Bush administration the Pentagon and Congress persistently opted for a "Cold War lite" strategy rooted in strategic pluralism. During the George H. W. Bush and Clinton years, talk did abound of realigning U.S. military strategy, operations, and tactics to comport with the new threat paradigm of the post–Cold

War era. Indeed, a so-called revolution in military affairs and force transformation became the catchwords and phrases of those years, talk similarly embraced and pursued by the George W. Bush administration. But as students of the U.S. military have argued, real transformation never occurred where it mattered most during the Clinton and Bush years: in the budget requests of the U.S. military and the funding priorities of Congress for force structure (i.e., the mix of weaponry —tanks, ships, airplanes, and submarines—necessary to meet threats). By the end of the Clinton presidency, former vice chairman of the Joint Chiefs of Staff, Adm. Bill Owens, recalls, "Military service planners [had] sought, with considerable success, to reduce U.S. military forces without jeopardizing their Cold War-era organization, internal force ratios, doctrine, or mission allocation."[23]

Witnessed, in the process, was the triumph of what public management scholars Michael Barzelay and Colin Campbell call "responsive competence" (maintaining political support) over fiscal and strategic competence (matching resources to strategic needs).[24] Initially, spending priorities were justified on the grounds that the former Soviet Union might yet revive, an argument championed by Richard Cheney, then secretary of defense, but backed by the military. When this scenario failed to develop, the Pentagon and its congressional allies mounted a full-court press to move toward leap-ahead technologies for preempting future peer competitors while pursuing Cold War lite weapons planning. Emerging ultimately was a strategic doctrine that tried to do all things at once. Known as "1-4-2-1," this doctrine envisions a force structure capable of defending American territory, deterring hostilities in four critical regions of the world (e.g., the Middle East), swiftly defeating foes in two simultaneous wars (e.g., in the Middle East and North Korea), and decisively overthrowing a government in one of these two wars.

Nor were these warfighting scenarios bereft of self-serving rationales as political pressures mounted for ever-deeper budget cuts. Consider the U.S. Navy's dilemma. The fleet's "blue water" dominance (i.e., its ability to project power globally on the open sea) looked unnecessary after the demise of the Soviet navy, thus prompting calls for sizable cutbacks in the carrier fleet. Moreover, becoming a "green water" (littoral areas) or "brown water" (inland areas) navy, as some now called for, was a transition unwelcomed by submariners, long the dominant profession in the service during the Cold War. Likewise, and already bearing the brunt of downsizing, many in the U.S. Army looked for a new rationale to staunch the personnel hemorrhage underway. Thus, as military analyst and strategist Thomas Barnett of the U.S. Naval Institute writes, the military services "were simply searching for the toughest list of tasks they could come up with to justify the largest and niftiest package of military capabilities possible. That is the budget game in a nutshell."[25]

While defense intellectuals, service chiefs, and civilian appointees at the Pentagon debated all this, however, military service members had more to worry about. During the Clinton years they repeatedly found themselves deployed in a series of life-threatening, ambiguously defined, and sometimes seemingly open-ended contingency operations dealing with situations in places such as Bosnia, Haiti, Iraq, Kosovo, and Somalia. What is more, these were missions for which young soldiers were conspicuously untrained, as "rebuilding replac[ed] destroying and consensus-building replac[ed] precision strikes."[26]

Hard enough on service members and their families, these deployments in pursuit of what Clinton's last secretary of state, Madeleine Albright, called "coercive diplomacy" were seen by many in the military as diverting resources from key warfighting needs.[27] To such critics they represented persistent financial drains on the military's still declining budgets during the Clinton years. These slimmer U.S. forces were engaged between 1990 and 1997 alone in forty-five small-scale military operations around the world, many of which involved costly, open-ended commitments of resources. The costs of the war in Kosovo alone, for example, exceeded $5 billion in 1999. As such, paying simultaneously for more frequent deployment of units in the field (i.e., increased operational tempo, or "op tempo"), military readiness, and future force modernization grew impossible.

One thing that "gave" in the face of these contingency operations and budget cuts was weapons modernization. Nor was this situation helped as procurement dollars "migrated" to Pentagon operations and maintenance budget accounts as a consequence of either chronic underestimating of costs or overestimating of "peacetime" savings.[28] In the long term this weapons "procurement holiday" only further depleted military coffers. Not only did the maintenance costs for aging weapons and systems increase, but their availability rates decreased. So, too, did programmed depot maintenance costs, incidents of equipment failures, and accidents rise. Thus, even when projections of $4.5 trillion in budget surpluses by 2010 looked possible in the late 1990s, and as Congress approved Clinton administration nominal budget increases of $112 billion per year between FY 2000 and FY 2005, some defense intellectuals fretted over what they saw as a "defense train wreck" coming in the twenty-first century.[29]

Relatedly, long-term strategic thinking in the Pentagon continued throughout the post–Post Cold War era to be shaped by a faith that costly technology was a key part of dealing with any scenario envisioned. Writes Col. Thomas Hammes of the Marine Corps, whether the Clinton administration's revolution in military affairs, the military's Joint Vision 2010 or 2020 planning documents, or the second Bush administration's "network-centered" military transformation, the dominant paradigm saw expensive technological evolution as the touchstone of military doctrine.[30] In the interim, however, the Pentagon left the military to scrape for resources among dwindling budgets (until 1998) to fight the new threat environment of failed states, transnational terrorists, insurgents, and the rogue states that harbored and abetted them.

A Gap Dwarfing Fulda?

Summarizing the untoward consequences of these dynamics through the first term of the George W. Bush administration, Barnett writes of a stunning misalignment of our military spending priorities with the real threats facing the United States:

> We knew we needed a greater capacity within the [military] ranks for nation building, peacekeeping, and the like, but instead of beefing up those assets to improve our capacity for managing the world as we found it, the Pentagon spent the nineties buying a far different military—one best suited for a high-tech war against a large, very sophisticated military opponent. In short, our military strategists dreamed of an opponent that would not arise for a war that no longer existed.[31]

Indeed, ten years after the fall of the Berlin Wall in 1989, 26 percent of U.S. active duty forces still were stationed overseas, and a navy unchallenged on the open seas still had over 50 percent of its surface assets deployed overseas. Moreover, in 2000, U.S. troops still were configured at Cold War levels: one hundred thousand each in the western Pacific and Europe, and about twenty-seven thousand in the Persian Gulf.[32] So frequent, enduring, and costly had operational tempo become by late 1998 in places like Bosnia, Haiti, Iraq, Kosovo, and Somalia that the chairman of the Joint Chiefs of Staff, Hugh Shelton, told Congress that military readiness levels were about to begin a "nose dive that might cause irreparable damage to this great force we have created, a nosedive that will take years to pull out of."[33]

Nor, however, does Congress escape blame. As former Senate National Security Advisor Winslow Wheeler describes, members of Congress repeatedly have reduced funding for military readiness in the post–Cold War era while claiming they were increasing funding. This occurred because of "egregious, pork-and-irrelevancy-laden" defense authorization and appropriations processes wherein members earmark dollars for their districts.[34] In this process members of Congress use defense authorization, appropriations, and military construction bills—as well as supplemental funding bills—to earmark dollars for such state-specific projects as bridge repairs, loan guarantees for power transmission lines in North Dakota, a special-needs learning center in Washington state, and a museum and memorial for the USS *Intrepid*. Not only have billions of dollars in earmarks neither been asked for by the military nor debated in full by relevant committees, but they have come out of the military's operations and maintenance account.[35]

Nor did it help the military that, despite campaign indications to the contrary, the new Bush administration submitted an FY 2002 budget request to Congress asking for no new funding beyond what the Clinton White House had submitted. Rather, Bush's secretary of defense, Donald Rumsfeld, called first for a bottom-up doctrinal review. Meanwhile, President Bush sought to meet his campaign promises to the military by paying for them out of cost savings from existing service budgets, not from new money. Confronted on this approach during a Senate Armed Services Committee hearing in early 2001, Rumsfeld aired his frustration: "If you think of the comments of this committee today, almost every comment of concern has been about an area that needs more money: shipbuilding, airplanes, maintenance, infrastructure—you name it. Where's it [funding] going to come from? I mean, where is it going to come from? It can't constantly be more."[36] He then became eerily prescient: "Let's be honest, if there were a crisis, we'd be right up to 8 or 10 [percent of gross domestic product in spending] in a minute [from 3 percent levels], and we could afford it just fine."[37]

On September 11, 2001, the prospect of crisis turned rhetoric into tragic reality, followed by U.S. invasions of Afghanistan and Iraq, years of sustained counterinsurgency warfare in both nations, and the turning of Clinton-era budget surplus projections into soaring budget deficits. Thus, one need not accept the arguments of Barnett and others that the 1-4-2-1 force-structuring premise was shortsighted to appreciate the predicament in which it placed efforts to create a corporate sense of responsibility for greening the U.S. military in the post–Cold War era.[38] The doctrine of ensuring that the United States remains a "peerless" high-tech military power amid constrained military budgets and "hot" and "cold" contingency military operations around the world made the military intensely wary of anything they perceived as diverting resources from these purposes. As we shall see in subsequent chapters, they thus saw expending ENR resources on any project, scope, or pace other than their own as a diversion of resources and a threat to military readiness and modernization. Although able to portray such a zero-sum game among ENR, military readiness, and weapons modernization to Congress and presidents, however, greening opponents could *not* control how shifts in strategic, operational, and tactical doctrine placed military operations more squarely than ever in the crosshairs of ENR regulators.

The Etiology of a Dilemma in Organizational Change for the Postmodern Military

Presidents of both political parties have upped the environmental compliance, cleanup, conservation, and pollution prevention ante for the U.S. military over the past half century. Only one day after triumphantly waving the famous "Dewey Defeats Truman" headline over his head, for example, President Truman issued an executive order (EO) requiring federal agencies to take all "practicable" actions to "cooperate" with states and localities enforcing air pollution regulations. Building on Truman's initiative, President Eisenhower in 1958 moved to extend his predecessor's EO to cover water pollution at federal facilities. Despite these orders, however, the decade of the fifties witnessed only scant and tentative state enforcement and minimal military compliance, a situation prompting President

Johnson in 1968 to urge Congress to "take steps this year" to address the "growing urgency" of noncompliance at federal facilities.

Johnson's missive, however, went unheeded, with the next serious escalation of the compliance stakes left up to President Nixon. In the waning days of his administration, Nixon issued an EO calling upon federal facilities to eliminate air and water pollution and to comply with *substantive* pollution standards just like any other person under the law. Left unscathed by Nixon's order, however, was the immunity of federal facilities from the *procedural* requirements of state and local laws and regulations. These included requirements to obtain permits, undergo inspections, and provide emission monitoring reports. No trivial matter, state regulators and environmental activists correctly noted that giving federal facilities exemptions from ENR procedural requirements effectively left them immune from regulation. Permit enforcement was the only practical way regulators could determine any installation's contribution to air or water quality in any given area. Perhaps, argued federal facilities, but making them comply with state procedural regulations was unconstitutional. Thus, unless Congress waived sovereign immunity privileges for federal polluters, states had no legal recourse.

In 1978 President Carter issued EO 12088 instructing federal facilities to meet both the substantive and procedural ENR regulations facing them. Yet left unrebutted through the Carter years were the persistent claims of federal facilities that the sovereign immunity doctrine made them immune from fines and administrative orders issued by either federal or state regulators. Then the Reagan Justice Department (DOJ) enunciated a "unitary executive theory" that remained dispositive throughout the George H. W. Bush, Clinton, and George W. Bush years: Federal interagency disputes over enforcement of ENR laws are disputes *within the executive branch* for the president (rather than the courts) to resolve.

More precisely, because federal agencies like the DoD are "subparts of a unitary executive branch, [they] cannot sue each other because 'the executive cannot sue himself.'"[39] Such a suit would also violate Article 3 of the U.S. Constitution, because a "justiciable controversy" requires two parties in conflict (whereas the federal executive constituted only one party). Relatedly, federal or state fines also were said to violate the Antideficiency Act by requiring federal agencies to spend money that Congress had not already appropriated. Ostensibly to circumvent these problems, the unitary executive theory created a formal process whereby the DOJ and the Office of Management and Budget (OMB) were formally charged with resolving agency disagreements. The former resolved legal issues, whereas the latter resolved management and policy issues.

Thus, by the time the Soviet empire dissolved in 1991, a series of presidents over the prior four decades had tried, to varying degrees and with little success, to create a corporate sense of responsibility in the Pentagon for ENR protection. Bequeathed to the post–Cold War era as a consequence was a regulatory regime that allowed the military needs of the Cold War to take precedence over ENR protection. It was also a system designed to preclude transparency and shield federal agencies as much as possible from state regulatory authority. Finally, it was a system that centralized power in the hands of any president's appointees at the OMB or DOJ to ensure that costs of meeting ENR requirements were left as much as possible to federal officials rather than to the states, the courts, or citizen activists.

The Post–Cold War Conundrum

Without question, the scope, pace, and intensity of trying to green the U.S. military services soared by leaps and bounds with the end of the Cold War. At least rhetorically, both the George H. W. Bush and Clinton administrations committed to go beyond compliance (e.g., by embracing innovation, process redesign, and pollution prevention strategies) to make the federal government in general, and the U.S. military in particular, world leaders in cleanup, compliance, and pollution prevention. In this regard, the Bush administration's major legislative contribution was its role in enacting the FFCA of 1992, whereas the Clinton administration's efforts were packaged in a persistent series of administrative and legislative initiatives.

The FFCA was a direct assault by Congress on the unitary executive theory. Among other things, it allowed for the EPA to assess both administrative orders and civil penalties against hazardous waste polluters such as the military services, as well as to initiate judicial enforcement actions against them.[40] Likewise, amid the more notable initiatives of the Clinton administration was his 1999 EO 13148, "Greening the Government through Leadership in Environmental Management." This EO renewed and made more stringent the pollution control goals and timetables of a series of Clinton EOs issued beginning in 1993 regarding toxic releases (EO 12856), pollution prevention (EO 12843), and ozone-depleting chemicals (EO 12969).

Significant enough in their own right, the salience to the military of these initiatives spiraled as the Clinton Pentagon launched three major, disparate, yet interrelated initiatives during the 1990s. These envisioned nothing less than a perestroika in U.S. military thinking and operations if institutionalized within the services. In cascading importance, they were incorporating environmental security into national security strategy; revamping operational doctrine to accommodate asymmetric threats by rogue states and terrorists; and creating a faster, more mobile, and more lethal military.

Environmental Security.   Prior to the Clinton administration, concerns about environmental security were rife among key members of critical committees on Capitol Hill. Most notable among these were then–U.S. senator Al Gore (D-TN) and Senator Sam Nunn (D-GA), chairman of the Senate Armed Services Committee. As deputy under secretary of defense for environmental security (DUSD[ES]) Sherri Wasserman Goodman's former boss, Senator Nunn, put it in 1990 in a floor speech, "I am persuaded that there is also a new and different threat to our national security emerging—the destruction of the environment. The defense establishment has a clear stake in countering this growing threat. I believe that one of our key national security objectives must be to reverse the accelerating pace of environmental destruction around the globe."[41]

But as alluded to above, environmental security also was a controversial concept among defense intellectuals and within the Clinton Pentagon. Using the inelegant term "securitizing" ENR concerns, these critics vowed that expanded definitions of national security rendered the word "security" meaningless. Doing so, they averred, prompted three interrelated dangers: a militarization of ENR policy, too extensive a justification for using the military abroad, and a backlash against the United States for doing so.[42]

Nonetheless, in short order, Gore asked the CIA to undertake a study of the environmental causes of "state failures," and Deputy National Security Advisor Sandy Berger convened meetings addressing environmental security issues. Meanwhile, Goodman began making the case at the Pentagon for linking environmental security to the new threat paradigm. In 1993 she averred that ENR scarcities in poorer developing nations can interact with political, social, and cultural factors and policies to produce instability and terrorism.[43] Similarly, CIA director George Tenet stated in 1997 that "our attention is increasingly focused on, and our resources committed to . . . disruptions in the supply of food and clean water which threaten deaths from starvation and disease, refugee flows impacting on neighboring states, murderous ethnic and civil conflict, and even state disintegration."[44]

Further informing this green offensive, Goodman argued throughout her eight years as DUSD(ES) that military commanders could use "the tools of environmental security to shape the strategic context, influence our battle space and enhance operational and combat effectiveness."[45] Indeed, when the Pentagon adopted what it called its "shape, respond, prepare" doctrine, she tried mightily to link greening to that doctrine. In that doctrine, the military's role was to shape the character of the international environment by establishing a forward military presence, performing joint training and peacekeeping exercises with allies and nongovernmental organizations, and entering security assistance arrangements against potential foes. The military also was to respond to security threats through a global military presence prepared to win wars "decisively to minimize casualties."[46] Preparing for a dangerous world meant modernizing for military superiority against any potential foe. Goodman contended that greening might contribute to these aims by, for example, eliminating adverse environmental conditions (e.g., contaminated water), forging cooperative agreements with other nations to protect the environment, ensuring that training continue uninterrupted by ENR-related lawsuits, making weapons systems more reliable, and avoiding the costs of cleanup in future years.

Propelled by such thinking, the official U.S. national security strategy issued in 1996 by the Clinton administration mentioned that "a number of transnational problems which once seemed quite distant [to the military], like environmental degradation, natural resource depletion, rapid population growth and refugee flows, now pose threats to our prosperity and have security implications for both present and long-term American policy."[47] Two years later, for the first time in history, environmental security was formally incorporated into the national security strategy as a component of U.S. strategic doctrine.

During these years the DoD also joined the North Atlantic Treaty Organization's Committee on Challenges to Modern Society and entered into a memorandum of understanding with EPA and the Department of Energy (DOE) that eventually involved such things as nuclear waste cleanup in the Arctic Sea from Soviet and (later) Russian naval vessels. At the same time, the CIA set up its Global Fiducials Program, collecting and declassifying data allowing scientists to track changes in global climate conditions. Meanwhile, the administration's commission on U.S.–Russian relations (cochaired by Gore and Russian prime minister Viktor Chernomyrdin) stressed that environmental problems were linked directly to the future stability and security of Russia.

Downsizing, Defunding, and Realignment. Ironically, even the downsizing and reconfiguration of force structures envisioned by the new threat paradigm, as well as the shape, respond, and prepare strategy designed partially to cope with it, created additional ENR challenges and conflicts for the U.S. military during the Clinton years. Complicit as well was the largely falling and flat funding for this transformation during the same period. These put substantial pressures on the services to make their forces "more lethal and less personnel-intensive through the exploitation of high technology."[48]

The rub for ENR protection, however, was that newer, faster, and more powerful jet fighter engines and armor divisions with greater maneuverability, stealth, and lethality also tended to be louder, flew lower to the ground or damaged it more directly, and emitted more pollutants. Weapons platforms like the F-22 Raptor, the F/A-18E/F, the Crusader Artillery System, and the Abrams M1-A2 tank required greater amounts of battle space for training and testing. Moreover, this happened precisely when urban development, sprawl, and commercial competition for airspace were expanding near many of the military's training areas.

A typical U.S. Army brigade training realistically for combat consists of five thousand people and twenty-five hundred vehicles distributed across an area of fifty by one hundred kilometers. In contrast, a World War II brigade required an eight-by-twelve-kilometer battlefield to train and operate effectively, whereas one operating and training battlefield for Desert Storm required a grid of fifty by sixty-five kilometers.[49] As training activities expanded, a vocal, well-organized, and litigious set of stakeholders living near military bases began to challenge base expansions. In the process they joined with national environmental groups, state regulators, national associations, and like-minded members of Congress to excoriate U.S. military actions that they said endangered public health, safety, and the environment.

Consonant with the military's longstanding mantra that warriors need to "train as they fight," military leaders responded that ENR statutes and regulations were dangerously impeding the military's ability to train. In fact, and as noted in chapter 1, the military coined a term—*encroachment*—for anything in its judgment "that impedes its ability to conduct realistic combat training."[50] Included among these, again, were environmental regulations, presidential orders, nearby airports with civilian aircraft landings and takeoffs, and urban growth that "destroys habitat for endangered species, forcing the animals onto military lands."[51]

To others in Congress, as well as in state and local governments, who worried about the threat of military bases being slated for closure or realignment in their districts, cities, and states, greening took on added meaning. With the Base Realignment and Closure (BRAC) Commission continuing its earlier rounds of base closures during the George H. W. Bush administration, they worried that stringent cleanup standards at contaminated bases would inordinately slow the transfer of these properties to public and private developers. Relatedly, and anticipating that BRACs would negatively impact local economies in major ways, members of Congress in a position to do so tried preemptively to "BRAC-proof" local bases. Some earmarked defense projects for their bases, making it more difficult to justify shutting them down or realigning responsibilities in future rounds. Others jousted among themselves to get the Pentagon voluntarily to realign responsibilities to bases in their districts in order to make it more difficult to close or realign them in future rounds. Moreover, BRAC-proofing combined with higher-than-anticipated cleanup costs to reduce significantly the cost savings predicted for reinvesting in readiness needs.[52] This shortfall, in turn, further pitted ENR, military readiness, and weapons modernization in a zero-sum contest for resources.

Revamping Operations.   Not only did the expanded space the military required to train for combat under the new threat paradigm combine with the shape, respond, and prepare strategy to bring greater ENR scrutiny to their operations, but so too did revised operational doctrines. The U.S. Navy's newly revised homeporting policies, for example, occasioned environmental controversy, as did the service's need to train near coastal areas to practice the offshore maneuvers that the new threat paradigm required. Specifically, the service's plans to homeport the last three of its nuclear-powered *Seawolf*-class submarines (in New London, Connecticut) were challenged in lengthy legal battles by New York's attorney general. At issue was the service's proposed dredging and disposal of over a million cubic yards of contaminated material in Long Island Sound to allow ships to berth. Relatedly, the navy's plans to homeport *Nimitz*-class aircraft carriers in San Diego beached for a time on legal challenges that the environmental assessment required under the National Environmental Policy

Act (NEPA) failed to consider the cumulative ENR impacts of navy activities in the area. The navy's training lanes also were put at risk until the California Air Resources Board determined how ozone emissions from its ships were affecting smog levels in southern California.[53]

Even without the new threat paradigm, of course, the challenges that ENR statutes and regulations posed for the U.S. military services as they trained the way they fought were immense in the early years of the post–Cold War era. For example, to comply with the Endangered Species Act (ESA), facilities like the army's National Training Center and the MHAFB in Idaho had to "work around" protected endangered desert turtles, pronghorn sheep, and gnatcatcher birds. Similarly, red-cockaded woodpeckers restricted training on U.S. Army and Marine Corps bases throughout the Southeast, and allegations of adverse effects on marine mammals, migratory birds, and human beings reduced the U.S. Navy's ability to use low-frequency sonar equipment and live-fire training.

But the training necessary to operationalize the new threat paradigm further exacerbated these challenges. Offshore operational capabilities, for example, require for realism maneuvers that place the military squarely within the regulatory purview not only of the ESA but also of statutes such as the Coastal Zone Management Act. Similarly, the homeporting of ships prompted the Pentagon to press Congress for nationally uniform discharge standards. Otherwise, the military argued, different requirements from state to state would sorely complicate naval operations.[54] Likewise, when the U.S. National Park Service released a 1994 study of the negative effects of military overflights on parklands, the Pentagon wanted time to challenge the study's conclusions. Researchers had concluded that low-level overflights by military aircraft caused physiological and behavioral responses jeopardizing the survival of wildlife in the national parks.[55]

Also, taking aim at overflights of its refuges, the U.S. Fish and Wildlife Service (FWS) supported legislative amendments to the National Wildlife Refuge System Administration Act of 1966 to give authority to refuge managers to halt military operations that were incompatible with the use of any refuge.[56] To these efforts in the mid- to late 1990s were joined others by the Bureau of Land Management (BLM) and (again) the FWS, typically in the wake of court suits by citizen groups living near training and testing ranges. The BLM, for instance, sought to halt navy training flights over public lands near the Naval Strike and Air Warfare Center in Nevada.[57] Similarly, when the army proposed to expand its National Training Center at Fort Irwin in California's Mohave Desert, the FWS challenged its authority to do so until the future of the endangered desert tortoise was assured.[58]

Old and new military tactical needs also prompted military violations of air and water quality regulations. Indeed, heavy use of obscurants (smoke), flairs, chaff, strafing, and open (air) burning/open detonations of explosives led to the closing of hundreds of outdoor military firing ranges and more than eleven hundred indoor ranges during the 1990s.[59] Preemptions of military training activities because of the ENR threats they posed also occurred. For instance, the Marine Corps was denied permission by the National Park Service to stage a seven-hundred-troop landing near the Golden Gate Bridge in California for four-day exercises using state-of-the-art equipment. Regulators worried about the effects of the landing and simulations involved on wildlife (especially birds and marine mammals off the coast) and sensitive sand dunes in the area, as well as on air emissions and sediment disturbance.

Meanwhile, the U.S. Air Force persistently had to worry about having to curtail critical air-to-ground combat training at bases near urban areas because of unexploded ordnance leaching toxic substances into groundwater supplies, noise abatement regulations, and skies too crowded for safety. Or, pushing on to the next generation of high-technology warfighting aircraft after the F-22, consider the Joint Strike Fighter. As deputy assistant secretary of the navy for environment and safety Elsie Munsell summarized the dilemma in 1999: "Because of the aircraft's operational requirements, it is going to have one huge and very powerful engine. . . . It makes more noise than anything we've got in the inventory, and it puts out more [nitrogen oxides] than anything in our inventory."[60]

Early in the post–Cold War era, these challenges seemed remote. But early wake-up calls for the military came, for example, when three civilian employees at Fort Benning, Georgia, were indicted on criminal charges for ESA violations. Even more eye-popping to the military, EPA shut down training completely in the late 1990s, when ordnance-leaching chemicals threatened groundwater supplies at the Massachusetts Military Reservation on Cape Cod, and the U.S. Navy was forced to shut down its bombing range on San Clemente Island (off California) four days a week during the loggerhead shrike's breeding season. Likewise, the U.S. Army's major training installation at Fort Hood, Texas, and the Marine Corps's training facility at Camp Pendleton, California, were forced during George W. Bush's first term to take steps to do workarounds of threatened or endangered species (e.g., rare plants and tidal estuaries). These caused what critics called "an impossibly truncated mismatch of the land needed and available for combat training."[61]

Consider, as it were, the fate of base commanders in the wake of these developments. Faced more persistently with enforcement of applicable federal, state, and local ENR laws in the post–Cold War era, base commanders had to be more familiar than ever with nearly twenty federal environmental statutes and approximately ten thousand pages of regulations. Each page of a federal rule, in turn, spawned another ten pages of state and/or local regulations. Further complicating the matter, federal, state, and local regulators have overlapping authority and, in some cases, impose inconsistent requirements.

Sometimes these requirements conflict within the same statute. For example, CERCLA's rules for protecting public health and safety can conflict with its requirements for restoring natural resources.[62] Sometimes they vary among statutes, and battles arise over which standards and requirements apply in given situations.

For the military (as well as for the states, environmentalists, and Native Americans pressuring the services for redress), the most pressing, persistent, and taxing of these statutory conflicts during the post–Cold War era have involved determining whether the corrective action provisions of the Resource Conservation and Recovery Act or Section 120 of CERCLA are dispositive at given sites.[63] At other times, ENR requirements vary among international agreements. Heavily dependent on ozone-depleting chlorofluorocarbons for coolants, for example, the military pondered phasing them out as per the Montreal Protocols of 1987 and replacing them with hydroflourocarbons. The 1992 Kyoto Convention on Global Climate Change, however, banned the use of hydroflourocarbons.

Nor were base commanders the only ones finding their Cold War moorings untethered by these operational changes. In Maryland, for example, a federal judge assessed criminal penalties against three civilian managers for hazardous waste violations at the army's Aberdeen Proving Grounds.[64] Found guilty of illegally storing, treating, and disposing hazardous waste in *United States v. Dee, Lantz, and Gepp* (1991), the defendants were sentenced to three years of probation and a thousand hours of community service. Some considered this penalty too weak. Others felt that it was not inflicted as high in the chain of military command as it would have been in the private sector under the Responsible Corporate Officer doctrine.[65] But as Art Linton, a veteran EPA federal facility coordinator in Atlanta, recalled, "This case was a turning point—no more business as usual."[66] Moreover, following on the heels of *United States v. David Carr* (1989), where a range foreman at Fort Drum, Kentucky, was found guilty of failing to report a hazardous waste spill, military base personnel were beginning to understand that they—not their superiors—would pay the price for ENR violations in the post–Cold War era.[67]

Those still not getting the message, however, would do so. In 1991 and 1992 federal and state prosecutors copped six convictions (one by court-martial) and pursued three additional indictments of individuals for violating environmental laws affecting aspects of national defense. These included convictions for such things as (1) making false statements on discharge monitoring reports (*United States v. Pond*; *United States v. John Curtis*; *United States v. Woodward*; and *California v. Hernandez*), (2) unlawfully transporting and/or disposing of hazardous materials (all the former cases plus *California v. Sam Lam*), and (3) permitting timber cutting in critical habitat (*United States v. Dunn*).[68] Moreover, the penalties imposed grew more severe. Pouring antifreeze into a storm drain at a navy auto repair shop drew a one-year probation and a five-hundred-dollar fine (*United States v. Cletus Bond*).[69] Likewise, falsifying documents combined with illegally disposing of hazardous waste brought fines, reductions in rank, and hard labor (*Woodward*). Falsifying a sludge test to comply with an NPDES permit brought a five-thousand-dollar fine and eighteen months probation (*Hernandez*).

Consequently, the message was clear by the time Bill Clinton became president. If the national security state could not itself develop an environmental ethic, the courts would hold at least some of its members liable for not doing so. Moreover, if the unitary executive theory precluded the DOJ and EPA from taking sister agencies to court, the Federal Tort Claims Act, the Federal Employees Liability Reform and Tort Compensation Act of 1988, and the nation's hazardous waste laws did not preclude them from taking legal action against individuals acting either within or outside of their official duties. Standing a "world apart" was no longer an option. Or was it?

Shaping, Responding, and Preparing the ENR Battlefield

To appreciate how all these shocks and minishocks interacted at the base level, and to begin appreciating the military's shape, respond, and prepare approach to gaining as much stability, predictability, and security as it could in the post–Cold War era, consider events at the MHAFB. In 1992 Idaho's congressional delegation was elated that the BRAC Commission had decided to house and train the 366th Air Expeditionary Wing at MHAFB. Equally pleased, the Air Force seized on the reassignment to justify a long-desired expansion of training space for its existing aircraft and pilots. In short order, however, these supporters of base expansion found themselves allied with Idaho governors in a pitched battle against various coalitions of grassroots environmentalists, ranchers, and the Shoshones and Paiutes of the Duck Valley Indian Reservation. Also eventually joining the opposition to the conventional air force methods used to calculate the ENR impacts of this Enhanced Training in Idaho (ETI) project were the BLM, the Idaho Fish and Game Commission, regional and national nongovernmental organizations (e.g., the Foundation for North American Wild Sheep and the Wilderness Society), and U.S. Senators Ben Nighthorse Campbell of Colorado (D, later R), Daniel Inouye of Hawaii (D), and Harry Reid of Nevada (D).

At issue, initially, were the land expansions necessary to accommodate the housing and training of the 366th. The dispute was joined when a local group, the Owyhee Canyonlands Coalition, contested in court the ecological wisdom and need for the ETI project. Incorporating twenty-five thousand acres in high desert country along the Owyhee River Canyon in southern Idaho, ETI lands were among the most pristine high desert areas remaining in the country and home to the country's largest population of bighorn sheep and desert antelope. The coalition claimed that training operations would have a devastating ecological effect unless the air force took sustained, persistent, and aggressive steps to mitigate their impacts. Simultaneously, the Shoshones and Paiutes living on the Duck Valley Indian Reservation contested use of the airspace above their reservation for ETI training. As Senator Inouye put their dilemma most graphically nearly six years later, "I've received literally dozens of letters from affected tribes telling me that in the midst of their religious ceremonies they have to hit the ground because the planes are flying so low and the sonic boom was so bad."[70]

As NEPA requires, the air force had conducted an environmental assessment in 1992 analyzing the impact of the addition of a composite wing at MHAFB to see if a full-scale environmental impact statement (EIS) was needed. But instead of assessing the cumulative impact of the addition of the 366th, the base's ongoing activities, and the ETI, the air force said it was only willing to do a separate environmental assessment for the ETI. Known as *piecemealing* environmental studies, this tactic (i.e., treating interrelated activities as separate) camouflaged the overall negative impacts of air force operations thus limiting the transparency of its decisions and operations. Piecemealed in the process was the "audience" paying attention to these decisions, wanting to participate in them, and holding the military accountable to ENR laws. Indeed, an earlier air force report warned that a joint EIS on the composite wing and the training range would produce environmental objections that could seriously delay the projects.[71]

Ultimately, a federal court magistrate agreed that the 366th composite wing and the training range were "inextricably intertwined," and that the Air Force disingenuously had used the bed-down of the composite wing at MHAFB to justify what it had always wanted to do (create the Idaho Training Range).[72] By 1996, however, an undaunted air force had strategically rethought the parameters and location of the lands needed and petitioned for new and expanded training responsibilities. In doing so, it counted on the Idaho congressional delegation (led by Senator Dirk Kempthorne [R] in a Congress now controlled by Republicans) to advance its aims. Now the air force wanted to house and conduct training for eight B-1B supersonic bombers and to relocate the Thirty-Fourth Bomb Squadron from Nevada to MHAFB as well.

These BRAC-proofing additions all required an increase in the use of local airspace plus supersonic and high-subsonic, low-penetration flights over southwestern Idaho and Nevada. Proposed, in all, was a twelve-thousand-acre expansion with airspace extending into Nevada to "provide aircrews with a realistic target array that allows simultaneous attacks from any axis."[73] Enhanced bomber training, in turn, required a three-hundred-acre primary ordnance impact area, a tactical range, five simulated bombing ranges, and thirty emitter sites arrayed along the terrain, plus the use of flares, chaffing, strafing, and low-level supersonic and subsonic maneuvers.

Not surprisingly, the Owyhee Canyonlands Coalition again cried foul. Most galling again to them was the air force basing its environmental assessment solely on the Idaho Training Range. In this case, the service eschewed simultaneously addressing the cumulative impacts of the composite wing and the training range (as the court magistrate had ordered), and it failed to consider the impacts of the B-1B bomber plans and their related activities. Nor did it help the air force's credibility in this piecemealing effort when a separate environmental assessment said that the B-1Bs would not train at supersonic speeds. Quipped an incredulous interviewee, "Why . . . would you bring in planes that train supersonic to an area that you can't fly supersonic?"[74]

Next came an air force inspector general report challenging the data analysis underpinning the rationale for base expansion. The air force had claimed that the Idaho Training Range was necessary for the greater efficiency and enhanced readiness it afforded. Without expanding MHAFB, the air force argued, the 366th had to fly one to two hours from Idaho to Nevada, Utah, and Oregon to train, wasting fuel and squandering precious training time.[75] In challenging the air force's cost-benefit analysis, however, the inspector general offered an alternative: Using an existing range in Utah would meet the service's goals more efficiently than expanding MHAFB.[76]

Nor was this the only computational sleight of hand plied by the air force as the MHAFB controversy progressed during the Clinton years. The Idaho Fish and Game Commission, for example, criticized the air force for failing to consider the impacts of airspace expansion on "relatively undisturbed native vegetation [and] on wildlife not previously exposed to low-level or supersonic overflight disturbance."[77] The commission also alleged that the air force's studies of training were "legally indefensible," pointing out that a 1997 air force planning document had stated that "current data collection methods [on noise impacts . . . are] extremely vulnerable to human error."[78] Finally, when considering mitigation options, the EIS merely averaged noise levels from overflights, instead of calculating the effects of excessive periods of noise.

Representing a state that would be losing BRAC-proofing training hours at Nellis and other bases, Senator Jack Reid (R) of Nevada welcomed these findings. They fit neatly into his battle to stymie the Idaho delegation's efforts to add the MHAFB expansion as a rider to the FY 1999 defense authorization bill. Joined by Senator Inouye, as well as by other senators from neighboring states affected by the Idaho base expansion, Reid argued that U.S. readiness could be maintained with a smaller ecological footprint by using other bases. At risk of "ruination," he claimed, were wilderness areas on the Idaho, Nevada, and Oregon borders.

Although significant congressional opposition arose to Kempthorne's base expansion language, the Senate nevertheless approved his amendment. But when the Air Force released its final EIS in 1998, a coalition of environmentalists, sportsmen, and recreational users in Idaho known as the Greater Owyhee Legal Defense filed suit. This coalition argued that the EIS once again did not meet NEPA standards because, among other things, it failed to consider adequately the effects of noise and chaff on wildlife. The air force responded that its analyses "represent the best available technology and are legally defensible."[79]

In the end, the air force got its base expansion, its B-1B bomber and 366th training, and its ETI when it proposed a series of mitigation efforts acceptable enough to the plaintiffs that all court suits were dropped in late 1999. Victory had not come easily in the face of unyielding shocks (e.g., the end of the Cold War) and minishocks (BRAC) that challenged business as usual in the air force. Neither had it come without persistent counteroffensives by the air force.

Conclusion

After reviewing the extent of behavioral change asked of the military on so many fronts (strategic, operational, and tactical) and within such budget constraints in the post–Cold war era, one might conclude that creating a corporate sense of responsibility for greening the U.S. military was doomed to failure. Yet, progress of a kind and degree chronicled in chapter 1 was made. However, as we shall see, these advances were premised less on the power and inculcation of ideas than on the pursuit and protection of political, organizational, and personnel prerogatives.

As we shall also see, this is not to say that ideas did not matter. To the contrary, proponents of the greening initiatives discussed in this book were as principled about and committed to the idea of ENR protection as opponents of those initiatives were principled and committed to the idea of ensuring national security. It is to say, however, that the offensives mounted by greening proponents pursuing these initiatives were filtered through the lenses of political, organizational, and personal ambition more broadly. And similarly animated were the counteroffensives mounted by opponents of these particular greening initiatives.

As the events just chronicled at MHAFB illustrate, greening proponents quickly learned that progress throughout the post–Cold War era typically meant jousting with protean, powerful, and persistent elements of the political economy that buttressed the armed services' Cold War ethic of sovereignty, secrecy, and sinecure. Likewise, opponents of these greening initiatives learned that ongoing shifts in the political, social, and economic context of military operations in the post–Cold War era meant that unprecedented challenges to that political economy were underway and new tactics protecting their prerogatives would have to be devised. Moreover, everyone learned that many of the battles involved would have to be waged at a corporate level within the Office of the Secretary of Defense itself, a topic discussed in chapter 3.

Notes

1. James Rosenau (with Paul R. Viotti), "Military Establishments in the Aftermath of the Cold War: A Theoretical and Comparative Analysis" (paper presented at the annual meeting of the American Political Science Association, Washington, DC, September 3, 1993), 1.

2. Ibid., 13.

3. Stephen Skowronek, *Building a New American State: The Expansion of National Administrative Capacities, 1877–1920* (Cambridge: Cambridge University Press, 1982).

4. James G. March and Johan P. Olsen, *Rediscovering Institutions* (New York: Free Press, 1989), 22 and 65 (emphasis added), respectively.

5. This is a quote from defense policy analyst Larry K. Smith. He served as a counselor to President Clinton's first two defense secretaries, Les Aspin and William Perry. Smith is quoted in Joe Klein, *The Natural: The Misunderstood Presidency of Bill Clinton* (New York: Broadway Books, 2002), 49.

6. See, for example, Thomas P. M. Barnett, *The Pentagon's New Map: War and Peace in the Twenty-First Century* (New York: G. P. Putnam's Sons, 2004); Klein, *Natural*; Benjamin Ginsberg, Walter R. Mebane Jr., and Martin Shefter, "The Presidency, Social Forces, and Interest Groups," in *The Presidency & the Political System*, 5th ed., ed. Michael Nelson (Washington, DC: CQ Press, 1998), 358–73; Charles A. Stevenson, *SECDEF: The Nearly Impossible Job of the Secretary of Defense* (Dulles, VA: Potomac Books, 2006).

7. Dana Priest, *The Mission: Waging War and Keeping Peace with America's Military* (New York: W. W. Norton, 2003), 44. Also see my preface in this book for details. Charles Stevenson writes that Vice President Gore was friends with Secretary Cohen and, hence, was heavily involved with the Pentagon during the Cohen years. He also argues, however, that there was "no daylight" between himself and the senior military, especially the commanders-in-chief and the Joint Chiefs of Staff. Writes Stevenson, Cohen "didn't want to get out in front of them. Indeed, he tended to line up *behind* them." He also got "'buy in' from the Chiefs for administration policy" and always "learn[ed] in advance the position the Chiefs wanted to take." See Stevenson, *SECDEF*, 108–9. Finally, not only did Cohen spend a great deal of each month away from the Pentagon physically, he also served as a conduit for Republican views from Capitol Hill and appointed Republicans to his Defense Policy Board.

8. For an excellent summary of the connection between the environmental movement of the 1960s and the New Left political agenda, see Robert Gottlieb, *Forcing the Spring: The Transformation of the American Environmental Movement* (Washington, DC: Island Press, 1993), especially chap. 3.

9. Dennis L. Soden, ed., *The Environmental Presidency* (Albany: State University of New York Press, 1999).

10. James Gustave (Gus) Speth, *Red Sky at Morning: America and the Crisis of the Global Environment* (New Haven, CT: Yale University Press, 2004).

11. Samuel P. Huntington, *The Soldier and the State: The Theory and Politics of Civil-Military Relations* (Cambridge, MA: Belknap Press, 1981), 11.

12. Both the Base Force Concept and the Bottom-Up Review were touted as bottom-up reviews of the military's strategic operational and tactical doctrines in light of the end of the Cold War. Congress requires the DoD to prepare a Quadrennial Defense Review after each presidential election. Among other things, the review projects the size, organization, and equipment needs of the military services over the next fifteen years.

13. Richard J. Newman, "Can Peacekeepers Make War?" *U.S. News and World Report*, January 19, 1998, 40.

14. Located between the former East German border and Frankfurt, West Germany, the Fulda Gap was considered the quickest way for an invading force from the Warsaw Pact (the military alliance of the Soviet Union and its satellite nations) to attack the industrial heart of West Germany.

15. Keith B. Bickel, "Buying Smart," *Blueprint* 5 (Winter 2000): 31; Adm. William A. Owens, "Revolutionizing Warfare," *Blueprint* 5 (Winter 2000): 26.

16. Included among these threats are computer viruses that can disrupt communications and intelligence networks, chemical (e.g., mustard and VX nerve gas) and biological agents (e.g., anthrax) distributed at bases and ports to disrupt military operations, aluminum reflectors capable of confusing radar targeting, and heat generators able to foil heat sensors.

17. For an insightful discussion of how the U.S. Air Force dealt with these changing circumstances and issues, see Michael Barzelay and Colin Campbell, *Preparing for the Future: Strategic Planning in the U.S. Air Force* (Washington, DC: Brookings Institution Press, 2004).

18. David H. Carstens, "Bringing Environmental and Economic Internationalism into U.S. Strategy," *Parameters: US Army War College Quarterly* (Spring 2001): 99.

19. The doctrine of dynamic uncertainty has a pre–Civil War vintage in the United States and abroad. In his classic, *The Soldier and the State*, Samuel P. Huntington refers to this ethos as "strategic pluralism." In contrast to an ethos of "strategic monism" (defined in this paragraph of the text), strategic pluralism advocates a "wide variety of forces and weapons to meet a diversity of potential security threats" (418).

20. Ibid.

21. Jack Goldstone, "Environmental Scarcity and Violent Conflict: A Debate," *Environmental Change and Security Project Report, Issue 2* (Washington, DC: Woodrow Wilson Center, 1996), 66–71.

22. Geoffrey D. Dabelko, "The Environmental Factor," *Wilson Quarterly* 23, no. 4 (1999): 17. They were joined by Gro Harlem Brundtland, former prime minister of Norway and author of the United Nation's Commission on Sustainable Development, and Mikhail Gorbachev, former president of the Soviet Union.

23. Adm. Bill Owens (with Ed Offley), *Lifting the Fog of War* (New York: Farrar, Straus, and Giroux, 2000), 39.

24. Barzelay and Campbell, *Preparing for the Future*, 130–31.

25. Barnett, *Pentagon's New Map*, 91.

26. Priest, *Mission*, 19.

27. Ibid., 52. Albright's concept is encapsulated in the famous line to Colin Powell, then chairman of the Joint Chiefs: "What's the point of having this superb military that you're always talking about if we can't use it?" Basically, it involved a belief in "limited warfare for limited ends," or the projection of U.S. military power abroad for limited purposes to help shape events and for humanitarian purposes. It was the opposite of the so-called Powell doctrine that limited military involvement to situations where the ends were clear and massive overwhelming firepower was used. For Albright, incremental use of military power proportional to the situation was needed.

28. Operations and maintenance funding includes salaries and benefits for military and civilian personnel; the price of operating and maintaining the armed forces; and the costs of operating and maintaining all of the services' real property, installations, and facilities. As Charles Stevens points out, operations and maintenance funds often are used as "bill payers" for weapons modernization and to minimize the impact of cuts in force structures because the latter two mean gains or losses in employment in congressmembers' districts.

29. Daniel Gouré and Jeffrey M. Ranney, *Averting the Defense Train Wreck in the New Millennium* (Washington, DC: CSIS Press, 1999). Over the next thirty years, they argued, merely maintaining the status quo would require all existing weapons platforms to be "recapitalized" (i.e., replaced) because of aging.

30. Col. Thomas X. Hammes, *The Sling and the Stone: On War in the 21st Century* (St. Paul, MN: Zenith Press, 2004). Hammes notes that the "technology drives warfare" premise has been softened a bit, beginning with Joint Vision 2010, but that it still remains front and center in the Pentagon's Vision 2020 thinking regarding "information age" military forces predicated on advancement in computer technologies.

31. Barnett, *Pentagon's New Map*, 4.

32. Owens, *Lifting the Fog of War*, 39.

33. Gen. Henry H. Shelton, chairman of the Joint Chiefs of Staff, "Readiness of U.S. Armed Forces" (statement before the Senate Armed Services Committee, Washington, DC, September 29, 1998), 1, http://www.fas.org/man/congress/1998/98092901_plt.html (November 1, 1998).

34. Winslow T. Wheeler, *The Wastrels of Defense: How Congress Sabotages U.S. Security* (Annapolis, MD: Naval Institute Press, 2004), 53.

35. Ibid. Legislators also often fudged revenue neutrality on these state-specific earmarks by claiming offsetting savings in operational costs through so-called good government reforms that always failed to materialize. When they did not, operations and maintenance accounts again were left with drastically reduced funding.

36. James Dao, "As Defense Secretary Calls for Base Closings, Congress Circles the Wagons," *New York Times*, June 29, 2001, http://www.nytimes.com/2001/06/29/politics/29MILI.html (June 29, 2001).

37. Jackson Diehl, "B-1 Blundering," *Washington Post*, July 9, 2001, A17.

38. See, for example, John Arquilla and David Rondfeldt, "Cyberwar Is Coming," *Comparative Strategy* 12 (November 1, 1993): 141–65; Hammes, *Sling and the Stone*; Martin van Crevald, *The Transformation of War* (New York: Free Press, 1991); William S. Lind, Keith Nightengale, John F. Schmitt, Joseph W. Sutton, and Gary I. Wilson, "The Changing Face of War: Into the Fourth Generation," *Marine Corps Gazette*, October 1989, 22–26.

39. Joshua E. Latham, "The Military Munitions Rule and Environmental Regulation of Munitions," 2004, 3, http://www.bc.edu/bc_org/avp/law/lwsch/journals/bcealr/27_3/04_TXT.htm (June 25, 2004).

40. Stephen Dycus, *National Defense and the Environment* (Hanover, NH: University Press of New England, 1996), 42.

41. Kent H. Butts, "Why the Military is Good for the Environment," in *Green Security or Militarized Environment*, ed. Jyrki Kakonen (Aldershot, UK: Dartmouth Publishing, 1994), 87.

42. See, for example, Paul Benjamin, "Green Wars: Making Environmental Degradation a National Security Issue Puts Peace and Security at Risk," *Policy Analysis* (April 20, 2000): 1–25.

43. Sherri Wasserman Goodman, DUSD(ES), "The Environment and National Security," remarks prepared for presentation at the National Defense University, Washington, DC, August 8, 1996, http://www.loyola.edu/dept/politics/hula/goodman.html (August 10, 1996).

44. George J. Tenet, Acting Director, CIA, statement before the Senate Select Committee on Intelligence, Hearing on Current and Projected National Security Threats to the United States, Washington, DC, February 5,1997, http://www.fas.org/irp/congress/1997_hr/s970205t.htm (February 5, 1997).

45. "NSC Weighs Raising Environment Threats in Draft 1998 National Security Plan," *Defense Environment Alert (DEA)* 6, no. 8 (April 21, 1998): 4.

46. Michael O'Hanlon, *How to Be a Cheap Hawk: The 1999 and 2000 Defense Budgets* (Washington, DC: Brookings Institution Press, 1998), 21.

47. Goldstone, "Environmental Scarcity and Violent Conflict."

48. Chris Demchak, *Military Organizations, Complex Machines: Modernization in the U.S. Armed Forces* (Ithaca, NY: Cornell University Press,1999), 1. Demchak argues that higher levels of weapons complexity actually do just the opposite, especially given the tendency for them to require more organizational complexity to ensure their certainty of operation.

49. "DOI, DoD Outline for Congress Key Elements of Fort Irwin Expansion Plan," *DEA* 9, no. 3 (January 30, 2001): 8–10.

50. "Encroachment Likely to 'Loom Large' in 2005 Base Closure Round," *DEA* 10, no. 17 (August 13, 2002): 3.

51. Ibid.

52. Members of Congress became irate when the Clinton administration allowed two military bases (one in California and one in Texas) to avoid BRAC closure. Critics charged that Clinton had violated BRAC processes in order to cull political favor in two states with large numbers of electoral votes as he prepared for the 1996 election campaign.

53. "Navy, New York Settle Long Island Seawolf Dredging Lawsuit," *DEA* 4, no. 1 (January 10, 1996): 9–10; "Navy Issues Plan for Homeporting Nimitz-Class Carrier Near San Diego," *DEA* 4, no. 1 (January 10, 1996): 10–11; "Navy to Help Fund California Study on Air Emissions from Ships," *DEA* 5, no. 13 (June 17, 1997): 14.

54. "Navy Gains Senate Armed Services Support for Uniform Discharge Standard," *DEA* 3, no. 14 (July 12, 1995): 3.

55. "Park Service Releases Overflights Study Following DoD Delay," *DEA* 2, no. 21 (October 19, 1994): 10–11.

56. "Military Fears Wildlife Refuge Bill Could Undermine DoD Authority, *DEA* 3, no. 16 (August 9, 1995): 14. This act was eventually amended in 1997 as the National Wildlife Refuge System Improvement Act, PL 105–57.

57. "BLM Orders Navy to Halt Training Flights Over Public Lands in Nevada," *DEA* 5, no. 5 (February 26, 1997): 7.

58. "Administration Preparing Legislation for Fort Irwin Expansion," *DEA* 8, no. 6 (March 21, 2000): 7.

59. In open burning disposal, flame or heat is used to ignite what becomes a self-sustained combustion process. In open detonation operations, disposal occurs by using a controlled series of explosions.

60. "Navy Working to Avert Environmental Problems with JSF," *DEA* 7, no. 16 (August 10, 1999): 10. As such, it could be barred from flight in these areas for violating noise and nitrogen oxide emissions standards.

61. Katherine Seelye, "Pentagon Seeks Exemption from Environmental Laws," *New York Times*, March 30, 2002, http://www.nytimes.com/2002/03/30/politics/30ENVI.tyml (March 30, 2002).

62. "Trustees Voice Concerns Over EPA Ecological Risk Management Guidance," *DEA* 6, no. 24 (December 1, 1998): 11.

63. Dycus, *National Defense and the Environment*, especially chap. 4.

64. *United States v. Dee, Lantz, and Gepp*, 912 F.2d 741 (4th Cir. 1990), *cert. filed*, 59 U.S.L.W. 3631, No. 90–877, 1991.

65. Christopher Harris and Patrick O. Cavanaugh, "Environmental Crimes and the Responsible Government Official," *Natural Resources and Environment* 6, no. 1 (1991): 21.

66. Art Linton, Coordinator, Federal Facilities Office, U.S. EPA Region IV, interview with author, Atlanta, GA, June 2, 1992.

67. *United States v. David Carr*, 880 F.2d 1550 (2d Cir. 1989); *United States v. Dee, Lantz, and Gepp*.

68. *United States v. Pond*, Cr. S-90-0420, D. Md. (April 17, 1991), 21 Env. L. Rep. 10444 (1991); *United States v. Curtis*, 988 F.2d 946 (9th Cir. 1993), *cert. denied*, 114 S. Ct. 177 (1993); *United States v. Woodward*, 469 U.S. 105 (1985); *California v. Hernandez*, No. 25148 Riverside Mun. Ct. (May 11, 1992); *California v. Lam*, (Cal. State) (May 29, 1992); *United States v. Dunn*, 480 U.S. 294 (1987).

69. *United States v. Bond*, Cr. 91-0287-GT, S.D. Cal (April 9,1991).

70. "Reid, Inouye Try to Block Kempthorne's Idaho Air Force Range Expansion," *DEA* 6, no. 10 (May 19, 1998), 5.

71. "Court Report Says Air Force Plans Violate Environmental Law," *DEA* 2, no. 21 (October 19, 1994): 6.

72. "Air Force Faces Legal Setback in Plans for Idaho Training Range," *DEA* 3, no. 10 (May 17, 1995): 17–18.

73. "Air Force to Study Impacts of Enhanced Training at Mountain Home," *DEA* 4, no. 3 (February 7, 1996): 10.

74. "Environmentalists in Air Force NEPA Case Add New Claims," *DEA* 4, no. 25 (December 4, 1996): 19.

75. "Idaho Congressional Delegation Ready to Push for Expanded Air Force Range," *DEA* 6, no. 3 (February 10, 1998): 15–16.

76. "Environmentalists Revive Arguments Against Air Force's Idaho Range Plan," *DEA* 4, no. 18 (September 4, 1996): 17–18.

77. "Idaho Sets Parameters for Air Force Range Expansion Plans," *DEA* 5, no. 16 (July 29, 1997): 11.

78. Ibid.

79. "Environmentalists Sue Air Force, Idaho Over Planned Range Expansion," *DEA* 6, no. 9 (May 5, 1998): 12.

CHAPTER THREE

About-Face at the Pentagon?

In 1987 the inspector general of the Department of Defense reported that the department's environmental and natural resources efforts to date had been stymied by a stunning failure to demonstrate their high priority within the military services. Moreover, progress on the greening front would be uncertain unless four objectives were achieved: policies that were excessively fragmented had to be integrated; effective management structures, which did not at that time exist, had to be developed; communication bottlenecks rife at all levels of DoD had to be eliminated; and inadequate guidance and resource support had to be redressed.

Presented with these findings at a hearing of the House Energy and Commerce Committee's Subcommittee on Environment, Energy, and Natural Resources, an exasperated Reagan appointee, the DoD's deputy assistant secretary for the environment, Carl J. Schafer, sparred with an equally flummoxed Congressman Mike Synar (D-OK):

> *Synar*: What are you doing [about getting into compliance]? Don't tell me about the problems. Tell me what you're doing.
>
> *Schafer*: We are doing everything we can. We have issued policies from my office on each and every one of these subjects.
>
> *Synar*: Policies?
>
> *Schafer*: Yes, sir. That's my function. We are pulling together the policy on these things. We have issued policy. It is easy to say it is fragmented, but camels can't fly.[1]

Or could they? After all, academics and major corporate leaders (e.g., at Monsanto and 3M Corporation) routinely were touting how the greening of business could be a win-win situation. The environment got cleaner *and* corporate profits soared.[2] More broadly, the comments of Richard Clarke, chairman and chief executive officer of Pacific Gas and Electric Company, were hardly atypical at this time: "A strong global economy is sustainable only if it integrates economic, social, and environmental well-being."[3] Thus, with some of the nation's most egregious corporate polluters making the transition to a beyond-compliance ethic in their organizations, the new Clinton administration talked of doing the same in the U.S. military.

This chapter focuses on the patterns of politics driving, and subsequently driven by, major, crosscutting, and context-defining offensives launched by the Clinton administration to create a corporate sense of responsibility for greening the U.S. military in the Pentagon. Each began before the Republican takeover of Congress in 1995 but played out in various iterations throughout the Clinton years. Each in turn spawned counteroffensives by opponents. Reviewed first is the historical–structural misalignment for these purposes inherited by the Clinton administration from the Cold War era. Chronicled next are Deputy Undersecretary of Defense for Environmental Security (DUSD[ES]) Sherri Wasserman Goodman's efforts to do three things: (1) shift ENR responsibilities from the military services to the OSD; (2) better align DoD's personnel, financial management, logistics, information technology, and procurement systems to the new strategic, tactical, and greening emphasis of the post–Cold War era; and (3) create cross-agency councils to promote green values within the Pentagon. Combined, the tensions produced sent mixed signals from the Pentagon to military leaders and their subordinates about the priority given to greening efforts and wrought a significant yet still halting, halfway, and patchwork record of progress in institutionalizing a green ethic within the Pentagon.

The Historical–Structural Mismatch at DoD

As rational choice institutionalists predict, proponents and opponents of various statutes tend to riddle them with ambiguities, inhospitable implementing agencies, and fragmented implementation structures that can create perverse incentives.[4] Their aim is to ensure that they can influence the substance, scope, and pace of implementation in the future. Likewise, students of public administration, public management, and bureaucracy long have appreciated that an agency or program's power suffers when located deep within the administrative labyrinth of an organization with multiple responsibilities. These agencies tend to undergo frequent reorganizations, and they are without ready access to key decision makers specifying their budgets, staffing, and decision rules.[5] As we shall see in later chapters, this was true when it came to assigning responsibility for implementing many of the major ENR statutes that the military faced. Congress, after all, had assigned responsibility for implementing the Endangered Species Act to the FWS in the prodevelopment Department of the Interior (DOI), and the National Environmental Policy Act to a weak Council on Environmental Quality.

Likewise, despite EPA administrators under both Reagan (William Ruckelshaus and Lee Thomas) and George H. W. Bush (William Reilly) wanting federal facilities to be leaders in cross-media regulation, only two of ten regional offices (Region VIII in Denver and Region IV in Atlanta) had a "focal point" within their organizations for regulating federal facilities by the time Clinton took office. As Jack McGraw, then acting administrator (Region VIII–Denver), observed, federal facility coordinators became organizational "eunuchs":

> Coordinators were largely paper shufflers reviewing papers and so forth. They
> were placed in the Environmental Services Division, or in the Associate Regional

Administrator's office, or sometimes they were placed in the external [or public rela-
tions] office. . . . [The regions] were required to have one, and were allocated a slot.
But a number of regions used them as fillers. They had people they didn't know what
to do with, so they were placed in that slot.[6]

If the federal facilities regulatory regime inherited by the Clinton administration was organizationally disadvantaged, the compliance ethic at DoD was
plagued by a sinewy organizational culture inherited from the Cold War. As political scientist Erwin Hargrove explains, agencies typically create "heroic myths"
(i.e., stories) about how their successes are achieved.[7] These then are reified as
widely shared beliefs about what is important to the organization, how it achieves
its mission, and what values it shares in pursuing it. As Hargrove also documents,
however, organizations quite easily can become "prisoners" of their own myths
when the environmental challenges they face change, making timeworn, accustomed, and successful behaviors fostered by that myth dysfunctional.

Such was certainly the case in the Pentagon when it came to pressures to
green the U.S. military in the post–Cold War era. For starters, building a corporate sense of responsibility for a beyond-compliance ethic meant creating what
the military calls a sense of "jointness" of ENR thinking, initiatives, and operations within the Pentagon. But a commitment to coordinated action among the
services (what the military calls "fighting purple") was a notion foreign to the
Pentagon during most of the Cold War.[8] Indeed, "Live and let live" might be
said to have been the unofficial credo among them. Produced amid this antipa-
thy toward fighting purple, in turn, were self-images among the services that
did two things: (1) further hindered efforts at corporate thinking when it came
to greening the U.S. military during the Clinton years, and (2) predisposed the
services to trust their own technoscientific judgments and to challenge those of
ENR regulators throughout the post–Cold War era. Together, these produced
and buttressed the Cold War culture, or heroic myth, of sovereignty, secrecy, and
sinecure alluded to in chapter 1.

"Servicism," Self-Image, and Heroic Myths in the Pre-Clinton Era

A lack of jointness had not come from want of trying by secretaries of defense
and presidential administrations of both political parties during the Cold War.
Since the titular "unification" of the military services in the National Security Act
of 1947, jointness of military operations was a central aim of America's post–
World War II defense strategy. Still, the 1950s witnessed sustained and persistent
interservice rivalry, functional balkanization rather than coordination within the
military's regional commands, and a divorcing of authority and responsibility for
the OSD, the Joint Chiefs, and regional commanders.[9]

To be sure, Robert McNamara's (President Kennedy's first secretary of defense) reforms in the 1960s enhanced his power immensely relative to service

chiefs. In doing so, he set the substance of the services' force structures until President George H. W. Bush's secretary of defense, Richard Cheney, issued his 1991 Future Year Defense Plan, and he brought more technical rationality to weapons purchases. But McNamara's centralization efforts left in their wake bad feelings on the part of the military, feelings that subsequent defense secretaries were loath to arouse again. Thus, since McNamara, no defense secretary, until Donald Rumsfeld under President George W. Bush, took on the services with McNamara's zeal.

These tendencies toward autonomy were even fostered throughout the Cold War by many of McNamara's successors—most notably, Melvin Laird during the Nixon administration and Casper Weinberger during the Reagan years— who strengthened the military departments relative to the OSD.[10] Rampant, as a result, was a dysfunctional commitment to what scholar Samuel Huntington calls "servicism" and James Locher, former assistant defense secretary, calls "service supremacy."[11] The services, writes Locher, "wielded their influence more to protect their independence and prerogatives than to develop multiservice commands capable of waging modern warfare . . . and blunted efforts to make their separate forces, weapons, and systems interoperable."[12]

During the Reagan presidency, the Goldwater–Nichols Act of 1986 was designed partially to avert these pathologies, but it had come up short in many ways. Among other things, the act was designed to strengthen "jointness" among the historically fragmented services, with their service-centric requests for weapons systems. Yet as political scientist James Lebovic's analysis of defense spending between 1981 and 1993 reveals most compellingly, the military services continued to advance the same "active" stance toward weapons acquisition that they held in the era before Goldwater–Nichols.[13] Further fortified in the process were what military expert Carl Builder called the services' distinct "self-images."[14] As Builder describes them, these self-images included an enduring cultural tendency to deny the legal authority of others over their operations, to be the final authority on technical issues, to be wary of innovations that afforded uncertainty on the battlefield, and to oppose the transparency of service operations.

Although all the services nurtured these images, the U.S. Navy valued them more and guarded them most zealously against outside influences. Chairman of the Joint Chiefs and air force general David Jones once stated that the navy would prefer "to be given a mission, retain complete control over all the assets, and be left alone."[15] Researchers attribute this cultural predisposition to several factors. First, the navy sees itself as the legatee of the British navy's claim to supremacy on the oceans, with its ship commanders historically operating independently "beyond the horizon." The navy also was the most strategically independent of the services, having, through log rolling, its own army (the Marine Corps), air force, and navy. Nor did the navy value external analyses of its warfighting requirements or of how to use its assets generally. In the navy's judgment, techniques like operations research (making existing systems more efficient or effective), systems analysis (using modeling to choose among alternative weapons systems), or requirements analysis (determining how many and what size weapons) were decidedly more fallible in making these judgments than U.S. Navy experience and traditions.

Not surprisingly, the U.S. Air Force's heroic self-image propounded air power as the decisive instrument of war and, like the U.S. Navy, viewed its personnel as experts to be left alone to ply their trade. Ensconced also in the air force's Cold War doctrine was the idea that air power "can exploit speed, range, and flexibility better than land and sea forces, and therefore, it must be allowed to operate independently of these forces."[16] Revered, too, was acquiring for its pilots the most technologically advanced aircraft available, flown in ways they thought best, and put through their envelope-pushing paces as only air force pilots could. Equally unsurprising, the air force had built a substantial in-house analytical capacity to support its operational, developmental, and acquisition decisions. As such, the service also was genetically "hardwired" to rely on its own technical analyses rather than those done by others.

The U.S. Army, meanwhile, saw itself largely as the servant of others, reacting and adapting to whatever national warfighting needs emerged. This is a self-image that military scholars attribute to the army's inability to define war on its own terms.[17] During the Cold War this translated into a resource acquisition strategy that was equally reactive: Once a strategy was articulated, usually by others, the army identified risks to be overcome and what it needed to make that strategy work.[18] By the time Clinton took office, moreover, the army had grown accustomed to dealing with inadequate resources at the start of every war and, thus, to making do with what it had until adequate funding arrived. Therefore, spliced into the army's DNA was a predisposition to use "creative" accounting in the form of borrowing and shifting resources from account to account to "hold the fort" until adequate resources arrived.[19] In turn, the army's historical approach to systems, operations, and requirements analysis is best summarized as "getting a single answer (often a number) rather than illuminating the alternatives in the face of recognized uncertainties."[20] The army's approach was also geared more toward plugging numbers into DoD's preexisting systems, with "detail and scope prized . . . at the expense of clarity or understanding" for the recipients of that information.[21]

These were all self-images, of course, that would make the services bridle when confronted by ENR regulators, local ENR activists, other national ENR groups, and whistle-blowers. These combatants came armed with their own technoscientific risk assessments, environmental impact statements, and statutes to push, prod, and litigate as they tried to green the services. Equally riling culturally to the military was the complexity that greening threatened to add to already complex weapons systems.

As the writings of classical military scholars such as Sun Tzu and Karl von Clausewitz illustrate, two of the most galling fears of warriors since time immemorial are what they call "self-imposed surprise" and "friction." And one of the most self-imposed sources of surprise and friction perceived by a risk-averse military comes from letting themselves become victims of complex weapons systems that do not work in combat as advertised. Moreover, as scholar Chris Demchak cogently summarizes, fear of a "rogue" (i.e., unexpected) series of events in battle means that a paradox of weapons complexity exists: The more technologically complex a weapons system, the greater the complexity of the organizational structure needed to avert battlefield surprises.[22]

Infamous among Vietnam War veterans, for example, were the jamming of M-16 rifles and the inability of F-4 Phantoms armed with AIM-9 air-to-air missiles to duel effectively with Soviet MiG-21s in close-in "knife fights."[23] Likewise seared into the military's collective memory were persistent problems with keeping complex weapons "mission-capable." The technologically sophisticated Apache helicopter, for instance, was notorious for failing to perform all its missions at least half of the time and none of its missions about one third of the time.[24] Similarly woeful figures were available during the Reagan era for other sophisticated weapons platforms, such as the Abrams M-1 main battle tank and M2/3 Bradley fighting vehicles. Indeed, a typical European field exercise lasting five to six days in either 1981 or 1982 rendered nearly half of the eighty-plus tanks of the armor battalions involved "non-mission capable."[25]

The rub for the services, of course, is that greening weapons systems threatened to increase their complexity even further. Similarly off-putting was the administrative complexity occasioned by ENR acquisition and regulatory regimes. Disruptive of established organizational structures, interactions, and routines, these new structures, processes, and procedures threatened resource distribution (i.e., succor) among the services. As I will discuss in greater detail in chapter 9, for example, full ENR cost-cycle accounting could advantage or disadvantage weapons systems dear to the hearts of the various services when procurement priorities were set.

Greening Gone Purple?

This is not to suggest that structures, processes, and procedures for dealing with ENR issues were not put in place by the Pentagon during the Cold War. Nor, consistent with variations in their self-images, is it to suggest that the services walked in lockstep on this front. The navy, for example, began its formal efforts in the early 1970s by creating an environmental support system with a distinct funding account for environmental cleanup projects. It also started its installation restoration program in 1980, four years before Congress required the services to do so. So, too, had the army established an installation restoration program in the mid-1970s, albeit one significantly smaller than the navy's. Meanwhile, the air force leapt far ahead by taking a proactive stance on pollution prevention, seeing it as a tool for avoiding costly compliance and cleanup actions.

It *is* to say, however, that the services shared a lack of command emphasis on the environment as well as a deep-seated aversion to outsiders telling them how far, fast, and technically to approach the task. Woefully lacking also were corporate organizational structures, processes, and procedures for combating environmental problems. At the same time, the services faced a surfeit of ENR responsibilities that far outstripped resources allocated for these purposes. Moreover, any efforts to address ENR issues were viewed as tangential to the military's primary mission; were readily traded off whenever they threatened military training; and were never incorporated or institutionalized in a corporate sense within the organizational, administrative, or accounting structures of the OSD at the Pentagon.

This, in turn, meant that even the most ENR-committed services, service personnel, or contractors were disproportionately rewarded at the end of the day for combat-related contributions (e.g., weapons production) rather than ENR protection. Military analyst and Lt. Col. Kent Hughes Butts put the realpolitik of the situation best in 1991 as the Soviet empire gasped its last breath. In arguing that the services' environmental programs could be improved greatly without additional resources if only command emphases improved, Butts wrote of the absence of "real priorities" regarding ENR protection:

> [Base] commanders are faced with a multitude of priorities. To be successful, installation commanders must satisfy the priorities of senior leadership at MACOMs [Major Commands] and [service] headquarters. Installation commanders are very perceptive and can identify their leaders' priorities with great acuity. They know that there are *paper priorities* and *real priorities*. Paper priorities are "We must do this because it is important; however, we can't adequately resource it at this time." Such priorities are supported by well-written letters to place on bulletin boards or show visitors. Real priorities shine like the sun; their communication to the installation commander is forceful and clear, and the installation comptroller will find a healthy budget line for such priorities and a celeritous, responsive staff officer at his MACOM to cover shortfalls if they occur.[26]

In sum, the military created ENR-related programs before the end of the Cold War, but ENR protection was never something that the warfighting and training missions of the armed forces worried about. Neither did it become a key element in the services' strategic, operational, and tactical doctrines. Moreover, whenever pressed by regulators to raise ENR protection in priority, the military's national security mission became the "bloody shirt" to ensure that the Pentagon controlled how, how much, and how fast the services complied with the nation's ENR statutes.

Teaching Camels to Fly?

With these historical–structural misalignments clearly in mind, the Clinton administration began its campaign of offensives to create a corporate sense of responsibility for greening within the Pentagon. As Samuel Huntington suggests, however, "People who act the same way over a long period of time tend to develop distinctive and persistent habits of thought. Their unique relation to the world gives them a unique perspective on the world and leads them to rationalize their behavior and role. This is particularly true where the role is a professional one."[27] And no more heroic organization existed with a unique professional perspective on the world and a capacity for rationalizing its behavior than the DoD.

The Goodman Offensive for Greening Purple Begins

Moving quickly on the ENR front, Clinton's first secretary of defense, Les Aspin, created the Office of the DUSD(ES). In doing so, the former congressman and respected defense intellectual tried symbolically to raise the Pentagon-wide profile, significance, and rewards of incorporating ENR values into the day-to-day operations of the U.S. military services. Wasting little time, DUSD(ES) Goodman and her team hit the ground running. She announced an ambitious agenda for advancing the corporate sense of responsibility for environmental security emphasized rhetorically by Aspin and the Clinton White House. In testimony before the Senate Subcommittee on Military Readiness and Defense Infrastructure in mid-1993, for example, she defined her commitment to environmental security as "ensuring responsible environmental performance in defense operations and assisting to deter or mitigate impacts of adverse environmental actions [on] international security."[28]

To realize these goals while ensuring military readiness, Goodman outlined for the committee a strategy that she called "C^3P^2 plus technology." This acronym stood for aggressively accelerating "compliance, cleanup, conservation, pollution prevention, and technology development" in "common sense" ways that would both be cost-effective and balance ENR considerations against military readiness needs. Premised on a ten-year forecast of likely challenges, choices, and opportunities facing Goodman's office, the C^3P^2 plus technology agenda meant ensuring that, first and foremost, the military services complied with the law. This, she averred, was critical to military readiness, because it ensured continued access to whatever air, land, and water resources the services needed for realistic troop training and weapons testing. Her agenda, with pollution prevention its centerpiece, also protected the quality of life of U.S. troops and their families by ensuring that environmental, health, and safety regulations were met on military bases. Finally, she committed her office to incorporating better environmental characteristics into all weapons systems acquisitions. Here, she cast a special eye toward lowering costs, improving performance, and avoiding battlefield risks, surprises, and rogue sets of events.

All this notwithstanding, Goodman's office still reported formally to the Office of the Under Secretary of Defense for Acquisition and Technology. Thus, she continued to fight for greening resources in an organizational culture where the dominant coalition consisted of engineers steeped in traditional acquisition and technology development. Goodman also began her tenure with a fragmented structure within the Pentagon and the military services that worked against developing a corporate identity. Take, for example, the relationship between the four pillars of Goodman's C^3P^2 plus technology strategy and existing installation (i.e., base) management structures. To green military bases successfully, installations management and environmental security had to be integrated. Yet they were located under separate under secretaries when Goodman took office, a situation not remedied until the George W. Bush administration. Additionally, although her Program Integration Office executed the planning, programming, and budgeting system and managed technology efforts, each of the military services had their own versions of these units.

Neither did the structurally balkanizing tendencies defying a corporate greening strategy end here. Not only were the armed forces' programs plagued by many of the same structural foibles but also responsibilities for performing them had intentionally been scattered across a wide range of funding accounts and organizational units. These included disparate and uncoordinated accounts for operations and maintenance (i.e., funding for military readiness activities like training), military construction, procurement, research and development (R&D), military family housing, military personnel, the Reserves, the National Guard, and base closures. Nor did it help Goodman's aims that key ENR challenges were marginalized without advocates or expertise within existing Pentagon structures, processes, and procedures. For example, despite the growing importance of threats to drinking water from military operations, as well as the regulatory actions and lawsuits spawned by them, no single office in the Pentagon had a person dedicated to water contamination issues.

Before future chapters examine how Goodman fared in addressing such issues, three Pentagon-wide (i.e., corporate-wide) offensives launched by her are revealing and important to understand because they afford a larger context of constraints upon her C^3P^2 plus technology agenda. These offensives involved three central questions. First, how much could she advance civilian rather than service control over environmental policymaking and budgeting? Second, how would other efforts to develop a corporate culture affect Goodman's efforts to develop a corporate ENR ethic? And third, how effective would her efforts be to create parallel cross-agency and cross-service councils for coordinating and integrating ENR policies across the Pentagon?

The Civilian Control Offensive.   As military journalists Thom Shanker and Eric Schmitt cleverly put the dilemma of military reform, "The Pentagon is a building with five sides but a million angles."[29] Faced with the "million angles" of deliberately fractured administrative, responsibility, and accounting structures when it came to ENR protection within the Pentagon, Goodman launched three major and interrelated efforts to enhance civilian control over the services. These cut to the quick of existing service sovereignty, secrecy, and sinecure. Aimed at reducing the military's control over ENR personnel, Goodman first tried to centralize in her office environmental policymaking and budgeting for the services, as well as to create a cadre of civilian ENR professionals with career tracks untethered to the military services. Second, she tried to create DoD regional offices paralleling the EPA's regions and through which all service ENR activities would be filtered, reviewed, and coordinated. Finally, Goodman moved to create within her office a mechanism for consolidating all environmental R&D initiatives, thus reducing the services' influence over the substance, scope, and pace of greening.

A prime mover of Goodman's initiatives in these areas was her principal deputy assistant secretary for environmental defense, Gary Vest. A former top environmental policymaker for the air force, Vest believed that the services had to either get greener or put military readiness at risk of court suits. Thus, when Brig. Gen. Jed Brown, at the time the army's top career environmental policymaker, began circulating an early draft of a vision statement titled "Environmental Security in the Year 2003," Vest told him to make it even "stronger" in wresting control from the services.[30] The version that Brown subsequently circulated only five months into the Clinton administration did precisely that. In fact, the services immediately characterized its contents as nothing less than misguided and crass bureaucratic imperialism on the part of Environmental Security Office (ESO) staff.

In short order, the military's counteroffensive to Brown's vision statement began. Various service officials set out to persuade the House and Senate Armed Services committees that readiness and weapons modernization would be threatened if service personnel were left out of budget and policy decisions in these areas. Consider the stakes involved for the military. Under the proposal, "all environmental security positions not required for military command and control or deployment" would be converted to civilian positions. What is more, the services no longer would control the career prospects of their civilian personnel, a responsibility they coveted because of the not-so-subtle leverage it gave them over ENR decisions. Instead, a DoD career development and management program would be created within Goodman's office, one encouraging and facilitating movements across the services. What Vest and company envisioned, argued critics in the military, was base commanders across all the services losing "control over the environmental issues that affect operations on [their] bases."

Similarly brash and viscerally unpalatable to the various services was the vision statement's emphasis on filtering environmental policymaking through newly created regional DoD offices. To be sure, a few environmental regional offices already existed in several EPA regions, but these were operated and run independently by the various services. For example, the air force had established regional offices beginning in the mid-1970s, and the navy had established some in 1990. What *was* unprecedented, however, was the idea of regional offices coordinating all three services, in all ten EPA regions, and led by officials (environmental security regional officers) who would be deputy assistants reporting to Goodman rather than to the services. Likewise jarring to the services' self-images and interests, the proposal envisioned these service teams handling service-specific issues and working with military installation staff reporting to Goodman's regional officers. Her regional officers, in turn, would work with service teams on "policy or matters of common interest."

Accurately predicting that the Goodman-Vest-Brown vision statement would be a "major battleground," informed observers argued that Goodman would pursue the regional office proposal first, and "if she wins that battle, then the next step will be the civilian workforce." The good news for her was that the DoD was able in 1994 to establish a Regional Environmental Coordinators (RECs) Program. But with the services mounting a counteroffensive resisting implementation, nearly three full years of negotiations passed before DoD issued consolidated policies, roles, and responsibilities for the DoD RECs.

Thus, in what will become a familiar pattern in this book, the evolving definition of REC roles and responsibilities after these crises of authority was done largely on terms acceptable to the military services. Most significantly, control of the regions was left with the services rather than shifted to Goodman's office in the OSD. The services, not Goodman's shop, were responsible for creating the RECs. Moreover, the RECs were appointed by service secretaries and reported to them, not to Goodman, and a lead military service, not Goodman's office, became the executive agency representing DoD on environmental issues. Finally, absent consensus, settlement of disputes would be elevated to the lead military service.[31]

In contrast, both Vest and Goodman appropriately cite creation of the OSD's environmental and training programs as major successes of their tenure. Even here, though, progress was disappointing in meeting their initial goal to create separate career tracks for ENR professionals across the services and run by Goodman's office. Not unlike with the RECs, moreover, progress made on the environmental education, training, and career development fronts still came packaged in terms protecting the prerogatives and authorities of the military services.

Granted, DoD instruction document 4715.10 saluted the Pentagon's commitment to incorporating ENR concerns into the curricula at service and joint service schools. Also justly praised was the creation of an integrated environmental security school system within the military.[32] Noteworthy, too, the DoD pledged to ensure that military personnel working in nonenvironmental program areas received training and education, especially those working as installation commanders, in acquisition, and in contracting and financial management. What is more, the DUSD(ES) was given responsibility for many of these tasks.

Nevertheless, the responsibility structures for implementing major aspects of the training and development phases consolidated amid this crisis of authority often were fragmented, complex, and assigned partially to units with no history of supporting such efforts. For example, Goodman had to evaluate the adequacy of education and training programs in cooperation and coordination with the under secretary of defense for personnel and readiness, the military services, the Defense Logistics Agency, and the Defense Nuclear Agency. The final determination of adequacy (especially if disputes could not be resolved) was assigned again to the military services. In addition, not only did the service heads make these final judgments, but they, not Goodman's office, determined whether or not ENR personnel had career advancement opportunities.

Finally, and in terms of ENR research and development consolidation in the face of environmental technology programs scattered among the services in the Pentagon, Goodman tried to advance a corporate sense of responsibility by launching her so-called test-bed program in 1993. Seeing Goodman's initiative as an upstart contender for scarce R&D dollars, however, Anita Jones, director of DoD's Research and Engineering Office, successfully fought Goodman's effort during internal DoD reviews of the project. In launching her counteroffensive, Jones began her own (ultimately unsuccessful) effort to incorporate all service R&D and Defense Environmental Restoration Account (DERA) R&D under *her* office's purview.[33]

Meanwhile, the services and their congressional allies aggressively mounted another counteroffensive in Congress to stop a proposed shift in control over military R&D projects to the Strategic Environmental Research and Development Program (SERDP). In the FY 1994 and FY 1995 budgets, for example, the Senate Armed Services Committee stopped efforts by the Senate Appropriations Committee to consolidate service R&D programs under SERDP.[34] The SERDP, created by Congress to expedite and prioritize environmental R&D, was managed conjointly by the DoD, DOE, and EPA.

Consolidation of environmental R&D in SERDP thus struck at the heart of the services' control over environmental R&D in several ways. First, it meant taking responsibility for coordinating DoD environmental R&D from the military's Tri-Service Program (formerly the Tri-Service Environmental Quality Research and Development Plan). Second, and even more distressing to the services, transferring these responsibilities to SERDP meant that the EPA would now help manage the program. Finally, and at the heart of the proposal offered by SERDP's legislative "godfather" (and Goodman's former boss on the Senate Armed Services Committee), Senator Sam Nunn (D-GA), the military's propensity to "[push] weapons programs under the guise of environmental research" would be foiled.[35]

Recognizing the assault this proposal made on the self-image and succor of the military services and their contractors, Nunn and his allies told them not to worry. Only second-tier projects would be transferred to SERDP. The military, however, would have none of this and went swiftly on the counteroffensive to reframe the issue to their advantage. The SERDP's long-term research focus, they argued, would cripple their near-term efforts to get into the field innovative cleanup technologies addressing the distinctive needs of the individual services. Moreover, SERDP director Robert Oswald tried to narrow further the focus of the transfer of responsibilities to high-priority items that the military identified as critical. He also sought to establish a program office staffed by members of the services to get flag officer buy-in. This after opponents already had tried to weaken the directorship of the SERDP by making it a part-time position led by the director of R&D (Oswald) at the Army Corps of Engineers.

Nor did the military's counteroffensive stop there during the Clinton years. Launched under the rubric of Defense Secretary William Cohen's 1997 heralded Defense Reform Initiative (DRI) to bring the "best business practices" of the private sector to the Pentagon (see below), three other efforts to consolidate diverse functions were foiled. First, in a bold move, the Pentagon in 1998 proposed moving responsibility for SERDP cleanup and pollution prevention R&D programs from the OSD (and, again, from Jones's Research and Engineering Office) to the army. In this instance, however, Jones's internal resistance to realigning responsibility structures was joined externally (for different reasons) and successfully by environmentalists and the ranking Democrat on the Senate Armed Services Committee, Charles Robb (VA).[36]

Second, when Goodman proposed later that same year to centralize funding for pollution prevention across weapons systems and have her office prescribe funding for pollution prevention testing in each service's five-year program objectives memorandum, army and air force opposition scuttled the proposal. Third, and decidedly less bold, was a DRI-related proposal by Goodman to consolidate under her purview the SERDP, with its basic and applied research focus, and the Environmental Security Technology Certification Program, with its field validation responsibilities. Again Jones successfully resisted this alignment of strategy and structure. This crisis of authority resulted in a structural consolidation and accommodation that was a decidedly looser "partnership" arrangement between the two units. Left was a still functionally fragmented SERDP–Environmental Security Technology Certification Program–Defense Environmental Restoration Program implementation structure, with separate parts controlled by DoD's Research and Engineering Office, the DUSD(ES), and the services.

The Management Systems Offensive.   Commenting on the sorry state of DoD's management structures in the mid-1990s, an exasperated Jack Brook, director of Defense Information and Financial Management at what was then called the General Accounting Office (GAO), put it bluntly: "Here's this [organization] with 3 million employees and a trillion dollars in assets, and they're not accountable. They can't produce an auditable financial statement. They don't have cost records. They can't control their inventory. They're in bad shape. If they were a private company and didn't go bankrupt because of inefficient management practices, they wouldn't be allowed to sell stock."[37] Indeed, the Pentagon's 1995 assessment of its own management systems said the department's operations were plagued by "an antiquated bureaucratic organizational structure coping unsuccessfully with the complexities of modern government and business."[38]

Nor were the Pentagon systems necessary for supporting the greening of the U.S. military in any better shape. The situation confronting the Clinton team is summarized well in a litany of ENR-related problems identified by a 1991 DoD inspector general's report amid claims of progress by the George H. W. Bush administration:

> A lack of DoD directives to implement [ENR] laws; a lack of supplemental and de-tailing instructions for the DoD components [i.e., the military services]; late funding, which caused programs to lag; poor relations with states and the EPA; poor infor-mation flow—up, down, and laterally; poor cooperation among DoD components, although they share the same problems; no program consistency among DoD com-ponents; inconsistent personnel practices among the components; and inability to set consistent priorities for cleanup.[39]

As the post–Cold War era dawned, however, the good news for greening pro-ponents was that correcting these management system problems became increas-ingly attractive to Pentagon reformers. The bad news, however, was that offensives to reform these systems focused on how they affected military readiness and mod-ernization, not ENR concerns. The first Bush administration's Base Force Concept, as well as the Clinton administration's Bottom-Up Review, Quadrennial Defense Review, and Joint Vision 2010 report, all put severe strains on the Pentagon's man-agement systems. In effect, they created a mismatch in capacity with the services' responsibilities (i.e., a historical-structural mismatch) that the Pentagon feared could compromise national security. Indeed, some in the Pentagon said this mis-alignment of strategy and structure could hobble necessary shifts in the military's strategic, tactical, and operational doctrines.

Still, with ongoing reviews of these doctrines in the first term of the Clinton administration, a major effort to address the Pentagon's management system shortcomings in ways affecting greening did not come until 1997 with Secretary Cohen's DRI.[40] Consistent with Clinton's National Performance Review (NPR), Cohen said that applying best business practices would reduce OSD personnel by one-third through eliminating some functions and transferring non-core OSD functions to the military services or other defense agencies. In addition, the DRI included features to reduce overhead and streamline infrastructure at all levels of DoD and the military services, reform the acquisition process, and outsource or privatize support activities whenever alternative service suppliers existed. Other best business practices included consolidating excess support agencies, leveraging commercial technology, and reducing unneeded standards and specifications.

In short order, Goodman's office found itself squarely within the crosshairs of three major initiatives carrying the imprimatur of the DRI, initiatives that will be chronicled in greater depth in subsequent chapters. These actions both illustrated and further diminished the capacity of her office to win internecine struggles within the Pentagon. They included proposals to move environmental functions from Goodman's office to the army; to privatize or competitive source

various environmental functions carried out or overseen by civilian ENR workers in the services (e.g., BRAC and other cleanups); and to privatize water, wastewater, natural gas, and electric utility provisions at U.S. military bases.[41] By so
doing, the Pentagon anticipated saving approximately one-third of its $1 billion
per year nonrecurring environmental compliance and operations and maintenance costs as well as a portion of its $900 million recurring costs.[42] In the process
Goodman's office saw the transfer of thirteen of its ENR positions to the army
(eleven), the air force (one), and the Defense Logistics Agency (one). Included
among these were positions related to the advocacy of environmental restoration, conservation management, environmental R&D and technology, and conventional weapons demilitarization.[43]

Likewise, and as we shall see in greater detail in chapter 8, the DoD used the
DRI's focus on downsizing OSD and transferring "non-core functions" to the services to justify decentralizing its chemical demilitarization destruction program
from the OSD to the army. Then, in 1998, the Pentagon proposed decentralizing
authority for running its Technical Assistance for Public Participation program
from Goodman's office in the OSD to the army. Incensed, environmentalists
belittled the transfer as letting "the fox guard the henhouse."[44] Opponents of
greening, they argued, again were using the DRI's focus on "rationalizing administration" as a counteroffensive to enhance the autonomy of a service chronically
excoriated for its obstinacy and sleight of hand in, for example, ignoring citizens'
opposition to burning demilitarized chemical weapons.[45]

Local ENR activists also perceived DoD's proposals to privatize or competitive source environmental management positions and base cleanups as efforts
to "load shed" legal responsibilities to others for remedying environmental violations, monitoring wastewater discharges, meeting drinking water standards,
and paying potential fines and penalties. Perhaps these approaches might make
technical sense (they would later prove difficult to implement). But whether intentionally or inadvertently, they also signaled to those in the army, navy, and air
force that the environment was, as many in Congress had claimed since 1994, a
responsibility that others should shoulder. Critics complained that a more perverse incentive could not have been found against institutionalizing a beyond-
compliance ENR ethic within the U.S. military.

The Parallel Structure Offensive.   A well-established technique for circumventing structural fragmentation in organizations (public or private) is to create
parallel structures (e.g., councils or teams) to bring unity of purpose to otherwise disparate operations.[46] The Clinton years witnessed major efforts to use
parallel structuring in this fashion to advance greening. In early 1993, for example, Vest created the Defense Environmental Council (DEC) "to steer and coordinate . . . the work of top environmental officials [across] the services . . . and
to integrate the participation of all offices involved in environmental security
matters."[47] With Goodman chairing the council, Vest argued that she and John

Deutch, then undersecretary of defense for acquisition, would have a "means by which OSD can get good and timely advice and counsel" from the individual services on how to make environmental programs work best.[48] Vest, in turn, chaired two policy boards under the council, one for environmental safety and the other for installations, with eleven committees (e.g., on cleanup, compliance, and pollution prevention) reporting to the two boards. For its part, the council would have input into DoD's planned acquisition reform initiative (see chapter 9 for in-depth treatment) and a key role in implementing the recommendations of Aspin's Bottom-Up Review of the U.S. defense posture.

Or would they? Once again, Vest and Goodman poked the services in the eye. Although the council included members from environmental professionals in the services, representatives from operational warfighting units in the services were excluded. What is more, with the career chances of environmental officials still in the military's hands, they were prone to weighting heavily the concerns of their non-ENR superiors. In addition, and in combination with the greening offensives already discussed in this chapter (e.g., trying to centralize civilian control in Goodman's office), the services saw this move as yet another example of bureaucratic imperialism on Goodman's part. Thus, in short order, service resistance combined with events related to BRACs to prompt a counteroffensive by the military to marginalize the council in policy deliberations.

Perhaps most crippling amid all this was a major reorganization launched by Goodman's superior, John Deutch, only eight months after Vest first announced the DEC's creation. As noted earlier and detailed in subsequent chapters, pressure within Congress spiraled during Clinton's first two years to expedite the transfer of BRAC properties to local communities for economic development. To symbolize the administration's concern structurally, Deutch created an Office of Economic Security within the OSD, a move stripping Goodman's office of some installations-based activities that had to be integrated with ENR values to advance greening. Rationalized as "integrating the base closure and cleanup process with reuse and investment activities," many of the functions transferred to the Office of Economic Security were functions previously listed as Vest's ENR priorities for the DEC.[49] Included among these were installation management, construction management, and investment activities. In effect, key ENR responsibilities now were placed in the hands of a new unit far more concerned with expediting base transfers and economic development than with ENR protection.

Yet another reorganization that compromised Goodman's office under the rubric of the president's NPR, Deutch's initiative had additional ripple effects detrimental to greening. First, realizing there were "activities that involve both Economic and Environmental Security which require a high degree of cooperation, coordination, and partnership," Deutch's plan envisioned "partnership plans" worked out between Goodman's office and the new Office of Economic Security.[50] Thus, in trying to put Humpty Dumpty back together again, a series of agreements would have to be negotiated between the respective units, leaving consolidated structures in the wake of these crises of authority with ambiguous responsibilities and high transaction costs.

Significant in its own right for complicating the operation of Vest's DEC, Undersecretary Deutch's initiative also prompted a reorganization of Goodman's office, one that immediately drew the ire of environmentalists. Created was a new office led by an assistant deputy under secretary of defense for environmental quality and responsible for integrating cleanup, compliance, and pollution prevention. Although Vest denied the clear implications of the move, environmentalists understood fully what had happened. Functions that the Clinton administration had elevated with great fanfare to the deputy under secretary level in DoD were now demoted to the assistant deputy level. Indeed, environmental professionals in the military who appreciated Goodman's initiatives argued against the move, especially because it downgraded the pollution prevention emphasis she had earlier touted as the centerpiece of her C^3P^2 plus technology agenda.

In 1998 yet another offensive began using parallel structuring to advance a corporate sense of responsibility for greening within the Pentagon. In response to Cohen's DRI of the previous year, Goodman initially had engaged in some brinksmanship to rally help from supporters outside the Pentagon. She floated the idea that subsequent mandated cuts in staffing to her office might require a reconsideration of the office's four ENR pillars. Goodman eventually settled on keeping the pillars but did get in return from Deutch a "corporate board" comprised of senior leadership in her office to conduct "planning" and "oversee the execution" of her C^3P^2 plus technology agenda.[51]

Incredibly, the six offices that titularly reported to her (environmental quality, cleanup, safety and occupational health, program integration, explosives safety, and pest management) were essentially still going their own ways after six years of the Clinton administration. In the process they acted as competitors pitted against each other in a zero-sum (and often below zero-sum) struggle for resources, power, and influence within her office. The creation of the parallel structure notwithstanding, however, strategic ENR planning never fully materialized in her office in ways indicating that the sinewy program ties of the various offices could be overcome. Thus, despite the Herculean and notable accomplishments of Goodman's team in the face of immense obstacles over their eight years at the Pentagon, each of the six major program offices in the Environmental Security Office was still putting together separate strategic plan as George W. Bush took his oath of office in 2001.

Discussion

This chapter has recounted the state of the Pentagon's commitment to greening the U.S. military as the Clinton administration took office in 1993 as well as the patterns of politics associated with three major initiatives launched by Sherri Wasserman Goodman to begin addressing shortcomings she perceived in that legacy. These initiatives involved efforts to align corporate structures, processes, and procedures better with greening strategies by enhancing civilian ENR control, by redressing inadequate management systems critical to greening, and by creating parallel decision structures to ensure a role for greening proponents in readiness and weapons system decisions.

Goodman's initiatives were met by resistance from Pentagon actors reminiscent of the Cold War era, resistance premised on keeping control of the substance, scope, and pace of greening out of the hands of greening proponents. Resistance also meant trying to keep control of relevant information related to greening in the hands of the services and their civilian representatives while trying to protect established Cold War relationships with contractors and with each other. Respectively, and in terms of the services' heroic myth, these meant retaining as much sovereignty as possible, maintaining as much secrecy as possible, and preserving existing patterns of sinecure. And as subsequent chapters chronicle, changing circumstances and White House concessions to the military often left Goodman and her staff at a disadvantage in battles within the E-ring.

To be sure, some progress toward greening was made. But rendered in the process were structures, processes, and procedures geared more toward the military maintaining as much stability, predictability, and security of its traditional operations as possible. Discernible from these dynamics, too, is a persistent pattern of politics. To see how and why this is the case both substantively and conceptually, we return to the five research questions posed in chapter 1 and to concepts culled from the disparate theories reviewed there on organizational change.

Was There a Trajectory of Contestation?

Witnessed in this chapter was a clear trajectory (or arc) of contestation to the civil–military disputes involved. First, the shock of the end of the Cold War catalyzed perceptions of a historical-structural mismatch, which was followed by reform offensives that were rebutted by reform counteroffensives. Together these created crises of authority that could only be resolved through negotiation and ultimately the consolidation of structures, processes, and procedures that left any progress made uneven and subject to shifting political pressures. Moreover, throughout this trajectory of contestation, the patterns of politics witnessed were steeped in the pursuit of the political, organizational, and personal prerogatives perceived by proponents and opponents alike.

What Motivated the Participants' Behavior?

Taking each component of this trajectory in order, first came the proposition by a reform coalition (led by Clinton appointees within the OSD) that a historical–

structural mismatch existed. Most broadly, greening proponents contended that existing DoD structures, processes, and procedures within the OSD when Clinton took office were inadequate for creating a corporate sense of responsibility to meet growing external pressures on the U.S. military to green its operations in the post–Cold War era. This perception created the three minishocks or initiatives within the Pentagon that constituted a greening offensive by Goodman and her supporters.

Making "sense" of these post–Cold War pressures and how best to deal with them, Goodman's civilian control offensive was premised on a belief that continuing military control over the career chances of ENR personnel, DoD regions, and R&D was not up to meeting post–Cold War calls to green its operations. Likewise, Goodman's initiative to consolidate ENR research and development under her office rested on her belief that, if left in place, existing military structures, processes, and procedures would continue channeling R&D funding into warfighting-related projects or divert the monies to military contingency operations abroad. Equally inimical to new post–Cold War realities, in her view, were existing management systems and decision structures. These marginalized the compliance, cleanup, and pollution prevention values and information that a corporate sense of ENR responsibility demanded.

Still, disagreements reigned over what reforms, if any, were needed as Goodman sought to impose and diffuse her initiatives within the Pentagon. These disagreements were intensely fueled by and filtered through perceptions of principle, self-interest, and realpolitik, with perceptions of history, context, and contingency most telling. Respectively, these refer to such factors as organizational culture, inherited resources, structural arrangements, and constellations of power (history); the social, economic, political, and technological situation at any time (context); and how delays incurred by greening initiatives would affect warfighting missions (contingency). Moreover, they were framed, and reframed over time, as issues in ways calculated to advance these interests.

For Goodman, her staff, and external allies, for instance, advancing a Pentagon-wide sense of responsibility for a beyond-compliance ethic meant boosting the relative influence and strength of Goodman's historically disadvantaged office within the Pentagon (i.e., they had to change history-related misalignments). They also had to take advantage of changes they perceived in the social and political pressures facing the military in the post–Cold War era (i.e., take advantage of a more favorable context). Finally, they had to gamble that the threats of delays posed by lawsuits and fines now allowed by the FFCA of 1992 would make the services more receptive to greening (i.e., contingencies were now more favorable to them than during the Cold War).

For opponents of Goodman's initiatives, however, all that was needed to meet new and evolving post–Cold War challenges was to do more of what the Pentagon and the services were already doing, only better. Thus, in short order, opponents framed Goodman's initiatives as unnecessary, ill-conceived, and unbridled bureaucratic imperialism by Goodman and her staff. Consequently, in weighing and deciding to wage counteroffensives to them, opponents also viewed Goodman's initiatives through "filters" of organizational history, context, and contingency and saw major threats. Each of the initiatives threatened existing military (versus civilian) dominance of the substance, scope, and pace of greening; threatened the existing decision structures, processes, and procedures supporting that dominance; and posed potential delays that jeopardized core warfighting missions.

In coming to these conclusions opponents weighed such things as the extent to which each greening initiative had the potential to impact or impose delays on their unit's ability to perform its traditional core mission-related activities. The motivational power of this contingency factor was illustrated, for instance, when Goodman tried shifting ENR research and development to her office in order to stop its diversion to conventional weapons research. Relevant, too, for opponents was the military's historical superiority relative to Goodman's office within the E-Ring; in short, they had greater established power, access, and influence within the "building" than did Goodman's office. These translated into existing contextual differences in energy distributions (i.e., in the relative balance of power between or among the contestants) that clearly favored Goodman's opponents.

As such, opponents' calculations were straightforward: they were advantaged by and sought to protect existing decision structures. More precisely, those with official authority to make decisions related to Goodman's initiatives were unlikely to support massive change (i.e., decision structures were closed to outsiders). At the same time, they calculated that the esoteric management issues involved made it unlikely that Goodman's initiatives would become associated with other issues and thus draw allies to her cause (i.e., access structures were relatively closed).

But history alone was not destiny because the context at any given point in time mattered. Affecting opponents' decision calculi in mounting counteroffensives, for example, was the lack of issue salience to potential Goodman allies, especially after the 1994 congressional elections. Important, too, were the lack of proximity to everyday concerns of nontraditional members of the Pentagon's political economy as well as the improbability of other issues spilling over into these decisions to shift the balance of power toward greening (i.e., "proximity effects" were unlikely). Nor was Goodman's relative power position in Pentagon decision structures helped when disputes such as gays in the military and mangled missions in Somalia and Haiti diverted the White House's attention away from greening. Put more conceptually, the entry times of these disputes and events were unpropitious for her cause.

What Specifically Were They Fighting Over?

Wrought by this thrust-and-parry politics of contestation were crises of authority wherein the old order or regime was under challenge by Goodman's initiatives, but a new order was yet to be born. Consequently, the military's precise ENR responsibilities, let alone any need to commit to a beyond-compliance ethic, were left in abeyance until authority relationships were resolved. In turn, the targets or "fodder" for these battles fell into three broad categories (or sets) of rules: constitutional, collective choice, and operational.

In terms of constitutional rule sets, the primary battle occurred over a fundamental constitutional and jurisprudential principle: What is the proper balance of ENR civilian control over the military? Regarding collective choice and operational rule sets, the primary contests were over authority (who decides?), scoping (who is responsible for doing what?), position (who has the right to participate?), and payoff (who bears the burdens or benefits?) rules. Included were crises over who would have responsibility for training and rewarding ENR personnel (authority rules), whether EPA would have a role to play in SERDP (scoping rules), and whether Goodman's office would have input into such core mission decisions as strategic doctrine or Secretary Aspin's Bottom-Up Review (position rules).

Likewise illustrative were contests over whether persons reporting to Goodman or the individual services would make cleanup and other greening decisions in DoD regions (authority rules), whether and how DERA R&D funds would be allocated by Goodman's office (payoff rules), and what role the DEC process would play in acquisition reforms (scoping rules). Also involved explicitly or implicitly in each of these battles were contests over information and aggregation rules. Respectively, these included disputes over the kinds of information needed to evaluate service ENR personnel (information rules), and how Goodman's regional office was to collate information and integrate needs across the services to make regional decisions (aggregation rules).

What Strategies and Tactics Did They Use?

Witnessed throughout these crises of authority, too, were examples of various strategies and tactics reminiscent again in attitude and in aim of what the military used during the Cold War era. Within the general confines of its omnipresent zero-sum issue (re)framing of ENR–military readiness weapons modernization tradeoffs, plus the issue framing noted already in this section, these repertoires of contestation included some mobilization of external allies. However, opponents of greening initiatives focused most heavily on deinstitutionalization strategies. These were designed to reduce the capacity of regulators to function effectively.

Illustrative of mobilization strategies were efforts to mobilize key external and internal actors (e.g., Nunn, Deutch, the Armed Services committees, and local ENR activists) to both support and oppose SERDP and the creation of RECs. Regarding deinstitutionalization strategies, tactics such as devolution, deskilling, defunding, downsizing, and load shedding were rampant. Significant in this regard were efforts to devolve ENR responsibilities from Goodman's office to the military services, including efforts to devolve the chemical demilitarization program to the army. Also illustrative were efforts to shift certain key activities under BRAC from Goodman's more ENR-oriented shop to the new Office of Economic Security; to require the two offices to work together (thus diluting Goodman's authority); to privatize (i.e., load shed) controversial cleanup responsibilities and electric utility provisions; and to deskill, defund, and downsize her office (e.g., by cutting ENR positions from Goodman's office). It is important to note that these were done under the rubric of improving management practices as per Clinton's NPR and Secretary Cohen's DRI. Thus they were illustrative of objective shifting, a tactic used to justify or mask initiatives with controversial policy implications as mere technical management issues.

What Were the Implications?

In the end, the negotiation and bargaining necessary to resolve these crises of authority produced a consolidation of structures, processes, and procedures that were halting, halfway, and patchwork. Illustrative of this dynamic were the fractionated structures left in the wake of contests between Jones and Goodman and her staff over control of the SERDP, over the role and composition of the DEC, and over the reporting requirements of the RECs. What is more, these left the military woefully shy of the civilian accountability, transparency, and resource reengagement necessary to institutionalize an enduring beyond-compliance ethic. Rendered instead were structures, processes, and procedures geared more toward maintaining as much stability, predictability, and security of the services' traditional operations as possible. All this improved the ability of the Pentagon "camel" to fly compared with the status of ENR concerns in the Cold War era. Yet the battle over the initiatives covered in this chapter also left a strategy-structure misalignment that would become the leitmotif against which conflicts over the substance, scope, and pace of greening ensued during the Clinton years. Simultaneously, by sending an inconsistent message about its priority, they rendered problematic an enduring about-face when it came to nurturing a beyond-compliance ethic in the U.S. military absent sustained external pressures during Goodman's tenure and in the post-Clinton years. To begin seeing how and why this was the case, I turn in chapter 4 to the patterns of politics accompanying the development of such a mental schema among service personnel when it came to base cleanups during the Clinton years.

Notes

1. Seth Shulman, *The Threat at Home: Confronting the Toxic Legacy of the U.S. Military* (Boston: Beacon Press, 1992), 18–19.

2. Michael E. Porter and Claas van der Linde, "Green *and* Competitive: Ending the Stalemate," *Harvard Business Review* (September–October 1995): 120–34; Michael E. Porter and Claas van der Linde, "Perspectives: The Challenge of Going Green," *Harvard Business Review* (July–August 1994): 37–50.

3. Porter and Van der Linde, "Perspectives," 37.

4. Jonathan Bender and Terry Moe, "An Adaptive Model of Bureaucratic Politics," *American Political Science Review* 79, no. 3 (1985): 755–74; John Brehm and Scott Gates, *Working, Shirking, and Sabotage: Bureaucratic Response to a Democratic Public* (Ann Arbor: University of Michigan Press, 1997); David Epstein and Sharyn O'Halloran, *Delegating Powers: A Transaction Cost Politics Approach to Policy Making under Separate Powers* (Cambridge: Cambridge University Press, 1999); Thomas W. Gilligan, William J. Marshall, and Barry R. Weingast, "Regulation and the Theory of Legislative Choice: The Interstate Commerce Act of 1887," *Journal of Law and Economics* 32 (1989): 35–61; John D. Huber and Nolan McCarty, "Bureaucratic Capacity, Delegation, and Political Reform," *American Political Science Review* 98, no. 3 (2004): 481–94; John D. Huber and Charles R. Shipan, *Deliberate Discretion? The Institutional Foundations of Bureaucratic Autonomy* (Cambridge: Cambridge University Press, 2002); David E. Lewis, *Presidents and the Politics of Agency Design: Political Insulation in the United States Government Bureaucracy, 1946–1997* (Stanford, CA: Stanford University Press, 2003); Mathew D. McCubbins and Talbot Page, "A Theory of Congressional Delegation," in *Congress: Structure and Policy*, ed. Mathew D. McCubbins and Terry Sullivan (New York: Cambridge University Press, 1987); Terry Moe, "The Politics of Bureaucratic Structure," in *Can the Government Govern?* ed. John E. Chubb and Paul E. Peterson (Washington, DC: Brookings Institution Press, 1989), 267–329; Lawrence S. Rothenberg, *Regulation, Organizations, and Politics: Motor Freight Policy at the Interstate Commerce Commission* (Ann Arbor: University of Michigan Press, 1994); Barry R. Weingast and Mark Moran, "Bureaucratic Discretion or Congressional Control? Regulatory Policy Making by the Federal Trade Commission," *Journal of Political Economy* 91 (1983): 475–520; Amy Zegart, *Flawed by Design: The Evolution of the CIA, JCS, and NSC* (Stanford, CA: Stanford University Press, 1999).

5. Francis E. Rourke, *Bureaucracy, Politics, and Public Policy* (Boston: Little, Brown, 1984); Richard Tobin, *The Expendable Future: U.S. Politics and the Protection of Biological Diversity* (Durham, NC: Duke University Press, 1990); Jeanne Nienaber Clarke and Daniel C. McCool, *Staking Out the Terrain: Power and Performance among Natural Resource Agencies*, 2nd ed. (Albany: State University of New York Press, 1996).

6. Jack McGraw, acting regional administrator, Region VIII, U.S. Environmental Protection Agency, interview with author, Denver, CO, June 24, 1994.

7. Erwin C. Hargrove, *Prisoners of Myth: The Leadership of the Tennessee Valley Authority, 1933–1990* (Princeton, NJ: Princeton University Press, 1994).

8. Adm. Bill Owens (with Ed Offley), *Lifting the Fog of War* (New York: Farrar, Strauss, and Giroux, 2000), 219.

9. Edward N. Luttwak, *The Pentagon and the Art of War: The Question of Military Reform* (New York: Simon and Schuster, 1984); James G. Burton, *The Pentagon Wars: Reformers Challenge the Old Guard* (Annapolis, MD: Naval Institute Press, 1993); Fred Thompson and L. R. Jones, *Reinventing the Pentagon: How the New Public Management Can Bring Institutional Renewal* (San Francisco: Jossey-Bass, 1994); James Kitfield, *Prodigal Soldiers: How the Generation of Officers Born of Vietnam Revolutionized the American Style of War* (New York: Simon and Schuster, 1995); Col. David H. Hackworth, *Hazardous Duty: America's Most Decorated Living Soldier Reports from the Front and Tells It the Way It Is* (New York: William Morrow, 1996).

10. Richard A. Stubbing, *The Defense Game: An Insider Explores the Astonishing Realities of America's Defense Establishment* (New York: HarperCollins, 1986).

11. Samuel P. Huntington, *The Soldier and the State: The Theory and Politics of Civil-Military Relations* (Cambridge, MA: Belknap Press, 1981); James R. Locher III, *Victory on the Potomac: The Goldwater-Nichols Act Unifies the Pentagon* (College Station: Texas A&M University, 2002).

12. Locher, *Victory on the Potomac*, 15.

13. James H. Lebovic, "Riding Waves or Making Waves? The Services and the U.S. Defense Budget, 1981–1993," *American Political Science Review* 88, no. 4 (1994): 839–52. See Locher, *Victory on the Potomac*. Also see Kenneth R. Mayer, *The Politics of Defense Contracting* (New Haven, CT: Yale University Press, 1991) for an excellent empirical analysis of the political economy of these dynamics.

14. Carl H. Builder, *The Masks of War: American Military Styles in Strategy and Analysis* (Baltimore: Johns Hopkins University Press, 1989).

15. James L. Lacy, *Within Bounds: The Navy in Postwar American Security Policy* (Alexandria, VA: Center for Naval Analyses, CAN 05 83 1178, July 28, 1983), 536. Jones was chairman of the Joint Chiefs of Staff from 1978 to his retirement in 1982.

16. *Basic Aerospace Doctrine of the United States Air Force,* AFM 1-1, March 16, 1984, A-6.

17. See, especially, Adm. J. C. Wylie, *Military Strategy: A General Theory of Power Control* (Westport, CT: Greenwood Press, 1967).

18. See, especially, Stephen K. Scroggs, *Army Relations with Congress: Thick Armor, Dull Sword, Slow Horse* (Westport, CT: Praeger, 2000); Builder, *Masks of War.*

19. See, for example, Richard Betts, *Military Readiness: Concepts, Choices, Consequences* (Washington, DC: Brookings Institution Press, 1995).

20. Builder, *Masks of War,* 106.

21. Ibid., 105.

22. Chris Demchak coins this term to characterize the "sense of shock, often felt as betrayal, when a nasty surprise occurs." These might include the jamming of M-1 rifles during the Vietnam War, higher-than-average rates of breakdowns and repairs for computerized equipment, and shortages of replacement parts for complex weapons. Chris Demchak, *Military Organizations, Complex Machines: Modernization in the U.S. Armed Services* (Ithaca, NY: Cornell University Press, 1991), 21.

23. Kitfield, *Prodigal Soldiers,* 79.

24. Ibid., 393.

25. Demchak, *Military Organizations, Complex Machines,* 47, fn 13.

26. Lt. Col. Kent Hughes Butts, "Environmental Security: What Is DoD's Role?" Occasional Papers (Carlisle Barracks, PA: Strategic Studies Institute, U.S. Army War College, 1993), 25; emphasis added. This despite the army and the air force having established deputy assistant secretary-level positions related to the environment. The rub was that in the army and the air force, environmental concerns competed for resources against safety and occupational health concerns (deputy assistant secretary of the army and air force for environment, safety, and occupational health). The navy had an assistant secretary for installations and environment, with installation maintenance concerns dominating environmental protection. Various iterations of these offices continue today, plus ENR subunits dealing with ENR responsibilities within each service. Likewise, the military has established environmental centers (e.g., the army Environmental Center and the air force Center for Environmental Excellence) that evolved beyond fragmented Cold War predecessors. All these today can take advantage of the Defense Environmental Network & Information Exchange (DENIX) to gain the latest in ENR "best practices."

27. Huntington, *Soldier and the State,* 61.

28. Sherri Wasserman Goodman, statement before the U.S. Senate Committee on Armed Services, Subcommittee on Military Readiness and Defense Infrastructure, Washington, DC, June 9, 1993, 2.

29. Thom Shanker and Eric Schmitt, "Rumsfeld Set to Advise Bush on Picking Top Military Man" (Final: "Choice of Top Military Man Weighed as Strategy Changes"), *New York Times,* July 23, 2001. Also available online at http://www.nytimes.com/2001/07/23/politics/23CHIE.html (July 24, 2001).

30. The following quotations regarding this dispute are from "Services, DOD Tangle on Civilian Control of Environmental Program," *DEA* Prototype (September 15, 1993): 3.

31. The U.S. Army is the DoD REC for EPA Regions IV, V, VII, and VIII; the U.S. Navy is the DoD REC for EPA Regions I, III, and IX; and the U.S. Air Force is the DoD REC for EPA Regions II, VI, and X.

32. Paul G. Kaminski, Under Secretary of Defense (Acquisition and Technology), "DoD Instruction 4715.10 Environmental Education, Training, and Career Development," April 24, 1996, https://www.denix.osd.mil/denix/Public/ES-Programs/Education/Policy/note1.html (July 5, 2004).

33. "DoD Backs R&D Shop in Turf War Over Environmental Technologies," *DEA* 1, no. 2 (November 3, 1993): 6.

34. "Executive Director Slot at SERDP May Presage Research Consolidation," *DEA* 1, no. 4 (December 1, 1993): 15.

35. "Senate Debates Expanded Role of DOE, EPA in DoD Environmental R&D," *DEA* 1, no. 1 (October 20, 1993): 19.

36. "In reversal, DoD Agrees to Retain Public Participation Functions," *DEA* 6, no. 9 (May 5, 1998): 10; also see "Citizen Input, Technology Programs Raise Eyebrows on Capitol Hill," *DEA* 6, no. 6 (March 24, 1998): 19.

37. Katherine Barrett and Richard Greene, "The Pentagon Paupers," *Financial World* 22 (October 24, 1995): 44.

38. Department of Defense, "Part V: Defense Management (Financial Management Reform)," *1995 Annual Defense Report*, 1995, http://www.defenselink.mil/execsec/adr95/fm_.html (January 5, 1996).

39. Shulman, *Threat at Home*, 116.

40. The Clinton–Gore "reinventing government" initiatives, of course, were undertaken earlier and had important impacts on program processes like cleanups. These will be documented extensively in future chapters. Here I focus solely on Pentagon system reforms. Referred to formally as the National Performance Review (NPR), reinventing government involved the adoption of best business practices. Proponents claimed these would heighten economy, efficiency, and program benefits as well as foster greater innovation, higher customer satisfaction, and better results for taxpayers. Best business practices included downsizing agencies, flattening hierarchies, decentralizing authority, privatizing noncore functions, reengineering processes, and linking budgets to performance.

41. "Need for Modernization Funds Drives DoD Push for Privatization," *DEA* 7, no. 7 (April 6, 1999): 7–8. Competitive sourcing occurs when government employees are given the chance to compete with the private sector in bidding for contracts before they are privatized.

42. "DoD Extends Deadline to 2003 for Services to Privatize Utilities," *DEA* 7, no. 1 (January 12, 1999): 16.

43. "Army Audit Agency to Examine Environmental Functions Moving to Army," *DEA* 6, no. 2 (January 27, 1998): 3–4.

44. "Citizen Environmental Organizations Boycott Range Rule Meeting," *DEA* 5, no. 26 (December 16, 1997): 7.

45. "DoD Plans Complete Transfer of Chemical Demil Funding Authority in FY99," *DEA* 5, no. 26 (December 16, 1997): 4–5.

46. Robert T. Golembiewski, "Public Sector Organization: Why Theory and Practice Should Emphasize Purpose, and How to Do So," in *A Centennial History of the American Administrative State*, ed. Ralph C. Chandler (New York: Free Press. 1987), 433–74.

47. "DoD Launches Senior-Level Environmental Oversight Council to Devise Joint Civilian-Military Policies," *DEA* 1, no. 3 (November 17, 1993): T-6.

48. Ibid.

49. "DoD Strips Environmental Security Office of Key Installation Functions," *DEA* 2, no. 14 (July 13, 1994): 10.

50. Ibid., 11.

51. Office of the Undersecretary of Defense, "Department of Defense Office of Environmental Security Corporate Board Charter," March 2, 1998.

CHAPTER FOUR

Base Cleanups, Sovereign Impunity, and the Expansion of the Beaten Zone

Gen. Ulysses S. Grant, commander-in-chief of the Union forces during the Civil War, felt no hesitation in placing himself within what military riflemen call the "beaten zone": the elliptical pattern (or "cone") formed by machine-gun rounds striking either the ground or the target. Nevertheless, Grant had several brushes with serious injury if not death during the war, in particular at Fort Harrison, Petersburg, Shiloh, and Vicksburg. Indeed, at Fort Harrison and Vicksburg, shells burst near him as he wrote dispatches in the open. This prompted one soldier who witnessed his composure under fire to exclaim, "Ulysses don't scare worth a damn!"

The EPA, environmental groups, the states, and nongovernmental organizations in the United States can be excused for substituting the "U.S. military" for "Ulysses" in that sentence when it came to the Pentagon's nonchalance in complying with ENR protection laws during the Cold War. As discussed in prior chapters, the armed services and their allies in Congress had positioned the military well beyond the beaten zone, allowing the services to keep control of the substance, scope, and pace of greening efforts.

By the time Bill Clinton assumed the presidency in 1993, the nation was far from understanding the sobering legacy that this attitude had bequeathed to taxpayers. Three things *were* clear to Clintonites, however. First, the scope of the problem was large. Late in the George H. W. Bush administration, the DoD estimated that its military bases in the U.S. alone harbored nearly 20,000 toxic waste sites covering nearly twenty-seven million acres of contaminated property. In fact, 81 percent of federal facilities on the National Priorities List (NPL) belonged to the DoD. And by 1992 the DoD was involved in some phase of the cleanup process at nearly 1,800 military bases at home and abroad.

Second, contaminants at these sites included low-level radioactive waste, unexploded ordnance (UXO), acids, nitrates, heavy metals, fuels, and cleaning solvents. Proportionally, contamination from fuels and solvents (e.g., gasoline, diesel and jet fuel, cleaning compounds, and degreasers) were found at 60 percent of DoD sites. Likewise, toxic and hazardous wastes (e.g., heavy metals such as lead and mercury, chemical munitions residues, explosive compounds, and caustics like cleaners, paints, and strippers) were the primary problem at 30 percent of DoD sites. Further compounding the problem, 8 percent of DoD sites were plagued by UXO, and 2 percent suffered low-level nuclear waste contamination from equipment treated with radium (e.g., dials and gauges).

Third, the ultimate scope of the problem was unclear and cost estimates were spiraling. In 1985, for example, the DoD estimated cleanup costs at $5 to $10 billion for a universe of 400 to 800 contaminated sites. Yet by 1988 the DoD had reported 12,000 potential sites, with estimated cleanup costs totaling $8.5 to $12.8 billion over the next five to seven years alone. Then, less than a year later, DoD revised its estimates (in 1987 dollars) upward to between $11 and $15 billion, including $2 billion for the army's Rocky Mountain Arsenal in Colorado. But even these figures had to be revised drastically by the end of 1989. The number of sites identified increased by 24 percent, to 15,257, and cleanup costs soared as high as $42.2 billion. Moreover, the Pentagon still lacked even reasonable "guestimates" about the severity of contamination at its nearly 7,000 formerly used defense sites scattered in the United States and abroad. Nor did these estimates include the costs of remedial actions at base closures to get them transferred into private hands for economic development under BRAC I, II, and III.

At the same time Democrats *and* Republicans in Congress, environmental groups in Washington, and grassroots ENR activists near military bases complained that the Pentagon's cleanup efforts were too slow, confrontational, and lacking in good faith. In particular they felt that the military was deliberately slowing down cleanups by "studying the problem to death." In response, two major efforts to ameliorate these problems occurred during the early 1990s. The first, the Community Environmental Response Facilitation Act (CERFA), was launched by Congress in the last year of the Bush administration. The second was President Clinton's base closure Community Reinvestment Program. Launched by the White House in mid-1993 by executive order, this program was typically referred to as his Fast-Track Cleanup Program.

Under CERFA the DoD had to identify so-called clean parcels on the 1988 and 1992 list of base closings under BRAC so that these properties could be transferred as expeditiously as possible to communities for development. Moreover, Congress gave the services only until April 14, 1994, to identify these parcels, with EPA concurring on the designation of NPL sites and states concurring on non-NPL sites. Once certified, these clean parcels would be suitable for transfer or lease (known respectively as Findings of Suitability to Transfer and Findings of Suitability to Lease) for economic development by communities and private investors. Similarly, Clinton's Fast-Track initiative was designed to help speed the economic recovery of communities affected by BRAC. This was especially important to the Clintonites for two reasons: The country already was in a recession and base closures were occurring in so-called Gun Belt states rich in both Cold War facilities and presidential electoral votes (e.g., California, Florida, and Texas).

To be sure, the magnitude of the Sisyphean cleanup task facing the military grew more rather than less daunting by the time George W. Bush took office in

2001. Since 1994, for example, the number of waste sites needing cleanup on active, closed, transferred, or transferring military bases grew from 24,898 to 28,538. Nonetheless, by the time Clinton left office, the DoD reported that cleanup responses were complete at nearly 60 percent of closing bases and that 30 percent of these properties were in the hands of public and private sector developers.

As this and the next two chapters chronicle, however, Clinton's success came amid internecine Pentagon warfare as well as with a stiff price for ENR protection. First, the offensives of some Clinton appointees challenging the Cold War ethos of sovereignty, secrecy, and sinecure again rubbed many within DoD as a power grab that justified retaliation. Second, the military was bent on shaping, responding, and preparing the ENR battlefield to ensure that whatever progress did occur was done on the services' terms. As Craig Hooks, director of the EPA's Federal Facilities Enforcement Office, put it late in the Clinton administration, "DoD appears to want to retain unilateral decision-making on milestones, budget, and cleanup issues, and at every turn, it puts the burden on the community and EPA if involvement is sought."[1] Third, this counteroffensive by the military and its allies put tremendous downward pressure on environmental standards. Greening proponents *had* wanted speedier cleanups, but they also wanted cleanups that sufficiently protected public health, safety, and the environment. Yet combined with adroit zero-sum issue framing regarding ENR protection, military readiness, and weapons modernization, the focus on speed created enormous pressure to choose "compromise remedies that [could] be completed within that year's funding, rather than selecting a more complete cleanup that [would] take several years of funding."[2]

To begin illustrating how and why this occurred in this contentious arena of civil–military relations, this chapter reviews three fundamental cleanup issues that had to be resolved during the Clinton years. First, should EPA's "fencepost-to-fencepost" policy at contaminated military sites prevail? Second, were the RCRA or CERCLA (i.e., Superfund) site evaluations, cleanup standards, and procedures to apply to cleanups at active DoD sites? Third, regardless of the answers to the previous two questions, were the additional applications of best business practices going to advance or undermine greening in the U.S. military?

The Fencepost-to-Fencepost Scoping Challenge

By the time Bill Clinton took office U.S. military leaders were fearing the loss of their historical control over the substance, scope, and pace of cleanups at DoD bases. Wrote Lt. Col. Kent Hughes Butts of the army in 1993, the public's embrace of an environmental ethic and Congress's push toward reregulation of the environment posed a "significant threat to [the military's] operational independence."[3] Indicative of this growing dilemma for the Pentagon was the EPA's fencepost-to-fencepost policy in making Superfund determinations at military sites. Fencepost-to-fencepost approaches meant that lands the Pentagon did not want to part with after the 1988 BRAC round commenced downsizing would be unattractive to potential developers because of their NPL listing. The DoD's ultimate success in redefining EPA's policy, in turn, rested on the conjunction of four interrelated events: an unyielding BRAC schedule, pressure from local communities to transfer parcels more quickly for development, assaults by Congress on cleanup budgets, and the increasingly apparent technical challenge of cleanup for land transfers.

By All Means . . . Fence Me In

CERCLA, and subsequently the Superfund Amendments and Reauthorization Act of 1986 (SARA), charged EPA with assessing the levels of contamination at both public and private sites across the United States. To this end the EPA developed a numerical scoring approach known as the hazardous ranking system. Sites acquiring contamination scores exceeding 28.5 were put on the NPL as being the most seriously contaminated in the United States. When sites at military facilities attained such a score, DoD had to negotiate an interagency agreement with EPA and the states for cleaning up the site, thus opening up the remedial investigation/feasibility study and remedy selection processes.[4]

The rub, however, was that at private facilities, the EPA scored contaminated waste sites for cleanup on an individual rather than a cumulative site basis. That is, regulators did not add the scores for various "hot spots" on a company's property to determine an overall score. Nor did they treat all the property abutting a contaminated area as an NPL "site"; only those areas actually contaminated were listed as a site. In contrast, at military sites, the EPA looked at available data, identified the four to six most contaminated sites, and added those scores together. If their cumulative score exceeded 28.5, the agency placed the entire installation on the NPL list.

The uniqueness of the nature of the threat from the military's detritus and the Pentagon's shoddy recordkeeping during the Cold War were major factors in the EPA's logic. Barred from doing its own soil sampling by an executive order endorsed by the Pentagon during the last decade of the Cold War, the agency was forced to rely on information provided by the DoD. Finding the DoD's sampling inadequate, the EPA said that "operational" prudence dictated erring on the conservative side when scoping military as opposed to private facilities. So too, however, did "political" prudence and bureaucratic convenience dictate such a Superfund policy, as any underestimation of risk made by the EPA in listing sites would come back to haunt them. At least initially, however, advantage also accrued to the military; until pressure began mounting from Congress and President Clinton for accelerated transfers, declaring an entire base a Superfund site actually improved an installation's ability to compete for DERA resources.

The Sound of Concrete Cracking

These arguments and strategies, however, progressively lost their political allure to all parties with each passing year of the Clinton administration. Disenchantment began slowly in the final years of the first Bush administration as congressional angst mounted over the slow pace and lack of prioritization of cleanups at military sites. In response the services began arguing that the EPA's fencepost-to-fencepost policy hindered the transfer of base properties. Moreover, with an impatient Congress beginning to cut DERA funding significantly in FY 1993 and FY 1994 after a highly critical DoD comptroller audit of the cleanup program showed unused appropriations (see below), the services tailored their counteroffensive message accordingly.

Suffering already from unfavorable comparisons with the quicker pace of cleanups at private sites, for example, the military attacked the EPA's policy for masking the progress the services *were* making at military bases. As an illustration, even though the military might be cleaning up contaminated sites on a base, the base as a whole remained listed as a Superfund site until all the individual sites on the premises were cleaned up. The Pentagon argued that if military sites were treated in the same way as private sites, cleanup comparisons would not put military facilities in such a negative light. At private sites compliance rates were calculated on the basis of the number of sites cleaned, not on the cleanup status of all sites on a facility.

The services also seized upon the agency's fencepost policy as a reason for burgeoning estimates of cleanup costs, estimates for which the new Republican majority in Congress routinely took them to task throughout 1995 and 1996. With demands from the White House and Capitol Hill mounting that the EPA and the military better prioritize cleanups in the face of funding constraints (discussed in greater detail in the next two chapters), DoD's Patricia Ferrebee told President Clinton's Commission on Risk Assessment and Risk Management, "We're [DoD's cleanup office] very concerned that we're putting priority [on sites that do not pose] the greatest risk." But they were forced to, she continued, because the EPA's fencepost policy was "elevating hundreds of relatively low-risk sites" to Superfund status, "thereby taking resources away from cleaning up high-risk sites."[5] Nor was the military alone in making these claims. Investigators at the GAO, for example, concluded in 1994 that although "the majority of the 7,448 contaminated sites on DoD's high priority installations [were] not Superfund type sites . . . all but a few of these . . . were given high priority status simply because they [were] located on a military installation with a small number of badly contaminated sites."[6]

Meanwhile, the Clinton administration was feeling pressure to reassess the fencepost policy from electoral-vote-rich Gunbelt states. During President Clinton's first year in office, states such as California, which already had shouldered the burden of the 1988 and 1991 BRAC rounds, were desperate to get parcels more quickly into the hands of developers. With this concern in mind, James M. Strock, then California EPA secretary, petitioned Clinton's EPA not to place six additional BRAC bases in California on the NPL. Argued Strock in a letter to EPA administrator Carol Browner, "For [an entire] closing base to be placed on the NPL is to be effectively 'blacklisted' [for redevelopment] in the eyes of the public and private sector due to the perception that serious levels of contamination exist throughout the facility."[7]

The Ego Meets the Superego

With such momentum mounting for changing the EPA's policy, and with the DoD already attacking it, a new front was opened by the "superego" of the Pentagon: the DoD comptroller.[8] The comptroller pulled no punches: Sherri Wasserman Goodman's shop had fundamentally mismanaged cleanup dollars at military sites. Specifically excoriated were three interrelated funding trends in Environmental Security Office (ESO) cleanup programs, trends partially attributable to the EPA's fencepost policy. These were an "underexecution of funding for cleanup," an "overexecution of funding for studies," and the "shift[ing] of unexecuted funds to lower priority environmental studies."[9]

Already outrageous enough to key members of Congress, things only got worse when the comptroller stated that what *was* spent on cleanups in FY 1993 and FY 1994 was less than the original amounts requested by the Pentagon for those years. To wit, and in an action with even broader implications for ESO's already precarious stature within the Pentagon, the comptroller proposed cutting ESO's budget request for its cleanup and compliance programs through FY 1997 by 15 percent (or approximately $530 million).[10] Moreover, this came after the Congressional Budget Office warned the Pentagon in 1994 that continued "limited progress in cleaning up [rather than merely doing site investigations at] the 18,795 contaminated sites on the military's 1,800 installations" was likely to result in "drastic budget cuts."[11]

All this was like manna from heaven to members of Congress already upset with ENR funding. Important members of the Senate Armed Services Committee such as Senator John McCain (R-AZ) (although he later changed his mind), for example, argued that ENR programs overseen by Goodman's office were "nondefense related." They wanted already allocated funding for these purposes shifted to military readiness accounts and future ENR funding to come from the budgets of the EPA and other regulators. Likewise, fourteen House Republicans, including Virginia's Herbert Bateman, chair of the Readiness Subcommittee of the National Security Committee, urged the DoD to strip environmental funding from its budgets. Calling cleanup expenditures a "threat to readiness," they argued that the "funding for these non-defense programs roughly corresponds to the dollar amount cited by [DoD] Deputy Secretary [John] Deutch for additional [weapons] modernization cuts. . . . We urge you to first consider reducing or canceling non-defense programs . . . prior to any reductions, cancellations, or delays in weapons modernization."[12]

Moreover, even under previous Democratic control, Congress already had produced a $400 million cut to DERA in the FY 1995 defense appropriations bill. Congressman Vic Fazio (D-CA), for instance, voiced the outrage of his colleagues with extensive cleanup needs in their states that unobligated cleanup funds for BRAC accounts totaled nearly $1.9 billion as of September 30, 1993, funds primarily in air force hands.[13] Fazio and the bipartisan coalition he led on the House Appropriations Committee proclaimed that a lack of will, not resources, was slowing cleanups at BRAC sites. What is more, and speaking in zero-sum funding terms, Fazio observed, "If the Navy determines it needs more allocated funds to close bases under BRAC III, the Department has the flexibility to re-allocate funds between the Air Force and Navy."[14]

For their part Goodman and her allies within the OSD vigorously disputed the comptroller's report. For example, her direct superior, Paul Kaminski, under secretary of defense for acquisition and technology, shot back that if DoD "does not request full funding, the department is subject to fines and penalties—and subject to lawsuits."[15] Goodman also appealed for time, arguing that a lack of accurate recordkeeping during the Cold War, not a lack of will, was holding up cleanup progress. Absent good records, the painstaking process of exploring what, where, and how much contamination was on a base (i.e., site investigation) had slowed the process. In fact, the DoD had proposed increased funding for site cleanup from $600 million to $859 million, making FY 1994 the first year in the Pentagon's history that requests for cleanup funding surpassed requests for site investigation expenditures.

It did not take long for greening proponents in the states and among environmentalists to rush to Goodman's aid, albeit taking a different tack. "The problem is not with the Environmental Security office," argued one observer, "but with branches of the Pentagon that have been responsible for the pollution and don't consider cleaning up their own mess as part of their mission."[16] There is, opined another, "a fundamental misunderstanding among many in the Pentagon of the importance of environmental programs [to military readiness]. . . . The military outside of the environment office does not believe spending money on environmental programs is warranted."[17] Likewise, a state official pulled no punches in attacking the comptroller's actions. "They're [the comptroller] acting illegally," he charged. "It's one thing for Congress to cut back, but another thing for DOD to slit its own throat."[18]

On the other hand, of course, the services and Goodman's competitors in the OSD were hardly sad to see her office come under attack for mismanagement. As noted in chapter 3, Goodman's efforts to centralize authority for environmental policy in the ESO and establish ESO regional offices were perceived accurately as direct assaults on the services' traditional sovereignty in this area. Likewise, when the Defense Science Board warned in a subsequent 1995 draft report that environmental regulations threatened military readiness if ignored by the military, other Pentagon officials said that the report was orchestrated by the ESO to justify its continued existence in the wake of congressional efforts to end its programs.[19]

What *was* incontrovertible by this time, however, was the building of bipartisan pressure in Congress to have the military make the most effective use of reduced funding. As Michael West, a Republican staff member on the House Armed Services Committee, framed this priority-setting issue: "If military bases were regulated like towns and counties, which they closely resemble, the savings [from ending EPA's policy] would run into the billions of dollars. Fenceline-to-fenceline regulation (primarily under RCRA and . . . CERCLA) is responsible for a significant portion of DoD's National Priority List (NPL) and [for] corrective action requirements that simply do not exist elsewhere [i.e., at private sites]."[20] Nor did it hurt the opponents' cause when GAO investigators reported that environmental base contamination, predicated on the EPA's fencepost policy, was the greatest obstacle to transferring BRAC properties for economic development.[21]

With these political winds at their backs, allies on the Senate Armed Services Committee inserted wording crafted by the military in the committee report for the FY 1995 defense authorization bill. Stipulated was that the Pentagon and EPA were to review the fencepost policy. Making clear the committee's preferred outcome, the report read, "The decision to list entire installations on the NPL [means that] thousands of minimally contaminated sites fall under the CERCLA study process [that might otherwise not] and this may not be the most expeditious and effective way to cleanup installations on a timely basis."[22]

Further adumbrating the success of the military's cause was a subsequent 1995 report issued by Clinton's Federal Facilities Policy Group (FFPG, aka, the Rivlin–McGinty report). The FFPG was convened initially in 1993. Its members included representatives of federal agencies and was cochaired by Alice Rivlin, then the deputy director of the OMB, and Kathleen McGinty, then the chairperson of the Council on Environmental Quality and former Senate aide to Vice President Al Gore. No doubt buttressed by the seismic shift in the political landscape of the 1994 election sweeping conservative Republicans into key committee chairmanships, the eventual FFPG report (*Improving Federal Facilities Cleanup*) curiously contained two major priorities espoused by Speaker of the House Newt Gingrich (GA) (and discussed more fully in chapter 5). These were the need to relax cleanup standards at BRAC properties by embracing future land use as a cleanup criterion, and to eliminate EPA's fencepost-to-fencepost policy.[23]

Arguing almost verbatim a position taken by the Republican leadership in Congress in proposing further cuts to the DERA budget, Rivlin made it clear that cleaning up federal facilities from fencepost-to-fencepost to residential standards was "neither feasible nor affordable." Eight months earlier Gingrich had advocated zoning areas of bases for industrial development and relaxing more stringent cleanup standards in those zones. His point, made before a variety of audiences, was the same as Rivlin's: Cleaning up *all* portions of a base "to the level where a school could be built" made little sense.

Nor was the military's position on the EPA's fencepost policy harmed when peak associations like the U.S. Conference of Mayors and the International City Management Association turned up the heat on Congress to expedite cleanups. Central to their members' frustrations, again, were the impacts of the next BRAC round. San Diego mayor Susan Golding (R), cochair of the U.S. Conference of Mayors, put the dilemma best for cities facing closing bases, slow environmental cleanups, and ongoing assaults on DERA and BRAC cleanup funding: "It is now clear everyone underestimated the costs of cleanup. . . . [If] the government is serious about hazardous waste cleanup, [Congress needs to allocate more money or] ease the environmental regulations" applied to cleanups.[24] Ultimately, the Conference of Mayors endorsed a two-part transfer authority that cut to the quick of EPA's fencepost policy: Clean properties on a base could be transferred at once to "put immediate life" into properties that would otherwise lie vacant.[25]

With the Congressional Budget Office predicting a "dim future" for defense cleanups absent fundamental reform and technological breakthroughs, the military's supporters were able to place a DoD-supported provision into House draft Superfund legislation that allowed for the demise of the fencepost-to-fencepost policy. As we shall see in chapter 5, however, success did not come fully until 1996, when Congress expanded the definition of uncontaminated parcels in the FY 1997 defense authorization bill. In the process, the services' position on the EPA's fencepost-to-fencepost policy became law.

How Clean Is Clean?

The demise of the EPA's fencepost-to-fencepost policy was only the tip of the iceberg for advancing the military's cleanup agenda in the mid-1990s. A variety of obstacles remained, including how much cleanup was necessary at any given site. The answer to that question, in turn, depended on what statute, RCRA or CERCLA, was applicable. Known as the "how clean is clean" question, the issue was an acute one for a resource-challenged and overcommitted military desperate to meet readiness and weapons modernization funding challenges. The stricter the standards applied, after all, the longer, more costly, and less in control of its cleanup destiny the Pentagon became. Much like the fencepost policy, however, the services' stance on this issue varied during the Clinton years as their perceptions changed about how best to assure the stability, predictability, and security of military operations.

We'll Take CERCLA Any Day

If the fencepost policy issue largely was resolved in the military's favor by mid-1995, the statutory muddle slowing cleanup at federal facilities was far from resolved. Most responsible for that muddle was an issue rooted in the corrective action authority afforded by Congress in the 1984 Hazardous and Solid Waste Amendments. Under these amendments, federal facilities seeking treatment, storage, and disposal permits for hazardous waste disposal had to prove to the EPA that they had cleaned up previous releases before a permit was issued, regardless of when the releases occurred. Congress, as such, expanded RCRA's focus from dealing solely with ongoing permit activities *before* pollution occurred to dealing as well with pollution that occurred from *earlier* treatment, storage, and disposal permit activities (thus formerly and exclusively under the rubric of Superfund). In doing so, however, Congress also presented military base commanders with two disparate sets of regulators, regulatory processes, and regulatory standards during the Cold War. Open to interpretation, in the process, was whether Congress intended the states to play a consultative role, as per CERCLA, or a regulatory role, as per RCRA, when it came to selecting corrective actions on military bases.

Nor, given the stakes involved for the military, the states, and environmental groups, would the answer to this question grow any less salient in the post–Cold War era. If CERCLA did not trump RCRA, state (rather than federal) standards, timetables, and compliance judgments would drive cleanups at federal facilities. What is more, because RCRA permitted state regulators to impose stricter standards than federal regulators, DoD could face more costly cleanups. Also, whereas CERCLA required that any remedy selected had to be cost-effective, RCRA, contrary to the military's interests, did not require costs to be factored into remedy decisions. Finally, the disparate ways that the two statutes treated cleanup costs and approaches made RCRA unappealing to the military. Not only were cleanup remedies more limited under RCRA than under CERCLA, but RCRA made it distinctly more difficult to tailor remedial actions to fit into ongoing activities at military bases.

All this, of course, prompted the military in the early post–Cold War era to continue claiming that Congress intended CERCLA to preempt RCRA at military sites. Nor was it surprising that its position on this issue grew more uncompromising as Congress began to assault the Pentagon for slow cleanup progress, exorbitant costs, and tardy transfers of BRAC properties. As such, the military also fought efforts during the early Clinton years to transfer any CERCLA-granted authority to anyone but the EPA administrator. Moreover, facing litigious environmental activist groups near its bases, the military argued that Congress specifically had barred preenforcement judicial reviews of federal cleanups (Section 113[h]) in favor of postenforcement judicial reviews (a position a federal court would later rule against).

Neither was it surprising that state regulators and environmental groups took issue with these points. Their argument was straightforward: Section 120 of CERCLA, as amended by SARA in 1986, was clear that nothing in CERCLA impaired the obligation of federal facilities to comply with "applicable or relevant and appropriate requirements" (ARARs) of state laws. And RCRA regulations were ARARs if generation, treatment, storage, and disposal of RCRA-related hazardous wastes were taking place at CERCLA sites.[26] Further buttressing this argument, the states contended, was Section 120(I) of CERCLA, which stated that nothing in Section 120 excused federal facilities from complying with RCRA requirements. Even more basically, states continued to argue that their authority and responsibilities in cleanups at military bases did not depend on their proving that CERCLA justified their actions. These were embedded incontrovertibly within RCRA.

Unpersuaded, and to gain additional leverage, the services complemented their efforts to have CERCLA trump RCRA in the early Clinton years by trying to gain further regulatory relief under CERCLA. Moreover, as BRAC land transfers became an ever more dominant issue in Congress and in local communities during the 1990s, these DoD missives began paying off. For example, the White House even incorporated some of the military's aims for regulatory relief in various Superfund reform packages that it sent to the Hill. In turn, the DoD offered the military's own independent set of amendments to its congressional allies to attach to defense authorization bills (bypassing less friendly ENR congressional committees primary jurisdiction) when Clinton's reforms of CERCLA stalled in Congress.

In this instance, and as noted in the previous section, House and Senate Armed Services committees debated amendments to CERCLA that would permit only contaminated portions of bases to be listed by EPA on the NPL. Likewise, concerned about the imposition of fines and criminal liability "hang[ing] over the heads of base commanders," the military supported an ultimately unsuccessful effort by allies such as Senator Bennett Johnston (D-LA) to amend the 1992 FFCA accordingly.[27] Meanwhile, allies on the House National Security and Commerce committees pressed for Superfund proposals designed, among other things, to eliminate duplication of RCRA and Superfund cleanup standards at Superfund sites.[28]

As an illustration, Rep. Michael Oxley (R-OH), chairman of the House Commerce Subcommittee on Commerce, Trade, and Hazardous Materials, pushed a variety of amendments to Superfund proposed by the military, including requiring states to follow federal cleanup requirements at RCRA sites. At issue, raged the National Association of Attorneys General (NAAG) in rebuttal, was the "sovereign immunity" defense discussed in chapter 2 and waged so persistently by the military during the Cold War. The services argued that states are forbidden to impose more costly cleanup standards unilaterally on federal facilities.[29]

From Antagonists to Partners?

As legislative stalemate over Superfund and RCRA reform dragged on, as cleanup budgets grew tighter for needed site investigation studies, and as Browner's and Goodman's relationships with new Republican committee chairs soured, an administrative strategy for speeding up cleanups grew increasingly attractive to the White House. Most significantly, a team of high-level appointees was created, including representatives from the EPA, DoD, DOE, DOJ, OMB, the Council on Environmental Quality, and the Council of Economic Advisors. Dominated by cost-conscious rather than ENR-promoting concerns, the interagency taskforce proposed cross-agency "partnerships" for reconciling disputes over cleanups at federal facilities.[30]

The practical and political appeal of this approach to the Clintonites spiraled in the wake of a series of studies reporting horror stories on how interagency disagreements over site characterizations were slowing cleanup. Studies of the 1988 and 1991 BRAC rounds, for instance, showed that the military had listed about half (121,200 of the 250,100) of the total acres involved as uncontaminated. Yet the EPA and state regulators concurred with this assessment on only 34,499 of these acres.[31] At the root of the problem, the federal cross-agency team concluded, was that each part of the site investigation process involved several reports and plans prepared by contractors and requiring multiple reviews by the principals and by state regulators.[32]

With ENR interests seriously outgunned on Clinton's interagency task force, and fully cognizant of the implications of this "new partnership" on federal regulators' leverage over their more powerful Pentagon polluters, proponents of greening the U.S. military fought back. For instance, several EPA regions (e.g., Region V) expressed strong reservations to Administrator Browner about the partnering idea. How could something like this work, others wrote diplomatically, when "the potential value of partnering is appreciated in some DoD locations, [but] it is not widely practiced throughout DoD, nor is it universally understood and accepted as a way of doing business"?[33]

Resurrecting Sovereign Immunity

While the rhetoric of partnering proceeded apace, the services simultaneously escalated a counteroffensive to challenge RCRA on sovereign immunity grounds during 1997 and 1998. Outraged, the states mounted an equally sustained, albeit unsuccessful, effort to broaden Superfund's waiver of sovereign immunity. Stunningly reminiscent of its Cold War posture, the DoD's position was characterized by the NAAG as follows: "Generally DoD denies that CERCLA effects a waiver of immunity from state actions at all" and thus "refus[es] to recognize its responsibility to comply with state environmental laws to the same extent as private parties[,] forc[ing] state regulators to either litigate or compromise their authority."[34]

To redress these claims, NAAG submitted a package of reforms to sympathetic staff members on Oxley's subcommittee calling for greater state authority at federal facility sites in general and at BRAC sites on the NPL in particular. "As you know," wrote President Clinton in a letter to NAAG supporting these initiatives, "we will remain vigilant against efforts to undermine environmental protection at federal facilities, to hinder the states' legitimate role in protecting their citizens, or to frustrate the cleanup effort through severe budget cuts."[35] Endorsed by forty-one state attorneys general, including every state association jousting with the military over ARARs, the NAAG report and Clinton's letter brought a swift reaction from DoD.

After its allies on the Senate Armed Services Committee stymied an amendment to CERCLA allowing states to sue the federal government, the DoD next "partnered" with DOE to torpedo subsequent reform efforts.[36] Responding to another request from the Armed Services Committee to assess with DOE and EPA the impact of broadening sovereign immunity waivers, the services said the existing waiver was "working well" and played their ace in the hole. Environmental standards were slowing down land transfers to communities for redevelopment and reducing cost savings from BRAC. Moreover, "after more than a decade of effort and a nearly $1.7 billion investment, the Department of Defense has achieved response complete [*sic*] at 15,265 of the 27,454 contaminated sites [remaining]. We cannot support legislative provisions [like this] that could undermine this significant progress."[37]

Reviving an effective Cold War mantra, the military also alleged that private actors and the states would abuse the amendment through raids on the federal treasury. "Other parties may view [DoD] as having 'deep pockets' of taxpayer dollars for performing expensive remedies that exceed the CERCLA standard," the Pentagon claimed, "but the [DoD] does not . . . have the resources to address every site to this extent."[38] Moreover, not only could "the states . . . use this authority to reorder cleanup budget priorities and schedules," they also might argue that state enforcement or citizen suits could be initiated "before the remedy is implemented, despite the pre-enforcement review bar to such challenges, established by CERCLA section 113(H)."[39] Also, for good measure, the services argued that the DoD should retain lead authority at these sites.

Responding to these allegations, NAAG argued back in similar Cold War–era language: In fighting the expanded waiver of sovereign immunity, the military still was trying to be treated differently from private polluters. Additionally, rather than increasing costs, empirical studies indicated that states had "a record of *saving* federal facilities money with cost-cutting suggestions."[40] Moreover, if existing waiver language was working well, it was doing so largely in the interests of the U.S. military. More precisely, the services had won court case after court case challenging the states' application of ARARs.

Indeed, by 1999, so successful were the military's arguments before the judiciary that proponents of the broader waiver grew fearful that the FFCA would be totally eviscerated by the courts. As such, members of Congress such as Diana DeGette (D-CO) and Charles Norwood (R-GA) of the House Commerce Committee, and Dan Schaefer (R-CO), one of the original sponsors of the FFCA, stepped up efforts to broaden the government's waiver of sovereign immunity in both CERCLA and the Clean Water Act. As they put it in a letter seeking cosponsors for their bills, "While states can theoretically apply environmental standards to federal facilities, they often encounter endless litigation by the federal operators (especially the military and DOE) and face probable defeat in trial."[41]

Rethinking the CERCLA Advantage

With so many issues evolving in ways advantaging the military services, their preference for regulation under CERCLA seemed to serve them well. But as pressure spiraled from Congress to expedite land transfers of BRAC properties to community developers, the services' preference for CERCLA in *all* instances began losing its allure. Thus, by early 1995, Goodman was arguing before the BRAC Commission that CERCLA "contains obstacles to economic redevelopment, requires costly remedies that vary from jurisdiction to jurisdiction, and fosters adversarial relationships between federal and state regulators."[42] Indeed, by the late 1990s, even capacity problems among regulators that the military once saw as advantageous under Superfund began to look like liabilities.

A strategy-structure mismatch that festered throughout the Clinton years, for instance, was the precarious state of risk assessment capacity within the EPA, at the Agency for Toxic Substances and Disease Registry in the Department of Health and Human Services, and in the states. Between 1980 and 1995, for example, the EPA's risk research budget—excluding funding for construction grants—plummeted from 20 percent to 7 percent of the agency's total budget.[43] Likewise, the Agency for Toxic Substances and Disease Registry, charged with advising EPA on public health concerns at Superfund sites by developing toxicological profiles of substances commonly found at them, was incurring substantial funding cuts. Not surprisingly under these circumstances, the agency increasingly was chided by critics in Congress and the environmental community as being "cursory," "inconsistent," and tardy in its assessments.[44] Normally an advantage to the military when cursory reviews found little risk, the tardiness and inconsistency factors soon became a liability at sites scheduled for BRAC transfers.

Likewise, with CERCLA requiring total cleanups (or "permanent remedies") of sites *before* transfer, the Pentagon reversed course and fought battles to have RCRA apply because it did not have such a stipulation. Also, when it was not seeking a shift to RCRA, the military aggressively sought to gain exemption from aspects of CERCLA. For example, these aims occasioned a heated and prolonged battle among the army, EPA, and the California EPA at Fort Ord. The army insisted that UXO-contaminated lands it was trying to transfer to the BLM be exempted from Superfund (in this case, kept out of the remedial investigation process). Army and Pentagon leaders felt that to do otherwise would create a precedent in favor of CERCLA versus RCRA at other bases. This is not to say that the military ever completely eschewed its preference for CERCLA. It *is* to say, however, that the military would selectively embrace or reject CERCLA and RCRA during the Clinton years with arguments that often contradicted each other in whole or in part, depending on the services' perception of their interests at any given time.

The Best Business Practices Challenge

The services also would selectively embrace or reject other efforts involving cleanups by seizing upon broader efforts by the Clinton administration to apply best business practices within the Pentagon and the services. Although typically trumpeted by reformers as mere technocratic "tools" for improving efficiency, best business practices arguments pursued under the administration's National Performance Review (NPR) and Defense Reform Initiative (DRI) routinely were again used to advance the substantive policy interests of some and diminish those of others. Most illustrative of this tendency relative to site cleanups were (1) unsuccessful efforts by the military to tear down the fences surrounding DERA and BRAC funding in order to move resources toward military contingency operations, (2) successful efforts by the military to devolve responsibility for DERA funding accounts to the services from the OSD, and (3) successful efforts by the services to cut funding for reimbursing state and public oversight in Defense-State memoranda of agreement (DSMOAs).

Tripping over DERA and BRAC Fences

As noted in chapter 1 the primary funding mechanism of the DoD's environmental program is the DERA. Although initially rather small in funding relative to the ultimate scope of the problem revealed in the post–Cold War era ($150 million in FY 1984), DERA had risen to $1.96 billion in annual funding by the end of FY 1994. Moreover, a Baptist-bootlegger coalition in Congress feared that the services might raid DERA either to help fund activities dearer to their hearts (e.g., readiness or weapons modernization) or, conversely, to redirect funding from other projects to pay for litigation-driven cleanups. As such, Congress set up an important "fence" around DERA prohibiting reprogramming of funds for purposes other than base cleanups.

To some in the Pentagon and Congress after the Republican takeover in 1995, the time had come to break down the DERA fence under the rubric of a best business practices (BBP) approach to military operations. The BBP justification was straightforward: Dollars should flow wherever they are needed most. The rhetoric of BBPs, however, was only a fig leaf covering true intentions. The immediate impetus for their concerns was finding funding to pay for military operations, first in Haiti and then in Bosnia. Catching members of environmental committees off guard, the House National Security Committee, in its markup of the FY 1996 defense authorization bill, attached a provision that would have officially breached the DERA fence. This provision allowed the military to shift up to $200 million annually from DERA to military operations, as well as to "higher priority" program areas within DoD. Seen by opponents as a cynical attempt to use these operations to set a precedent that could lead to dismantling DERA, a conference committee dropped the provision after opposition by Senator McCain (who by then had backed off his opposition to nondefense-related funding) and a coalition of House members. As one House member put it, DERA easily could become a "slush fund" if the fence were torn down. Added another environmentalist at the time, "The overall signal [if the DERA fence were breached is] that cleanup is somehow an elective activity that [the military does] when [they] feel like it."[45]

Not surprisingly, Goodman joined this chorus, sharing with an equally aroused and vocal coalition of cleanup contractors the fear that diversions of DERA funding would, variously, jeopardize cleanup schedules, make DoD cut back on cleanup contracts or be unable to pay for present contracts, and make the military liable to additional lawsuits. DERA, after all, already was strapped for cash and would become more so after subsequent cuts of $200 million in FY 1996 and approximately $30 million in FY 1997. In addition, even committee members who were otherwise unsympathetic to greening worried that, if the DERA fence were breached, the courts might "force the financing of environmental restoration activities out of operations and maintenance funds, even at the cost of a significant impact on the Department's readiness."[46]

Still, McCain and others exacted their own pound of flesh for their support of Goodman's position. A proviso was included in the FY 1996 defense authorization bill that by then was a common refrain from a Congress bent on speeding up cleanups in the wake of pending BRAC closures. Specifically, "by 1997, no more than 20 percent of the annual funding for DERA 'should be spent for administration, support, studies, and investigations.'"[47] Further constraining the Pentagon's discretion and putting downward pressure on cleanup standards, House and Senate conferees stipulated that the military "not let ongoing environmental cleanup efforts preclude reuse opportunities at closing military installations."[48]

Devolving DERA to the Services

The military and their congressional allies had yet another card to play, however, when it came to DERA. Under the best business practices rubric of the NPR, the military sought to devolve the DERA account out of the OSD and to the services. Placing responsibility for DERA within the OSD, however, was originally seen in 1986 as a way to ensure a sense of corporate purpose, vision, and coordination for ENR cleanups within the Pentagon. By the mid-1990s, however, a resource-stretched DoD clothed its rationale for devolving DERA responsibilities to the services in tried-and-true best business practices principles related to cost-effectiveness, priority setting, and results-oriented management.

Ratifying a set of recommendations offered in an internal NPR-prompted study conducted by the military, Deputy Defense Secretary John Deutch announced in early 1995 that creating a more efficient, accountable, and results-oriented cleanup program was best realized by devolving responsibility for cleanups to those closest to the problem. This in turn meant breaking up the central DERA account and creating separate cleanup accounts managed, funded, and monitored, respectively, by the army, air force, and navy.[49] Moreover, he announced that the military would implement the devolution administratively until its approval by Congress. Left unstated, of course, was that DERA devolution gave more leverage to the services in negotiating with state regulators over cleanup remedies. They, rather than OSD, would now have the power to decide which sites would get priority funding, resources the states badly wanted.[50]

Neither, however, did the neutral, technocratic, NPR-justified logic underpinning Deutch's rationale for devolution blind proponents of greening to the policy and programmatic threats that devolution raised. Most disquieting to them was the following sentence in DoD's request to Congress to approve DERA devolvement: "As the [services] identify requirements they will continue to look for the most cost effective method of fulfilling those requirements to avoid funding environmental restoration *at the expense of mission requirements.*"[51] Nor were their concerns assuaged by the DoD's assurances that "indiscriminate transfer [of funds] by the department" would not occur. Any proposal to shift funds would have to be approved by national defense, rather than more ENR-sympathetic, congressional committees.[52]

Likewise, state regulators feared that devolution would disrupt the cleanup process and that their input into cleanup remediation would be marginalized. For instance, Mary Jean Yon, president of the Association of State and Territorial Solid Waste Management Officials (ASTSWMO), wrote to the Senate Armed Services Committee: "We question how placing environmental cleanup budgets in direct competition with other service requirements [as they would in the shift] will affect the Defense Environmental Restoration Cleanup program; how the maintenance of various funds will affect the DoD prioritization process[;] . . . how . . . other pertinent stakeholders will participate in this process; and . . . whether there will be suitable flexibility built into the process to ensure that DoD will be able to meet all of its commitments."[53]

Meanwhile, support for such concerns increased both within and outside the Senate Armed Services Committee. As one congressional staffer stated bluntly, "DERA loses . . . if you relegate DERA to a service level, in effect, cleanup [does have] to compete with other programs."[54] Added another worried observer, "This [competition] is likely to result in a net decrease in funding for environmental accounts" generally. "There aren't a hell of a lot of believers out there" in the military chain of command who see any advantage to investing in the environment to get future savings.[55] In addition, members of Congress chagrined by the military's end-run of ENR committees worried that DERA devolvement would impede Congress's ability to oversee adequately the management and use of cleanup funds. They were joined by others warning that devolving DERA would make congressional earmarking of funds for pet cleanup projects easier than when the OSD could keep tabs on the account and say no to them.

Congress subsequently refused to ratify DERA devolution in the FY 1997 defense authorization bill *unless* DoD submitted a report that adequately justified devolvement. The report would also have to ensure the military's commitment to consistent and accountable funding and identify how "administrative efficiencies" would produce overall savings. Seizing yet another opportunity to diminish the ESO's capacity to oversee the services and to create a corporate sense of responsibility for greening the armed forces, opponents demanded that any report include the amount of "administrative savings" acquired to date at the ESO under Deutch's plan.

Once issued, the report buoyed the spirits of greening opponents appreciably. They were pleased to learn that the share of the DERA expenditures Goodman's office controlled and dispensed already had fallen appreciably by the end of FY 1997 from $5.64 million to $2.98 million since Deutch launched his initiative in FY 1995. In addition, ESO professional staff involved in cleanups had been cut by 17 percent. So informed, Congress subsequently approved DERA devolution to the military services in the FY 1997 defense authorization bill.

Deconstructing the DSMOA Grant Program

Consistent with arguments of BBP proponents such as Deutch and (later) Defense Secretary William Cohen, the services did take a harder look at the costs involved in managing the cleanup program after DERA devolution. But realized in the process were the fears of many devolvement opponents. As EPA Region IX federal facilities cleanup branch head Dan Opalski later described the process four full years into devolution: "Take a real close look and check the scales to see where the authority [really] is [i.e., with the military services, not regulators]."[56] Added Opalski, although the military services had promised transparency throughout the devolution process, they had not lived up to this and other commitments. And nowhere were the pyrotechnics set off by these actions better illustrated than when the now DERA-managing services began implementing the DSMOA program.

In passing Section 211(b) of SARA in 1986, Congress had hoped that the DSMOA program would encourage state and DoD partnerships, leading to cooperative cleanup agreements at active and closing bases and thus overcoming the distrust between state regulators and the military that had accrued during the Cold War.[57] Also, to help ensure that limited resources did not prevent the states from performing oversight functions in a timely manner (and thus hold up transfers), DSMOA grants from the Pentagon were established to reimburse the states for eligible services performed.[58] In exchange for its largesse, however, the military got a precious and disturbing concession from the states: they used a "vastly 'more amicable' oversight protocol [i.e., less stringent state testing and soil sampling] than the alternative—enforcement of *state* hazardous waste laws against" a facility. As one Louisiana official put it, everyone knew that the "states [dependent on DSMOA funds] tend to be more reasonable" than the EPA.[59]

Yet as readiness needs spiraled amid increased operational tempo, McCain and others in the Senate began questioning why state oversight costs should come out of DoD's budget rather than from state coffers. Thus, despite Goodman warning that "we'd set back" to the Cold War era the progress the services had made in calming their relations with state regulators, Congress by 1995 already had cut requested DSMOA funding by 50 percent. Moreover, they stipulated that DSMOA dollars could not fund regulatory enforcement activities.[60] To which the ASTSWMO responded that state regulators would no longer be able to support active participation or oversight of DoD remediation of contaminated sites, thus slowing down cleanups and base transfers.[61] "This will bring us back to the dark ages," added a California cleanup official. "If there's no [DSMOA] funding for the state, we don't have the staff to participate" in overseeing DoD cleanups.[62]

Embracing this welcome opposition from the states, an embattled Goodman appealed in early 1996 to the five states most dependent on DSMOA funding for help (Alaska, California, Massachusetts, Texas, and Washington). On cue, and putting their case in terms Congress would understand, they averred that cuts were increasing transfer times for parcels and decreasing BRAC savings, as well as reducing jobs, in congressional districts.[63] However, seizing upon the new authority they acquired after DERA devolution, the military services immediately trumped Goodman's efforts. Justifying their actions in terms of cleanup costs competing with readiness and other tasks now in service budgets (as critics had predicted), the military told states to provide base-specific data on oversight cost reimbursement requests. Then, after comparing DSMOA requests at the base level across states and facilities, the services began aggressively challenging the DSMOA funding requests from various states.[64] Critics charged that the services' motives were driven less by a desire to cut costs than by a wish to use their authority over DSMOA to cow the states and reduce state oversight of military cleanups.

While conflicts over DSMOA requests continued, states also excoriated DERA devolvement for negatively impacting their input into site characterization and cleanup remedial planning. Argued Clarence Smith of the Illinois EPA in 1998, "We get mixed signals from the services. . . . Some of [them] are better than others about involving states in cleanup plans for a given year." After DERA devolvement, Smith continued, state regulators often felt "left out . . . [because t]he services go to the [Army] Corps [of Engineers] rather than to the states."[65] DSMOA is a "great instrument that connects us all," added Tim Nord of the Washington Department of Ecology one year later, but it now failed to get the states and DoD to begin working toward "common goals." As Nord put it, "We [the military and state regulators] say the words, but we don't necessarily advance . . . partnering."

Nor was comity advanced after state regulators charged the services with using DERA devolvement to ask "nitpicking" questions about DSMOA requests in order to cut their reimbursement costs. Yes, John Fairbank of Maryland's Department of the Environment conceded, the DoD (through DSMOA) had made "a distinct move away from the 'DAD' [decide, announce, and defend]" mantra of the Cold War era, but they still used DERA devolvement as leverage for their own ends. Nor were these impressions short-lived. In 2001, an ASTSWMO study reported that DSMOA devolution had frustrated faster cleanups and transfers of military sites. Stubbornly inconsistent policies and requirements across the military services existed, with the navy the only service having issued DSMOA implementation guidance four years after devolution. Moreover, the services too frequently treated state regulators as "arm's-length" contractors rather than as partners.[66]

Discussion

Military strategist A. A. Vandergrift has observed that in battle, "positions are seldom lost because they have been destroyed, but almost invariably because the leader has decided in his own mind that the position cannot be held."[67] Much the same might be said of the contestants vying over the scope, standards, and management practices of cleanups at U.S. military bases during the Clinton years. To be sure, the "beaten zone" had been expanded for the services. Yet rendered in the process were structures, processes, and procedures geared more toward the military maintaining as much stability, predictability, and security of its traditional operations as possible.

Was There a Trajectory of Contestation?

Discernible, again, was a trajectory of contestation consistent with that witnessed in chapter 3. Observed are perceptions of historical-structural mismatches followed by greening offensives and counteroffensives. These led to crises of authority that were resolved only after prolonged bargaining and negotiations, which in turn spawned decidedly misaligned and fractionated greening structures, processes, and procedures. These altered the status quo, but compromised large-scale organizational change. In the process, these consolidated structures produced equally halting, halfway, and patchworked results across the U.S. military which could be selectively marshaled to praise or critique the services' progress in greening. Ensconced also in them were the seeds of future civil–military conflict, as well as multiple access points allowing the combatants to fight again another day. Finally, throughout this trajectory of contestation, the patterns of politics witnessed were steeped once again in the pursuit of the political, organizational, and personal prerogatives perceived by proponents and opponents alike.

What Motivated the Participants' Behavior?

Taking each component of this trajectory in order, first came perceptions of historical–structural mismatches spawned by the shock of the end of the Cold War, only this time related specifically to cleaning up contamination on U.S. military bases. To proponents of these greening initiatives, scoping, statutory, and management approaches inherited from the Cold War era were not up to the cleanup challenges facing the military in the post–Cold War era. More precisely, they were inadequate in the wake of the strategic, doctrinal, and operational minishocks cascading through the Madisonian system in the post–Cold War era to ensure a speed up of actual cleanups, while still protecting public health, safety, and the environment. These placed military operations in the crosshairs of an aroused public, regulatory community, and litigious set of grassroots groups.

Against this leitmotif Goodman launched an offensive to speed up cleanups in ways that would satisfy these pressures without compromising public health and safety or military readiness. In turn, strong counteroffensives were mounted once again by the military and its allies to Goodman's efforts to impose and diffuse her cleanup offensive. These disagreements, too, were fueled by and filtered through shifting perceptions of principle, self-interest, and realpolitik, with perceptions of history, context, and contingency most telling. Moreover, as part of this sense making, they were framed (and reframed over time) as issues in ways calculated to advance these interests.

By the mid-1990s, for instance, EPA's fencepost-to-fencepost policy, which had suited the military fine as a means to hold on to base properties, shifted to a counteroffensive by the services. In the process the military reframed EPA's policy as a cost-effectiveness and regulatory-unreasonableness issue. This occurred as pressures for transfers mounted and calls for prioritizing cleanups came from the White House and Congress because of shifts in issue status related to salience, proximity, and boundary effects. In order, these refer to changes in perceptions of the importance of the issue, changes in how directly stakeholders were affected by it, and related issues spilling over to alter the audience paying attention to the issue.

Also evident in effecting behavior were shifting perceptions of the threat to existing military dominance over the substance, scope, and pace of cleanups (i.e., organizational history); of the extent to which existing structures, processes, and procedures supporting that dominance were under assault because of changes in the political, social, or economic circumstances they faced at any given time (i.e., contextual factors); and of the ability of greening initiatives to enhance the power of the states to delay cleanups and thus threaten military missions (i.e., contingency factors).

Consider, for example, how the military initially preferred CERCLA to RCRA regulations because of the lesser stringency and greater cleanup flexibility afforded by the former and because of the enhanced authority that RCRA gave to states inherently less sympathetic to the military's mission. But as pressures for base transfers heated up the policy debate, the military reframed the issue in its counteroffensive as CERCLA working against local economic development. Thus the services' perceptions of the constellation of power they faced from regulators (i.e., from existing decision structures) changed, shifting balances of political power (i.e., energy distributions) in their favor.

More precisely, this happened as the military sensed that state and local officials would be more amenable to facilitating base transfers on its terms. In effect, shifts again occurred in issue salience, boundary effects, and primacy effects as political, social, and economic conditions shifted. Respectively, states and localities grew more interested in transfers, economic development and unemployment concerns were increasingly perceived as jeopardized by cleanup regulations, and the speed of base transfers took precedence over potential future harms.

Also witnessed in the chapter is how "portfolio management" (i.e., the trading off of policy emphases as circumstances changed) affected the patterns of politics animating cleanup offensives and counteroffensives at U.S. military sites. The chapter chronicles, for example, how the otherwise ENR-oriented Clinton administration scaled back the zeal of its cleanup offensives and changed its issue framing to fit shifting political, economic, and social developments. This came in response to the Republican takeover of Congress, as well as to the mounting costs of cleanup and the need for priority setting enunciated by Gingrich and the Rivlin-McGinty committee. Dilution of regulatory effort also came amid congressional cuts in funding, concomitant pressures to expedite base transfers, and continuing needs to reform management systems within the Pentagon.

What Specifically Were They Fighting Over?

Again wrought by this thrust-and-parry politics of contestation were crises of authority wherein the old regime was under challenge, but a new order was yet to be born. Consequently, the military's precise regulatory responsibilities, let alone any need to commit to a beyond-compliance ethic, were left in abeyance until authority relationships were re-established. Moreover, the targets or "fodder" for these battles fell once more into three broad categories (or sets) of nested rules: constitutional, collective choice, and operational. Included as fodder for contestation over constitutional rule sets were battles over such fundamental and jurisprudentially ripe issues as the appropriate relationship between states and the federal government when it came to cleanup standards. And looming throughout the background of these issues were those related to the unitary executive theory and the Antideficiency Act. This, as the military tried to maintain the supremacy of federal over state regulators when disputes arose, and to never let issues die over the constitutionality of fines from other federal agencies. Specifically, contests targeted rules regarding whether Congress had waived sovereignty immunity for federal facilities. What is more, these shifting disputes over whether or not military base cleanups fell within or outside the rubric of state regulatory authority were essentially battles at the constitutional level over exit and entry (how are things classified for regulatory purposes?) as well as authority (who decides?) rules.

In terms of collective choice and operational rule sets, the primary crises of authority in this chapter involved exit and entry, information (what kinds of information are needed for decision making?), aggregation (how is that information best integrated to make decisions?), and payoff (who bears the costs and benefits?) rules. Respectively, these were illustrated by crises of authority over (1) whether DERA and BRAC fences should be torn down to move resources toward readiness needs, (2) whether and how military sites should be scored for Superfund status and whether the services had to meet procedural or merely substantive state requirements, (3) what costs qualified as reimbursable for DSMOA funding and how the information-informed decision rules and requirements of state versus federal statutes interacted to affect cleanup standards, and (4) whether and how the states were accurately reporting costs of oversight for DSMOA indemnification and where cuts to DSMOA funding were to occur. Also serving as fodder for battles spawning crises of authority were such scoping (who had responsibility to act?) and authority rules as whether the services or OSD should control DSMOA funds and the DERA account.

What Strategies and Tactics Did They Use?

Witnessed throughout these crises of authority, too, were examples of various strategies and tactics used by the military, repertoires of contestation that again were reminiscent in attitude and in aim of the Cold War era. These included issue (re)definition, ally mobilization, delegitimation, and deinstitutionalization strategies. Again, and within the general confines of its omnipresent zero-sum issue framing of ENR military readiness–weapons modernization tradeoffs, the chapter shows the military reframing cleanup from a safety to an economic development issue. The services also consistently portrayed themselves as willing to comply with cleanup regulations, but only so far as compliance did not jeopardize readiness.

Also present in the chapter are the military's persistent efforts to engage in the demobilization of its foes or their actions by pursuing statute shopping, as well as to engage in their delegitimation through congressional committee shopping.

The former refers to the military's efforts to seek regulation under whatever statute gave them the most regulatory relief and, hence, the less environmentally aggressive constituencies that came with them. Also illustrative of demobilization tactics were claims by the military that they should be treated the same as private polluters, thus implying that what they asked for was quite reasonable. The latter involves the services effectively claiming that ENR committees lacked jurisdictional primacy in terms of legislative referrals when it came to military matters.

Most notable in terms of statute shopping are the military's evolving but persistent challenges regarding CERCLA versus RCRA. Most illustrative of committee shopping are DoD's attempts to get allies on the Senate Armed Services Committee to insert authorization language requiring that the fencepost policy be revisited by EPA with Pentagon input. Illustrative, too, is the assistance the military sought from allies on both House and Senate military committees to devolve DERA authority to the services and to get allies in the House to put language into bills that would require states to follow federal cleanup requirements at RCRA sites. In turn, of course, greening proponents also tried mobilization of allies. Consider, for example, how Goodman joined contractors in challenging efforts to tear down the DERA fence and how she appealed for support to states heavily dependent on DSMOA grants.

More generally, delegitimation (i.e., undercutting the legitimacy or authority of opponents) is illustrated by the military's repeated claims for sovereign immunity from lawsuits, and its attacks on the appropriateness of EPA's Superfund risk-ranking processes. Illustrative, too, are questioning the legitimacy of treating military sites differently from private sites and the comptroller's allegations of mismanagement by Goodman's shop. Moreover, these efforts were complemented by the military again adopting the repertoire of contestation used so effectively in chapter 3: deinstitutionalization of the capacity of regulators to pursue greening efforts aggressively. Most indicative of this tactic were the Pentagon's devolving of DERA accounts to the services, as well as congressional funding cuts before and after the DoD comptroller's allegations of ENR program mismanagement in the Pentagon.

To these deinstitutionalization efforts one also can add funding cuts to the Agency for Toxic Substances and Disease Registry that hindered toxic assessments (i.e., pursuing defunding tactics), as well as the Pentagon invoking the NPR and DRI as rationales for devolving DERA and DSMOA to the services from OSD (i.e., engaging in objective shifting). And to these objective-shifting tactics can be added resource dependency and delaying tactics. For example, DSMOA itself helped increase the dependency of state regulators on the military for resources while delaying the issuance of guidance documents for DSMOA implementation after devolution similarly advantaged the military over the states. Put more conceptually, the energy loads and energy distributions between the military and its state regulators were shifted toward the former, with a commensurate chilling effect on the latter.

What Were the Implications?

In the end the consolidation of administrative, responsibility, and accounting structures wrought by the negotiated settlements to these interacting crises of authority left them halfway, halting, and patchworked. In the process base clean-ups did accelerate appreciably but with downward adjustments in protective standards for public health, safety, and the environment. In turn, all this once more left the military woefully shy of the accountability, transparency, and re-source reengagement necessary to institutionalize a beyond-compliance ethic in the military. Rendered problematic in the process, too, was enduring organiza-tional change absent sustained external pressures in the post-Clinton years. But the (ir)resolution of the three cleanup questions chronicled in this chapter are only part of the story. To illustrate why and how this is the case, I turn in chapter 5 to the patterns of politics affecting contaminated base transfers. These also sent muddled messages about the priority of developing a beyond-compliance ethic in the U.S. military during the Clinton years.

Notes

1. "EPA to Issue Policy on Cleanup Milestones Without DoD Concurrence," *DEA* 6, no. 17 (August 25, 1998): 16.
2. "Base Cleanup Teams Bogged Down by Community Demands, Funding Issues," *DEA* 7, no. 3 (February 9, 1999): 12.
3. Lt. Col. Kent Hughes Butts, "Environmental Security: What is DoD's Role?" Occasional Papers (Carlisle Barracks, PA: Strategic Studies Institute, U.S. Army War College, 1993), 1.
4. Gordon M. Davidson and Christopher Grundler, "EPA's Federal Facility Hazardous Waste Compliance Program," *Federal Facilities Environmental Journal* 1, no. 1 (1990): 55–67.
5. "New DoD Evaluation Process Aims at Ranking Sites for Cleanup Dollars," *DEA* 2, no. 24 (November 30, 1994): 7.
6. GAO, *Environmental Cleanup: Too Many High Priority Sites Impede DoD's Program,* GAO/NSIAD-94-133, May 4 (Washington, DC: GAO, 1994), 9.
7. "EPA Expected to Reject California Request," *DEA* 1, no. 5 (December 15, 1993): 14.
8. Samuel P. Huntington, *The Soldier and the State: The Theory and Politics of Civil-Military Rela-tions* (Cambridge, MA: Belknap Press, 1981), 439.
9. "DoD Comptroller Slashes $530 Million from Cleanup, Compliance Request," *DEA* Special Report (December 8, 1994): 1.
10. As Huntington wrote in the 1950s, the comptroller was the "'garrison in the conquered city,' giving powerful representation to an essentially unmilitary and alien element within the [Defense] Department" (Huntington, *Soldier and the State,* 439).
11. "Congressional Budget Office Sees Dim Future for Defense Cleanup," *DEA* 2, no. 8 (April 20, 1994): 12.
12. "Rep. Dornan Calls for Halt to DoD Spending on Environment," *DEA* 3, no. 6 (March 22, 1995): 9.
13. Fazio represented a district that included Sacramento, home of Mather Air Force Base, a base placed on the NPL list in 1982 and slated for closure in the 1988 BRAC round.
14. Pacific Studies Center, "Base Closure Cleanup Derailed from Fast Track by Budget Cuts," *Citizens' Report on the Military and the Environment* 1, no. 1 (March 1994): 1.
15. "DoD Comptroller Slashes $530 Million from Cleanup."

16. "DoD Comptroller Plan to Slash Environment Spending Under Attack," *DEA* 2, no. 25 (December 14, 1994): 6.

17. Ibid.

18. Ibid.

19. "Defense Science Board Panel Says Regulations Threaten Readiness," *DEA* 3, no. 5 (March 8, 1995): 3, 7–9.

20. Michael A. West, "The 104th Congress and Federal Facility Environmental Activities: A Preliminary Assessment," *Federal Facilities Environmental Journal* 6, no. 2 (1995): 4–5.

21. "Environmental Contamination Major Obstacle to Base Reuse, GAO Says," *DEA* 2, no. 24 (November 30, 1994): 11–12.

22. "Senate Directs EPA, DoD to Rethink Method for Adding Bases to Superfund List," *DEA* 2, no. 14 (July 13, 1994): 12.

23. For Gingrich and Rivlin quotes on this issue, see "Gingrich Calls for Easing Cleanup Standards at Some Military Facilities," *DEA* 3, no. 4 (February 22, 1995): 5.

24. "Nation's Mayors Urge DoD to Quicken Pace of Cleanup at Closing Bases," *DEA* 3, no. 3 (February 8, 1995): 10. Senator McCain subsequently backed away from his earlier position by better defining what he meant by "nondefense-related" items in the DoD's budget. Indeed, by early 1995, he clarified in a letter to Secretary of Defense William Perry that he supported full funding of the military cleanup. "GOP Senator Stresses Support for Funding DoD Cleanup, to 'Clarify' Stance," *DEA* 3, no. 3 (February 8, 1995): 4.

25. "Nation's Mayors Urge DoD to Quicken Pace of Cleanup at Closing Bases."

26. Hilary Noskin, Rita Carnes, and Paul Schumann, "When Does RCRA Apply to a CERCLA Site?" *Federal Facilities Environmental Journal* 3, no. 2 (1992): 173–78.

27. "DOE Won't Back Plan to Amend Federal Facility Compliance Act," *DEA* 3, no. 18 (September 6, 1995): 3.

28. "House Panel Devising Superfund Reform Proposal for DoD Cleanup," *DEA* 3, no. 18 (September 6, 1995): 4–5.

29. Ibid.

30. DoD, *Defense Performance Review: Environmental Security Committee, Final Report*, M-U 42214-147, July 15 (Washington, DC: DoD, 1993), 4.

31. GAO, *Environmental Protection: Challenges in Defense Environmental Program Management*, testimony, GAO/T-NSIAD-95-121, March 24 (Washington, DC: GAO, 1995), 8.

32. Ibid., 12. They asserted that the site characterization process at McCord Air Force Base in Tacoma, Washington, was typical. Between 1988 and 1991, document preparation, revisions, and negotiations at McCord involved twenty-five documents with multiple versions and reviews. Each version cost anywhere from twenty to thirty thousand dollars.

33. GAO, *Environmental Protection*, 4.

34. "Sovereign Immunity Report from NAAG Counters DoD Claims," *DEA* 7, no. 16 (August 10, 1999): 17.

35. "Attorneys General Float Federal Facilities Reforms to Oxley's Staff," *DEA* 3, no. 25 (December 13, 1995): 15.

36. "DoD, DOE Report Opposes Explicit Waiver of Superfund Sovereign Immunity," *DEA* 7, no. 4 (February 23, 1999): 16.

37. "Text: Excerpts of Sovereign Immunity Report," *DEA* 7, no. 4 (February 23, 1999): 16.

38. Ibid., 19.

39. Ibid., 19, 17.

40. "Sovereign Immunity Report from NAAG Counters DoD Claims"; emphasis added.

41. "Reps. DeGette, Norwood Urge Strengthening Sovereign Immunity Waivers," *DEA* 7, no. 2 (January 26, 1999): 17.

42. "DoD Seeks Legislation to Allow Use of DERA Money at Newly Closing Bases," *DEA* 3, no. 6 (March 22, 1995): 4.

43. "EPA Science Board Highlights Plight of Agency Research Program," *Inside EPA Weekly Report* 15, no. 19 (May 13, 1994): 11–12.

44. "Health Assessment Agency Seeks Major New Role in Superfund Cleanup Decisions," *Inside EPA Weekly Report* 14, no. 20 (May 21, 1993): 10, also 1.

45. "Lobbying Shifts to Senate to Protect DERA 'Fence'," *DEA* 3, no. 12 (June 14, 1995): 7.

46. "DoD Reasserts Opposition to House Plan to Tear Down DERA 'Fence'," *DEA* 3, no. 19 (September 20, 1995): 10.

47. "Defense Conferees Reach Agreement, Bill Passes House and Senate," *DEA* 3, no. 26 (December 27, 1995): 11.

48. "House-Senate Conferees Cut $200 Million from DoD's FY96 Cleanup Request," *DEA* 3, no. 20 (October 4, 1995): 5.

49. "Dismantling DERA Will Force More Efficient Use of Cleanup Dollars, DoD Says," *DEA* 4, no. 8 (April 17, 1996): 30, 26–29.

50. "Navy, State Officials Renegotiating Cleanup Agreements at California Sites," *DEA* 4, no. 6 (March 20, 1996): 10.

51. "Excerpts: DoD Report to Congress on DERA Devolvement," *DEA* 4, no. 8 (April 17, 1996): 27; emphasis added.

52. "House Panel Votes to Eliminate 'Fence' around DERA Funds," *DEA* 3, no. 11 (May 31, 1995): 3.

53. "Text: ASTSWMO's Letter on Devolvement," *DEA* 4, no. 15 (July 24, 1996): 24.

54. "DoD Makes a Case for Breaking Up DERA into Separate Services Accounts," *DEA* 4, no. 6 (March 20, 1996): 9.

55. "Dismantling DERA Will Force More Efficient Use of Cleanup Dollars," 30.

56. "Protracted California DSMOA Debate Affecting Cleanups, EPA Official Says," *DEA* 7, no. 3 (February 9, 1999): 11.

57. The DSMOA funding level was limited to 1 percent of total cleanup costs for active bases and 1.5 percent for BRAC bases—thus further distorting priorities.

58. These costs are reimbursed through Headquarters, U.S. Army Corps of Engineers, for eligible services in support of environmental cleanup at listed installations. These included, but were not limited to, such oversight costs as state review of technical documents, site visits, identification and explanation of ARARs, RAB expenses, and support for public participation.

59. Both quotes are from "California's Cleanup Oversight Charges Raise Eyebrows at Navy," *DEA* 6, no. 4 (February 24, 1998): 14; emphasis added.

60. "Congress Backs $1.42 Billion for Cleanup in $243 Billion DoD Appropriation," *DEA* 3, no. 24 (November 29, 1995): 11. It could only fund scientific and technical activities provided by the states.

61. "States to Battle Senate Armed Services Cut to Cleanup Oversight," *DEA* 3, no. 15 (July 26, 1995): 7.

62. Ibid.

63. "Five States Spell Out Impacts of Cuts in DSMOA Funds," *DEA* 4, no. 6 (March 20, 1996): 15.

64. "California's Cleanup Oversight Charges Raise Eyebrows at Navy," 13–14.

65. This and the following two quotes are from "States Give New DSMOA Process Mixed Reviews, Say Problems Still Remain," *DEA* 6, no. 22 (November 3, 1998): 8.

66. "States Say Report Will Not Solve Problems with DSMOA Program," *DEA* 9, no. 18 (August 28, 2001): 5–6.

67. He is quoted in U.S. Marine Corps, *Warfighting: The U.S. Marine Corps Book of Strategy* (Washington, DC: U.S. Marine Corps, 1989), 2.

CHAPTER FIVE

Guns, Dogs, Fences, and Base Transfers

During Sparta's war with Argos, King Cleomenes (520–491 BC) negotiated a thirty-day truce with Argos that he violated nightly by ravaging their fields. Cleomenes never understood the fuss over the violations, Cicero reports, because of a technicality: The truce stipulated *days*, not *nights*.[1] As the previous chapter began describing, those trying to ensure that closed, realigned, or realigning military properties in the post–Cold War era were available for reuse and redevelopment without compromising public health, safety, and the environment knew how the people of Argos felt by the end of the Clinton administration.

As important as the gains noted in chapter 4 were to the U.S. military in shaping, preparing, and responding the base cleanup "battlefield" to the services' liking, a spate of more technical cleanup and transfer issues involving priority setting, base reuse, and land transfers also had to be resolved. Indeed, these were critical as part of greening proponents' ongoing offensive to speed up actual cleanup (not just studies) of contaminated properties. As in chapter 4, how and in what ways this second tier of issues were resolved again tested the patience, persistence, and political aplomb of proponents of greening the military.

Challenged in the process was the resiliency of the military's Cold War ethic in the post–Cold War era. As I will also demonstrate in this chapter, a parsing of language that would have made King Cleomenes blush drove these debates. Combined with the dynamics chronicled in the previous two chapters, the strategies and tactics used again sent consistently mixed signals about the priority to be given to greening efforts in the U.S. military. Moreover, they cumulatively left a halting, halfway, and patchworked set of structures, processes, and procedures whose misalignment further complicated the institutionalization of a green ethic in the services.

To see how and why this was the case, in this chapter I review the patterns of politics driving and driven by three major and interrelated sets of decisions affecting how best to transfer properties. First, what methodologies and criteria should determine the order of base cleanups at DoD sites? Second, regardless of order, under what circumstances, using what types of conveyances, and held accountable in what ways for public health and safety could the military transfer properties to communities for redevelopment? Third, regardless of conveyance instrument, could the services cut their costs and still protect public health and safety by using institutional controls?

The Relative Risk Ranking Challenge

With tens of thousands of polluted sites spread across the nation, the Pentagon had worked since 1986 to prioritize cleanups on a "worst first" basis. And so confident was the military in its finished defense priority model (DPM) that representatives fully expected a panel of the National Academy of Sciences (NAS) to endorse their model roundly in 1991. Reminiscent of the military's heroic self-image and hubris, one Pentagon spokesperson even told the NAS panel that "as far as [the Pentagon is] concerned, the key task for the Academy is merely to add some credibility on Capitol Hill and out there [i.e., among the general public]" to DoD's model.[2]

To the Pentagon's chagrin, however, panel members disparaged the complex, quantitatively driven, and seventy-five-variable-informed model as poorly conceived, misspecified, and underspecified. Said one member sarcastically, the DPM was no more than "a process of getting numbers to derive more numbers to go to a table to get a further number all in an effort to rationalize a comparison of apples and oranges."[3] Indeed, when asked by NAS panelists how a cleanup "site" was defined and cross-site comparisons made, Pentagon briefers responded that they were not sure how to compare a "large, relatively benign problem to a smaller, more hazardous one."

Likewise, when panelists asked why the DPM did not include important cultural and regional differences in such things as fish consumption or bathing patterns, the briefers responded, "We want to be as accurate as we can . . . , [but] we have to weigh how much additional information will benefit the precision of the score." But even when measured accurately, NAS panelists complained that some factors were weighted in ways incommensurate with their potential dangers. The model relegated unexploded ordinance (UXO), for example, to the bottom of its site cleanup priority list, as it did the potential harm from the burning of chemical weapons at its disposal facilities. Moreover, even when all relevant variables included and weighted accurately in the model, NAS panelists argued that data gaps precluded prudent comparisons.

All this was music to the EPA's ears as Clinton took office. Methodological problems with the model aside, agency administrator Carol Browner wanted the growing clamor for priority setting from Congress and President Clinton to produce a system consonant with the NPL ranking system of the EPA. Yet definitely more to the liking of many governors, mayors, and environmentalists was a "litigation-first" (also known as "enforcement-first" or "loudest-first") approach to priority setting. They preferred to take their chances with lawsuits rather than risk having their sites ranked low by *anyone's* technocratic model. Moreover, lawsuits typically resulted in interagency agreements and federal facility agreements negotiated by EPA and state regulators with military base commanders.

The rub, of course, was that a litigation-first approach also meant that cleanup priorities were linked largely to whoever got to the courthouse door first or got the U.S. military to concede points the services normally would not have conceded to avoid suits, fines, or other penalties. Also, from a technical perspective, these early interagency agreements and federal facility agreements often were flawed, either under- or overestimating the scope of the problem. This was the case because, for perverse but understandable reasons, many interagency agreements and federal facility agreements had set up remedies, schedules, and milestones *before* adequate site characterization had taken place.

Why would they do this? With congressional opprobrium growing over the slow pace of cleanups, the military, EPA, and environmental activists benefited in several ways from premature agreements in the early years of the post–Cold War era. To begin with, the EPA listed a facility as "in compliance" as soon as an agreement was signed, even though remedies were not in place. Thus, the agency's enforcement numbers looked better when examined by Congress. Concomitantly, the interagency agreement process advantaged the military services. Given the power asymmetries between the EPA and DoD, as well as EO 12580 delegating remedial response authority to the DoD, the services were for all practical purposes in de facto control of cleanups.

Internecine Warfare Begins

By the time the Clinton administration arrived in Washington, however, this arrangement was looking decidedly less attractive to the U.S. military. As noted in prior chapters, every passing year of that administration saw the EPA and the military's disenchantment grow. This occurred as cleanup costs spiraled, congressional funding cuts ensued, operational tempo increased in pace and duration, and Congress and the White House excoriated the slow pace of cleanups and BRAC transfers.

Even before Clinton took office, however, a director of EPA's federal facility operations in the first Bush administration, Christopher Grundler, proposed initiating a national stakeholder dialogue on site remediation at federal facilities. Convened ultimately during the Clinton years by the Keystone Dialogue Group of Denver, Colorado, and comprised of representatives from thirty-seven stakeholder groups, the EPA, state regulators, and the Pentagon, the "Keystone group" issued an interim report in 1993. Known formally as the Federal Facilities Environmental Restoration Dialogue Committee, the Keystone group's recommendations on priority setting sorely disappointed advocates, like the U.S. military, of a national risk-based, priority-setting model. Offered instead was a three-tiered, priority-setting scheme that was enforcement led rather than relative risk prioritized. It also relied on a "fair share" allocation system for meeting site remediation milestones nationally in federal facility agreements and interagency agreements whenever funding shortfalls existed. That is, all facilities had to share equally in any funding cuts made by Congress, regardless of the severity of risk at a site.[4]

Adopting and implementing this recommendation soon ran pell-mell into hard feelings, controversy, and the funding challenges of the 104th through 106th Congresses. Stung by the recommendations and not surprisingly angry about being excluded from the Keystone dialogue, the military services publicly attacked the report as geared more toward public relations than accomplishment. Typical were the comments of Philip Sheuerman, legal counsel for the U.S. Army Materiel Command. Chiding the Keystone recommendations in a critique guaranteed to resonate with members of Congress already impatient with the pace of cleanups at military sites, Sheuerman wrote that "we should remember that every dollar spent on *process* [like the Keystone dialogue emphasized] is a dollar taken from actual remediation."[5]

For Sheuerman and other critics, the fair-share component of the agreement dodged the issue of setting priorities—the ostensible reason for the dialogue group. To which Keystone participants such as George Hoffer, EPA Region X federal facilities coordinator, retorted, "Yes, the concept of fair share is intellectually and scientifically poor, but it was *politically* doable. If you don't have fair share, you have the state of Tennessee going after South Carolina for money for Oak Ridge to be taken from cleanup monies at Savannah River. [Also], how do you build a risk model that gets the concerns of different Indian tribes built into it?"[6]

As noted in chapter 4, however, President Clinton's Federal Facilities Policy Group (FFPG, aka the Rivlin–McGinty report) and the Republican Speaker of the House were by then arguing that a "top-down" national priority scheme was critical. Also noted in that chapter, however, was the virulent response of state regulators, ENR activist groups, and their congressional allies to the Rivlin–McGinty report. More precisely, critics initially argued that FFPG deliberations were shrouded in "secrecy" and limited to federal agencies, with environmentalists and state regulators lambasting Rivlin's initial ground rules forbidding participants to "speak to anyone about the group's activities."[7]

Then, upon release of the FFPG report in 1994, critics said that it was "not [about] improving cleanups. . . . It [was] . . . about saving money. . . . It [didn't] address [at all] how public health would be affected."[8] Others assailed the report as taking a "watered-down" or "least common denominator approach," for "not providing any aggressive response to Gingrich-led initiatives that would damage environmental programs," and for saying that interagency agreements and federal facility agreements "must be changed as a result of financial constraints."[9] Still others were inherently suspicious of raising quantification of risk as the definitive criterion in policy judgments.

The DoD Risk-Ranking Reaction

Against this leitmotif, the Pentagon set about devising a new risk-ranking model. Announced in 1994 after consultation with the EPA, the Relative Risk Site Evaluation Framework (RRSEF) sorted contaminated sites into one of three categories based on relative risk to public health, safety, and the environment: high, medium, or low. A site's ranking, in turn, depended on the nature and concentration of risk, pathways and rates of risk migration, and the potential for human or ecological "receptors" to be exposed to these risks.

Any close reading of the DoD's *Relative Risk Site Evaluation Primer* indicates how far the Pentagon went to accommodate critics' concerns. Consonant with the Keystone group's prescriptions, for instance, RRSEF did not produce a single absolute risk value for any site. The framework also factored interagency agreements and federal facility agreements into site rankings and afforded a dialogue with stakeholders concerning site conditions.[10] But a close reading also suggests that the Pentagon tried to design implementation structures, processes, and procedures to maintain the military's control over ranking decisions.

The DoD, for example, was responsible for training EPA and state regulators on the intricacies of applying the framework at military sites. Likewise, each service was authorized to apply the RRSEF framework on its own terms, with vague guidance documents from the OSD to the services. Each service then redelegated lead responsibility for conducting risk-ranking assessments to base commanders, with guidance documents again vague. Combined with tight time constraints for having the framework inform FY 1996 funding requests, this meant scant opportunity for regulatory agencies and the public to be involved, a stakeholder-involvement decision left up to installation leaders steeped in a "decide, announce, and defend" approach to decision making.

In signing off on the RRSEF, a politically outgunned EPA nonetheless noted that it would not rely exclusively on the DoD's risk-based comparisons when developing the agency's own cleanup priorities. Also, the military would have to afford summaries of "the costs, relative threats, and improvements to public health and the environment from [any] remedial alternatives [offered]" before sign-off by EPA regions. Moreover, though "encouraging" (but not requiring) EPA regions to use risk-based approaches (like the RRSEF), such an approach would only be a *"primary point of departure* in categorizing cleanup activities."[11]

How advantageous this negotiated RRSEF was for the military, however, became clear in 1996. By that time, critics pointed out that a big gap existed between how the relative risk model was sold and its implementation, gaps reminiscent of the military's Cold War culture of sovereignty, secrecy, and sinecure. Not only were stakeholders not playing the significant role in the RRSEF process that the military had promised, but significant variations existed across EPA regions. Moreover, the services were ranking sites without EPA reviewing the original data used when doing rankings, creating an information asymmetry favoring the military's choices.

Joining this rising chorus of discontent with the military's implementation of the RRSEF, the EPA complained about the inadequacy of site characterizations at military bases and the services' tendency to choose cleanup technologies that their own data indicated were inadequate. Most upsetting to the agency, cleanup remedies such as "containment," "fencing," or "natural attenuation," rather than the permanent remedies required by the 1986 Superfund Amendments and Reauthorization Act, were selected significantly more often for military sites than for private Superfund sites where the EPA conducted remedial investigation/feasibility studies.

The Strategy-Structure Mismatch for Relative Risk Assessment Continues

Even under the best of circumstances, hope of implementing the RRSEF with fidelity to green values also had to redress existing strategy-structure misalignments. To be sure, each of the services instituted extensive environmental training programs for base commanders and their personnel. In addition, doing well in these courses, and predicating base commander evaluations partially on avoiding ENR violations, became meaningful components of career advancement. Yet although some of the services provided formal classroom instruction to military personnel, others only provided informal training on an "as-needed" basis.[12] Nor would this situation improve much during the Clinton years. In the most systematic study done during the early 1990s, for example, the GAO found significant shortages of DoD environmental personnel, high rates of turnover, and minimal expertise to carry out effective RRSEFs.[13]

Nor did the capacity of EPA and state agencies improve significantly enough during the Clinton years to breed confidence among greening proponents. Guidance from the EPA was commonly absent or inconsistent, requests for risk-ranking data varied over time and across EPA regions, and data gaps persisted.[14] Indeed, the GAO reported in 1997 that incomplete data existed at 1,040 of the 2,070 facilities listed on the EPA's Federal Facilities Docket.[15] Still lacking, as well, until late in the Clinton administration, was EPA guidance to regional officials about which federal facilities to evaluate first among those backlogged. Additionally, cries of unequal treatment did not abate when critics learned that EPA *had* developed guidance for nonfederal private sector NPL candidates. Nor were many states better prepared for oversight. As Lynn Goldman, assistant administrator for the EPA's Office of Prevention, Pesticides, and Toxic Substances, summarized the situation, "some states have no capacity [at all to do risk assessments], not a single toxicologist [on staff]."[16]

With or without adequate expertise or oversight, the military services claimed in 1997 that relative risk evaluations were completed for approximately 75 percent of their sites. Of these, 54 percent were ranked as high risk, with the remainder ranked either medium or low risk. Moreover, those ranked as high risk were receiving about 83 percent of DoD's cleanup budget. Still, the RRSEF did not rank sites within categories. When challenged by critics, the military argued that facility officials could "usually identify the worst sites within categories."[17] This, of course, also left priority setting more to military base commanders than to either the Pentagon's civilian leadership in the OSD or to EPA, state regulators, and citizens groups.

The FUDS Conundrum

Further indicative of the military's historical control of cleanup priority setting was the tendency of the Army Corps of Engineers to marginalize state officials in the relative risk ranking of formerly used defense sites (FUDS), in decisions not to take further action at them, and in claims that FUDS were exempt from state laws.[18] As such, a spirited offensive by state regulators to open up the Corps of Engineers' risk-ranking process began during the first term of the Clinton administration. Moreover, this campaign was given additional urgency by a 1996 Congressional Budget Office study estimating that no less than 8,000 FUDS required immediate cleanup attention. Led initially by the ASTSWMO, the states sought greater input into an expedited FUDS cleanup process.[19]

In response the Corps of Engineers initially reiterated its Cold War position that FUDS were exempt from state law, thus rendering state involvement unnecessary and perhaps even illegal. But with UXO detection more commonplace, and with an embattled EPA issuing threats of administrative orders and fines (see below), DoD finally requested increased congressional funding for FUDS cleanup. These entreaties produced annual budget increases of $30 to $50 million for FUDS cleanups over the remainder of the Clinton years.[20] Thus by 1999 the DoD was touting the significant progress made at FUDS, noting how approximately 5,500 sites no longer were awaiting determinations about suitability for transfer or leasing for development.

Still, the DoD's Sherri Wasserman Goodman estimated that even with Congress's increased largesse, the Corps of Engineers would need until 2060 to cleanup FUDS.[21] Moreover, funding increases notwithstanding, the states rapidly grew disenchanted with the Corps of Engineers's site characterizations on FUDS. Reminiscent again of the DoD's Cold War culture, half of respondents to a 1996 ASTSWMO survey of state regulators said that *they* had to take the initiative to get information out of the Corps of Engineers, and the other half characterized communication from the corps as sporadic.[22] In addition, only eight states said they had participated in the service's out-year planning and priority-setting cycle; thirty states said their involvement was "lacking" or "inadequate."

Things only worsened in early 1999 when studies of corps determinations regarding "no further action" needed for cleanup at FUDS found evidence of gross misfeasance (if not malfeasance) in site characterizations. Performing site recharacterizations in six states, researchers found that thirty-two of the sixty-six "no further actions" issued by the corps actually required further action. Identified, for instance, were distressingly high levels of asbestos, polychlorinated biphenyls, UXO, leaking underground storage tanks, groundwater contamination, and trichloroethylene. Especially problematic was a failure to take soil samples or to consider state applicable or relevant and appropiate requirements (ARARs) in setting cleanup standards. Most chilling, the corps's site characterizations typically involved little more than "drive-by" or "windshield" assessments, site walk-throughs, or telephone interviews with FUDS operators.

Into this breach stepped the EPA, asserting that it would exert authority over FUDS cleanups.[23] Also pressuring EPA to act were state associations and activists living near FUDS. The latter wanted the states rather than the EPA to take over cleanup at FUDS and to ensure that detonating UXO stopped being the Corps of Engineers' preferred method of cleanup. As one citizen activist stated, the "drive to convert military property into tax-generating residential or commercial lots is causing corners to be cut, [and] as a result, detonation is being utilized before the extent of buried UXO is even known."[24] Not surprisingly, the states needed little prodding. The Environmental Council of the States, for example, demanded that the Pentagon "acknowledge in writing [the] states' regulatory authority, role, and responsibility" for cleanup at FUDS.[25]

Faced with losing control over the substance and pace of FUDS cleanup, the corps's immediate response was to blame regulators for "unrealistic" cleanup requirements. Nonetheless, hoping to stop EPA and the states from revamping administrative and responsibility structures that protected the sovereignty of the military, the corps announced plans in 2000 to "reengineer" the program. Offering no specifics, the army said only that, consonant with Secretary of Defense William Cohen's DRI, it would advance a sense of "corporate responsibility" for the FUDS program by increasing OSD's oversight and revising its guidance to the corps.[26] Critics scoffed that the planned launch of a reengineered FUDS program in February 2001 only bought the Army time to see if a less environmentally predisposed George W. Bush won the 2000 election.

The Slippery Slope of Future Land Use

Similarly placing downward pressures on cleanup standards and complicating priority setting was the Community Environmental Response Facilitation Act (CERFA), discussed in chapter 4. Recall how a consensus had developed that the military should identify areas on each base scheduled for BRAC transfer that "offered the greatest opportunity for reuse and redevelopment" and transfer that property to cities for development.[27] Yet just prior to the 1994 midterm elections, a DoD task force concluded that considerably more resources were needed to do an effective job of identifying and transferring those properties by stipulated deadlines. Also slowing progress was the process of developing community reuse plans by local reuse authorities (LRAs).[28] Although Congress had envisioned that they would expedite BRAC transfers predicated on future land-use decisions, LRAs were not able to keep pace in developing reuse plans with the military's now-accelerated cleanup process (see below for more details).

Still, military-friendly groups like Business Executives for National Security pressed Congress for legislation allowing community reuse plans to drive priority setting. Under this "best first" cleanup strategy, the highest priority for cleanup would go to the "most commercially viable properties."[29] Dubbed by some the "most attractive for reuse first" criteria for priority setting, by the late 1990s this approach was refined subtly, albeit meaningfully, by DoD in its political and financial interests to become the "most visible reuse first" criteria.

Importantly, there was again more to the military's gradual evolution from a "worst first" to "most visible reuse first" cleanup prioritization scheme than responding in visible ways to congressional pressures for quick transfers. As Tim Fields, the EPA's deputy assistant administrator for solid waste and emergency response, noted, the military understood it was "cheaper to clean up a *closed* facility because of the push to get the site ready for productive reuse[, as] closing bases use an *expedited* cleanup plan."[30] A wary Fields added, "There may be a need to accommodate community reuse and shift our priorities for cleanup from the 'worst first' to the 'most attractive for reuse first'."[31]

Others joined Texas attorney general Dan Morales (D) in seeing future land use itself as integral to pushing cleanup standards (and, hence, DoD's cleanup costs) downward even more. Throughout the Clinton years, Morales argued that future land use combined with early transfers (see next section) were thinly veiled "attempts to subsidize economic redevelopment of bases by allowing the cleanup standards to be loosened." These standards, added Morales, are "moving too quickly to short-term solutions [that are] more *budget-based* than health and safety-based."[32] But the EPA, DoD, and the military services moved ahead, driven by the ambiguous future land-use criteria that Morales and other critics found so laden with DoD mischief. Trading off risk-based priority setting for less costly cleanup standards afforded by future land-use determinations was too financially and politically attractive to resist.

The Base Reuse and Leasing Challenge

The order of cleanups aside, two equally challenging, conflict-producing, and interrelated cleanup and land transfer questions with dire consequences for greening the U.S. military further animated the Clinton years. First, when were contaminated properties suitable to transfer for reuse? Second, how were they best conveyed into private hands for reuse?

The Suitability-for-Transfer Conundrum

With pressures for transfers mounting amid precarious funding, the military was not content with the halfway, halting, and patchworked victories chronicled thus far.[33] The services also sought to wring additional concessions advantageous to their positions from both CERFA and President Clinton's Fast-Track initiatives to accelerate transfer of BRAC properties for redevelopment. Taking Fast-Track first, the services immediately went after one of their longstanding nemeses, the National Environmental Policy Act (NEPA). Specifically, they successfully lobbied House and Senate Armed Services committees (again, rather than ENR committees) to permit the DoD to stop doing two environmental impact statements, one for disposal and one for reuse of base properties. Then, administratively, DoD issued guidance stipulating that the twenty-four to twenty-eight months allowed for environmental impact statement preparation be cut to twelve months. Next, during 1995 and 1996, Senator David Pryor (D-AK) offered legislation narrowing the scope of environmental impact statements that had to be performed before military lands could be transferred.[34]

The military also proposed revamping existing interagency agreements and federal facility agreements. As noted, many of these had been signed hastily during the Ronald Reagan and George H. W. Bush years to get EPA's and the military's compliance numbers up in the face of growing congressional scrutiny. Costly and leading to enforcement-driven priority setting, these pacts were now renegotiable in a more favorable environment for the military. Resource-strapped regulators were now under the gun to approve site characterizations produced largely on DoD's terms and with incomplete information.

Were these initiatives not distressing enough to them, greening proponents were equally aghast at the way the military *and* the EPA were implementing CERFA. Recall from chapter 4, for example, how Congress gave the services only until April 14, 1994, to identify parcels suitable for transfer for development, with EPA concurring on the designation of those sites on the NPL list and states concurring on non-NPL sites. By late 1993, however, several EPA regions had rejected the DoD's efforts to get clean parcel designations, calling them too hastily done, inadequately documented, and tardy.[35] What riled environmental activists even more over the coming years, however, was the decision by the EPA to redefine *administratively* the meaning of "clean" to include parts of base properties with minute levels of contamination. Part and parcel of Clinton's initiative to accelerate transfers, this action made it easier to qualify military lands for transfer by substituting a "de minimis" criterion for its longstanding "zero release" standard.[36] But in doing this EPA ignored language in CERCLA specifically ruling out parcels containing contaminants as suitable for transfer.[37]

Why such a sudden alignment of interests between regulator, regulatee, and an avowedly green White House? As one state regulator explains, the services' persistent administrative and legislative push to expand the clean parcel definition was predicated on their hopes of "pump[ing] up the number [of land transfers] under CERFA."[38] In doing so they (as well as the EPA and White House) could "show" Congress how aggressively they were trying to convert parcels. Indeed, using this relaxed definition of contamination in mid-1994, DoD declared as "uncontaminated" approximately three hundred parcels on sixty installations nationwide, all of which had previously failed to qualify under the zero-release standard.

Expediting Transfers or Transferring Expediently?

Still lacking amid the move toward de minimis standards, however, was a *legislative* imprimatur for using them to expedite property transfers. Thus, by early 1995, groups such as the U.S. Conference of Mayors were importuning Congress for relief in this and other land transfer matters. "Since communities [still] cannot develop sites until they are cleaned," the conference argued, "it is recommended that the federal government either allocate more money for cleanup or change the regulations for military bases."[39] And no more tenacious and powerful an ally existed to aid this campaign during the Clinton years than the U.S. military.

The following were central to the military's campaign. First, the services stepped up their efforts to amend administratively and legislatively Section 120 of CERCLA to allow land to be leased rather than transferred outright (i.e., deeded) to developers before they were totally cleaned. Second, the military tried to find ways to incorporate input from stakeholders while maintaining the stability, predictability, and security of core military functions. Finally, the services again explored the load shedding of cleanup responsibilities to the private sector.

Interpreting CERCLA Creatively. Through 1995, the Pentagon continued to wage a concerted and multifront campaign against CERCLA, contending that it was slowing down the transfer of properties by anywhere from two to six years.[40] By then, however, the services were taking a different tack: they insisted that long-term leases of these properties to developers were *not* transfers. This interpretation would allow them to convey properties for development without heeding CERCLA's requirement for total cleanup before transfer. Moreover, facing parallel congressional pressures to expedite transfers, Clinton's EPA initially joined the military in this campaign.

Even before the Clinton administration took office, the Pentagon had pressed Congress for a legislative clarification of CERCLA in the FY 1993 Defense Authorization Act. Specifically (and rife with load-shedding implications), the military wanted authority to transfer properties to communities and private developers prior to cleanup whenever the new owners promised to finish the cleanup, comply with all standards, and abide by any other agreements made. Repeatedly rebuffed by Democratic congresses, the DoD now successfully importuned the EPA through 1995 to permit administratively the transfer of contaminated properties by lease rather than by deed before total remedies were in place at Pease Air Force Base in New Hampshire (the first BRAC closing base), Lowry Air Force Base in Colorado, and California's Mathers and Norton Air Force Bases, Presidio (U.S. Navy), and Fort Ord (U.S. Army).[41] Lawsuits challenging the actions quickly followed.

Although the specifics of lawsuits at various bases varied, the plaintiffs (as well as many state regulators and environmental activists) shared one common belief: Leasing before cleanup was completed would leave states and localities holding the bag for cleanup costs. Again, Texas Attorney General Morale's concerns are illustrative: "In light of the Antideficiency Act and other barriers to the ensuring of sufficient funding for cleanups, the requirement of base cleanup [by the military] *before* transfer provides the one sure means of ensuring that there will indeed be cleanup of the facility to be transferred."[42] Added the National Association of Attorneys General (NAAG), the DoD was likely to invoke sovereign immunity after leasing these properties, thereby blocking state enforcement actions against the services.

Nor were NAAG's concerns diminished after the courts began ruling that the Pentagon's leasing proposal violated federal environmental laws. Trying yet another angle, the DoD asked Congress in 1995 and 1996 for an amendment to Superfund that would permit the services to transfer properties by deed prior to the construction of a cleanup remedy.[43] But the Superfund reauthorization bill to which this proposal was attached eventually stalled in an increasingly polarized Congress for the remainder of the Clinton administration. Also stalled was a parallel initiative by the military to apply RCRA rather than CERCLA to transferring bases, thus entirely mooting CERCLA's prohibitions against transfers before total cleanups were completed.

Foiled by greening proponents in Congress, a characteristically indefatigable military next tried to attach its proposal to the Senate's FY 1997 defense authorization bill. This was a strategy again designed to circumvent less friendly environmental committees in Congress. Distressing enough to greening proponents, four other aspects of this bill and the decision process leading up to its passage were especially galling. First, the military responded to a query by its allies on the Senate Armed Services Committee about its liability after transfers.[44] Asserted the Pentagon, "Additional response action required as a result of a change in land use . . . [should be] borne by the party seeking the change."[45]

Second, and in a move redolent of the military's Cold War culture, the amendment to the 1997 defense bill proposed that the military be exempt from even the admittedly ambiguous sovereign immunity waiver in CERCLA. This amendment, of course, was immediately challenged by a bipartisan group of attorneys general from cleanup-challenged states such as California (Dan Lungren–R), Colorado (Gayle Norton–R), Michigan (Frank Kelly–D), Minnesota (Hubert Humphrey–D), and Washington (Christine Gregoire–D). Pointing out the military's success in challenging the sovereign immunity waiver at FUDS, Gregoire and Humphrey argued that "in jurisdictions where these [court] decisions are followed, states could be foreclosed from using their laws to ensure that federal agencies address past contamination, even if the contamination were previously undiscovered or undisclosed."[46] Added Representative Dan Schaefer (R-CO), "Without an ironclad assurance that states can enforce the ultimate cleanup of these sites, the good idea quickly becomes a curse on communities . . . [because] federal entities will initiate transfers and disappear from the liability mix, leaving private entities with full responsibility."[47]

Third, and relatedly, proponents of greening bridled that the military consistently showed a cynical pattern reminiscent of its Cold War ethos. Depending on what best advanced their short-term interests, the services either wanted or didn't want to be treated like private polluters. In this instance, the Pentagon insisted the services be treated like private polluters. All the military wanted, officials claimed, was "to put base closure property on the same footing as private property, which can be sold" prior to a completed remedy and which had lowered costs appreciably. To which Sam Goodhope, a state regulator on the Defense Environmental Response Task Force, responded, "Private parties can't get out of their obligations by not putting enough money [in their] bank account."[48]

Finally, critics screamed when yet another effort to "end-run" less DoD-friendly ENR committees occurred in 1996. But this time an apoplectic White House and Clinton appointees in the Pentagon joined them when the military tried to dodge them as well. Attempting to "undercut" an agreement painstakingly worked out by the Clinton administration, the services began "negotiating [directly] with the Armed Services Committee," cutting a separate deal that had "the potential to cut regulatory agencies out of the picture" entirely.[49]

Amid all this, a series of GAO studies further aroused the fears of greening proponents that accelerating transfers was creating a "race to the bottom" in terms of relaxed cleanup standards and shoddy work. On the positive side, investigators found that by "September 1995, DoD had obligated 96 percent of available [cleanup] funds, [a figure] substantially higher than the 50 percent rate two years earlier." But this occurred without any additional expertise added to site characterization efforts and despite GAO noting that earlier lower obligation rates were due partly to a lack of "necessary expertise to better estimate [cleanup] requirements."[50]

Nor were their fears allayed when, in 1997, the services' allies on the House National Security Committee again sought to push Superfund amendments and specific cleanup relief for military sites through a proposed Defense Reform Act. For one thing, they did so without the knowledge of Goodman's office.[51] For another, Chairman Floyd Spence (R-SC) decided not to link this bill with the FY 1998 defense authorization bill until it reached the floor. This was a not-so-veiled effort to circumvent sequential referral to environmental committees that had foiled earlier efforts to get the expedited transfer language approved.

With or without victories, the military spent the remainder of the Clinton years in new or resuscitated pursuits of regulatory relief. Incorporating the military's preferences, for example, the Pentagon drafted language for a prospective Defense BRAC Act of 1999 limiting the services' vulnerability to NEPA lawsuits to sixty days after required actions were either taken or not taken.[52] Moreover, as state regulators and developers feared, once transfers were allowed the military began challenging the standards that locals applied to cleanups. As Colorado's assistant attorney general for the environment, Dan Miller, recounted in 2004, "Developers and communities [had] to clean up with their own money and hope to get it back" from the Pentagon.[53]

The Community Participation Conundrum.   As these debates raged the citizen participation structures created by various statutes (e.g., CERCLA and the Superfund Amendments and Reauthorization Act) also provoked battles over the reuse and land transfer process. Moreover, they did so in ways advantaging the military services through efforts reminiscent of the Cold War era to limit transparency. Consider the confused, ambiguous, and overlapping nature of the administrative and responsibility structures regarding transparency in base transfers set by congressional statutes and independent military actions.

As originally envisioned under CERCLA, technical review committees (TRCs) were designed to involve local communities in cleanup decisions at military sites. Community-appointed members of TRCs (joined by regional EPA, business, and service personnel) were allowed to review documents and comment on cleanup plans. In turn, Restoration Advisory Boards (RABs) were co-chaired by a representative from the military installation in question *and* a local community member. Their responsibilities were twofold: (1) to represent the diverse elements in an affected community, and (2) to serve as a point of contact with the military installation for citizens more generally in a community.[54] Moreover, RABs, with support from the Technical Assistance for Public Participation program, were to go beyond the review and comment responsibilities that TRCs afforded. They were to give advice on remedy alternatives, selection, and (as noted) prioritizing cleanup sites.

Meanwhile, the DoD's BRAC Cleanup Teams (BCTs) were comprised of representatives from the DoD, state regulatory agencies, and the EPA. The BCTs were to be the primary forum for developing BRAC cleanup plans to facilitate reuse, coordinating closely with base transition coordinators and LRAs.[55] In turn, and as noted above, LRAs were to create redevelopment plans for the properties and be the community's point of contact with the military.

The apparent inclusivity of this participatory structure notwithstanding, feelings of exclusion and tension mounted among some in local communities. Local governments, after all, still had no direct representation on BCTs, and BCT meetings were basically closed meetings where cleanup decisions were made. Contractors and local government officials could be invited to portions of these meetings, but they could attend only under the conditions set by BCT members. Thus, by 1997, nonmembers were demanding either observational or full membership on BCTs. Strenuously opposed, the military argued that RABs alone were the vehicles for local input, that only military and regulatory representatives on the BCTs were legally accountable for decisions made, and, consequently, that other groups could not have input into those decisions.[56]

Groups representing local governments not only found these excuses lame (e.g., membership on the BCT would make them just as accountable), but they knew that "sometimes community members [e.g., local citizens of RABs] ha[d] different opinions than local governments." Moreover, "while RABs [sometimes did] include local government representation, there ha[d] been cases where local government officials ha[d] been kicked off the RAB by other members."[57] Nor did it take long before these problems came famously into bas-relief at, of all places, the army's Fort Ord training base in California. The base had been touted by the army as a model of how federal, state, and local officials could partner with citizens to expedite reuse decisions and land transfers. Yet Fort Ord officials were roundly criticized for excluding the base's RAB from major decisions involving UXO cleanup before transfers. In rebuttal, Fort Ord officials declared that final authority regarding "treatment of UXO is something that has been delegated to [the Army] and doesn't need approval" from federal and state regulators or citizens.[58]

Thus, by mid-1995, some members of the base's RAB were pointing to a "continuing pattern": The army was leaving them to "operate in a vacuum" by refusing to discuss the status, nature, or methods of cleanup at Fort Ord.[59] Asked one RAB member, "Why can't they just give us a presentation in simple language about what is being transferred, what's planned, and the cleanup methods being used?"[60] They were even joined in their frustration by the National Oceanic and Atmospheric Administration (NOAA) after the army refused to investigate the possibility that UXO from Fort Ord was present in the Monterey Bay. And when the army did conduct its own investigation, NOAA said that the service inadequately sampled the water body.[61]

Subsequently, the army not only dismantled the RAB at Fort Ord as "ineffective" and "dysfunctional" but also did the same at McClellan Air Force Base in California.[62] Predictably, citizen groups said the service's rationale for unilaterally taking this precedent-setting step was disingenuous: The RABs were working entirely as they should by questioning army remedial cleanup decisions at closing bases (see *Curt Gandy et al. v. U.S. Department of the Army et al.*). Unfazed, army spokespersons responded that RABs were not required by law; they were only a manifestation of DoD policy. Hence, the services had the discretion to dismantle RABs that were not, in their sole judgment, functioning effectively.

"We're just wondering who's next," said one citizen activist challenging the military's action at McClellan. Added another, "It's a huge mess . . . [a] typical kind of thing [one expects when] agencies don't know jack about dealing with the public."[63] Nor were these isolated concerns. By the end of the Clinton administration, a confederated national RAB caucus had formed, one calling for a national dialogue on public participation to help redress what the group saw as a retreat from the early participation principles enunciated by the military.[64] "Too often," the caucus alleged, "opportunities [to participate] only allow citizens to give rubber-stamp approval of government decisions, [and] citizens demand that honest and substantive input into government decision-making" be revived.[65] Conceding that commitment varied across military bases, Associate Director Renee Wynn of the EPA's Federal Facilities Restoration and Reuse Office responded that changing behavior in the military was much like child rearing: "We must constantly remind them of the direction we want them to take."[66]

Toward Privatization? With these structurally induced transaction costs mounting for the military amid cries for quicker transfer of properties for redevelopment, the services began looking once more to the private sector for load-shedding relief. Couched again in Cohen's DRI, full privatization of military cleanups became a mantra at the Pentagon and in the military services in the late 1990s. Goodman argued that early transfer authority was insufficient for getting land transfers done "faster, cheaper, and simpler." Increasingly pressured to expedite transfers but strapped for resources, Goodman averred in 1999: "I know it [cleanup] can be done cheaper and faster in the private sector. I fully believe that."[67] Thus, going well beyond previous calls for early transfers of assets to new owners if they promised to pay cleanup costs, Goodman now proposed getting totally out of the business of cleanups.

In the end the challenge would be to convince federal and state regulators of both the environmental and financial benefits to be derived from full privatization. And this would prove no mean task. By the spring of 2000, for example, the International City Management Association (ICMA) said it would not support privatization of cleanups without formal assurances by the Pentagon that the military services would do two things they were reluctant to do: commit to earlier stakeholder participation in the privatization process and premise privatization on locally developed land-use plans.[68] In a more practical constraint, the DoD learned the difficulty of expanding the pool of cleanup contractors (and thus getting competitive bidding on contracts) due to the financial risks associated with cleanups and liabilities.[69]

The Institutional Controls Challenge

The final component of the services' quest for property transfers before total cleanup was their proposal to use institutional controls (also known as land-use controls) at hazardous waste sites. Designed to reduce risk by limiting access to contaminated sites rather than actually cleaning them up, institutional controls use such contrivances as zoning restrictions, fences restricting access (and sometimes guarded by dogs), deed restrictions, and habitat modifications. Moreover, institutional controls can mix governmental regulations like zoning and permitting with proprietary controls like easements and covenants to restrict the use of real property.

Institutional controls were hardly a novel idea in the late 1990s. In 1994, for example, interest in them began mounting within the military and among communities anxious to transfer BRAC properties. Moreover, interest grew as the costs and technical complexities of UXO cleanup became clear (see chapter 6 for an in-depth look at this dilemma). Thus, caught between the need to transfer properties before cleanups were pursued, completed, or technologically possible while ensuring public safety at the lowest possible cost, the Pentagon considered institutional controls at some of the military's most difficult and potentially costly UXO-contaminated sites.

As they did so, however, institutional controls began drawing the sustained scrutiny, first, of nonfederal researchers from the ICMA, NAAG, the Environmental Law Institute, and Resources for the Future. None opposed these techniques in principle, but each proffered warnings. Researchers from the institute, for example, found that institutional controls helped to reduce risk but noted a variety of ways in which they could fail over time (e.g., breaches of security). Likewise, Resources for the Future found that institutional controls were selected at Superfund sites only at the consent decree stage rather than during the remedy selection phase. Consequently, "the public 'doesn't really have a role'" in designing them or in pointing out their weaknesses.[70] They also found too little thought given to how institutional controls were implemented and monitored in the long term. Meanwhile, NAAG legal researchers cautioned that institutional controls were not substitutes for the permanent treatments required by law. Still others warned that although deed restrictions might hold the military's feet to the fire in fulfilling its responsibilities, state and federal regulators would lose enforcement powers. This might happen because only parties to deeds were legally entitled to enforce them, and regulators would not be parties to institutional controls.

Thus, by late 1997, even those positively disposed to institutional controls were having second thoughts. The DoD's Defense Environmental Response Task Force wanted the military to demonstrate that institutional controls were enforceable before properties were transferred.[71] Moreover, many of the military's critics argued that the services again were only trying to avoid state and federal oversight. Nor did two subsequent actions by the EPA do anything but exacerbate these suspicions. First, with resources short, the agency announced it would rely on the Pentagon's data and analysis regarding contamination and institutional controls monitoring. Second, it allowed the services to provide developers with a general rather than precise description of the nature, extent, and area of contamination near properties. Reinforced in the process were perceptions that the Pentagon could hide problems for which others would later pay.

Chastened, the EPA began over the next two years (1998–99) to refine its interim guidance for institutional controls at closing bases.[72] Yet once·issued, the battle over institutional controls among EPA, the military, and ENR activist groups grew acerbic. By 1999, for instance, Lenny Siegel of the Center for Public

Environmental Oversight spoke for many critics in characterizing institutional controls as "a way for responsible parties—that is, polluters and property owners—to get away with less than complete treatment or removal." Neither were critics' and regulators' suspicions allayed when the services and their congressional allies pressed the EPA to halt release of its revised guidelines until they talked further.

Critics saw this request as yet another attempt by the military to stall regulations on institutional controls until it could gain final say over the adequacy of institutional controls chosen at any site. Challenging the EPA's plan to require federal agencies to inform the agency about the kinds of institutional controls they were putting into place, the Pentagon claimed that the EPA wanted to preempt it from developing its own guidance on implementing institutional controls. The military also attacked the EPA's claim that it alone had the authority to decide if deed restrictions were sufficient and to make the military clean-up sites to meet health and safety standards. CERCLA, the Pentagon argued, afforded only a consultative role to EPA, a distinction that military lawyers (in a not-so-veiled threat) said the courts might have to resolve. Countered an EPA official, "It is EPA's responsibility to ensure that all parts of a remedy, including institutional controls, are protective" of public health and safety.

Stalemated, the military's counteroffensive postponed final EPA guidance until just two months before the Clinton administration left Washington. Seemingly carrying the day, EPA persisted in "establish[ing] criteria . . . to evaluate the effectiveness of institutional controls that are part of a remedy or are a sole remedy" for transferring Superfund properties for reuse.[73] But these came one month after DoD issued its own land-use control guidance document for Superfund site transfers. They also were done amid warnings by researchers that EPA should take even more aggressive steps to ensure that the agency's regions followed this guidance, "because EPA's regions don't usually follow headquarters' recommendations." What is more, they occurred in the wake of warnings by Jim Woolford, EPA's director of the Office of Federal Facilities Restoration and Reuse, that the agency could consider itself lucky if institutional control failure rates did not exceed "50 percent . . . over the next 50 years."[74]

One cannot overstate how prescient these early warnings were. A study released in mid-2000 by the ICMA discovered that the military had used institutional control solutions in 70 percent of its sixty-seven BRAC Records of Decision.[75] Perhaps even more disturbing for public health and safety, researchers found a sizable knowledge gap concerning institutional controls among base transition coordinators, LRAs, and local governments. Most had little knowledge about what types of institutional controls were used, what entity monitored and enforced them, or who funded the oversight of any facility. Moreover, the National Research Council reported that natural attenuation (i.e. decay)—a key component of institutional controls at many military sites—had major flaws.[76] The technique was appropriate for only a very limited number of contaminants, did not so much destroy as immobilize certain metals, and, for some compounds, produced other hazardous byproducts. Meanwhile, the ELI issued a report stating that its research on four Superfund sites using institutional controls found their long-term effectiveness highly suspect. For example, some of the institutional controls listed in applicable Records of Decision remedial requirements were not implemented; the EPA's consultation with state and local regulators in monitoring and oversight was uneven at best; and EPA regions had not made oversight of institutional controls "a regular, consistent, and routine part of staff responsibilities."[77]

Discussion

At the battle of Shiloh in April 1862, a wounded soldier who had been told to leave his weapon and go to the rear soon returned, saying, "Gimme another gun. This blame fight ain't got any rear."[78] As this chapter again has illustrated, proponents of transferring military properties for economic development in ways maximizing public health, safety, and the environment can be excused for feeling much the same way by the end of the Clinton years. Chronicled were familiar patterns of politics as the military services and their congressional allies countered this offensive by repeatedly and successfully pursuing ENR regulatory relief, in this case by gaining expedited land transfers of base properties. On the one hand, these politics foiled the services' cultural tendencies to rely on their own technical models to set cleanup and land transfer priorities. On the other hand, the military's efforts to shape, prepare, and respond to the greening battlefield in this policy arena ultimately protected its control over timing, method of remedy selection, and the extent of health, safety, and environmental protection afforded once lands were transferred.

Was There a Trajectory of Contestation?

Discernible, again, was a trajectory of contestation in this arena of civil–military relations consistent with that identified in previous chapters. Witnessed were perceptions of historical-structural mismatches followed by greening offensives and counteroffensives. These led to crises of authority that were resolved only after prolonged bargaining and negotiations, which in turn spawned decidedly misaligned and fractionated greening structures, processes, and procedures. These altered the status quo, but compromised large-scale organizational change. In the process, these consolidated structures produced equally halting, halfway, and patchworked results across the U.S. military which could be selectively marshaled to praise or critique the services' progress in greening the transfer process. Ensconced in them, too, were the seeds of future conflict, as well as multiple access points allowing the combatants to fight again another day. And once more, the patterns of politics witnessed throughout this trajectory of contestation were steeped in the pursuit of the political, organizational, and personal prerogatives perceived by the combatants.

What Motivated the Participants' Behavior?

Taking each component of this trajectory in order, first came perceptions of historical–structural mismatches spawned by the shock of the end of the Cold War. In this instance, the historical-structural mismatches involved minishocks related to the need to downsize the now woefully overbuilt base infrastructure inherited from the Cold War. Also as in prior chapters, disagreements reigned over what reforms were needed. These arose as Goodman sought initially to impose and diffuse her initiatives within the Pentagon for speeding transfers while ensuring the maximum protection of public health, safety, and the environment.

These disagreements were intensely fueled by and filtered through sensemaking perceptions of principle, self-interest, and realpolitik, and they were (re)framed over time as issues in ways calculated to advance these perceived interests. For greening proponents, base transfers had to be done in ways protecting public health, safety, and the environment. But for greening opponents, the key was to expedite, prioritize, and ensure cleanups and base transfers for economic development in ways that saved money for the military's readiness needs.

As their offensives and counteroffensives mounted, greening proponents persistently tried to impose and diffuse their preferred options by framing the issues as negatively as possible for the services. The military, argued proponents, was hiding behind sovereign immunity arguments; willfully compromising public health and safety; and trying to shift cleanup costs to states, localities, and private developers. In response the services tried to enact an environment better suited to their aims. They did so by framing the issues in their counteroffensives as, respectively: eliminating inefficiencies and misallocations of resources that took funding from military readiness; reducing regulatory unreasonableness and impracticality, because zero tolerance of contamination was an unrealistic standard; and advancing the public's interest in revitalizing economic development in local communities.

Also illustrated in the chapter is how filtering of information and issue framing were, in turn, affected by combatants' shifting perceptions throughout the offensives and counteroffensives mounted. Once again, organizational history, the existing organizational context, and organizational contingencies related to the impact of delay were primary filters of these perceptions. These included sense-making perceptions of the threat to the historical balance of forces controlling the substance, scope, and pace of land transfers (e.g., the ability of its historical political economy to control events); the extent to which existing decision structures, processes, and procedures supporting that dominance were perceived as under assault because of changes in the political, social, economic, or technological arenas at any given time (i.e., the context had shifted); and the ability of greening initiatives to delay or threaten the military's core warfighting mission (i.e., contingency factors had shifted).

Also not unlike prior chapters, shifting perceptions of issue status and constellations of relative power at any given time informed the decision calculi of the actors involved. The military, for example, only reacted against the EPA's established litigation-first strategy once the federal facility agreement and interagency agreement processes that helped inflate compliance numbers got in the way of expediting transfers and it began losing de facto control over cleanups within the federal government. Similarly motivated was the EPA's shift away from its CERCLA zero-release standard in favor of a de minimis one, as well as the embrace of future land use as a cleanup criterion in the wake of Gingrich's endorsement and the recommendations of the Rivlin–McGinty committee.

Relatedly, the chapter offers repeated illustrations of portfolio management, with the zeal of the combatants' offensives and counteroffensives calibrated in terms of shifts in issue images and, hence, in access structures (i.e., the facility of other issues to be linked to them). These included shifts in issue salience (the relative importance of issues), boundary effects (the ability of issues to become linked to other issues), proximity (who is impacted by given issues), and decision structures (who has the authority to participate in decision making). Indeed, the Clinton administration is seen as repeatedly (re)calibrating its priorities in imposing and diffusing its cleanup and transfer offensives to shifting political, economic, and social factors, as well as to perceived balances of forces.

In this vein the concept of fair share that emerged from the Keystone process is illustrative, as are the EPA's reinterpretation of institutional control guidelines and its breach of CERCLA's prohibition of transfers if parcels contained any level of contaminant, no matter how small. In each instance, the boundary and proximity effects (for localities and their congressional patrons) of base transfer pressures, the salience of the Rivlin–McGinty report, and the mobilization of state associations against the military avoiding more complete treatments and removals were dispositive.

What Specifically Were They Fighting Over?

Wrought once more by this thrust-and-parry politics of contestation were by now familiar crises of authority wherein the old order was under challenge by greening initiatives, but a new order was yet to be born. As noted in previous chapters, the military's precise regulatory responsibilities, let alone any need to commit to a beyond-compliance ethic, were left in abeyance until authority relationships could be resolved. Moreover, the targets or "fodder" for these crises again fell into three broad categories (or sets) of rules: constitutional, collective choice, and operational.

In terms of nested battles over constitutional rule sets, the primary battle occurred over fundamental constitutional and jurisprudential principles involving federalism and the appropriate relationship between the federal government and the states. Also looming throughout the background of these issues again were those related to the unitary executive theory and the Antideficiency Act. This occurred as the military sought to maintain the supremacy of federal over state decision makers when disputes arose. Nested, too, within this battle were conflicts over the making of collective choice and operational rule sets. Included among the former were crises of authority over what constituted appropriate risk-ranking methodologies, the interpretation of Clinton's Fast-Track Cleanup Program and CERFA, and the development of guidance documents for base commanders seeking to transfer "clean parcels" for economic development. Meanwhile, at the operational level, battles took place over what constituted sufficient monitoring by the military once institutional controls were put in place.

More conceptually, the primary crises of authority across these rule sets involved entry and exit rules (how are things classified for regulatory purposes?), information rules (what kinds of information are needed for decision making?), aggregation rules (how is that information best integrated to make decisions?), scoping rules (who is responsible for doing what?), authority rules (who decides?), and payoff rules (who bears the costs and benefits?). Taking these in order, battles over entry and exit rules were joined over when sites were clean enough for transfer or merited high or low priority for cleanup. Likewise, crises of authority involving information and aggregation rules included what (and when) information had to go into risk-ranking models or studies related to institutional controls, and whether drive-by or windshield surveys were sufficient at FUDS. Apparent too were challenges of scoping, authority, and position rules. These included, respectively, crises of authority over who had functional responsibility when additional contamination was discovered after land transfers; whether authority for UXO cleanups at FUDS should be shifted to the EPA or the states; and what the appropriate level and type of participation was among BCTs, RABs, and LRAs. Also targeted throughout were payoff rules, including who would pick up the tab for costs incurred during cleanups or after transfers and what priority-setting criteria were acceptable. In the latter, moving toward "most visible reuse first" meant fewer resources for sites that might have fared better under a "worst first" strategy.

What Strategies and Tactics Did They Use?

Witnessed throughout these contests, too, were examples of various strategies and tactics reminiscent in attitude and in aim of what the military used during the Cold War era. Within the general confines of its omnipresent zero-sum issue framing of ENR military readiness–weapons modernization tradeoffs, plus the issue framing noted already in this section, these repertoires of contestation included the military's efforts to redefine RAB participation as conditioned on cooperative behavior. Illustrative also in this regard were the services' efforts to reframe local reuse plans as obstacles to land transfers, and to redefine interagency agreements and federal facility agreements as misallocating scarce cleanup resources.

Nor did the military stop there, with multiple examples again of ally (de)mobilization and load-shedding repertoires. The former included the prodding of military allies in Congress to promote future land use, efforts to get friendly legislators to introduce language allowing transfers before cleanup whenever the new owners promised to finish the job, asking that base closure properties be put on the same basis as private properties, and attempts to exempt the military from CERCLA's sovereign immunity waiver. Equally indicative were efforts by the military to apply RCRA rather than CERCLA standards to avoid the enhanced state scrutiny and accompanying mobilization of DoD critics this entailed (statute shopping) and to limit the timing of the services' vulnerability to NEPA lawsuits (constituency shopping). Examples of the latter included hiving off controversial and costly cleanups through early transfers and the use of institutional controls. In turn, these strategies were met by the countermobilization strategies of greening proponents (e.g., NAAG, the Texas attorney general, and state governors) who were worried about a shift-and-shaft strategy on cleanups and property transfers.

The military and its allies were also not shy about using delegitimation, deinstitutionalization, and disinformation strategies as these crises of authority played out. Respectively, these tactics involved undermining the authority of opponents or their actions, undermining the capacity of regulators to act aggressively, and providing false information. Indicative of delegitimation strategies, for example, were not only the aforementioned claims for sovereign immunity that the military so routinely made but also the use of committee-shopping strategies. Illustrative were the military's repeated efforts to avoid ENR committees (e.g., on the Defense Reform Act) and the White House by working through allies on House and Senate Armed Services committees. Meanwhile, in addition to the significant congressional defunding of cleanup operations discussed in chapter 4, deinstitutionalization tactics included speeding up FUDS's reviews without affording commensurate resources to do them; leaving some RABS in the dark when it came to cleanup methods being used at sites and disbanding "uncooperative" ones; and delaying the issuance of guidance documents for risk-ranking FUDS. Likewise illustrative of deinstutionalization repertoires was the Army Corps of Engineers's promise to reorganize under the DRI instead of reforming its processes, a classic instance again of objective shifting as actions with controversial policy implications were couched as mere technical management issues. Finally, disinformation strategies came packaged in this chapter in the "cooking" of risk analysis numbers at FUDS.

What Were the Implications?

In the end the consolidation of structures, processes, and procedures inevitably produced by bargaining and negotiation in resolving these crises of authority wrought the same kind of misalignments of strategy (i.e., creating a green corporate ethic) and structure witnessed in prior chapters. Moreover, these halfway, halting, and patchworked structures, processes, and procedures left dubious the extent to which properties were being transferred in ways adequately protecting public health, safety, and the environment. They also left the military woefully shy of the accountability, transparency, and resource reengagement necessary to institutionalize a beyond-compliance ethic in the military. In the process underwhelming messages were sent about the priority of developing a beyond-compliance green ethic capable of shifting mental models and schema in the military. As such, future progress would be susceptible to the vagaries of external pressures for greening the land transfer process. Nor does this base cleanup story end here. As I discuss in chapter 6, greening proponents involved in the development of a munitions rule at U.S. military bases during the Clinton years also came to appreciate the plight of the citizens of Argos battling King Cleomenes.

Notes

1. Andrew P. Peabody, trans., *Ethical Writings of Cicero: De Officiis (On Moral Duties); De Senectute (On Old Age); De Amicitia (On Friendship), and Scipio's Dream* (Boston: Little, Brown, 1887).

2. Seth Shulman, *The Threat at Home: Confronting the Toxic Legacy of the U.S. Military* (Boston: Beacon Press, 1992), 43.

3. Quotes regarding the NAS reaction are from ibid., 49.

4. Thus if Congress appropriated only 80 percent of what the DoD requested for meeting all its milestones, each site would receive 80 percent of what it had requested. In a bow to DoD's preference for risk-based priority setting, however, the Keystone group did allow departments to request a different allocation scheme predicated on risk-based factors. But if they took this route, the EPA and the states would be free to prosecute violations of milestones at sites that did not absorb their fair share of cuts.

5. Philip Sheuerman, "First, Do No Harm: The 'Keystone' Initiative," *Federal Facilities Environmental Journal* 4, no. 2 (1993): 137; emphasis added.

6. George Hoffer, Superfund, Federal Facilities Branch, Region X, EPA, interview with author, Seattle, WA, March 25, 1994; emphasis added.

7. "Keystone Members Pressing for Input into White House Task Force," *DEA* 2, no. 8 (April 20, 1994): 20.

8. "OMB Director Designate to Remain Co-Chair of Policy Group Until Fall," *DEA* 2, no. 14 (July 13, 1994): 25.

9. "White House Cleanup Report Draws Criticism from Private Sector," *DEA* 3, no. 22 (November 1, 1995): 15–16.

10. Robert Turkeltaub and William D. Rowe Jr., "Relative Risk Site Evaluation within DoD's Cleanup Program," *Federal Facilities Environmental Journal* 7, no. 3 (1996): 47–58.

11. "Text: EPA Description of Federal Facility Reforms," *DEA* 3, no. 25 (December 13, 1995): 13; emphasis added.

12. Turkeltaub and Rowe, "Relative Risk Site Evaluation within DoD's Cleanup Program," 54.

13. GAO, "Environmental Cleanup: Case Studies of Six High Priority DoD Installations," report to the chairman, Committee on Governmental Affairs, U.S. Senate, Washington, DC, GAO/NSIAD-95-8, November 1994.

14. GAO, "Federal Facilities: Consistent Relative Risk Evaluations Needed for Prioritizing Cleanups," report to the Chairman, Committee on Government Reform and Oversight, House of Representatives, Washington, DC, GAO/RCED-96-150, June 1996.

15. Ibid., 10.

16. Lynn R. Goldman, "Risk Assessment Planning at the EPA," remarks during discussion at *Inside EPA* Conference on Environmental Risk Assessment: Politics and Policymaking, Doubletree Hotel, Arlington, VA, November 1–2, 1994.

17. GAO, "Federal Facilities: Consistent Relative Risk Evaluations Needed for Prioritizing Cleanups," 14.

18. FUDS are locations, often operated by contractors, where military functions such as ammunition manufacturing and military vehicle production occurred, but have since ceased (with many of the sites now owned by private parties and in use for a variety of activities, including commercial airfields, industrial facilities, and residential development). See "Justice Department Will Approve Unilateral Cleanup Orders at Some FUDS," *DEA* 7, no. 8 (April 20, 1999): 7–8.

19. "ASTSWMO Task Force Dubs Devolvement, FUDS Cleanups Top Priorities," *DEA* 4, no. 10 (May 15, 1996): 20; "State Waste Managers Pursue Greater Involvement in FUDS Cleanups," *DEA* 4, no. 12 (June 12, 1996): 18.

20. "Senate Appropriators Boost Defense Cleanup Spending, Sanction Devolvement," *DEA* 4, no. 13 (June 26, 1996): 6–7.

21. "Environmental Security Office Seeking Major Increase to FUDS Budget," *DEA* 8, no. 22 (October 24, 2000): 4–6.

22. "State Waste Managers Pursue Greater Involvement in FUDS Cleanups."

23. "Cal/EPA, Federal Officials Seek Improved UXO Management Policy," *DEA* 7, no. 17 (August 24, 1999): 14.

24. Ibid.

25. "ECOS Urges DoD to Recognize State Authority for FUDS Cleanups," *DEA* 8, no. 18 (August 29, 2000): 7–8.

26. "FUDS Cleanups 'Grossly Underfunded,' Army Corps Officials Say," *DEA* 8, no. 8 (April 18, 2000): 7–8.

27. CERFA, Section 2(2).

28. LRAs were comprised of individuals selected by local or state officials to advocate community interests. They were responsible for creating redevelopment plans for transferred properties.

29. "Reuse Should Drive Cleanup Priorities, Business Group Says," *DEA* 3, no. 6 (March 22, 1995): 16.

30. "EPA Studying Costs of Cleanup at Open vs. Closed DoD Facilities," *DEA* 3, no. 6 (March 22, 1995): 8; emphasis added.

31. Ibid., 9.

32. "Texas Attorney General Attacks Views of Federal Base Task Force," *DEA* 3, no. 1 (January 11, 1995): 11–12; emphasis added.

33. See, for example, "Lawmakers Look for Silver Lining Under Cloud of Closures," *Congressional Quarterly Weekly Report*, March 7, 1992, 546–49. Although Congress had appropriated $758.6 million for BRAC cleanups for FY 1992, those funds covered only the 1989 BRAC round, leaving the 1991 round totally unfunded. Then, when President George H. W. Bush offered $160 million of a $1 billion supplemental for 1991 BRAC cleanups, the funds were rescissions from existing programs important to members of Congress rather than additional funds.

34. "Sen. Pryor Offers Measure to Ease Interim Leasing at Closing Bases," *DEA* 3, no. 18 (September 6, 1995): 11.

35. "EPA Regions Rejecting Some Clean Parcel Requests for Lack of Data," *DEA* 1, no. 6 (December 29, 1993): 10.

36. "Text: EPA Memo Lays Out Lenient Definition for Clean DoD Parcels," *DEA* 2, no. 9 (May 4, 1994): 4–5.

37. Section 120(h)(4)(A) of CERCLA was the specific prohibition.

38. "EPA May Allow Public Use of Mildly Contaminated DoD Sites," *DEA* 2, no. 7 (April 6, 1994): 6.

39. "Mayors Urge Streamlining of Base Transfer and Cleanup Process," *DEA* 3, no. 5 (March 6, 1995): 12.

40. "DoD to Develop Policy to Implement Transfer-by-Deed Amendment," *DEA* 4, no. 17 (August 21, 1996): 3. That is, if the military had to wait for a remedy to be installed.

41. "First Circuit Lays Out Schedule in Pease AFB Case," *DEA* 3, no. 1 (January 11, 1995): 11.

42. "Texas Attorney General Attacks Views of Federal Base Task Force," 12; emphasis added.

43. "DoD Exploring Privatization Options for BRAC and Other Cleanups," *DEA* 7, no. 7 (April 6, 1999): 3–4.

44. The Defense Environmental Response Task Force is a DoD federal advisory committee charged with developing recommendations for BRAC closing bases.

45. "Military Not Responsible for Additional Cleanup Costs, DoD Tells Congress," *DEA* 4, no. 10 (May 15, 1996): 3.

46. "State AGs Press for Changes to 'Transfer by Deed' Amendment," *DEA* 4, no. 13 (June 26, 1996): 4.

47. "House Passes Transfer-by-Deed Amendment with Slight Modifications," *DEA* 4, no. 16 (August 7, 1996): 6.

48. "States, Feds Face Off on Transferring Property Prior to Cleanup," *DEA* 4, no. 10 (May 15, 1996): 22.

49. "Revised 'Transfer by Deed' Amendment Receiving Mixed Reviews," *DEA* 4, no. 14 (July 10, 1996): 4.

50. "Reducing Cleanup Costs at BRAC Sites is Difficult, GAO Says," *DEA* 4, no. 20 (October 2, 1996): 23.

51. "House Defense Authorizers Pursue Major Environmental Revisions," *DEA* Special Report (June 9, 1997): 1.

52. "DoD Seeks to Limit Time for Filing NEPA Lawsuits at Future Closing Bases," *DEA* 7, no. 7 (April 6, 1999): 8.

53. Peter Eisler, "Cleanup Fights Stall New Uses for Old Bases," *USA Today*, October 14, 2004, 3, www.usatoday.com/news/nation (April 23, 2006).

54. "Fact Sheet: Restoration Advisory Boards," http://www.afcee.brooks.af.mil/pro act/fact/may02a.asp (February 17, 2003). Comprised of volunteers selected in an open nomination process to represent an affected community's "diverse interests, concerns, and values," more than three hundred RABs existed (mostly at BRAC bases) by the time George W. Bush assumed the presidency.

55. Ibid.

56. "Local Governments May Call for Representation on Base Cleanup Teams," *DEA* 5, no. 4 (February 12, 1997): 10–11.

57. Ibid., 11.

58. "Environment Officials Plan Response to UXO Exemption at Fort Ord," *DEA* 2, no. 18 (September 7, 1994): 20; "Army Reasserts Position as Final Authority in Fort Ord UXO Dispute," *DEA* 3, no. 21 (October 18, 1995): 5–6.

59. "Army Accused of Hampering Cleanup Advisory Board," *DEA* 3, no. 1 (January 11, 1995): 19.

60. Retorted others on the RAB, however, "There are some members of the board that have a better technical understanding who are impatient and disruptive" (ibid.).

61. "NOAA Preparing for Showdown with Army Over Fort Ord Cleanup," *DEA* 2, no. 24 (November 30, 1994): 14–15.

62. "Army Disbands Fort Ord Advisory Board Due to 'Ineffectiveness'," *DEA* 7, no. 11 (June 1, 1999): 22.

63. "Citizens Plan to Sue Over Disbanding of McClellan RAB in California," *DEA* 8, no. 12 (June 6, 2000): 11. In actuality, EPA Region IX officials agreed with the DoD's action to dismantle and reform the RAB.

64. "RABS Overcome Some FACA Hurdles, Miss Out on Law's Benefits," *DEA* 7, no. 1 (January 12, 1999): 14.

65. "RAB Caucus Calls for National Dialogue on Public Participation," *DEA* 7, no. 15 (July 27, 1999): 18. Also significant in limiting citizen participation on RABS was the military trying to circumvent the Federal Advisory Committee Act (FACA). As one observer notes, "The Defense Department avoids triggering FACA with its RABS by seeking facts and information rather than advice and recommendations, seeking individual advice rather than group consensus, avoiding strict agency management and control, and avoiding repeated meetings. . . . In particular, as long as DoD seeks individual rather than consensus advice, it's safe." See, "RABS Overcome Some FACA Hurdles," 14.

66. "RAB Caucus Calls for National Dialogue on Public Participation," 18.

67. "DOD Exploring Privatization Options for BRAC and Other Cleanups," 3.

68. "Cleanup Privatization Needs Thorough Public Input, Groups Say," *DEA* 8, no. 8 (April 18, 2000): 8–9.

69. "DOE Finds Substantial Barriers to Cleanup Contract Reform," *DEA* 8, no. 23 (November 7, 2000): 12.

70. "Researchers Express Caution Over Use of Institutional Controls," *DEA* 4, no. 25 (December 4, 1996): 18. This was the case because negotiations over consent decrees only involve the regulating agency or agency and the responsible party or parties.

71. This resulted from research chronicling how institutional controls and land-use controls "may not be sufficiently enforceable in all states." "DoD Advisory Board Seeks Enforcement of Institutional Controls," *DEA* 5, no. 14 (July 1, 1997), 20.

72. The following quotations regarding the debate over institutional control policy are from "Despite DoD Criticisms, EPA Will Issue Interim Closing Base IC Policy," *DEA* 7, no. 9 (May 4, 1999): 3. The EPA's interim guidance document was known formally as the "Policy Towards Landowners and Transferees of Federal Facilities." The revised guidance document was known formally as the "Institutional Controls and Transfer of Real Property Guidance under CERCLA Section 120(h)(3)(A), (B), or (C)."

73. "EPA Issues Final Interim Land Use Controls Policy for BRAC Sites," *DEA* 8, no. 3 (February 8, 2000): 10.

74. "EPA Issues Final Version of Institutional Controls Guidance," *DEA* 8, no. 23 (November 7, 2000): 11–12.

75. Records of Decision are public documents that explain which cleanup alternatives will be used at Superfund sites.

76. "NRC Report Finds Current Attenuation Protocols are Inadequate," *DEA* 8, no. 4 (March 21, 2000): 14–15.

77. "Institutional Controls May Fail, Unless Improvements Made," *DEA* 8, no. 13 (June 20, 2000): 19.

78. George F. Will, "Winning the 'Three-Block War'," *Washington Post*, April 14, 2004, p. A25.

CHAPTER SIX

Missiles, Mayhem, and the Munitions Rule

Homer writes in the *Iliad* that when Mars rushed into Achilles's soul in his battle with Hector, "the springs of fate snap[ped] every lock tight."[1] As the two previous chapters on base cleanups have illustrated, however, the U.S. military in the post–Cold War era conceded nothing to fate. Rather, like the principles informing the Clinton administration's strategic military doctrine in the 1990s, fate was something to shape, prepare for, and respond to in order to protect as much stability, predictability, and security of the military's core operations as possible. Moreover, the only thing "locked tight" was the military's determination to control the substance, pace, and extent to which responsiveness, transparency, and the reallocation of resources related to base cleanups took place.

Nor would this predisposition wane in a third major component of cleanup debates during the Clinton years: how best to regulate the treatment, storage, and disposal of active or spent munitions at U.S. military bases.[2] One of the special concerns Congress had in debating the merits of the FFCA of 1992 was discerning how best to protect civilians and military personnel from the explosive *and* toxicological threats posed by live or spent munitions on active and closed, transferred, or transferring military bases.[3] Moreover, with passage of the FFCA jeopardized over this important issue, Congress left it to the EPA to develop a "munitions rule" dealing with these issues. One major component of that rule would be a "range rule" regulating UXO.

The technical complexity alone of developing these rules was formidable. Multiplying the challenges, however, were the high stakes involved for the White House, the military, federal and state regulators, and environmental activists. Depending on their specifics, these rules might require of the services greater, modest, or trivial behavioral changes; more or less transparency of their munitions-related operations; substantial or insubstantial costs (financial, political, and cultural); and enhanced or diminished control of the pace, scope, and substance of greening at their bases. Commensurate with those stakes, the EPA, states, and environmental activists mounted persistent offensives throughout the Clinton years but were unable to gain agreement on the range rule component of the munitions rule amid the military's counteroffensives. Left again amid the aftermath of these crises of authority were the same kinds of fragmented structures reported in the preceding chapters. Bequeathed, too, were the kinds of halting, halfway, and patchworked efforts and results that proved so unfavorable to institutionalizing a beyond-compliance ethic in those episodes.

To illustrate these civil–military dynamics, I review in this chapter the patterns of politics driving and driven by three major, interrelated, and contemporaneous sets of decisions affecting development of the munitions rule. First, when, how, and determined by whom were conventional and chemical military munitions a solid or hazardous waste subject to the RCRA and, hence, to state rather than federal standards? Second, what was an adequate level of UXO safety on rangelands? Third, how much consultation with the states was necessary in developing and implementing the range rule as a key component of the munitions rule, including who had final say when disputes arose among the parties?

When Is Ordnance a Waste?

Under RCRA, there are two types of waste that require regulation: those specifically listed in Subpart D as solid waste and those with any of the four characteristics listed as hazardous in Subpart C of the statute. The four characteristics associated with the latter include ignitability, corrosivity, reactivity (i.e., explosivity), and toxicity.[4] From their perspective environmental activists and state and federal regulators had no doubt that military munitions fell clearly within either the solid or hazardous waste regulatory ambit of RCRA. Since 1980, in fact, munitions *had* been subjected routinely to RCRA's solid waste regulations and permitting requirements. But although everyone agreed that the "shelf life" (i.e., the point of obsolescence, damage, or excess) of military munitions was finite, at issue during the Cold War era was *when* munitions became solid or hazardous waste.[5]

Under then-current RCRA regulations munitions were considered "products used for their intended purpose" and did not become solid waste subject to RCRA regulations until they were "discarded or intended for discard."[6] Also deferring to the military, the EPA had not treated munitions as wastes subject to RCRA regulations *before* they went to treatment, storage, and disposal facilities. Moreover, the agency deferred to the Pentagon's Defense Explosives Safety Board (DESB) to devise procedures for handling these "products," deference which meant that explosive and not toxicity threats were the only concerns before disposal.

Hardly sanguine about this "self-certification" process as the Cold War wound down, state regulators and environmental activists pressed Congress between 1990 and 1992 to mandate independent oversight of the military's storage of munitions on U.S. bases. Nor did they find it acceptable for the EPA alone to conduct this oversight; state regulators had a legal role to play under RCRA. For their part, the military countered with by then familiar sovereign immunity claims that they only had to comply with state ENR standards and not their procedures. Moreover, George H. W. Bush's Pentagon argued that RCRA imposed permitting and procedural burdens that would severely complicate and endanger the military's management of munitions and its training processes. Also foisted upon the services would be costly and redundant procedures. This because the EPA's standards for hazardous waste regulation were already "comparable" to DESB regulations for storing munitions, whereas the Pentagon's existing standards and procedures were "sufficient" when it came to treatment, storage, and disposal.

The EPA, environmentalists, and most state regulators profoundly disagreed. If private polluters made the same arguments about "comparability" and "sufficiency," they would be rejected outright. Moreover, even if standards and procedures were comparable to the EPA's, self-regulation as the military envisioned would result in illegalities. RCRA storage requirements, for instance, required secondary containment whenever liquid wastes were stored outdoors, whereas DoD requirements did not (e.g., at mustard gas storage sites). Likewise, whereas RCRA prohibited storing wastes for more than a year unless they were unstable, Pentagon regulations put no time limits on storage. Nor were the DESB's protocols sufficiently protective of all dangers posed by ordnance. Although renowned experts on explosivity, board members lacked expertise on toxicity, a major shortcoming because leaching of toxic chemicals from munitions is a distinct threat.

Equally contentious were by-now de rigueur debates over application of CERCLA and RCRA cleanup standards (see chapter 4), only this time as they applied to UXO cleanup. By the early 1990s, moreover, the consequences of not resolving these debates were increasingly clear. Incidents involving severe injuries and deaths to military personnel and unwary civilians on transferred properties previously certified as clean became focusing events, garnering the attention of regulators and local communities.[7] Still, the Pentagon never wavered during the remainder of the George H. W. Bush presidency, prompting (unfulfilled) hope among greening proponents that the FFCA might clarify these issues in their favor.

Into the FFCA Bog

During congressional debates over the FFCA between 1990 and 1992, the first Bush administration initially proposed letting EPA consult with the Pentagon and the states to set national treatment, storage, and disposal standards for handling munitions. Long championed by the military, national standards would reduce the possibility that inconsistent state standards could complicate its training operations. The rub, again, was that the military wanted the DESB rather than the EPA to be the lead agency on the standards-setting project. Thus aided by its allies on the Senate Armed Services Committee, the Pentagon got a draft bill designating itself, and hence the DESB, as lead agency.

Ultimately, however, House and Senate conferees bucked the military by assigning lead agency status to the EPA. As Bush originally had proposed, the agency was to consult with the secretary of defense and "appropriate state officials" as it developed a munitions rule resolving RCRA issues. The FFCA also contained "agency forcing" language stipulating that no more than six months after George H. W. Bush signed the act (i.e., by April 1993), the EPA had to propose interim regulations specifying when munitions became hazardous wastes subject to RCRA's treatment, storage, and disposal requirements. The agency then had until April 1994 to issue a final munitions rule.

The Clinton Offensive Begins

But what did it mean to "consult" with the secretary of defense and "appropriate state officials" when developing the munitions rule? Wary state regulators and ENR groups again saw mischief afoot. The term *consult,* they feared, was a familiar code word reestablishing the military's Cold War dominance of federal interagency deliberations. Moreover, when the first interim rule deadline passed without action, environmental activists concluded that their fears were, if anything, understated. If faster progress were not made on the interim rule under the new Clinton administration, the Military Toxics Project (MTP) and the Aberdeen (Maryland) Proving Ground Superfund Citizens Coalition promised that the EPA and military would find themselves in court.

Shortly thereafter, and citing increased responsiveness from both the EPA and military in the wake of its action, the MTP decided temporarily to back off from filing a lawsuit (a decision it would later reverse). By then, the group's comfort levels was partly a function of EPA congressional testimony related to the range rule component of the munitions rule. "Munitions on a firing range," the agency stated, "have been 'abandoned' [and hence are subject to RCRA standards]."[8] Greening proponents also were buoyed by the EPA's dismay when Pentagon guidance to the services in 1994 stated that munitions did not become a waste subject to RCRA standards until "after DoD has ruled out [such things as] future use, sales, [and] reprocessing."[9] Still discomfiting to them, however, was the EPA's comfort with the military's sovereign immunity arguments. "If DoD carries out a cleanup under Superfund authority," agency officials testified, "the cleanup must meet applicable or relevant and appropriate RCRA standards [as well, but] *a RCRA permit isn't required.*"[10]

Two weeks later, however, EPA officials denounced the military's mounting inflexibility during munition rule talks. Then, pouring fuel on the fire, the Pentagon announced its *own* interim draft munitions guidance, a document that did not incorporate EPA's positions. Equally galling to agency officials, the Pentagon's guidance came *after* the agency's unequivocal warnings that any military base following such "legally flawed" guidance would risk fines and lawsuits for violating RCRA.[11] Troubling, too, were a series of practical implementation questions. What recourse would regulators have if the military were slow in starting the review process for a specific munition? How would they know when munitions were discarded?

Seemingly backing off a bit on the guidance as the controversy heated, Sherri Wasserman Goodman responded, "We'll wait until EPA's policy has been implemented, then we'll develop a policy consistent" with it.[12] Greening proponents were convinced, however, that Goodman was losing internal battles in the OSD and needed some additional leverage. That came when MTP leaders informed the EPA and the Pentagon that they were preparing to refile their lawsuit, a court action that the group would not agree to drop until July of 1994. At that time, EPA agreed in principle to issue a draft munitions rule by October 31, 1995, and a final rule by October 31, 1996, fully two years behind schedule.

In the interim, and consistent with its counteroffensives in previous chapters, the military hardened (as did regulators) its position on the munitions rule and prodded congressional allies for help. Moreover, it did so up to and after EPA provided a draft munitions rule to it, and other stakeholders, for comment in late May 1995. For example, the team leader for DoD's munitions rule working group, the U.S. Army's Rosemary Queen, played the readiness card with Congress and supportive peak associations as talks with the EPA again bogged down. In a briefing calibrated to arouse members of the American Defense Preparedness Association on Pearl Harbor Day, Queen offered a bleak future if ENR regulators got their way: "Additional regulating of munitions may compromise the effectiveness" of the U.S. military.[13]

Deconstructing the Draft Munitions Rule

When the EPA finally announced its draft munitions rule, the effectiveness of the military's counteroffensive was startling. As one MTP member bridled, clearly the "pen was in DoD's hand." Another, however, saw a method to the agency's madness: "They're trying to see how ballistic we'll go[, so] . . . we'll go as berserk as possible." Nor were critics' concerns assuaged when EPA officials conceded that the draft regulation does "[favor] the military's position . . . because there are many areas of agreement between EPA and DoD."[14] Specifically, on the key issue of when munitions become wastes subject to RCRA regulations, the draft rule largely took the military's position: Munitions were not waste prior to actual disposal.[15]

Excluded from RCRA regulation, "as products used for intended purposes" rather than wastes, were open burning/open detonation activities. Similarly excluded until disposal was use of munitions in the "training of troops and explosives experts, including training in proper destruction of excess propellant; use in research and development, evaluation, and testing of munitions; and recovery, collection, and on-range destruction of unexploded ordnance and contaminants during range clearance at active or closing ranges." The EPA's draft munitions rule also endorsed the military's position that RCRA regulations were redundant, arguing that the "services' safety record in storing munitions has been good."[16] And riling ENR activists and state regulators even more, the EPA agreed to defer to DoD if the military could write a range rule acceptable to it for munitions cleanup on closed, transferred, and transferring bases. Greening proponents insisted that such a rule would have to incorporate a risk-ranking model integrating both explosive and toxicity risks. But reversing the EPA's original position that munitions on these bases fell within RCRA's regulatory rubric, this version of the larger munitions rule would have allowed DoD's range rule, once issued, to preempt RCRA standards.[17] If deemed not acceptable, an EPA version of the range rule would go into effect in the interim.

Officials at the EPA were quick to point out that the services did not get everything they wanted in the draft munitions rule. For one thing, the DoD's authority on the range rule was contingent on the EPA approving whatever range rule the military developed. Moreover, the EPA's draft noted that UXO "clearly fits within the CERCLA definition of 'hazardous substance,' independent of whether it is considered a solid waste."[18] Thus, contrary to the military's arguments, CERCLA's strictures applied to UXO on Superfund sites, a ruling that negated self-regulation by the services.

Proving the EPA's arguments correct that the military had not gotten everything its way, the DoD's counteroffensive picked up steam rather than attenuated. One month after the EPA submitted its proposed munitions rule to the OMB for review, the Pentagon submitted its own version to OMB for review. Nor did the services limit their counteroffensive to external regulators and critics. In mid-1995, they lodged a formal complaint that Goodman's principal negotiator, Gary Vest, had given away too much and not gotten enough in return.[19]

Characterized by one independent cleanup expert as a "blatant attempt [by the military] to circumvent regulation," DoD's draft munitions rule provoked furious EPA officials to turn to the White House for help (especially to Vice President Gore).[20] But ENR activists were equally furious with the EPA's draft rule. Noting how "particularly disappointing" it was for a Democratic administration to issue such a document, many went on the offensive.[21] If the Pentagon's final munitions rule supported the DoD's positions, court suits would quickly follow. But as one ENR expert put the Herculean task facing these groups and state regulators, the "magnitude of DoD's counteroffensive on the munitions rule emphasizes a historically disheartening fact: It [the military] can easily outgun EPA—throwing significantly more resources at the issue whenever it wants."[22]

Indeed. Once the EPA released its proposed final munitions rule in late 1995, after weeks of feverish meetings among DoD, EPA, and White House officials, the final version differed little from the draft rule.[23] In addition, and indicative of the level of distrust (other interviewees said "paranoia") among the parties, some state regulators even feared that the services had enough leeway in the rule to engage in "sham" training exercises in order to avoid cleaning up munitions.[24] Granted, EPA did ask stakeholders to comment further on whether it should prohibit the states from issuing munitions regulations that were broader or more stringent than those set by EPA.[25] But it did so noting that Congress had expressed a clear preference in the FFCA for a uniform munitions standard, thus buttressing the military's position. The EPA also urged the states not to adopt parts of any final munitions rule that might be forthcoming but to adopt the rule in its entirety to ensure comparable standards.

With even some EPA staff charging that "DoD officials strong-armed the agency" and that the EPA had "caved to DoD," a crisis of authority ensued over the next sixteen months, with heated charges and countercharges, threats of lawsuits, and political skullduggery.[26] ENR activists chastised the EPA for "caving in" to the Pentagon on the range rule and promised to "rais[e] a lot of [legal] hell on a local and national level" to stymie what they saw as "EPA giv[ing] up jurisdiction [to write the rule] to DoD." Opined one irate member of the Military Production Network, "It's the fox guarding the henhouse."[27] Added representatives of the MTP, "Congress did *not* intend for DoD to write *any* portion of this rule."[28] Relatedly, Lenny Siegel of the Center for Public Environmental Oversight averred that the EPA was "challenging the concept of parity [among the parties] every time it suggests that the Defense Department be allowed to write its own rule." He added that any attempt to foil transparency would inevitably produce "a situation where severe restrictions [on military operations would become] the only option" for state regulators.[29]

Meanwhile, disgruntled state officials focused their opprobrium on the dangers of the EPA's proposed preemption of state regulatory authority. Yet most saw the EPA as less a villain than an outgunned agency crying out for political help. As one state ENR regulator trying to mobilize his colleagues put it, "Nobody [in the EPA] favored the preemption option [letting the military write the range rule]. . . . [Carol] Browner is going to need some political cover [to fight this] . . . and that has got to come from the states."[30] And come it did. In addition to pressure mounted by governors such as Evan Bayh (D-IN), John Kitzhaber (D-OR), and Mike Leavitt (R-UT), groups such as ASTSWMO persistently challenged efforts to preempt state authority. Indeed, as talks dragged on in mid-1996, ASTSWMO president Mary Jean Yon expressed members' continuing frustration: "State managers believe strongly that while DoD clearly has expertise in the safe use of military munitions, [only] *states* have the expertise and authority to regulate solid and hazardous waste."[31]

Unfazed, the military services dug their heels in further, launching a concerted, expanded, and multifaceted public relations, legislative, and administrative campaign to support their positions on the munitions rule. During the first four months of 1996, for example, even a territorially minded Goodman, fearful of losing oversight responsibility to EPA, urged her environmental staff to "seize every opportunity" to show the stringency of the military's explosivity standards for munitions handling.[32] Likewise, as state opposition to national standards mounted, she argued that "only a change in the law [allowing them would] ensure that military safety and training will not be jeopardized."[33]

The services also hedged their bets in case the EPA wavered on the range rule or on national standards. Again trying to marginalize ENR committees in

Congress and take enforcement leverage away from state regulators, the military tried to use the FY 1997 defense authorization bill to advance the services' agenda. Upon the military's urging the Pentagon proposed a strategic package of amendments to (among other things) bar states and localities from enforcing munitions regulations if they were more stringent than the munitions rule. Simultaneously, the Pentagon pressed the DOJ for an opinion declaring any state preemption provision illegal. Ultimately, the services abandoned their legislative proposal on preempting more stringent state standards. They feared it was making negotiations on the munitions rule more difficult. Clear, too, eventually was that Pentagon pressure on DOJ for a favorable decision was equally self-defeating, and this appeal also was dropped.

With these crises of authority continuing unabated, another chasm opened on the UXO front, this time with the Army Corps of Engineers. Specifically, although the corps argued that UXO did not fall within the regulatory rubric of CERCLA, officials used the statute to justify doing accelerated (i.e., less rigorous) cleanup actions that they contended were "Superfund-like." Moreover, they wrapped these claims rhetorically in the mantra heard from Capitol Hill and the White House for "faster and cheaper" cleanups generally. CERCLA and RCRA, the corps argued, were too costly and time consuming; CERCLA "lite" and RCRA "lite" would accomplish quicker cleanups more cost effectively.

Incensed, EPA officials as late as 1999 scolded the Corps of Engineers for this rhetorical sleight of hand. They argued, as well, that even if accelerated response were considered analogous enough to satisfy CERCLA's goal of permanent remedies, "using time-critical/emergency responses as the sole response paradigm" was becoming an inappropriate "default approach for the Services."[34] These, after all, rested on the still unreliable institutional controls discussed in chapter 5. Nor were the EPA's qualms limited to the corps's actions or held only by these officials. They were joined by state regulators, ENR activists near closing bases, and other federal regulators. The BLM, the FWS, and the National Park Service, for example, worried that the DoD would "shift" UXO-contaminated properties to them and "shaft" them with cleanup costs and liabilities. As Doug Bell of the EPA's Federal Facilities Restoration and Reuse Office characterized these fears, "There is potential for serious deficiencies with accelerated response," including "constructing a fence around a UXO-contaminated area—to reduce risk but never com[ing] back and actually remov[ing] the UXO."[35]

Sticking to Their Guns?

This Sturm und Drang notwithstanding, the EPA's final munitions rule was issued in February of 1997 (three years late) with little change from its proposed rule, thus indicating the largely overwhelming success of the military's counteroffensive. Indeed, DoD compliance officials said that the military was quite "pleased with the rule because it incorporates almost everything the Defense

Department sought."[36] This, again, is *not* to suggest a total victory for the DoD. For example, the rule also specified four conditions under which munitions were waste.[37] What is more, greening advocates took some solace in the cleanup responsibilities the EPA assigned to the military when munitions landed outside ranges, insisting that these errant munitions be immediately treated as waste.

Still, by delaying the effective date of the munitions rule until August 12, 1997, the EPA also gave the military additional time to work out differences in range rule language before the agency's federal rules trumped DoD standards. Moreover, the immediate outcries and threats from state regulators and citizen activists showed the significance of the concessions made to the military. As one state regulator noted with exasperation, "The substance of the rule is they [the states] can't regulate because nothing is ever hazardous waste."[38] Bequeathed again in the EPA's concessions were structural, process, and procedural consolidations related to determining when munitions were a waste. These left halting, halfway, and patchworked structures, processes, and procedures on the ground that would sorely complicate the greening process.

How Safe Is Safe Enough?

As noted in the previous section, and as originally envisioned, a range rule dealing with UXO cleanup on closed, transferred, and transferring bases had to be developed and included as a component of the munitions rule. But as negotiators groped their way toward a final munitions rule in the mid-1990s, controversial drafts of the munitions rule allowed the DoD—with the Army Corps of Engineers taking the lead—to develop a final range rule that the EPA had to approve. Otherwise, a range rule developed by the EPA would go into effect, something that the military wanted to avoid at all costs.

One major and controversial aspect of any range rule developed was how best to assess risk on UXO-contaminated ranges. As counteroffensives by the military mounted over the contents of the risk model informing that decision, ENR regulators and activists tried to get concessions from the Pentagon by leveraging the military's desire to avoid an EPA interim range rule. Recall from chapter 5 that the Army Corps of Engineers's original risk-ranking model for prioritizing *all* cleanups—the Defense Priority Model—had been castigated as inadequate and subsequently revised. Offered in its place by the Pentagon was the Relative Risk Site Evaluation Framework, a broader-based model that also drew brickbats from proponents of greening before and after implementation problems arose with it. Much the same would happen with UXO risk models.

In this instance the Corps of Engineers developed the relative risk ranking (R^3) model for priority setting on UXO-contaminated properties. The rub, however, was that no models existed in the early 1990s that combined risks from explosions (the DESB's forte) and risks from toxics leaching (the regulators' forte) from munitions. Some state and federal regulators, in fact, thought integrating the two was "nearly impossible."[39] Moreover, they feared that the DoD would make a feint in this direction but ultimately weigh explosive risks more heavily than environmental risks in any model the corps offered.

Thus, when the DoD offered its interim R^3 model dealing mostly with the risks of explosion calculated by DESB, the battle was joined. Crafted as a compromise by the Army Corps of Engineers, the proposed rule did stipulate that chemical risks would be handled under the EPA's existing chemical risk models.[40] Still, consistent with the military's approach to its earlier ill-fated defense priority model, the R^3 model was based solely on quantitative risk assessments. Like its reaction to that earlier model, the EPA argued that too many variables in the model were unknown, unmeasurable, and impractical to operationalize. Thus, instead of the corps's preferred risk *assessment* approach, the EPA again mounted an offensive to get the military to develop a more comprehensive risk *management* approach that analyzed, selected, implemented, and evaluated actions crafted to reduce risk. Almost instantly state regulators joined the dispute, adding fuel to the fire. As one state regulator put it, "We have to validate the model [i.e., see if the model accurately predicts known levels of UXO hazards]. That's where the rubber meets the road."[41]

Or would they? As it turns out, yes, after labyrinthine counteroffensives on the military's part. As debate over the munitions rule continued to unfold in the mid-1990s, for instance, military officials persuaded the Pentagon to try to undermine the EPA's position on the risk-ranking component of the range rule. DoD did so by unsuccessfully appealing to OMB to expedite its review and find the R^3 model adequate. OMB officials told the Pentagon that they would expedite review of the military's range rule only if it came to OMB with the EPA's backing. Thwarted and running out of time before the munitions rule was issued placing an interim EPA version of the range rule in effect, the military asked the EPA to accept DoD's interim range rule on closed bases. Failing this, the Pentagon unsuccessfully importuned the EPA to delay issuing the munitions rule.[42]

Under the gun, the Army Corps of Engineers next said it would take regulators' concerns into account in revising the R^3 model for final approval. But citing Congress's deadlines for issuing the munitions rule, military officials argued that they could not meet those deadlines if forced to actually test (i.e., validate) the model before approval. Nonsense, cried wary state regulators and environmental activists; the services were up to their old Cold War secrecy tricks. Moreover, by December of 1997, a "hopping mad" swath of state regulators were convinced of chicanery, as deadlines for state testing of the model's validity passed without the Pentagon giving them anything to test.

When the corps finally did issue its revised interim R^3 model, it offered a three-tiered approach to assessing explosive risks from UXO, one combining models developed by three separate units within the Pentagon: the Army Corps of Engineer, the Army Environmental Center, and the Naval Explosive Ordnance

Disposal Technology Division. This R^3 model not only reflected a consolidation of the perspectives of these three institutional actors as they pressed their programmatic interests but also tried to finesse several unresolved issues raised in the postmunitions rule imbroglio (discussed in the previous section).

Offered as a partial palliative to the EPA's initial concerns regarding quantification of risks, for example, tier 1 involved a qualitative risk evaluation of the type, density, and human exposure (given anticipated future land use) of UXO on a range.[43] Left unarticulated, however, was any discussion of the central question: How would the corps rate and weight explosive-versus-toxic risks? Analogized one critic, the corps "was [still] asking states to buy the car [i.e., the range rule] without seeing the engine [the risk-ranking method]."[44] Sensing a lemon, many state regulators and ENR activists also inveighed against the model's methods and assumptions. For example, although the model assessed the probability of three factors (the probability of encounter, the probability of detonation, and the likely consequences of detonation), regulators said these estimates simply could not be independently validated. Moreover, although the 1×10^{-6} risk level used in the model passed technocratic muster, no level of death or maiming was politically "insignificant." The UXO risk, as one EPA official put it, is not analogous to chemical risk assessment (as the corps's model implicitly assumed) because there is no target range of acceptable risk.[45] Still others in EPA regional and state regulatory offices worried that they would be liable if accidents occurred after their agencies approved the model.

Further exacerbating this crisis of authority was the corps's insistence on using two controversial data collection methods to inform its risk model. The first, known as "mag and flag," used low-technology metal magnetometers to identify and mark likely areas of UXO contamination. Critics seriously doubted the technological reliability of this approach, roundly excoriating the corps for not using more sophisticated and readily available methods. Just as controversial was the military's insistence on using two statistical grid sampling approaches it had developed on potential or actual UXO sites. The technicalities of each sampling method aside, however, the real issue was whether sampling of UXO sites was prudent given the severity and finality of the harms involved.[46]

In the military's eyes, however, "100-percent surveys" of sites for UXO were outlandish technically and budgetarily. Indeed, as conflicts over the Corps of Engineers's sampling methods spiraled during the last two years of the Clinton administration among EPA, state regulators, and grassroots ENR groups at several ranges (e.g., Fort Ord in California, Lowry Bombing Range in Colorado, and Naval Station Adak in Alaska), a widely cited paper by Robert Lubbert and Julian Chu of the corps criticized these surveys harshly. They saw a distressing "trend developing" toward unrealistic cleanup requirements imposed "from political [appointees and members of Congress] and higher headquarters."[47]

Nor did it help this crisis of authority over greening military cleanups when focusing events heightened the urgency of UXO issues.[48] Prompted by an incident where a civilian worker died handling scrap metal containing live ordnance, a letter from the EPA's Tim Fields to Goodman argued that events now made it clear that these issues had to be resolved before the issuance of a range rule. Added another EPA source, each of the agency's regions and offices dealing with the range rule saw UXO contamination as "simply a game of Russian roulette," and they urged quick action to "try to prevent a number of serious catastrophes that are looming." Fields also heaped opprobrium on the military's approach to site characterization at ranges, on the services' failure to apply the DoD's own DESB explosive safety standards on ranges, and on the services' continuing propensity to transfer UXO-contaminated properties to private actors. As one EPA operative summarized the dilemma matter-of-factly, "The problem here is that the military is not investigating military ranges."[49]

Shifting Tactics

The first telltale signs of the services shifting their counteroffensive tactics to gain more stability, predictability, and security of their core military operations on range rule issues occurred at individual bases rather than in service-wide guidance documents. At Lowry Bombing Range in Colorado Springs, for instance, the state of Colorado sued the corps to complete "parcel-by-parcel" visual surveys and UXO removal. This happened after live ordnance was found on transferred lands the corps had declared "clean" after statistical sampling. The corps finally agreed in 1999 to abandon grid sampling and mag and flag techniques at Lowry, switching to synthetic aperture radar to survey the entire range from an airplane.[50] Then, after "months of unfocused discussions with regulators" and "confused" talks among the parties, DoD officials announced that the corps would shift in the "short term" to emphasizing risk management over risk assessment.[51] Moreover, the army said that it would put "on hold" its use of an equation characterizing risk on the basis of probability of harm.[52]

Needless to say, references to concessions in the "short term" and to putting probability assessments "on hold" raised the antennae of state and federal regulators. Were these merely tactical retreats to be jettisoned once the EPA approved the range rule or until a possibly more sympathetic presidential administration arrived in Washington? Some insiders feared that the R^3 model might "appear again in several years after the range rule is promulgated."[53] Likewise unsettling to critics were comments by military officials that they still needed to have a quantitative approach to UXO risk analysis. "Otherwise," a DoD official claimed, "we'll be constantly going back to do more clearance."[54]

Nor were matters helped in 1999 when state regulators tried to validate the Corps of Engineers's by-then proposed interim range rule risk methodology. When Colorado regulators plugged actual data from some of their state's most seriously UXO-contaminated sites into the model, they were unable to get a ranking of "very high risk." Indeed, an army contractor at the time claimed that

99 percent of all sites using the risk tool fell into the medium category.[55] All this, however, was but the prelude to an even bigger storm. When the corps released in 1999 a "read-ahead" version of its final risk model, the model still included in its explosive risk safety tool the probabilistic parameters it had vowed to abandon, similarly weighted, and still added together.[56]

Not surprisingly, federal and state regulators, citizen groups, and Native American tribes were irate, declaring as before that the model was simply "too complicated" to be workable.[57] But their consternation was grounded more in a profound sense that the corps was stalling to see what the 2000 elections might bring. Thus, knowing how badly the services did not want to operate under the EPA's version of a range rule in the absence of an approved DoD-developed rule, EPA again threatened a veto of the DoD's range rule unless an acceptable risk management model was included. Acceptance, in turn, depended on the corps offering a risk model that was "final and functional" (i.e., tested).

With legislative stalemate rampant, federal and state regulator approval unlikely, and the results of the 2000 Bush-Gore presidential election in judicial limbo in late 2000, DoD retracted its risk model, as well as its proposed range rule, from further consideration. In the process, the corps announced that its proposed risk model was "pretty close to dead."[58] Made clear, too, however, was that gaining some version of a quantitative risk-ranking model remained the military's ultimate goal. The military's general culture propounding its own technical superiority, and the army's culture of "getting a single answer (often a number) rather than illuminating the alternatives in the face of recognized uncertainties," remained hard nuts to crack.[59]

The State Consultation Challenge

Difficult enough in their own right, the two preceding challenges relating to the greening of the munitions and range rules were played out amid a third, hotly contested issue: Who had final dispute resolution authority when disagreements arose over munitions cleanup on contaminated properties? Prior to 1996, the Pentagon successfully insisted on language requiring the military only to coordinate with state regulators. By late 1996, however, the scope of the EPA's conflict with the military over this wording expanded, with states certain the services were bent on language vagueness to marginalize state regulatory authority. State hackles were raised only further when the U.S. Army proclaimed that state regulators only had the right to disagree with the military's decisions on closed, transferred, and transferring bases.

All this, of course, was totally anathema to federal and state regulators, as well as to ENR activists. All were acutely aware of the formidable remnants of the military's heroic Cold War culture of sovereignty, secrecy, and sinecure. Still, trying to take this issue off the table as the deadline for the EPA's munitions rule neared without EPA and OMB approval of its range rule, the Pentagon agreed to substitute the word *concurrence* for "coordination." Although the military hailed this change as "expanding the role of states, federal land managers and [Native American] tribes," the states were unimpressed by this EPA-suggested change.[60] Nonetheless, state regulators bowed to the military while vowing to pursue the matter more contentiously during the rule's implementation.

Their thinking was that the concurrence language at least institutionalized a role (though still clouded) for the states, a role less ambiguous and with more authority than the term *coordination*. ENR activists, however, saw a decidedly more nefarious deal taking place: The states were settling for less restrictive munitions standards favored by the military services in return for enhancing their authority under concurrence. Yet as noted, once the DoD circulated its first draft range rule in 1997, the states (although declaring that the military services had made a "valiant effort" to address their concerns) had a host of issues with the substance, timing, and processes spelled out in the draft rule.[61] Moreover, many of these centered on the concurrence process.

Four issues in particular critically informed this crisis of authority over state roles. First, how much time would states have to concur when the services declared that permanent remedies were impractical? Second, when could states participate in developing future range management guidelines? Third, who would fund oversight of UXO cleanups? Finally, how could disputes on these issues be resolved? Taking these issues in order, the 1997 draft range rule afforded states forty-five days to review the military's decision on cleanup feasibility, with DoD allowed to *assume* agreement if a response was not forthcoming within that time period. As ASTSWMO lamented at the time, "We can't live with that [because states often] have such a limited staff" that they cannot adequately do the work within that time frame.[62]

Likewise, although states wanted to "be involved [in guidance development] right from the beginning . . . [rather than] at the tail end of the process," the draft rule only afforded the right to comment on any final guidance the DoD issued. At the same time, although the preamble of the draft stated that "it would be good [as the states wanted] to include" funding for UXO cleanup oversight in Defense-State memoranda of agreement, no express commitment to it existed in the rule itself.[63] As such, the military might be angling for an implicit concession by the EPA that UXO not be subject to state hazardous waste laws.[64] Finally, although the preamble referenced two of the states' preferred options for dispute resolution (either governors or the courts having final say when disagreements arose), the DoD did not mention them in the rule itself.

As debates over these issues raged on, both the military and EPA concluded (again incorrectly, as the previous section chronicled) that validation of the R^3 model, along with EPA and OMB approval of the range rule, was likely to take until late summer. Thus, to cover what officials inaccurately thought would be a brief interim period before the range rule was approved, the DoD and EPA finalized a set of management principles to serve as guidance for UXO clean-ups. Goodman called the six general principles (and eleven more specific UXO cleanup principles) a "significant accomplishment." Likewise, EPA's Tim Fields optimistically claimed that "we are well on our way to addressing the fundamental issues surrounding UXO."[65]

Or were they? Both the EPA and DoD negotiators tried, in effect, to avoid the dispute resolution issue by agreeing to "give substantial deference to the expertise of the other party."[66] In practice this meant giving greater weight to the DoD's opinions on explosives issues and more weight to the EPA's on health issues. But many state regulators and environmental activists framed this "balance of authority" rhetoric as the EPA abdicating its responsibilities under various ENR statutes. Specifically, they saw only ambiguous responsibility and authority structures, continued self-regulation of explosives issues by the military services, and the probability that a more powerful DoD would trump the EPA whenever disputes arose on toxicity issues. State regulators were equally chagrined by preamble language questioning the legality of governors having final dispute resolution authority."[67]

Moreover, as noted earlier, when the military announced its revised proposed final range rule in April 2000, the EPA, state regulators, and environmental activists went ballistic.[68] In specific regard to state consultation and citizen participation issues, this draft allowed the military to respond to imminent threats with temporary remedies without consulting with state regulators and stakeholders. Nor was CERCLA-equivalence realized by the revised rule's continued failure to afford adequate and meaningful levels of public participation. Indeed, the EPA argued that public participation would be virtually eliminated from the process. Moreover, even if it were not, transparency was not served by allowing the military alone to decide what qualified as "verified," "validated," or "readily available" information. The EPA and state regulators also belittled the DoD's failure to mention how a "particular response action would be selected over another," an issue directly related to who had the final say when disputes arose.

Although the EPA went officially on record as "concerned" about the tactics and language used in this version of the range rule ("This is not what [we] agreed to"), state regulators and citizen activists were absolutely "livid" and felt "betrayed."[69] Seeing the proposed final rule as yet another instance of the military's thumbing their noses at them, NAAG asked OMB to reject it on by-now familiar grounds. Specifically, they argued that the DoD lacked the authority to issue a range rule. Moreover, lest OMB see the situation otherwise, NAAG promised "significant federal-state conflicts if the rule were to go forward." Similarly, the Environmental Council of the States condemned the proposed range rule as "inconsistent with congressional intent to provide for a state role in UXO cleanup."[70]

Nor could the military's next action been better crafted to irritate ENR regulators and activists. With just two months left in the Clinton presidency and as

OMB continued reviewing the proposed final rule, the military's allies in Congress again tried for regulatory relief. As a result, the Senate version of the FY 2002 defense authorization bill included a provision that conspicuously omitted UXO as a hazardous waste under CERCLA. This not only outraged federal and state regulators as yet another surreptitious attempt to circumvent more hostile ENR committees but also ratified the military's longstanding claim for UXO exemption from CERCLA (in the face of the EPA's continuing opposition). "It's no strange coincidence," said one EPA official, that this provision surfaces "at a time when this issue is at the heart of the controversial range rule."[71]

This is not to say that regulators thought the range rule had not improved over the years. Officials such as James Woolford, director of the Federal Facilities Restoration and Reuse Office, said it had.[72] It *is* to say, however, that one of the most frustrating aspects of the 2000 draft final range rule to state regulators and ENR activists was the military's continuing claim that the Pentagon rather than regulators had final authority in a variety of UXO cleanup situations. Those with long memories wondered what had changed from the Cold War era. Those with shorter memories knew that none of this boded well for institutionalizing a beyond-compliance ENR ethic in the U.S. military in the years ahead.

Discussion

Nineteenth-century military pioneer Henry Halleck wrote after the Civil War about the difficulties associated with professionalizing the services: "There is an immobility here that exceeds all that any man can conceive of. . . . It requires the lever of Archimedes to move this inert mass."[73] As in the preceding chapters, the "inert mass" of the military establishment was forced to budge a bit when it came to the civil–military dynamics of munitions rule making during the Clinton years. Yet the critical Archimedean lever of power necessary for institutionalizing this key aspect of building a corporate sense of responsibility for greening the military was still elusive as George W. Bush was sworn into office as the forty-third president of the United States.

Was There a Trajectory of Contestation?

As in the preceding chapters, discernible was a now-familiar trajectory of contestation that began with perceptions of historical–structural mismatches, followed by offensives and counteroffensives, crises of authority, and subsequent misaligned consolidations of structures, processes, and procedures. Also as in prior chapters, these altered the status quo but compromised large-scale organizational change, produced uneven progress, and institutionalized a role for the combatants in resolving the future conflict that these halfway, halting, and patchworked structures would inevitably produce. Once more, also, the patterns of politics witnessed throughout this trajectory of contestation were steeped less in the power of ideas and more in the pursuit of the political, organizational, and personal prerogatives perceived by proponents and opponents alike.

What Motivated the Participants' Behavior?

Taking each component of this trajectory in order, first came perceptions of historical–structural mismatches spawned by the shock of the end of the Cold War, which in turn inspired minishocks related to how best to clean up closed, transferred, or transferring military ranges contaminated with UXO. Operant this time as the participants made sense of these changes and their implications for existing military and ENR concerns, greening reformers concluded that existing Cold War decision structures dominated by the military precluded realistic assessments of when munitions were a waste (and hence subject to RCRA). They also jeopardized accurate appraisals of public health risks (not just explosive danger), and marginalized key and litigious stakeholders whose values had to be accommodated in such decisions.

Also as in prior chapters, however, disagreement reigned over what specific reforms were needed as greening proponents sought to impose and diffuse their initiatives within the Pentagon and the military services. For example, the reforms proposed again were framed, and reframed over time, to respond to "issues" similarly crafted to advance the interests of the disputants. Moreover, one sees how this filtering (i.e., selective attention to and marshaling of "facts") and issue framing were affected by perceptions of history (i.e., by organizational culture, inherited resources, structural arrangements, and constellations of power), context (i.e., by the social, economic, political, and technological situation at the time), and contingency (i.e., by how delays incurred by greening initiatives would affect warfighting missions).

More precisely, for proponents of greening, the munitions rule had to treat munitions as waste as early as possible in the process to bring them under stricter and participation-enhancing RCRA regulations. It also had to be premised on risk management rather than risk assessment criteria and to leave final authority in the hands of regulators when disputes arose. As such, their offensives to impose and diffuse their positions sought to enact an environment more advantageous to their aims. They did so by framing the issues as sovereign impunity if the military got its way on RCRA and on final authority, as well as recklessness, endangerment, and arrogance if the military's risk models prevailed. In response, the counteroffensives of the military and its allies framed the issues as a lack of regulatory common sense, as technical superiority, and as implementation infeasibility.

Likewise, one again sees the importance of history in perceptions of how the munitions rule would threaten existing military dominance over the substance, scope, and pace of UXO cleanups. Put differently, threats existed to the political economy inherited from the Cold War. At the same time, perceived changes in the political, economic, social, or technological context that could alter existing decision structures, processes, and procedures supporting that dominance also affected behaviors. Finally, perceptions of the ability of greening initiatives to enhance the states' power to control the extent, nature, and pace of UXO cleanups affected the military's actions because of the potential mission-threatening delays they might cause (i.e., contingency factors).

Recall, for instance, how the military's counteroffensive again included the services' historical proclivity to make their own, largely quantitative, single-figure analyses the bedrock for decision making when ranking risks. Also illustrative in this regard were its constant efforts to circumscribe state and local regulatory and decision-making involvement in order to make DoD the final arbiter when disputes arose. So too were the military's insistence that the DESB's expertise was sufficient for evaluating both explosive and toxic threats, its refusal to have independent oversight of munitions stored on bases, and the corps' efforts to try to "outgun" the EPA when its prerogatives were threatened. Included, too, were the corps trying to protect statistical sampling as a risk-ranking tool, pushing for RCRA-lite and CERCLA-lite requirements, and pressing for self-certification when announcing its own ill-fated interim draft munitions rule.

As in previous chapters, one also sees classic examples of how portfolio management (i.e., tradeoffs made in light of existing circumstances) were both the product of and produced the patterns of politics witnessed in this chapter. Once again, too, the decision calculi for doing so involved perceptions of issue image and relative constellations of power at any point in time. Chronicled once more, for example, was how the otherwise ENR-oriented Clinton administration reined in the EPA. This occurred when it let the DoD "strong arm" the agency on most of the points of contention in the munitions rule, and most especially when the EPA decided to devolve responsibility for the range rule to the military. Put more conceptually, the White House failed to offset EPA's chronic energy-load deficit with DoD by weighing in with support for the agency. Yet as the crisis of authority progressed, Clinton's OMB backed the EPA's position that it would not approve any range rule submitted unless it contained a proven and acceptable risk-ranking methodology. Likewise, one sees the states engaged in portfolio management by accepting less stringent standards in return for a seat at the table. So too did the military temporize in temporarily marginalizing quantification as deadlines for the range rule got closer, a reduction in zeal witnessed as well when the EPA and DoD cobbled together interim management principles by "giv[ing] substantial deference to the expertise of the other party."

What Specifically Were They Fighting Over?

Wrought once more by this thrust-and-parry politics of contestation were crises of authority wherein the old order was under challenge, but a new order was yet to be born. Consequently, the military's precise regulatory responsibilities, let alone any need to commit to a beyond-compliance ethic, were left in abeyance until authority relationships were resolved. In these authority crises the targets or "fodder" for contestation again included nested battles over constitutional, collective choice, and operational rule sets. In terms of battles over constitutional rule sets, the primary battle occurred over fundamental constitutional and jurisprudential principles of federalism related to who had ultimate (federal or state) authority when disputes arose over the range rule. Also illustrative were contests over whether federal standards could preempt more stringent state standards. Moreover, looming throughout the background of these issues were those related to the unitary executive theory and the Antideficiency Act. This again because the military sought to maintain the supremacy of federal over state decision makers when disputes arose, and never let issues die over the constitutionality of fines from other federal agencies.

Debates over these constitutional rule sets then helped shape and inform subsequent crises of authority over the "nested" collective choice and operational rule sets that followed. These included, for example, battles over such collective choice rules as when UXO munitions became wastes under RCRA and CERCLA, over the most effective and equitable way to rank risks, and over the types of information the services had to provide citizens. Respectively, these were crises of authority involving entry and exit, aggregation, and information rules. Also fodder as a consequence were operational rules involving such military base-level decisions as determining whether DoD guidance documents were legitimate for base commanders to follow and the meaning of consultation at individual sites. More conceptually, these involved disputes over authority rules (in this case, what constitutes authoritative decisions?), scoping rules (in this case, who has responsibility for doing something?), and aggregation rules (in this case, how were opinions to be weighed?).

Nor were these the only instances of battles involving these, and other kinds of, rules. For instance, crises of authority arose repeatedly over information and aggregation rules. These included contests over what information could and could not be shared with states, over the relationship between explosive and toxic risks in models, and over whether CERCLA-lite and RCRA-lite approaches were acceptable. Regnant, too, were other contests targeting scoping and authority rules, plus payoff rules (who bears the costs and benefits?). These included military challenges to rules specifying whether federal standards could preempt more stringent state standards (authority rules), whether the EPA or DoD (specifically, the DESB) had functional responsibility for developing the range rule itself (scoping rules), and over how to prevent accelerated responses that allowed the military to put up fences but never accrue the costs of actual cleanups (payoff rules). Moreover, targeted indirectly throughout the contests waged over the application of CERCLA and RCRA standards were position rules (who can participate?) that would have limited citizen participation in, and the transparency of, cleanup and transfer decisions.

What Strategies and Tactics Did They Use?

Witnessed throughout these crises of authority, too, were examples of various strategies and tactics used by the military that again are reminiscent in attitude and in aim of the Cold War era. Not unlike in prior chapters, these repertoires of contestation included issue (re)framing, ally mobilization, delegitimation, deinstitutionalization, and disinformation strategies. Again, within the general confines of its omnipresent zero-sum issue framing of ENR military readiness–weapons modernization tradeoffs, examples of issue (re)framing strategies included the military portraying additional munition rules as redundant with DESB safety rules. Also illustrative were the arguments by Queen and others that additional rules might compromise military effectiveness, and even Goodman's efforts to portray national standards as jeopardizing training.

Regarding ally mobilization strategies on the military's part, one can point to the army's prodding of allies in Congress and in other federal departments and agencies to promote such things as exempting UXO from CERCLA. Also illustrative was the army pushing for amendments barring stricter state standards, pressing both the DOJ and EPA to shorten the time that any draft range rule would be applicable at military bases, asking to be treated differently from privates on comparability and sufficiency standards, and the DoD petitioning OMB to expedite its review of the range rule. Relevant, too, were the services claiming the redundancy of RCRA regulation (statue shopping). Counteroffensives like these, in turn, were met again by countermobilization strategies by greening proponents. These included efforts by ASTSWMO and NAAG, other federal regulators and agencies worried about a "shift and shaft" response by the DoD (e.g., the BLM and the FWS on institutional controls), and litigation efforts by populist ENR groups such as the MTP and the Military Production Network. And to these were added the EPA's appeals to Vice President Gore.

Likewise, and in addition to the aforementioned claims regarding sovereign immunity arguments, military efforts to delegitimate the authority of its opponents included the Pentagon trying to write its own munitions rule (without including the EPA's positions), the military's threats to move ahead later with its "read-ahead" version of the risk model, and its claims this time to be treated differently from private polluters. Moreover, to these again one can append the army's filing of complaints with Goodman that Vest had not negotiated a good enough deal with the EPA on the munitions rule. Witnessed again, too, was the military's penchant for committee shopping to avoid less sympathetic ENR committees.

Similarly illustrative and provocative, especially in light of severe funding shortfalls relative to the size of the UXO cleanup task, were additional efforts by greening opponents to deinstitutionalize regulatory capacity. They did so, for example, by trying to leverage statutory, administrative, and political deadlines to their advantage. These included withholding information until the last minute from state regulators (e.g., on the risk rule), trying to limit state concurrence timetables in the face of state resource shortages, and deferring action until after the 2000 presidential elections. Moreover, to all this the military added disinformation strategies, including doing risk analyses at UXO sites that understated the actual risks present when tested against known risks.

What Were the Implications?

In the end the administrative, responsibility, and accounting structures wrought by the negotiated settlements to these crises of authority were again left halfway, halting, and patchworked. This in turn once more left the military woefully shy of the accountability, transparency, and resource reengagement necessary for a beyond-compliance ethic to take root in the military. On the one hand, the patterns of politics witnessed amid these civil–military clashes foiled the services' cultural tendencies to rely on their own technical models to set cleanup and land transfer priorities. On the other hand, they did not "lock tight" a diminution of the services' control over the timing, method of remedy selection, and extent of protection afforded the public once lands were transferred. Nor would the signals sent by these crises of authority be sufficient to nurture the kinds of mental models and schema needed to institutionalize an enduring beyond-compliance ethic in the U.S. military, especially one that could weather a diminution of external pressures on the services for greening. Similar dynamics also would plague the greening of the military in other ENR policy arenas. To begin seeing how and why no epiphany on the order of "Mars rushing into Achilles's soul" occurred on the greening front during the Clinton years, I review in chapter 7 the patterns of politics accompanying the greening of the U.S. military in the natural resources management arena.

Notes

1. Maureen Dowd, "The Springs of Fate," *New York Times*, May 16, 2004, p. 13.

2. Defined broadly, military munitions (or military ordnance) include such things as explosives, pyrotechnics, chemical and riot control agents, smokes, incendiaries, and confined gaseous, liquid, and solid propellants. Devices containing these (as well as devices and components thereof) include bulk explosives and chemical warfare agents, chemical munitions, rockets, guided and ballistic missiles, bombs, warheads, mortar rounds, artillery ammunitions, small arms ammunitions, grenades, mines, torpedoes, depth charges, cluster munitions and dispensers, and demolition charges.

3. Closed bases are closed training ranges that remain under the military's control, but are put to a use incompatible with training range activities. Transferred bases are FUDS: They are no longer under the military's control but are the responsibility of community or private owners. Transferring bases include those scheduled for base realignment and closure and are properties in the process of being transferred to nonmilitary owners.

4. Reactivity refers to the potential to explode or detonate in the presence of a strong initiating force or when heated in confinement. Included are such compounds as HMX, perchlorate, RDX, TNT, and their transformation products.

5. The following discussion of differences relies heavily on "Text: EPA Issues Paper on Munitions Rule," *DEA* 2, no. 18 (September 7, 1994): 7–11.

6. Ibid., 7. The only exception involved M55 rockets containing chemical agents. These were considered "obsolete," because they could not be resold or reclaimed and, hence, were inherently waste subject to RCRA.

7. By 2004, nearly sixty people had been injured by UXO explosions on U.S. military bases.

8. "Text: EPA Issues Paper on Munitions Rule," 9.

9. "Superfund Language Could Impose Full Liability on Defense Contractors," *DEA* 2, no. 18 (September 7, 1994): 6.

10. "Text: EPA Issues Paper on Munitions Rule," 9; emphasis added.

11. "DoD to Stick with Munitions Policy EPA Says Could Result in Violations," *DEA* 2, no. 16 (August 10, 1994): 20. For example, base commanders were told that they did *not* have to consult with state and federal regulators before taking action at their facilities. Yet, as one EPA official noted at the time, "states have a [statutory] role in all this that [DoD's interim policy] totally ignores."

12. Ibid., 20.

13. "Army Official Warns Stringent Munitions Regs Could Jeopardize Operations," *DEA* 2, no. 25 (December 14, 1994): 15.

14. "Environmental Attorney Attacks EPA Draft Munitions Rule," *DEA* 3, no. 13 (June 28, 1995): 4.

15. For example, munitions removed from a rifle magazine "for the purposes of destruction or disposal, would become subject to RCRA transportation, storage, treatment, and disposal standards" (ibid., 4).

16. Ibid.

17. Contingent management occurs when the military services are permitted to substitute their rules, standards, and procedures for those of the EPA. See "Uncertainty Over EPA Stance on Closed Ranges Hampers Dialogue," *DEA* 4, no. 24 (November 20, 1996): 11.

18. "Environmental Attorney Attacks EPA Draft Munitions Rule," 4.

19. "Citizens, Environmentalists Outraged Over EPA Proposal, Vow a Fierce Fight," *DEA* 3, no. 23 (November 15, 1995): 4.

20. "DoD Submits Own Version of Munitions Rule to Administration," *DEA* 3, no. 19 (September 20, 1995): 5.

21. "Environmental Attorney Attacks EPA Draft Munitions Rule," 4.

22. "DoD Submits Own Version of Munitions Rule to Administration," 4.

23. For example, in a concession to critics, stockpiled weapons were not considered solid waste prior to disposal unless they deteriorated to a point where they could not be used or recycled, or until DoD or military authorities decided they were solid waste.

24. "States, DoD Air Conflicting Priorities Over Munitions Rule Implementation," *DEA* 5, no. 10 (May 7, 1997): 3–6, 26.

25. This discussion relies heavily on "Upcoming DoD Range Policy Would Supersede RCRA, EPA Says," *DEA* 3, no. 23 (November 15, 1995): 3.

26. "Defense Cleanup Expert: Rule Undermines Government-Citizen Partnerships," *DEA* 4, no. 1 (January 10, 1996): 8.

27. "Citizens, Environmentalists Outraged Over EPA Proposal."

28. "Citizens Group 'Reluctantly' Agrees to Delaying EPA Munitions Rule," *DEA* 4, no. 25 (December 4, 1996): 4; second emphasis added.

29. "Defense Cleanup Expert: Rule Undermines Government-Citizen Partnerships," 8.

30. "State Officials to Raise Concerns Over Proposed Military Munitions Rule," *DEA* 4, no. 2 (January 24, 1996): 7.

31. "State Environmental Officials Protest DoD Policy for Closed Ranges," *DEA* 4, no. 9 (May 1, 1996): 8; emphasis added.

32. "DoD's Goodman Sees Aggressive Public Campaign to Show Sound Safety Record," *DEA* 4, no. 2 (January 24, 1996): 3.

33. "Anything Short of Uniform Standard Will Hamper Mission, DoD Says," *DEA* 4, no. 7 (April 3, 1996): 3.

34. "EPA Warns Defense Department of Urgent Need to Address UXO Issues," *DEA* Special Report (May 6, 1999): 2.

35. "Regulators Remain Concerned About Range Rule Risk Methodology," *DEA* 7, no. 13 (June 29, 1999): 4.

36. "EPA Munitions Rule Draws Mixed Reviews from Stakeholders, DoD," *DEA* 5, no. 4 (February 12, 1997): 5.

37. These conditions included: when munitions identified for disposal leave storage, rather than when they arrive for disposal; when munitions are burned, incinerated, or treated prior to disposal; when munitions are so damaged, deteriorated, or leaking that they cannot be put back into service; and when an authorized military official declares them to be waste.

38. "EPA Munitions Rule Draws Mixed Reviews," 6.

39. "States Critical of DoD's Delay in Releasing Range Rule Risk Assessment Model," *DEA* 5, no. 25 (December 2, 1997): 7–8.

40. In particular, EPA's *Risk Assessment Guidance for Superfund* and its *Ecological Risk Assessment Guidance for Superfund.*

41. "States Plan to Express Views on New Risk Model in Comments on Range Rule," *DEA* 5, no. 26 (December 16, 1997): 5.

42. "Pentagon Scrambles to Gain Nod from EPA on Closed Ranges Policy," *DEA* 4, no. 9 (May 1, 1996): 9.

43. In tier 2, if the qualitative risk evaluation identified "significant" risk, evaluators would do a streamlined risk evaluation to ascertain a specific measure of the risk to humans. As part of the streamlined version, evaluators also would do range samples and site characterization analyses. Then, using a widely accepted EPA risk threshold, the DoD would designate any range having more than a one in a million (1×10^{-6}) chance of a person being killed or severely maimed as posing an "unacceptable" risk to safety. Finally, the third tier involved a highly detailed risk evaluation that would more fully characterize qualitative risks to humans identified in the first two tiers. Ranges with risks ranked below 1×10^{-6} would not need additional cleanup, whereas those with risks ranked between 1×10^{-4} and 1×10^{-6} were likely to need accelerated site-specific remedies to bring them up to acceptable levels.

44. "States May Reject Range Rule Risk Model, Hampering UXO Regulation," *DEA* 6, no. 5 (March 10, 1998): 5. The discussion of state regulator reactions is derived from this article, unless noted otherwise.

45. "Navy, Regulators Unveil UXO Screening Plan for Adak Island," *DEA* 7, no. 24 (November 30, 1999): 7–8.

46. "EPA Warns Defense Department of Urgent Need to Address UXO Issues."

47. "FUDS Cleanups 'Grossly Underfunded,' Army Corps Officials Say," *DEA* 8, no. 8 (April 18, 2000): 7. Taking Lowry Bombing Range as an example, Lubbert and Chu argued that "if every acre of the [range] were sampled, the cost would be $354 million[, but] there still would not be 100 percent certainty that all [UXO] was detected and removed."

48. "EPA Warns Defense Department of Urgent Need to Address UXO Issues"; "Draft DoD Report Aims to Address Loopholes in Range Scrap Policy," *DEA* 7, no. 16 (August 10, 1999): 15. In response, the Defense Logistics Agency issued regulations strengthening safety considerations, but loopholes existed within them.

49. "EPA Warns Defense Department of Urgent Need to Address UXO Issues," 1.

50. "Army Corps, Colorado Reach Agreement in Buckley Field Cleanup," *DEA* 6, no. 9 (May 5, 1998): 18.

51. "DoD Outlines Strategic Plan for Developing Range Rule Risk Methodology," *DEA* 6, no. 19 (September 22, 1998): 6–7.

52. "DoD Moving Away from Quantification in Risk Assessment Model," *DEA* 6, no. 19 (September 22, 1998): 8.

53. Ibid.

54. "DoD Outlines Strategic Plan for Developing Range Rule Risk Methodology," 6.

55. "Regulators Remain Concerned About Range Rule Risk Methodology." EPA officials said that this finding was not accurate, and was probably a function of the use of inaccurate algorithms.

56. "Range Rule Risk Methodology Too Complicated, Regulators Say," *DEA* 7, no. 19 (September 21, 1999): 9; "Citizens Appear to Favor Risk Management for UXO Clearance," *DEA* 7, no. 4 (July 13, 1999): 10.

57. "Range Rule Risk Methodology Too Complicated."

58. "Army Signals Range Rule Risk Methodology Will Likely Be Dumped," *DEA* 8, no. 26 (December 19, 2000): 17.

59. Carl H. Builder, *The Masks of War: American Military Styles in Strategy and Analysis* (Baltimore: Johns Hopkins University Press, 1989), 106.

60. "EPA, Pentagon Send Drafts of Munitions Rule, Range Rule to White House," *DEA* 4, no. 22 (October 23, 1996): 11.

61. "Crucial Issue Still at Stake for States in Range Rule Deliberations," *DEA* 5, no. 7 (March 26, 1997): 3.

62. Ibid.

63. Ibid.

64. "DoD, EPA Sign UXO Management Principles for Former Ranges," *DEA* 8, no. 6 (March 21, 2000): 4.

65. Ibid., 3.

66. Ibid.

67. Ibid.

68. Quotes in this section on EPA's reaction (except where noted) are from "Text: EPA Letter to OMB on Range Rule Issues," *DEA* Special Report (April 11, 2000): 1–4.

69. "Army Sends Range Rule to OMB But EPA Approval Not Certain," *DEA* 8, no. 6 (March 21, 2000): 8–9.

70. "ECOS Urges OMB to Send Range Rule Back to Defense Department," *DEA* 8, no. 18 (August 29, 2000): 22.

71. Ibid.

72. "Draft Final Range Rule is Inconsistent with CERCLA, EPA Says," *DEA* Special Report (April 11, 2000): 1–4.

73. Stephen E. Ambrose, *Halleck: Lincoln's Chief of Staff* (Baton Rouge: Louisiana State University Press, 1990), 87.

CHAPTER SEVEN

Natural Resources Management, Military Training, and the Greening of the Drone Zone

I was talking to God coming up that hill," said a fatigued and adrenalin-driven U.S. Army Ranger participating in the annual Mangoday Warrior Exercise at Fort Knox, Kentucky.[1] Mangoday is named after Genghis Khan's famed cavalrymen, who legend says trained beyond exhaustion and battled without fear. Aptly named, this exercise puts an elite corps of Ranger captains through five food- and sleep-deprived days of extensive marches and mock battles. Evident throughout the exercise are glassy-eyed soldiers in a heat-induced daze that civilians might call "sleepwalking" but that Rangers call the "drone zone."

Why put Rangers through the drone zone? John Turnquist, a U.S. Navy assistant general counsel for installations and environment in the Clinton administration, recites a time-honored military mantra: "We must train the way we fight because we will fight the way we train."[2] As Col. P. K. Keen, commander of the U.S. Army's Seventy-fifth Ranger Regiment, characterizes this training challenge, "The Army needs leaders who have the warrior spirit, first and foremost—who can close on the enemy and destroy him—but who are also smart enough and conceptual enough to maneuver in a battlefield full of civilians, watched by the media, a battlefield where the rules of engagement are highly restrictive but the combat is brutal nonetheless."[3]

Hardly anyone challenges this logic. What greening proponents strenuously contest, however, is when remnants of the military's heroic myth of sovereignty, secrecy, and sinecure surface to claim that ENR laws threaten that end. Most unpalatable to them is when these claims produce counteroffensives challenging the implementation of ENR laws on anything but the military's terms. Instead, greening proponents see the integration of ENR planning as pivotal not only with training but also with total installation management. Only then will the accountability, transparency, and resource reallocation necessary to morph the military's cold warrior ethic into a beyond-compliance culture occur in the post–Cold War era.

These post–Cold War civil–military concerns, of course, were hardly novel. Issues like these have arisen ever since the first V-2 rocket tests in 1946 at White Sands Missile Range in New Mexico.[4] Indeed, neighbors of military bases have experienced it all: the window-shattering noise of low-flying F-16s, F-111 Stealth fighters, and B-52 bombers; the destruction of errant Patriot missiles; and the wafting of pollution into their respiratory systems from open burning/open detonation of munitions. Yet during the Cold War, most neighbors either suffered silently or vacated or leased their properties in the name of national security when asked to do so by the services.

What was different in the post–Cold War era was that the "neighbors" were now closer, more numerous, less deferential, and more prone to use a bevy of ENR laws to help pursue their grievances (real or imagined). These laws included NEPA, the Federal Land Policy and Management Act, the ESA, the National Wildlife Refuge System Administration Act, the Archeological Resources Protection Act, the Migratory Bird Act, the Military Lands Withdrawal Act (MLWA), and the National Forest Management Act. Moreover, as noted in chapter 2, this occurred as high-tech weaponry and maneuvers required more (and more diversified) training, testing, and operating space; as heavier vehicles and longer-range weaponry inflicted more damage on natural resources; and as urban sprawl grew in Gunbelt states.

Not unlike in previous chapters, however, the military and its allies were not without options to deal with this encroachment dilemma. Again, throughout the Clinton years, they persistently mounted counteroffensives to garner as much stability, predictability, and security for their operations as possible from these ENR regulatory offensives. To see how, why, and with what consequences this was the case, this chapter examines the patterns of politics both driving and driven by four integrated natural resource management (INRM) questions. First, how successful could the Clintonites be in expanding the reach of ENR statutes to ensure INRM plans on military bases? Second, and in a by now familiar query, to what extent did the military have to gain formal *consent* from, or merely to *consult* with, federal and state regulators, as well as citizen groups, in creating these plans? Third, how much regulatory relief from the ESA could the armed forces wrest from regulators and the Congress if they pursued INRMs at their bases? Finally, could the military accelerate reauthorization of a major land withdrawal as a precedent for reducing congressional scrutiny?

The Integrated Training Area Management and Legacy Resource Expansion Challenge

The idea of ENR management at U.S. military bases was hardly a new one. Indeed, in his history of the role of the U.S. military in helping to create both Yosemite and Yellowstone National Parks between 1890 and 1916, Harvey Meyerson portrays the blue-coated Old Army as imbued with a culture of "ecological nationalism." Writes Meyerson in *Nature's Army*, the Old Army had "an institutionalized commitment" to both the protection of the public domain from intrusive exploitation by settlers and to the "scientific" exploration, mapping, and classification of the geography, flora, and fauna on the frontier. Some officers even "became amateur geologists, paleontologists, zoologists, botanists, and ornithologists." And why not? Their charge as soldiers included advancing nation building through a "distinctive earthy patriotism."[5]

Putting a halt to this, of course, was the creation of the National Park Service in 1916, and with it came a European-style professionalization of the U.S. military. This said, one must not infer that the services did not engage in natural resource management (NRM) on their bases throughout the Cold War. For example, during the height of President Reagan's military buildup, the services entered into a cooperative agreement with the Nature Conservancy to train base commanders in the importance of NRM. Likewise, Congress created the DoD's Legacy Resource Management Program during the George H. W. Bush administration, charging the military with preserving natural and cultural resources on their lands.

Still, these typically were more reactive than proactive planning efforts, were seen largely as tangential to the military's core warfighting mission rather than key sustainers of it, and mostly eschewed mounting an INRM effort. As envisioned by congressional supporters, for example, Legacy Resource funds were for ENR conservation work that the *military* deemed important but that did not fall under a legally binding interagency agreement or federal facility agreement (and thus were low priorities under the DoD's budgeting systems).[6] Launching the program in 1991, the Bush administration emphasized a biodiversity management initiative to make base-level personnel more aware of the impact of day-to-day operations on the environment.

But with the arrival of the Clinton administration in Washington, Deputy Undersecretary of Defense for Environmental Security Sherri Wasserman Goodman set out to ramp up the program appreciably. This would happen as part of her plan to advance more broadly a corporate sense for the relationship and importance of NRM to military readiness. She began her campaign by requesting $10 million in Legacy Resource funds for FY 1994 and by testifying before the Senate Armed Services Committee that her office would "give highest priority to programs and projects that reduce the chances of losing these irreplaceable resources [threatened and endangered species, habitats, and cultural resources]."[7]

Nor did Goodman stop with the Legacy Resource program. Targeted too was an expansion of the scope, ends, and means of one of the Pentagon's key NRM programs: the Integrated Traininig Area Management (ITAM) program. Begun in 1984 by the army, ITAM since had focused on natural resource conservation at sixty training grounds that were not eligible for DERA funds. Under ITAM, repair work and rotation of training on ranges were pursued, as were such rehabilitative and protective activities as soil erosion controls, environmental training for troops, and data collection and analysis on degradation of lands, species, and critical habitats.

Yet in Goodman's eyes, ITAM's potential was unlimited as a model for showing how environmental considerations could be integrated fully into the planning of military operations more generally.[8] Using ITAM's authorities, she wished to have the services develop INRM plans for managing land, forest, fish and wildlife, and outdoor recreation in ways that comprehensively protected soils, wetlands, plants, animals, habitat, ecosystems, historic buildings, and archeological sites and artifacts.[9] Goodman also hoped that a conservation ethic predicated on sharing NRM data widely among service personnel and the public would be built in the process. Thus, no more direct threat to the military's Cold War ethic of sovereignty, secrecy, and sinecure could have been imagined.

Goodman's 1994 Ecosystem Management Policy Directive was indicative of the behavioral change she contemplated for the military. All installations were to use ecosystem management to "(1) restore and maintain ecological associations that are of local and regional importance and compatible with existing geophysical components (e.g., soil and water); (2) restore and maintain biological diversity; (3) restore and maintain ecological processes, structures, and functions; (4) adapt to changing conditions; (5) manage for viable populations; and (6) maintain ecologically appropriate perspectives of time and space."[10] Each of these aims required levels of integration, cooperation, and coordination between ENR and installation management offices that far exceeded the capacities of existing and fractionated administrative, responsibility, and accounting structures at U.S. military bases. Indeed, throughout the Cold War, these functions were assigned to two separate offices at most bases, sending inaccurate signals that ENR protection was something separate from installation management.

Again, however, political "time and space" quickly intruded on these plans. After the 1994 congressional elections, the general funding assault on ENR programs in the military discussed in earlier chapters did not spare the ITAM program (see below). Nor were Goodman's efforts helped when, in trying to recapture the regulatory reform agenda from conservative Republicans, the Clinton administration pushed "regulatory relief" in its NPR initiative. Getting with the NPR program, the Pentagon proposed giving the military more *flexibility* in meeting NRM planning standards.

Consonant with the performance-based philosophy of reinvention and congressional realpolitik, Goodman's office set about writing less prescriptive and more outcomes-based regulations. The White House argued that these would lead to more cost-effective ENR outcomes, thus averting more draconian cuts by Congress to ENR programs. The political merits of this approach aside, the White House was sending clear signals: Arguments based on cost-benefit analyses could sway the extent to which Goodman's NRM efforts survived review by the OMB. What is more, mixed signals repeatedly were sent to the services even when the Pentagon pursued specific NRM reforms. Although, for example, the DoD began its biodiversity management initiative during the George H. W. Bush administration, it took five years for the Pentagon to issue even a handbook (*Conserving Biodiversity on Military Lands*) to ensure cross-facility and cross-agency consistency of approach. As one interviewee from the Nature Conservancy said at the time, "Within the Department of Defense, there are many people who would like to continue the push for [biodiversity] awareness" (e.g., Tad McCall), but others would not.[11]

Consequently, two devastating counteroffensives marshaled by greening opponents during the Clinton years put ITAM sorely in jeopardy. The first, in 1995, saw the army transferring responsibility for ITAM out of its environmental office and into its Office of the Deputy Chief of Staff for Operations and Plans. The army again used NPR as justification: "The training community should be responsible for the maintenance of their training lands, and . . . this action [allows] management of natural resources to be more fully integrated into Army training activities."[12] Second, as cynics predicted, the relative priority of operations versus "unfenced" NRM funding soon took its toll as the army next zeroed-out funding requests for ITAM in its program objective memorandum for FY 2000 to FY 2005.[13]

Ironically, until then Goodman's selling of the ITAM model for integrating training and ecosystem management had carried the day. While funding the program at half of the $72 million annually estimated to meet NRM needs, the Pentagon nonetheless seemed convinced that worsening land conditions could jeopardize training operations. But with NRM funding still considered a Class III (or lowest) budgeting priority in the Pentagon, with overall DoD budgets expected to remain flat amid operations in Bosnia and Kosovo, and with most environmental program funding coming from the department's operations and maintenance accounts, the army was no longer willing to take additional money from training to pay for ITAM.[14]

Greening proponents, of course, saw ominous signs. Observed one military ENR specialist, at the first sign of a "real budget crunch," ITAM was what the army dropped first.[15] This interviewee argued that postponing "repair work and rotation of training done under the program" would result in "medium to long-term" range deterioration that could jeopardize training. Moreover, in the short term, installation commanders would have to make a "lot of tradeoff decisions" among NRM programs.[16] Added others, "The visibility and clout of a strong central conservation message will be blunted . . . [and] the on-the-ground practical expertise of ITAM practitioners will be lost."[17]

Not surprisingly, Goodman seized upon these arguments, launching a counteroffensive to restore full funding to the program. Responding, Army Chief of Staff Gen. Dennis Reimer cut a deal. He promised to build ITAM back into the army's budget if the Defense Resources Board promised not to issue any directive in this program objective memorandum to restore funding.[18] Shortly, as Reimer promised, a miniprogram objective memorandum in April 1999 proposed restoring funding for ITAM for FY 2001 to FY 2005, with a slight increase from $30 to $32 million annually.[19] In addition, President Clinton's budget request for FY 2000 projected some restoration of ITAM for FY 2003 to FY 2005. Congress then allocated a still disappointing $18.7 million for ITAM in FY 2000.

But ITAM's on-again, off-again funding woes continued. In 1999 the OSD budget office (rather than the army) threatened to cut funding substantially for

ITAM in its FY 2001 budget request.[20] More precisely, its Program Analysis and Evaluation directorate recommended a $24 million cut in the army's budget, one zeroing out ITAM funding for active bases and leaving only $8 million for inactive bases. Greening proponents quickly noted how desperately misaligned the OSD directorate's decision was with two recent range management policies that Deputy Defense Secretary John Hamre was promoting. The directives called for clearing ranges and other ENR stewardship activities at active (and inactive) training facilities in the United States and abroad, activities fundable through ITAM. Not surprisingly, the army's financial management, environment, and training operations offices, as well as the OSD environment and readiness offices, began "forcefully objecting" to the cut.[21]

Yet a full year later both the army and congressional conferees still were trying to compensate for the program's fluctuating budget woes. In the army's next program objective memorandum carrying it through FY 2007, officials argued that the historically "critical" funding requirement of $30 to $32 million annually for ITAM was no longer sufficient. Seeking $41 million annually, the army settled instead for much less ($5.1 million on top of its base) from a decidedly unsympathetic Congress. Moreover, even these funds were accompanied by a sharp rebuke from the Hill: "Realign [existing] resources [if you want] to fully fund the ITAM program."[22]

Even were one trying, a better scheme for creating a halting, halfway, and patchworked system of greening in the NRM policy arena was impossible to conceive. Nor could a system of resource allocation have been better designed to prompt continuing battles among greening proponents and opponents. Of course, with army base commanders "consistently reporting reduced ITAM funding as a training readiness issue in the[ir] Monthly Readiness Report[s]," the canard of a readiness-environment tradeoff was clearly losing ground as the Bush administration took office in 2001.[23] Still, even at this juncture, the Clinton administration had not made any additional corporate effort to eliminate the "stovepiping" of training, environment, and installation management functions while maintaining a "fence" around NRM funding.

Nor was the Legacy Resource program any better situated by the end of the Clinton years. Granted, a major event in 1995 involving the application of Legacy Resource funding promised at least a model for advancing the cause of INRM planning. In February, the Pentagon and the DOI inked a memorandum of agreement establishing a joint ecosystem management effort in the two-fifths of the Mojave Desert under their respective jurisdictions. Known as the California Desert Mojave Ecosystem Initiative, the memorandum of agreement promoted cooperation, planning, and communication among the services and between the two departments to protect the diversity of species and habitats. It also aimed to do this while still maintaining the services' ability to conduct large-scale exercises and major weapons training.[24] In reality, the White House pressured the Pentagon into signing the memorandum of agreement to show good-faith effort with the California Desert Protection Act of 1994. And the price the services extracted from DOI for doing so was to leave final authority with the DoD whenever interdepartmental disagreements occurred during implementation of the initiative.

The Sikes Act Consultation Challenge

Enacted by Congress in 1960, the Sikes Act did not actually require planning, and its legislative opponents inserted enough ambiguity in its provisions to ensure that military readiness trumped resource management. Sikes, for example, instructed the secretary of defense to manage installations with NRM ends in mind but "consistent with essential military requirements to enhance the national security of the United States."[25] Consequently, integrating Sikes NRM planning with installation management was largely off the radar screens of the U.S. military during the Cold War. Thus aided by allies in Congress, Goodman launched myriad offensives throughout the Clinton years to amend the Sikes Act to *require* military bases to develop and implement INRM plans. Goodman and her allies ultimately *were* successful in persuading Congress to pass the Sikes Act Improvement Amendments (SAIA) in 1997. However, the services and their allies immediately launched counteroffensives to ensure the military's control over the substance, pace, and scope of INRM planning throughout the Clinton years.

Round One

Goodman's offensive to amend the Sikes Act to require INRM plans at military bases began in earnest in the 104th Congress.[26] She was joined by environmentalists and state regulators who pressed members of Congress not only to amend Sikes to require plans but also to require that the plans be "mutually agreed to" by both the FWS and state fish and wildlife agencies.[27] Seeing an opportunity to boost the low priority of NRM funding in the Pentagon's three-tiered budget formula, Goodman immediately supported Rep. Jim Saxton's (R-NJ) effort in the House Armed Services Committee to mandate INRM plans at all military installations. Nor did she oppose his plan to add state fish and wildlife agencies to the regulatory mix.

In return, however, Goodman proposed military-preferred language that would help keep the Pentagon in the driver's seat. More precisely, and reminiscent of OSD's munitions rule strategy, Goodman's language substituted "developed in *consultation* with" the states and the FWS for the original Sikes Act's language requiring that plans be *mutually agreed to* with these actors.[28] Knowing full well the practical implications of the military's wording, however, the FWS strongly objected to losing its authority. Among others, the agency was joined by a coalition of professional biologists and military NRM managers (the National

Military Fish and Wildlife Association, or NMFWA), state fish and wildlife agencies (the International Association of Fish and Wildlife Agencies, or IAFWA), the Wildlife Management Institute, and the National Rifle Association (NRA).[29]

In congressional testimony, Junior Kearns, president of the NMFWA, was assuaged somewhat by Goodman's rationale that the OSD's language would prevent unnecessary red tape, but R. Max Peterson, executive vice president of the IAFWA, said that "there's no teeth in consultation."[30] Moreover, although Saxton's proposal expanded the number of actors involved in INRM planning (and hence its transparency), state fish and wildlife agencies were not given the equal standing they had under present law. With the more partisanly split Senate Environment and Public Works Committee (EPWC) opposed to Goodman's amendment, the more conservative House committee ordered the DoD and FWS (significantly, without state participation) to "fight [it] out internally" and return with a joint recommendation.[31]

Under the gun, the DOI and Goodman's office agreed to compromise language. The FWS got its preferred "mutually agreed to" language retained in the bill, whereas the military got a dispute resolution process that would give it ultimate say over the contents of INRM plans. Ignored, however, were the states' concerns about retaining equal legal footing in plan development. Specifically, conferees decided that absent agreement at the installation level, a base commander could elevate the issue to the highest levels of FWS. Only then would state involvement occur. At that point, and if disagreement still existed, the affected state(s) and FWS could elevate the issue to the OSD within thirty days. If either failed to elevate the issue within that time, they "would waive any rights to complain."[32] If the issue was elevated, however, the DoD would be the final arbiter.

Still, congressional confirmation of the pact remained in doubt. Whereas military employees in the NMFWA felt that the compromise language took "most of the sting . . . out of DoD's view" that the services could act unilaterally, the state agency-oriented IAFWA remained opposed. Countered one IAFWA leader, "States 'understand national security issues [too, and w]e aren't trying to insert ourselves' into that process."[33] Yet neither would they "compromise the authority that is already provided to them under the [Sikes] act" as well as under other ENR laws.[34] At loggerheads, the 104th Congress failed to reauthorize the Sikes Act.

Round Two

With frustration mounting by 1997 after a delay in Sikes Act reauthorization, House Resources Committee Chairman Don Young (R-AK) joined members of the FWS in urging the Senate to pass a House version that had dropped the military's dispute resolution language. Reflecting Young's frustration, one puzzled committee staffer volunteered, "I don't understand why DoD is so intent on raising problems."[35] But redolent of Cold War–era sovereign immunity tactical concerns, the services countered that their operations "could conceivably be held hostage by [a] state or FWS through no fault of our own."[36]

Nonetheless, by mid-November a letter from Peter Walsh, Goodman's assistant deputy under secretary of defense for environmental quality, to IAFWA's Peterson stated that the Pentagon now was willing to give equal status to state agencies in INRM plan preparation. Wrote Walsh to Peterson, "I trust that with all interested parties now in agreement, the revised Sikes Act can now move quickly towards passage."[37] Seeing this as yet another instance of Goodman's office assaulting service prerogatives, however, the military again balked. Reinvigorated was the military's strong preference to leave INRM planning as voluntary at military bases and to not specify a dispute resolution process. According to one congressional interviewee, Pentagon officials in the OSD saw the military's concerns as "groundless," but they reopened the discussions anyway.[38]

Commenced in the process was an additional year and a half of tough negotiations before these details were worked out and SAIA finally enacted. For the military, the issue was clear: Although FWS and the states had legitimate authority over fish and wildlife, they should not have final say over "issues relating to or that could impact mission preparedness or readiness."[39] Equally critical to the states and FWS, however, was that the Pentagon not attain final authority in INRM plans to determine adequate habitat for fish and wildlife.

With the crisis of authority joined in this fashion, movement toward consolidation of decision structures, processes, and procedures first began in mid-1997. At that point, greening proponents in the House took a page out of the military's counteroffensive "playbook." Against strong opposition, they attached the Sikes reauthorization bill opposed by the military to the 1998 Defense Authorization Act. With this legislative sleight of hand, President Clinton now could threaten to veto the defense authorization bill unless progress on ending the stalemate was made. Facing this possibility, the Pentagon restarted negotiations with both FWS and state regulators, but without involving the services (most critically, the army).

Formally out of the loop but never absent avenues of influence, the military made it known to (and through) congressional allies on the House National Security Committee and the Senate Armed Forces Committee that they now preferred language specifying that all the actors would "work cooperatively" on INRM plans. But they would not concede final authority in dispute resolution. They also argued that the three-year deadline proposed for completing INRM plans was impractical and would disrupt ongoing conservation plans.

Partially incorporating but not totally reflecting the military's concerns, Goodman's office next proposed Sikes language that tried artfully to finesse the issue. INRM plans would have to be "cooperatively developed" but not mutually agreed to by all parties. Responded one FWS interviewee at the time, this would be okay only if "'cooperatively' means that the integrated plans have been completed with *agreement* from states and FWS."[40] Rebuffed by FWS on its language, the military next proposed wording that effectively disaggregated responsibility structures. Purporting to maintain the "existing [creative] tension" among the services, FWS, and state agencies over NRM at military bases, the new language reverted to saying that the parties would have to "mutually agree." However, they would have to mutually agree solely to those "portions of the plans that relate to generally applicable fish and wildlife laws."[41]

Military interviewees quietly downplayed the new language as "just a [tactical] play on words."[42] In effect, however, the FWS and states still would have to get the *military's* agreement whenever they tried to implement natural resource or environmental statutes that affected military operations. Onto this ploy, but bargaining from a position of institutional weakness, FWS and state agencies insisted that the plans "be prepared in a way that does not repeal or modify any federal natural resource laws, or enlarge or diminish any state authorities."[43]

With time in the congressional session again an issue, and with these linguistic ambiguities still rife and vigorously debated, the House passed a bill in late June that consolidated much of the preferred language of the diverse protagonists. In the process, however, responsibility structures were further fragmented in the military's favor. More precisely, the DoD retained ultimate authority to decide NRM planning issues that related to military readiness, whereas state regulatory authority could not be enlarged or reduced.

At this point, staff from the Senate Armed Services Committee and EPWC met with the FWS and Goodman's office, respectively, as each decided whether to add similar Sikes language to the Senate bill. In its meeting with the Senate EPWC staff, the FWS said that it was satisfied with the House bill. But taking a calculated guess that it could get even more control over the substance of the plans from allies on the Senate Armed Services Committee, the DoD claimed that the language regarding cooperation and coordination might stop them from completing all four hundred INRM plans by 2000 (as envisioned by the bill).

Nonetheless, in July 1997, the Senate passed SAIA as part of the defense authorization bill. The Pentagon was given until November 2001 to develop and implement INRM plans and to review them at least every five years with the FWS and state fish and game regulators "as to operation and effect."[44] However, the Pentagon also acquired the authority to develop a dispute resolution process through its own administrative processes. Thus not only would the military have final say when disputes arose but also the Pentagon would design the appeals process. What is more, although SAIA provided for military bases to share information with the FWS and state regulators on all aspects of their INRM plans (not just those affecting fish and wildlife), mutual agreement on all provisions was a *goal*, not a requirement.

The ESA Relief Challenge

With the SAIA language settling these crises of authority, the military's counter-offensives regarding INRM put them in a good position to control the substance, pace, and progress in this area. But their efforts to attain as much stability, predictability, and security of their training operations as possible did not stop there. Taking ENR regulatory relief up a significant notch, the services now asked Congress to give them regulatory relief from their perennial nemesis: the Endangered Species Act (ESA). Section 7 of the ESA required federal agencies to do what was necessary to protect listed species and their critical habitats. The ESA, however, afforded substantial discretion to the FWS to determine the meaning of such terms as "consultation" with other federal agencies, "jeopardy" of species, and "adverse modification" of critical habitats.

Into the ESA Bog

The military's counteroffensive to the ESA began inauspiciously during the Clinton years in 1994 with a series of bills introduced by one of the act's major opponents: Rep. Richard Pombo (R-CA). These bills proposed creating loopholes for developers and added new hurdles for listing endangered species. These hurdles were premised on the takings clause of the U.S. Constitution, with proponents arguing that ESA regulations constituted taking land without just compensation for landowners. Required too were cost-benefit analyses whenever a species was listed, thus making it more difficult for listings to occur. Supporters of Pombo's unsuccessful bills, including Senate Republicans Jesse Helms and Lauch Faircloth of North Carolina, also sought simultaneously to rekindle battles over the ESA at Fort Bragg in their home state.

Helms offered a rider to a defense supplemental bill to stop "the Federal Government and its bureaucrats from, first, preventing the Department of the Army from carrying out its national security mission and, second, wasting taxpayer dollars in the process."[45] Asked Faircloth, was the nation prepared to put protection of the "red-cockaded woodpeckers . . . before the preparedness of our troops?"[46] Although these senators agreed to pull their amendment once the chairman of the Senate EPWC, John Chafee (R-RI), agreed to hold a hearing on the bill, the army's top environmental official, Lewis D. Walker, argued successfully against the exemption for Fort Bragg.[47] But he made it clear that the ESA did pose training problems for the services at many of their bases.

Frustrated by the unsuccessful efforts of Pombo to gain relief for private actors that also might apply to them, the military and its allies launched more concerted counteroffensives of their own in 1997 and 1998.[48] Sought, for example, in the 1998 ESA reauthorization bill, was language allowing the military to avoid complying with any species recovery plans that conflicted with military actions.[49] Moreover, the military tried again to change the consultation process with FWS whenever adverse impact decisions were involved. Under the ESA, FWS could take as long as needed before responding to any claim by the military that its operations (e.g., training overflights or dropping of chaff) were not having an adverse effect on species or habitats. But with backlogs long and getting longer at the FWS because of the resource cuts noted earlier, the military proposed ESA language giving the agency only sixty days to respond. If the deadline was missed, the military's action automatically was approved. As one environmentalist observed, this change effectively gave the military "the authority to make the first call" (and most likely a trump card) on whether or not to consult with the FWS.[50] How so? With the number of military actions large and with FWS's resources incommensurate with its responsibilities, the agency would be unable to meet the sixty-day deadline.

Nothing would come of either bill, but the trajectory of the military's attitudes toward ESA consultation was clear. Moreover, these attitudes would be abetted by FWS itself in ways not contemplated by greening proponents at the beginning of the post–Cold War era. Animating this development were burgeoning citizen demands for use of public lands during the Clinton years, especially in the Gunbelt states of the Southwest. These demands ran headlong into land-use restrictions triggered by ESA that land managers such as the DoD, the Forest Service, and the FWS could ignore only at the risk of lawsuits. But with these, the already resource-challenged Forest Service and FWS became more entangled in interminable delays, this time in issuing endangered species permits.

Consequently, in late 1997, the Pentagon, DOI (on behalf of the FWS), and the Department of Agriculture (on behalf of the Forest Service) launched the so-called Southwest Initiative.[51] The initiative was heralded by proponents as a proactive step toward averting ESA conflicts that military training could not abide and congressional opprobrium that federal regulators could not long suffer. It provided for early and ongoing collaboration among the parties before conflicts arose over endangered species. Sought was early public participation in military land-use decisions, as well as sharing by federal agencies of up-to-date information on endangered species in affected areas. As one highly supportive military interviewee noted in the early days of the program, "This is a step in the right direction. . . . We've never really worked with domestic [regulatory] agencies" *before* conflicts arose.[52] This observer opined that a priority now could be placed on avoiding conflict before it starts.

Perhaps. But once again the services and their allies were bent on shaping and preparing to their advantage the context within which these decisions were made. In this instance, the Pentagon again took advantage, as it had in DSMOA (see chapter 4), of resource-starved regulators by creating a resource-dependency arrangement that redounded to the military's benefit. Under the Southwest Initiative, each of the parties agreed to *share* their limited resources in order to reduce the backlog of endangered species permitting. But the ability to share was clearly on the Pentagon's side, with regulators depending on the military to share its resources with them in order to reduce growing FWS backlogs. But then, in an instant, a court victory by environmentalists in *Sierra Club v. Glickman* overturned the rules of the game for everyone in the Southwest Initiative, and in NRM in general.[53]

The Military, the ESA, and the INRM Equivalency Test

Interpreting the previously arcane Section 7(a)(1) language of the ESA, the court ruled in *Glickman* that *effort* to comply with the ESA mattered when court suits were filed charging lax implementation of the law. Consequently, federal agencies had to use all their authorities (funding, permitting, and programming) to carry out activities necessary to conserve species. Immediately, the FWS notified the military that both regulators like itself and regulatory targets like the services now had to exhibit sufficient effort or be liable for damages accruing from ESA violations. To which the Pentagon's Senior Readiness Oversight Council retorted in the military's timeworn zero-sum framing of the issue: Environmental laws like the ESA posed serious threats to military training.[54]

An offensive of lawsuits filed by environmental groups against FWS during 1998 and 1999 then went beyond *Glickman's* focus on permitting by asserting that FWS also was dragging its feet in making critical habitat designations.[55] These decisions, of course, also threatened to impose additional encroachment problems for military bases should further habitat studies and negotiations have to follow. For its part, the FWS had long argued that "official" designations of critical habitat were duplicative and, thus, unnecessary. In its view, listing a species as threatened or endangered implicitly prohibited any action by the military, or any federal agency, that might harm the habitat of that species. Consequently, no added protection was afforded a species by the FWS expanding its already overtaxed resources to conduct formal critical habitat designations.

As legal pressures mounted on FWS and the military for more official designations of critical habitat during the 2000 presidential campaign, the FWS's initial response came in the form of a *Draft Policy for Evaluation of Conservation Efforts When Making Listing Decisions.*[56] What the military proposed, however, was authority to use INRM plans as substitutes for critical habitat designations required by the ESA. The services already had begun working for administrative relief along these lines prior to *Glickman.* But in its aftermath, the military's proposal took on added allure to an FWS looking for any way to reduce its workload. In short order, the agency said it would accept INRM plans as the official equivalent of designating land as critical habitat.

As the Natural Resources Defense Council and others in the ENR community argued, merely having an INRM plan did not mean that procedures were actually in place to protect a species or its habitat.[57] Still, a besieged FWS moved ahead administratively with its plan in spite of the controversy it spawned. Operating under a court-imposed deadline of October 2000, for example, the FWS excluded from critical habitat designation tens of thousands of acres of military training lands at the Marine Corps's Air Base Miramar, as well as at Camp Pendleton in California.[58] Nor, in its typical way, did the military give up totally on the legislative front. The services continued their counteroffensive to get language into the ESA stating that any land proposed for critical habitat designation that was *not* currently occupied (or inhabited) by a listed species had to meet a higher standard than occupied lands before it could be so designated.[59]

The Accelerated Land Withdrawal Challenge

The military's ability in the preceding cases to gain enough leverage to afford considerable stability, predictability, and security of its training operations in the face of Goodman's INRM offensives was impressive. But the story, again, does not end here. Expended, too, were additional efforts by the services to catch greening proponents off-guard and to establish lesser scrutiny of their operations by accelerating the reauthorization of the 1986 MLWA. This act provided for the withdrawal of six military training ranges for a period of fifteen years. Comprising nearly half (47 percent) of the military's training lands at the time, the six bases were Arizona's Barry Goldwater Range, Alaska's Fort Greely Maneuver Area, New Mexico's McGregor Range, and Nevada's Nellis Air Force Range, Fallon Naval Air Station, and Bravo-20 Bombing Range. The MLWA also required the military to do an environmental impact statement (EIS) before the original withdrawal could be renewed in 2001. In the process, the services had to demonstrate fidelity to the Engle Act, the Federal Land Policy and Management Act, the Migratory Bird Act, NEPA, and the ESA.[60]

As late as 1994, however, GAO investigators assessing the impact of training on natural resources at the six withdrawn ranges found the services "generally uncooperative." Equally distressing, the military often used a loophole in the Engle Act to avoid its requirement for congressional review of land withdrawals of more than five thousand acres. Technically a state agency, the National Guard was exempt from the Engle Act, because the law applied only to withdrawals undertaken by federal entities. Exploiting this distinction, the military sometimes avoided congressional scrutiny by "laundering" land transfers of more than five thousand acres as "state" rather than "federal" acquisitions whenever Guard units operated on a base. Moreover, they did so no matter how marginal the Guard presence was compared to other services.

Still chaffing at these mild constraints on discretion, however, the military began lobbying Senate allies in 1998 to rewithdraw the 7.2 million acres included in the MLWA three years early. Moreover, they importuned these allies to take the bold step of withdrawing these lands *indefinitely* for full-scale training. In addition, one of their allies on this issue, Senator John McCain (D-AZ), proposed language in the accelerated withdrawal that would have drastically cut short

NEPA's transparency and consensus-building processes altogether. This would be done by eliminating the MLWA's mandate to perform EISs before renewal was sought.[61] McCain's proposal also would have let the FWS and DoD alone decide how the withdrawn lands at four of the bases would be managed.

Dogged by mounting criticism from excluded state regulators and environmentalists, McCain later withdrew this offending language from his proposal. In short order, however, the Pentagon circulated an amended version that eliminated some especially controversial properties from the withdrawal. It still included an "indefinite extension" provision, plus a new proposal to take away oversight responsibility from the FWS. Correctly seeing this as yet another effort to regain self-regulation at bases with questionable commitments historically to NRM management, Grace Potorti of the Rural Alliance for Military Accountability quipped that putting the "DoD in charge of land management is like asking a plumber to fly a 747."[62]

Ultimately, Congress refused to transfer total land management authority to the military at five of the six bases. Attesting to McCain's influence on the Senate Armed Services Committee, however, total authority was transferred to the Air Force at the Goldwater Range in Arizona. This transfer of authority to Goldwater was no small victory for the military's battle against transparency, placing as it did over half of the total training area at the six bases in the military's hands. Moreover, it left the Goldwater facility in the hands of the same base management that grassroots ENR activists had been fighting in the courts for years over EIS controversies. Also, gaining extended withdrawals of twenty to twenty-five years at all the bases (as opposed to the original fifteen-year withdrawals), the halfway, halting, and patchworked structures, processes, and procedures that had compromised NRM management at Goldwater were left in place even longer.

Conclusion

As Robert Leonhard writes in *The Art of Maneuver*, well-trained professional military officers understand that the "player with tempo constantly forces the opponent to react defensively to a series of attacks, threats, and feints, all the while advancing his own plan. . . . His tempo serves as a shield against enemy attack."[63] No better characterization exists of the posture taken by the U.S. military during the Clinton years when it came to greening the drone zone. In the end, the status of INRM planning was better than it had been during the Cold War, with the military less able to control the tempo "as a shield against attack." But greening was still precarious in terms of its institutionalization in the administrative, responsibility, and accounting structures of the services. Nor did the patterns of politics witnessed send consistent messages that a beyond-compliance ethic was a priority for the U.S. military. As such, as in the preceding chapters, future progress on the NRM front in the post-Clinton years would be especially dependent on continuing external pressures on the services to move toward a beyond-compliance ethic.

Was There a Trajectory of Contestation?

Reminiscent of preceding chapters, discernible among the patterns of politics exhibited in this chapter was an arc or trajectory of contestation that began with perceptions of historical-structural mismatches, followed by offensives and counteroffensives, crises of authority, and subsequent misaligned consolidations of structures, processes, and procedures. These again compromised the kind of large-scale organizational change envisioned by greening proponents, produced uneven progress, and institutionalized a role for the combatants in resolving the inevitable future conflict that misalignments would spawn. Moreover, throughout this trajectory of contestation in this realm of civil–military relations, the patterns of politics witnessed were steeped less in the power of ideas than in the pursuit of political, organizational, and personal prerogatives.

What Motivated the Participants' Behavior?

Taking each component of this trajectory in order, first came perceptions of historical-structural mismatches spawned by the shock of the end of the Cold War, which in turn inspired minishocks related to how best to integrate NRM planning with installation management. Operant this time were minishocks occasioned by the interaction of such post–Cold War era developments as urban sprawl onto lands near military bases; the military's need for base expansion in order to train a faster, more lethal, and more mobile fighting force; and the mobilization of an aroused and litigious public and regulatory regime wielding laws like the ESA and NEPA to advance their aims. Moreover, this chapter also shows again how disagreements among greening proponents and opponents were intensely fueled by and filtered through perceptions of principle, self-interest, and realpolitik, with perceptions of organizational history, context, and contingency most telling. Revealed once more, too, was how the combatants framed and reframed issues over time in ways calculated to advance these interests. In the process, one sees again how selective attention to and marshaling of "facts" (i.e., "filtering") and issue framing by the combatants were crafted to advance their interests.

In launching and pursuing their offensives, for example, greening proponents framed the issues regarding the Legacy Resource Program and the Sikes Act broadly as nonzero-sum tradeoffs between ENR protection and national security. Likewise, they framed robust implementation of ESA and the MLWA as protection against the erosion of civilian oversight of military operations. Specifically, in regard to Sikes, ITAM, and the Legacy Resource Program, proponents of these greening initiatives insisted that NRM and installation management planning structures, processes, and procedures had to be better integrated to meet new demands in the post–Cold War era. Moreover, this had to be done with a "fence" protecting NRM funds from raids by the services for core military functions. Otherwise, not only would endangered species be harmed, but military training would no longer be able to proceed without legal interruptions. Likewise, in regard to ESA consultation and land withdrawals, greening proponents framed the issue as putting the fox in charge of the chicken coop if land withdrawals were accelerated and management devolved to bases like Goldwater. In response to these initiatives, the counteroffensives of opponents emphasized the threats to training, readiness, and protection of national security that delays occasioned by INRM planning, ESA consultation, and congressional reauthorization might pose.

The chapter also reveals again how the sense making, filtering, strategies, and tactics of the contestants were conditioned by organizational history, context, and contingency. Here, history deals with the military's inherited organizational cultures, political economies, priorities, and resources related to NRM planning. These, after all, had allowed military dominance over the substance, scope, and pace of INRM planning for decades. Context in turn deals with the general political, social, economic, and technology circumstances existing at any given time, and the extent to which these protected or jeopardized the existing decision structures, processes, and procedures supporting that dominance over NRM. Finally, contingency refers to the ability of INRM initiatives to delay or threaten the military's ability to control the substance, scope, or pace of NRM planning.

Recall, for example, how the military's counteroffensive again included the services' historical proclivity to circumscribe state and local regulatory and decision-making involvement to make the DoD the final arbiter when disputes arose. Similarly illustrative are how path-dependent and consciously crafted shortcomings of regulatory capacity placed the FWS in a disadvantageous regulatory position on ESA consultations. Demonstrated as well was how the historical priority of litigation-based priority setting rendered ecosystem management a Class III (later, Class II) priority in DoD budget planning. Consider how elements of the military's heroic myth like secrecy and sovereignty prompted a shifting of ITAM responsibilities from the Army's environmental office to its Office of the Deputy Chief of Staff for Operations and Plans as an NPR initiative, as well as the military's propensity to make NRM planning voluntary.

Equally powerful in conditioning the behavior of the contestants as they pursued offensives and counteroffensives were contextual and contingency factors related to issue images and how these affected relative constellations of power at any point in time. Consider, for instance, how contingency operations in Bosnia and Kosovo resulted in boundary effects that reduced the salience of INRM (and other natural resource) initiatives to the military. This resulted eventually in the Army zeroing-out funding for ITAM in its original program objective memorandum for FY 2000 to FY 2005, only to follow with stop-and-start financing after external political pressures were applied (e.g., by President Clinton). Likewise illustrative of shifts in energy loads is how the FWS's and the military's positions on critical habitat designations evolved in the wake of changing political saliency, proximity, and issue valence after the *Glickman* decision. Respectively, speeding up habitat designations became a priority for FWS (salience), the court's decision meant that the military and FWS had to prove they were doing all they could (proximity), and falling behind on these certifications placed both in a judicially and politically negative light (valence). Compromised in the process by critical habitat designation delays would have been the military's ability to "train the way it fights."

What Specifically Were They Fighting Over?

Wrought once more by this thrust-and-parry politics of contestation were crises of authority that hobbled INRM planning. As in prior chapters, the military's precise INRM responsibilities, let alone any need to commit to a beyond-compliance ethic, were left in abeyance until authority relationships were resolved. Moreover, in these authority crises, the targets or "fodder" for contestation again included nested battles over constitutional, collective choice, and operational rule sets. In terms of battles over constitutional rule sets, the primary battles got caught up in constitutional rights issues, and again over the Antideficiency Act and the unitary executive theory. In order, these consisted of property rights disputes over whether the ESA's implementation constituted violations of the takings clause; over how far the military could go in meeting NRM obligations without additional appropriated funding; and over the military protecting the existing federal appeals process when it came to dispute resolution.

These battles in turn shaped and informed subsequent crises of authority over ensuing "nested" collective choice and operational rule sets. Noteworthy, for example, were crises of authority involving authority rules. These included contests over the extent to which states were entitled to equal status with the military in decision making regarding Sikes and the ESA, as well as over how much ENR management responsibility should be decentralized to base commanders in MLWA reauthorization. Illustrative also were contests over who had final authority when disputes arose over such things as the content of INRM plans and the substance of the Southwest Initiative.

Difficult enough in their own right, these crises of authority were again accompanied by contests over entry and exit, payoff, information, and aggregation rules. Illustrative of those involving entry and exit rules were battles over what constituted critical habitats, as well as how firm the "fence" was around NRM funding. Witnessed, too, were crises targeting payoff rules, including the shifting burdens and benefits involved in the on-again, off-again funding of ITAM, as well as when Congress told the army to "realign their resources" for NRM before they could receive additional funds. Finally, contests targeted at information and aggregation rules were again central in this case, most profoundly involving the FWS's decision to allow the military's INRM plans to be functional equivalents of critical habitat designations.

What Strategies and Tactics Did They Use?

Witnessed throughout these crises of authority, too, were examples of various strategies and tactics used by the military that were reminiscent in attitude and in aim of the Cold War era. Not unlike in prior chapters, and in addition to the issue (re)definition strategies noted above, these repertoires of contestation included extensive ally mobilization and demobilization tactics. These included Senator McCain's work in the military land withdrawal case generally (ally mobilization), in devolving ENR management responsibilities to Goldwater base officials (de-mobilizing opponents by narrowing the scope of the conflict), and in altering the withdrawal proposal to deactivate opposition.

Likewise witnessed on behalf of greening were the mobilization of national and state associations (e.g., the IAFWA, the NMFWA, and the NRA) during contests over Sikes Act consultation to support the DOI's position. Meanwhile, countermobilization efforts were consistently apparent as the military sought to marshal allies on congressional committees in support of its positions, as well as through statute shopping by claiming the redundancy of legislation. In this instance, claiming that INRM plans under the Sikes Act reauthorization were re-dundant of (and, hence, could substitute for) EISs "demobilized" opposition by cutting down on the transparency of what the military was doing.

Visible also in the chapter were military repertoires of contestation involv-ing delegitimation and deinstitutionalization strategies as officials tried to alter existing power constellations to the services' advantage. Delegitimation efforts included persistent contestation of the wording in the Sikes Act concerning "consultation," thus denying the legitimacy of the states to participate equally in decisions. Illustrative, too, was the military arguing that states lacked the knowledge of national security necessary to be given equal or final authority in INRM planning matters affecting the services. And perhaps the ultimate in crafty delegitimation strategies was the military pressing successfully in the Sikes reauthorization bill for authority to design the administrative dispute resolution process.

Prevalent, too, were multiple examples of the deinstitutionalization tactics witnessed in prior chapters, especially deadline manipulation, objective shift-ing, defunding, and resource dependency strategies. These included the military claiming that collaboration with the states would jeopardize the services' ability to complete INRMs by statutory deadlines, as well as trying to accelerate land withdrawals to catch opponents flatfooted. As for objective-shifting tactics, one again sees the military using reinventing government initiatives to devolve NRM responsibilities to more military-friendly environments. Meanwhile, illustrations of defunding and resource-dependency tactics included the Congress's and the army's stop-and-start funding for NRM programs in program objective memo-randa (defunding), plus the army taking advantage of resource dependency in the Southwest Initiative.

What Were the Implications?

In the end, the consolidation phase of the trajectory of contestation again left halfway, halting, and patchworked structures, processes, and procedures in its wake. Granted, and as noted, the status of INRM planning in the drone zone was better than it had been during the Cold War. The military clearly was less able to control the tempo "as a shield against attack." But greening was still precarious in anything but purely reactive terms amid mixed signals about its priority and in terms of its institutionalization in administrative, responsibility, and accounting structures within which Mangoday or any other warriors toiled daily. In the process these patterns of politics left the military woefully shy of the accountability, transparency, and resource reengagement necessary to create the kind of mental models and schema necessary for institutionalizing an enduring beyond-compliance ethic during the Clinton years. As I chronicle in chapter 8, however, they pale in military ferocity and obdurance to those witnessed during efforts to green the chemical weapons destruction process during these same years.

Notes

1. Roberto Suro, "Warrior Spirit Put to the Test in Combat with New Twists," *Washington Post*, June 12, 2000, p. A01.
2. "Navy Challenged to Balance Readiness and Environment," *DEA* 7, no. 16 (August 10, 1999): 14.
3. Suro, "Warrior Spirit Put to the Test."
4. See, for example, Tad Bartimus and Scott McCartney, *Trinity's Children: Living Along America's Nuclear Highway* (New York: Harcourt Brace Jovanovich, 1991), 21.
5. Harvey Meyerson, *Nature's Army: When Soldiers Fought for Yosemite* (Lawrence: University Press of Kansas, 2001), 227.
6. "DoD Tentatively Approves Air Force Plan for Sonoran Desert Management," *DEA* 5, no. 23 (November 4, 1997): 5.
7. Sherri Wasserman Goodman, DUSD(ES), statement before the U.S. Senate Committee on Armed Services, Subcommittee on Military Readiness and Defense Infrastructure, June 9, 1993, 9 (hereafter cited as Goodman Statement).
8. "Army's FY00-05 Fiscal Projections Cut Environmental Programs," *DEA* 6, no. 13 (June 30, 1998): 3–4.
9. Goodman Statement, 8–9.
10. "DoD Touts Commitment to Biodiversity in Releasing New Handbook," *DEA* 4, no. 24 (November 20, 1996): 20.
11. Ibid., 21.
12. L. Peter Boice, "Conserving the Department of Defense's Natural and Cultural Resources: Recent Advances, New Challenges," 1998, https://www.denix.osd.mil/denix/Public/Library/NCR/Speeches/fedfac1998.html (January 11, 1999).
13. "Army's FY00-05 Fiscal Projections Cut Environmental Programs." Granted, all of Goodman's ENR programs were funded at only 82 to 85 percent of projected needs in that program objective memorandum, but the army's conservation programs were especially hard hit.
14. "DoD Seeks Stable Funding for Environmental Programs in FY99," *DEA* 6, no. 3 (February 10, 1998): 3–4. Thus, Class I projects—the highest priority—were those necessary to meet deadlines in a compliance agreement, for corrective action under a notice of violation, or to meet a statutory or regulatory deadline that had already passed. In short, these were litigation-driven. Next in

priority were Class II projects designed to meet future compliance deadlines. Left at the bottom in Class III, as a consequence, were land-use planning, conservation, and ecosystem protection projects.

15. "Army's FY00-05 Fiscal Projections Cut Environmental Programs," 3.

16. Ibid.

17. L. Peter Boice, "Meeting Current Challenges to DoD's Conservation Program," *Federal Facilities Environmental Journal* 7, no. 2 (Spring 1997): 33.

18. The Defense Resources Board is comprised of OSD's highest officials and was chaired at the time by John Hamre, deputy secretary of defense.

19. "Army's Future Budgeting Plans Look to Restore ITAM Program," *DEA* 7, no. 8 (April 20, 1999): 14–15.

20. "OSD Budget Office Threatening to Ax Army ITAM Program," *DEA* 7, no. 23 (November 16, 1999): 5.

21. Ibid.

22. "Conferees Direct Army to Study Alternatives to OB/OD of Munitions," *DEA* 8, no. 16 (August 1, 2000): 7.

23. Ibid.

24. "DoD to Enter Ecosystem Agreement for Major Training Facilities," *DEA* 3, no. 3 (February 8, 1995): 21. Included in the California initiative were some of the services' premiere training facilities: Fort Irwin National Training Center, Nellis Air Force Base, Edwards Air Force Base, Naval Air Weapons Station China Lake, and Twenty-Nine Palms Marine Corps Air Ground Combat Center.

25. "Text: DoD Letter Affirming Sikes Act Agreement," *DEA*, 3 no. 24 (November 29, 1995): 19.

26. "GOP Endangered Species Reform May Speed Reuse of Bases," *DEA* 3, no. 1 (January 11, 1995): 9.

27. "NRA Argues Against DoD-Proposed Changes to Sikes Act," *DEA* 3, no. 19 (September 20, 1995): 14–15.

28. "DoD to Seek Changes in Bill Mandating Resource Management Plans," *DEA* 3, no. 16 (August 9, 1995): 15.

29. "NRA Argues Against DoD-Proposed Changes to Sikes Act." According to the NRA, its 3.3 million members had "a vested interest in sound scientific management of the wildlife and their habitats" on military lands (15).

30. "Goodman Attacks Cuts to Environment Budget as Posing 'Unfunded Mandate'," *DEA* 3, no. 6 (March 22, 1995): 13.

31. "DoD to Seek Changes in Bill Mandating Resource Management Plans," 15.

32. "DoD, Interior Hammer Out Deal on Sikes Act Reauthorization," *DEA* 3, no. 21 (October 18, 1995): 19.

33. "State Wildlife Agencies Force Changes to DoD, DOI Compromise Language," *DEA* 3, no. 22 (November 1, 1995): 8.

34. Ibid. Also see "Defense, Interior Still at Odds Over Sikes Act Reauthorization Options," *DEA* 5, no. 12 (June 4, 1997): 5. DOI and the states were especially worried that the DoD would get language into the Sikes Act that would reduce their ability to enforce these other ENR statutes.

35. "State Wildlife Agencies Force Changes to DoD, DOI Compromise Language," 7.

36. "Military, FWS and States Seek Compromise on Sikes Act as Hearing Date Nears," *DEA* 5, no. 10 (May 7, 1997): 8. This was a persistent theme enunciated throughout each of the many years of the debate over reauthorizing the Sikes Act.

37. "Pentagon Pulls Plug on Sikes Act Agreement with States," *DEA* 3, no. 25 (December 13, 1995): 3.

38. Ibid.

39. "Defense, Interior Still at Odds Over Sikes Act Reauthorization Options."

40. "Military, FWS and States Seek Compromise on Sikes Act as Hearing Date Nears," 7; emphasis added.

41. "Defense, Interior Still at Odds Over Sikes Act Reauthorization Options."

42. "Military, FWS and States Seek Compromise on Sikes Act as Hearing Date Nears," 7.

43. "DoD, States Reach Sikes Act Compromise," *DEA* 5, no. 13 (June 17, 1997): 17.

44. "DoD Clarifies Review Requirement for Natural Resource Plans," *DEA* 12, no. 23 (November 16, 2004): 10.

45. "GOP Senators Seek Exemption from Endangered Species Act at Fort Bragg," *DEA* 3, no. 6 (March 22, 1995): 17.

46. Ibid., 18.

47. At the time, Walker was U.S. Army assistant secretary for environment, safety, and occupational health.

48. "Revised ESA Bill Gives DoD Insulation from Impositions of Proposed Law," *DEA* 5, no. 22 (October 21, 1997): 3, 19.

49. Specifically, the DoD's preferred language stipulated that to "the maximum extent practicable, the Secretary [of the Interior], in developing recovery plans, shall give priority, without regard to taxonomic classification, to recovery plans that . . . reduce conflicts with military training and operations" (ibid., 3).

50. Ibid., 19.

51. "DoD, Federal Land Managers Launch Endangered Species Strategy," *DEA* 5, no. 26 (December 16, 1997): 10. This initiative was also known as the Southwest Strategy.

52. Ibid.

53. *Sierra Club v. Glickman*, 156 F.3d 606, 619 (5th Cir.), 1998; "ESA Lawsuit May Force Expanded Species Protections in Water Permits," *DEA* 6, no. 22 (November 3, 1998): 19. Other regulatory agencies also were made potentially vulnerable to lawsuits by this ruling, and many thought that they would have to revamp their permitting processes in order to include species protection.

54. "Defense Department Faces Critical 'Encroachment,' UXO Issues in 2001," *DEA* 9, no. 1 (January 2, 2001): 20–21; "SROC Calls for Formal Coordination on Encroachment Issues," *DEA* 8, no. 25 (December 5, 2000): 12. The Senior Readiness Oversight Council is chaired by the deputy secretary of defense. It meets monthly and affords senior officials at the Pentagon an opportunity to review readiness issues collaboratively. Included among its members are the vice chairman of the Joint Chiefs, the chiefs of each service, the under secretaries of each service, and other key DoD civilian leaders.

55. "Critical Habitat Designation Redundant, Military Tells FWS," *DEA* 8, no. 6 (March 21, 2000): 20, 19.

56. "Army Urges FWS to Include Critical Habitat Issues in ESA Policy," *DEA* 8, no. 18 (August 29, 2000): 5.

57. "Environmentalists' ESA Suit Threatens Marine Corps Training," *DEA* 9, no. 1 (January 2, 2001): 3–4. In *NRDC v. U.S. DOI*, the court ruled that FWS had to designate critical habitat for the coastal California gnatcatcher by October 2000 (113 F.3d, 1121 [9th Cir.] May 21, 1997).

58. "Environmentalists' ESA Suit Threatens Marine Corps Training." The delay incurred in doing otherwise at Camp Pendleton, the Marine Corps argued, would have taken out nearly 40 percent of the land necessary for realistic training.

59. "Critical Habitat Designation Redundant," 19.

60. "Senate Rescinds Provision Renewing Range Withdrawals, Following Criticism," *DEA* 7, no. 11 (June 1, 1999): 6–9.

61. "Senate Armed Services Committee Approves Military Range Withdrawals," *DEA* 7, no. 10 (May 18, 1999): 3, 19.

62. "Activists Blast Plan to Transfer Land Management to Military," *DEA* 7, no. 13 (June 29, 1999): 5–6.

63. Robert Leonhard, *The Art of Maneuver: Maneuver Warfare Theory and AirLand Battle* (Novato, CA: Presidio Press, 1994), 16.

CHAPTER EIGHT

Safety, Security, and Chemical Weapons Demilitarization

Generations of soldiers in the U.S. Army's Eighty-second Airborne Division know the story well.[1] At the beginning of the Battle of the Bulge in World War II, German panzers were routing U.S. forces beating a hasty retreat in the Ardennes Forest. At some point in the retreat, a tank commander unfamiliar with the terrain asked a soldier for directions, and the following exchange ensued:

> *Soldier*: You looking for a safe place to park that thing?
> *Tank commander*: I sure am.
> *Soldier*: Well, pull in right behind me, 'cause I'm the Eighty-second Airborne, and this is as far as the bastards are going.

This story not only illustrates the power of heroic myths to inspire esprit de corps, a warrior culture, and a self-image among troops in the U.S. military, but it also captures the U.S. Army's attitude since the early 1980s on demilitarizing (i.e., disposing of) Cold War stockpiles of chemical weapons. To paraphrase the above, "We know how to dispose of chemical weapons safely, so just line up behind us 'cause this is as far as those bastard regulators are going."

The saga of chemical demilitarization during the Clinton years actually begins a decade earlier in Geneva with multilateral negotiations over chemical weapons disposal under the auspices of the United Nations. With these complex negotiations still ongoing, Congress enacted the National Defense Authorization Act of 1986 (PL 99-145), directing the Pentagon to eliminate U.S. stockpiled (obsolete) chemical agents and munitions. The Reagan Pentagon designated the army as executive agent of the program, with the assistant secretary of the army for installations and environment in the OSD in charge of policy and program oversight.

Then, in 1988, Congress created the Chemical Stockpile Emergency Preparedness Program. The program was charged with developing emergency evacuation plans at the nine designated army installations where chemical weapons were to be demilitarized. These installations were the Lexington Blue Grass Depot located in Kentucky; the Newport Army Ammunition Plant in Indiana; the Tooele Army Depot in Utah; the Aberdeen Proving Grounds in Maryland; the Umatilla Army Depot in Oregon; the Anniston Army Depot in Alabama; the Pueblo Army

Depot in Colorado; the Johnson Atoll Chemical Agent Disposal System southwest of Hawaii; and the Pine Bluff Army Arsenal in Arkansas.

Next, in 1990, came a widely heralded bilateral agreement between the United States and the Soviet Union to destroy the overwhelming majority of chemical weapons stockpiles, followed two years later by the enactment of the Chemical Weapons Convention (CWC). Ratified by the United States in 1997, the CWC required this nation and Russia to, among other things, destroy 45 percent of Category 1 (the highest "risk" category) chemical weapons by 2004 (without endangering humans or the environment), and all declared stockpiled chemical weapons by 2007. The CWC also permitted a five-year extension, if needed, for destruction of all stockpiles.

Yet by 2003 the United States had to ask for a three-year extension of the 2004 deadline, having by then disposed of only 26 percent of specified chemical agent and 39 percent of all chemical stockpiles. In that same year, the chemical weapons demilitarization program earned an "ineffective" rating on President Bush's Program Assessment Rating Tool, partly because chemical weapons destruction had begun at only two sites (Johnston Atoll and Tooele). Also responsible for that rating was OMB's judgment that the program had inadequate measures of progress and accountability. Then, in 2004, a GAO study concluded that, at best, the government would not be able to reach the 2007 destruction target until 2014.[2] Meanwhile, life-cycle costs of the program rose from 1986 estimates of $2.1 billion to $32 billion in 2005. Bad news enough in its own right, in April 2006, Donald Rumsfeld became the first secretary of defense to acknowledge that the United States would need an extension of the CWC deadline to 2012, and was unlikely even to meet the extended deadline.[3]

To what are these embarrassing delays, cost overruns, and lapses attributable? For starters, chemical weapons demilitarization is a difficult task. Even under the best of circumstances, the CWC's timetables were challenging due to the unprecedented scale, technical complexity, and risks of chemical weapons destruction.[4] The army was to destroy in a safe manner a stockpile comprised largely of two thousand M55 rockets containing VX or GB nerve gases; 8-inch, 4.2-inch, and 155-millimeter projectiles containing GB, VX, or mustard gases; reams of MC-1 and MK94 bombs; and more than forty thousand one-ton containers of GB, VX, and mustard gases. Moreover, with the exception of the newer binary chemical weapons begun in 1987, the entire arsenal was over twenty years old and deteriorating, with some mustard gas as old as forty-five years. In total, the stockpile in 1990 consisted of 31,496 tons of chemical agents.

Yet these delays and cost overruns also stemmed from a bouillabaisse of self-inflicted wounds traceable to army traits consistent with its heroic Cold War self-image. Most notable in this civil–military imbroglio were the service's predisposition toward creative accounting; getting single answers to complex and controversial technical questions; and "deciding, announcing, and defending" decisions rather than exploring alternatives. All of which led to an Army Audit

Agency report issued one month after Clinton left office, which charged that the program repeatedly "ignored cost, schedule and *environmental impacts* and violated rules both inside and outside the military in order to keep the program going."[5]

To illustrate how and why this was the case, this chapter focuses on the patterns of politics that drove and were driven by three major challenges related to chemical weapons destruction during the Clinton years. First, how safe and reliable was the army's preferred option of incineration for chemical weapons demilitarization? Second, could the states use their regulatory authority to get the army to revise or jettison incineration? Finally, how much transparency of demilitarization operations would the army and its allies allow?

The Safety and Reliability Challenge

As noted in chapter 3, the army's approach to system, operation, and requirement analyses during the Cold War was summarized best as "getting a single answer (often a number) rather than illuminating the alternatives in the face of recognized uncertainties." Moreover, the army tailored its analyses to internal rather than external audiences, and viewed the process as calculating answers to problems defined exclusively by its military professionals. Marginalized was "illuminating and understanding problems" as others might see them.[6] Nor did this "single answer" mentality erode after the army lost many of its better analytic staff in the early 1980s.[7]

Certainly, no more apt characterization could be applied to the army's relentless technical hubris when it came to chemical weapons demilitarization in the post–Cold War era. By the Clinton years, the army had decades of mostly unchallenged experience with this task and had settled in 1988 on incineration as the centerpiece of its chemical weapons demilitarization program. Later renamed the Office of Program Manager for Chemical Weapons Destruction, this office reported to the deputy assistant secretary for chemical demilitarization, and ultimately to the deputy under secretary for acquisition, technology, and logistics. But in crafting accounting structures for chemical weapons demilitarization programs, including the army's, the OSD retained policy oversight and funding responsibilities. Interestingly, this was the army's preference, fearing otherwise that program costs for incineration might be taken out of *its* budget rather than that of the DoD.

By the mid-1990s, however, the army's preference for incineration became decidedly misaligned with post–Cold War ENR sensibilities. Greening proponents touted incineration's potential health risks and lambasted the army's "half-hearted efforts" to explore alternatives.[8] Holding firm to incineration as its so-called baseline technology, however, the army countered that incineration alternatives were unproven, would jeopardize its ability to meet CWC deadlines, and might drastically escalate costs.

Framing and Reframing the Safety Issue

What prompted the army's allegiance to incineration during the Cold War? The technical merits of the decision aside, the political logic was compelling. Congress had banned chemical weapons disposal in oceans in 1984, opposition mounted in state legislatures without disposal sites to transporting chemical weapons elsewhere for burial, and pressures from ENR activists on the army grew during the 1980s to abandon its domestic "cut holes and sink 'em" program. The army complied but expressed concern over the instability of chemical weapons stockpiles unless an expeditious way was found to dispose of them. To the army, that expeditious way was incineration. Most worrisome, service officials claimed, was that aging rockets might leak or detonate accidentally, and the igloos storing them could rupture after airplane crashes, natural disasters, or terrorist attacks. Also troubling was the threat to civilian populations posed by the instability of M55 rockets loaded with VX and GB nerve gases, flammable fuses, burster charges, and propellants. M55 accidents might even cause "sympathetic" explosions of nearby rockets.[9]

In testing at its Black Hills Depot and Dugway Proving Ground, for example, the army found that an M55 explosion created a chain-reaction fire that released an estimated 3 percent of the toxic agent GB (roughly 570 pounds), plus 37 additional pounds of VX. Premised on these data, army technicians estimated what they called the lethality rate or "maximum credible event" for each of its nine disposal sites if an explosion occurred. Ignoring the variability of terrain and atmospheric conditions and assuming that only 2.5 percent of stored gases were released, a 1 percent lethality rate was likely among populations living within 4.5 to 27 miles of any igloo.[10]

Not surprisingly, these projections shattered the complacency of many citizens living near existing and future sites. Yet critics alleged that the army was strategically manipulating its models to exaggerate the instability of chemical weapons destruction in order to sell its incineration plans to the public: The quicker the army could burn chemical weapons, the shorter the stay in igloos and the less the risk of explosion. Nor were citizen fears about incineration assuaged when, in 1979, chemical smoke pots burning at the Lexington Blue Grass Depot in Kentucky created a toxic cloud that drifted over nearby Interstate 75. The incident sent more than forty people to the hospital with respiratory problems. The army's image suffered further when, for two weeks, officials denied responsibility.

Also distrust-inspiring during the 1980s were revelations that weapons volatility might not be as likely as the army claimed. By then, twenty-five- to thirty-five-year shelf lives for M55 rockets were well established in the literature, a fact confirmed in several studies commissioned by the army itself, but that program officials downplayed. Likewise undermined were army claims that chemical agents could not be separated from M55 rockets for safe and prolonged storage.

Indeed, a study the service commissioned by Arthur D. Little researchers said that separation *was* possible.[11] Nor did it help the army's cause that a National Research Council (NRC) study used by service officials to tout the instability of M55 rockets was premised on incomplete data the service had supplied. These were data that demonstrated a longer shelf life for the rockets and, hence, less need to move ahead with incineration.[12]

The Grassroots Revolt

With charges and countercharges spiraling, citizens in rural and economically dependent areas near existing and future stockpile sites grew ever more wary of deferring to the army's claims. Meanwhile, opponents provided expanded wind transport models showing that toxic fumes from incineration would actually extend over more densely populated (and hence more politically powerful) metropolitan areas, thus tripling to quadrupling the number of deaths predicted by the army's models. Included were urban and suburban populations in Salt Lake City near the Tooele Army Depot, in Atlanta and Birmingham near the Anniston Army Depot, and in Little Rock near the Pine Bluff Arsenal.[13]

Equally distressing was the army's attitude toward incorporating the concerns of these populations into disposal decisions. Granted, during the 1980s, it did follow NEPA processes by incorporating citizen participation into programmatic environmental impact statement scoping hearings at potential sites. But the issues broached in the programmatic environmental impact statement did not involve the choice of disposal technology. Tapped only was input regarding *where* incineration would take place: onsite or offsite.[14] Thus, as the Cold War wound down in the late 1980s, a litigious grassroots movement took root, one that dramatically altered the post–Cold War context of the army's incineration program.

Not surprisingly, after the I-75 incident the anti-incineration offensive began in Kentucky with a grassroots group that expanded to become known as Common Ground and, later, the Kentucky Environmental Foundation. Based near the planned Blue Grass Depot incineration site, the movement subsequently spread to anti-incineration groups near the first four scheduled host sites in Alabama (Pine Bluff), Colorado (Pueblo), Oregon (Umatilla), and Utah (Tooele). By 1989, the DoD had become so concerned about mounting opposition to incineration like this that it sponsored a conference in Maryland bringing together concerned citizens from Alabama, Colorado, Oregon, and Utah.

Yet so disgruntled did these citizens become with the army's "decide, announce, and defend" presentations at the conference that they joined with attendees representing Greenpeace, the National Toxics Campaign Fund, and the Sierra Club to form the Chemical Weapons Working Group (CWWG). Thus midwifed ironically by the conference was a group that became the army's most relentless grassroots opponent in the post–Cold War era. The group then gained additional anti-incineration allies, including the Vietnam Veterans of America Foundation, who shared a common animus toward the army's handling of Agent Orange claims against the government. They were joined next by Gulf War veterans' associations incensed by the military's position on Gulf War syndrome, as well as by anti-incineration groups from Russia.[15]

The Data Never Speak for Themselves

Unfazed, the army refused to back down from its position that incineration was the only proven technology that would allow the United States to meet CWC deadlines. But as Congress turned up the heat on the program in the early 1990s, the army altered its tactics by trying to demobilize key components of its opposition. Following a directive in the 1993 National Defense Authorization Act to report to Congress on alternatives to incineration while going full speed ahead with incineration, the army proposed in 1994 to allow neutralization as a backup to incineration of chemical agents at its two low-volume bulk storage sites, Aberdeen and Newport.

Officially, the two sites were chosen because they stored chemical wastes in bulk containers rather than in actual weapons (e.g., in rockets), thus making them the only safe locations for studying neutralization. Environmentalists countered that "no logical basis" existed for the army to make such a distinction.[16] Instead, they offered three reasons for hiving off the two sites in this fashion, two political and one pragmatic. First, Aberdeen and Newport (along with Kentucky) were seedbeds of incineration opposition. Second, and more pragmatically, these facilities were handling very small amounts of chemical agents and weapons.[17] Finally, and again more politically, part of the proposal required offsite transportation of chemical agents, transport that the army knew many members of Congress already opposed.

Nor did the army let the results of studies on neutralization at these sites or elsewhere deflect them from their position on incineration. For example, in 1996, a team of technical experts from the army and potential contractors selected neutralization (followed by onsite biodegradation) as the best of five alternative techniques for chemical weapons disposal. But service officials again played the scheduling card.[18] Despite making major progress in research on neutralization, the army pointed to major and likely time-consuming obstacles to the safe disposal of neutralized materials produced by the process.[19]

It is important to note that some of the army's positions during the Clinton years were validated by outside studies.[20] By the same token, however, whenever research findings contradicted its assurances that incineration would allow it to reach CWC deadlines, officials always questioned the reliability of the data informing them. For example, a 1998 study by Arthur Anderson identified a 95 percent probability that five of the nine chemical weapons incineration disposal sites would take many years beyond the 2007 CWC deadline to complete their work.[21] The army discredited the study as predicated on obsolete data. Nor, in 1999, were chemical weapons disposal program officials any less unwilling to challenge the army's own Soldier, Biological, and Chemical Command when it found that storing M55 rockets did *not* pose higher risks than incinerating them.[22] Moreover, these denials became surreal in 1997 when the DoD proudly announced a $600-million contract to a U.S. company building a nonincineration project in Russia. The project, the Pentagon said, would assist our former adversary "in meeting destruction milestones contained in the Chemical Weapons Convention."[23]

The Race to the Top Challenge

As noted, by 1994 events on the ground were making it increasingly clear that the substance, pace, and progress of the army's incineration program lay less under the control of the chemical weapons disposal program office than in the hands of stockpile states and localities. As one DoD interviewee observed, mounting state regulatory and legal challenges were "giving ultimate veto power to the citizens in whose backyard the plants will be built."[24] In effect these grassroots actors tried persistently during the Clinton years to begin a "race to the top" when it came to rules affecting chemical weapons demilitarization in the post–Cold War era. In response, however, the army mounted a determined counteroffensive "to storm the states into accepting incineration."[25]

Brushfires Spread at the Grassroots

To appreciate the fury unleashed in state legislatures by the incineration issue, consider the steps taken in four states slated for disposal sites: Colorado, Indiana, Kentucky, and Maryland. In Indiana, Kentucky, and Maryland, state legislatures focused on stopping incineration plants before they were built. Kentucky, already with the strictest laws on incineration in the nation, followed Colorado and Indiana in giving local governments the ultimate authority to offer or block construction of incinerators affecting their jurisdictions. Also, were actions like these not threatening enough to the army's plans, meeting the emission standards that these states began issuing far exceeded the existing technical capabilities of public or private incineration sites. This was no accident; state solons were trying to make it impossible for the army to meet them.[26]

Governors such as Evan Bayh (D) of Indiana also began petitioning Congress to slow down, if not halt altogether, the service's march toward incineration. Bayh's attitude, like those of other governors, was not helped by his state's repeated problems in getting safety information from the army, as well as by inconsistent reports on army destruction plans at Indiana's Newport facility. In mid-1996, Bayh wrote to Clinton's secretary of the army, Togo West: "In particular,

I am concerned that the pressure to meet deadlines will not allow for adequate time to test alternatives to incinerating the VX [nerve agent] . . . [and I] cannot at this time accept any decision that designates incineration as the desirable [disposal] method."[27]

Consequently, by the mid-1990s the army faced a multistate regulatory offensive against its incineration plan, one that only picked up steam over the remainder of the decade. By mid-decade, only Utah (Tooele) had approved the army's request for an RCRA permit. Moreover, the approval was only an interim permit. Nor did the situation at the grassroots in many states improve for the army by the end of the decade. Utah regulators were compelled to respond to a variety of problems at Tooele throughout the Clinton years. In late 1999, for example, the Utah Department of Environmental Quality required the army for safety reasons to slow incineration destruction of M55 rockets at Tooele to two rockets per hour.[28]

Likewise, in Oregon (at Umatilla) in 1996, the army felt that its RCRA permitting prospects were so problematic that it unsuccessfully applied for a federal waiver. Also throughout the Clinton years, state officials joined GAO and others in repeatedly questioning the adequacy of emergency preparation plans in Alabama (Anniston), Oregon, and Utah.[29] Characterizing the army's effort as a "misguided mission," Rep. Peter DeFazio (D-OR) chastised the "military brass" for truculently insisting, in the wake of disturbing whistle-blower incidents at Johnston Atoll and Tooele (see below), that "they . . . get rid of these chemical weapons their way [and] at their [own] pace."[30]

Nor were Alabamans or Arkansans any more sanguine, harboring as they did environmental justice as one of their greatest concerns. Joining state and county officials, many environmentalists and African Americans living near Pine Bluff in Arkansas said it was no coincidence that the army's incinerator was located in a poor, minority county that already ranked in the top 20 percent nationally for cancer hazards and airborne toxics.[31] Neither were emergency preparation plans any better in Pine Bluff than near Umatilla. As one planning meeting attendee described in late 2000, "We watched in shock and disbelief as Army personnel and FEMA [Federal Emergency Management Agency] officials" sparred over whether citizens should be evacuated immediately or whether evacuation for some should be coupled with sealing schoolchildren off in their schools and having others remain in their homes.[32]

Finally, the service's incineration troubles were already blossoming when Gilbert Decker, army assistant under secretary for research, development, and acquisition, insisted in 1996 that searching for incineration alternatives would delay the Pueblo Army Depot program anywhere from six to eight years. Responding for the local chapter of the Sierra Club, Chair Ross Vincent charged that Decker's assessment was only "the latest foolishness from the Army's spin doctors . . . the public here has been systematically under-informed and in some cases, outright misinformed."[33] Thus, by the end of the 1990s, Bill Owens, Colorado's

Republican governor, was pushing the DoD to do further, delay-enhancing, site-specific environmental risk assessments before deciding which technology to use at Pueblo.[34]

Throwing Legal Sand in the Works

Many of these concerns and regulatory offensives in the states in turn offered the means for a litigious environmental community to skewer even further the army's embrace of incineration. Indeed, the peskiest, most delay-inducing, and financially costly assaults on the army's incineration plans and schedules involved endless administrative and legal challenges by ENR activists who opposed the issuing of permits by state regulators to the army. State and federal courts actually found in favor of the army's positions on procedural grounds in the vast majority of these cases. But each of them exacted a huge toll by flummoxing the army's schedule, causing additional cost overruns, revealing embarrassing aspects of program mismanagement, and, hence, further eroding the army's credibility and congressional funding.

Too numerous to cover individually, the regulatory and legal offensives buffeting the army's incineration program from the mid-1990s on fit into three basic categories. One set of challenges inspiring lawsuits at Anniston, Tooele, and Umatilla attacked the aforementioned discrepancies between army claims and various research findings. In these cases plaintiffs and interveners (including most of the nation's "Big Ten" ENR groups) claimed the army was violating NEPA's charge to assess the costs and benefits of incineration alternatives accurately.[35] Examples cited by the plaintiffs include a 1996 NRC study critiquing the army for not applying explicit and consistent criteria and methodologies when assessing incineration alternatives, a 1997 NRC study finding that the Pentagon's low-level exposure standards for workers and the public were premised on inadequate and invalid data, another 1997 GAO study showing that the chemical weapons stockpile was "reasonably stable through 2013," and an internal 1999 army report finding that leaks at chemical weapons stockpiles were not increasing, as the service claimed they were.[36]

Against this steady drumbeat of research contradicting its claims, the army faced a second set of legal problems stemming from recurring problems at Johnston Atoll and Tooele, problems calling into question the safety of operations at other sites. One of the army's major contentions was that it could proceed more rapidly with incineration at later sites still trying to get state permits by applying "lessons learned" from earlier experiences. But learning obviously was *not* taking place, as the same contractors responsible for earlier problems were later at work creating similar problems at sites scheduled to come online (most prominently, the Raytheon Demilitarization Company and EG&G, Inc., at Umatilla and Anniston).[37]

Relatedly, a final category of regulatory and judicial claims was based on flaws identified by a series of whistle-blower incidents at Tooele. Included among these were three hundred safety-related issues noted at the site by Steve Jones, an EG&G manager. In Jones's subsequent legal appeals, charges were added of witness tampering.[38] Then, in 1996, Utah officials confirmed allegations by Gary Millar, an EG&G general manager at Tooele, that "thousands of environmental, safety, quality, and operational deficiencies" existed at the site.[39] Subsequently, in 1997, a former hazardous waste operations coordinator and environmental compliance inspector proved that she was demoted by EG&G "for attempting to enforce environmental, health, and safety regulations" at Tooele.[40] Finally, in 2000, a former permit coordinator at Tooele charged that EG&G pressured him to cover up major design flaws, dangerous practices, and health and safety risks.[41]

Congress Redux

Without downplaying these protean and powerful offensives against the army's incineration plans at the state and local level and in the courts, the impact of an unrelenting offensive by members of Congress from affected districts and states cannot be overestimated. For example, when site managers at several stockpile sites began eyeing transportation of chemical weapons (stockpiled and non-stockpiled) to Tooele and other states to avoid more restrictive state incineration laws, Rep. Karen Shepard (D-UT) successfully attached a rider to the FY 1995 defense authorization bill blocking this practice.[42]

Relatedly, environmentalists working with sympathetic defense appropriators also killed in conference a 1997 proposal by Senator Frank Murkowski (R-AK) to study the feasibility of transporting chemical weapons to centralized destruction centers.[43] Then, as costs for the chemical weapons demilitarization program rose astronomically and various army-allied members of Congress argued that building all scheduled sites was now cost prohibitive, Reps. Glen Browder (D-AL) and James Hansen (R-UT) stymied calls for studying cross-state transportation of chemical weapons that would likely dump wastes in their states.

Meanwhile, in the Senate, Orin Hatch (R-UT), Ben Nighthorse Campbell (D-CO, later, R), and Hank Brown (R-CO), along with Rep. Scott McInnis (R-CO), tried in 1994 to promote nonincineration research at all disposal sites.[44] This work finally paid off when, over army objections, Congress mandated in the FY 1997 Defense Appropriations Act that the army test at least two alternatives to incineration.[45] In the process, it created the Assembled Chemical Weapons Assessment (ACWA) program to do this kind of research.[46] Importantly, and fearing that ACWA initiatives could die aborning, Congress also stipulated that the army's Office of the Program Manager for Chemical Demilitarization (PMCD) could not manage ACWA because it had so tenaciously resisted alternatives to incineration in the past. In addition, ACWA officials were to report to the acquisitions and technology office in the OSD, which had an organizational incentive to pursue alternative research. Last, in a further assault upon still-visible remnants of the army's culture of sovereignty, secrecy, and sinecure, Congress added an

ACWA Dialogue Committee of stakeholders to help evaluate and choose potential incineration alternatives.[47]

Nor did it brighten the army's spirits when the Clinton administration in 1997 promised environmentalists to back deadline extension language in the CWC. This language stated that "2004 will have no relevance to the stockpile disposal program."[48] Such a development cut to the quick of the army's argument that incineration was necessary to meet 2004 CWC deadlines, but still left the 2007 deadline in play to buttress its position. By then, however, the army's credibility on the deadline issue had suffered severely. Still, army officials tried to make hay out of the information asymmetry they held over Congress due to the opaqueness of the existing demilitarization program structures. Neither was this asymmetry improved for greening proponents when, as the next section chronicles, Secretary of Defense William Cohen's DRI again propelled a Felliniesque restructuring of the oversight of the chemical weapons demilitarization program.

The Transparency Challenge

Justified in terms of Cohen's best business practices–informed DRI, the Pentagon and the army pursued a series of reorganization strategies between 1997 and 1999 related to the chemical weapons program. These began when, to the incredulity of environmentalists, the DoD's deputy secretary, John Hamre, announced that the Pentagon wanted to redelegate all chemical weapons program functions, oversight responsibilities, and funding authorities from the OSD to the army.[49] Inherent in this proposal was placing management of the base incineration (PMCD) and incineration alternative (ACWA) programs under the army. As a DoD spokesperson said at the time, the OSD was "trying to 'get out of the business of managing [program] activities' at the secretariat level . . . [we should] be 'involved in policy, not management of an activity.'"[50] Also consonant with best business practice rationales, devolution was justified as decentralizing authority to program managers "out in the field" in order to "streamline the lines of authority and the lines of communication" within the program.[51]

No matter how logical in terms of best business practices, such a reorganization would have created yet another instance during the Clinton years of the proverbial fox (in this case, the army) in charge of the chicken coop. As one flabbergasted CWWG critic noted, "You're putting the pilot program for ACWA directly in the camp of the very people who were specifically legislated out of this program," because no one trusted them to carry out its mission in the first place.[52] As noted, Congress had stipulated in 1986 that funding for chemical weapons destruction be placed into an OSD rather than an army account.[53] In turn, the 1996 Defense Authorization Act stipulated that the OSD retain funding authority over the program, whereas the 1997 Defense Appropriations Act stipulated that any program manager assigned to evaluate incineration alternatives *not* report directly to the army's baseline incineration program. The OSD, it proclaimed, needed to "be an honest broker between the Army and communities."[54]

With communities across the depot states claiming that the army failed to take seriously their concerns about incineration, critical congressional reaction to the Hamre proposal was swift. As one congressional interviewee warned, "DoD [meaning the OSD] cannot simply wash their hands of this program. They have to exercise both a policy and [management] oversight role with respect to the program."[55] Also distrusting the army's oversight of the ACWA program, incineration opponents on the Senate Armed Services Committee countered that moving responsibility to a new unit—the Defense Threat Reduction Agency— was more consistent with the DRI's best business practices than moving it to the army.[56] Interestingly, they were joined by the military's allies on the committee but for decidedly different reasons. They now feared that the service's funding for warfighting might be tapped at the rate of $1 billion a year to pay for the spiraling costs of chemical demilitarization.

Ultimately, in 1998, Congress did delegate oversight responsibility to the army, but did not go along with the Pentagon's plans to merge the ACWA and PMCD programs. But in a 1999 announcement "ending" the DoD's effort to get congressional approval for the merger, Ted Prociv, army deputy assistant secretary for chemical demilitarization, left open the possibility that the Pentagon might try again.[57] Even without the merger, however, the fears of greening proponents materialized. A 1999 independent analysis of the impact of oversight devolvement to the army concluded that it threatened "to disrupt progress severely."[58] Decrying the management frustrations that devolution had wrought, these experts contended that it had "forced the program and its former OSD leader down the chain of command . . . [leaving behind] . . . uncertainty as to lines of authority and responsibility." Not only was "bring[ing] this program into unity" the only way to meet the CWC deadline, they averred, but doing so required "dramatic changes" that would recentralize control within the OSD in order "to unify, simplify, and shorten the command structure at the top."[59]

The Funding Shell Game Begins

Amid the convoluted responsibility and accounting structures afforded by these consolidations, and facilitated by them, the lack of transparency of the chemical weapons program soon got the program into more trouble. This happened when the army again was caught applying the "creative accounting" methods so ingrained in its warrior culture. Ironically, these problems began for the army in 1998 after it asked permission from Congress to reprogram formerly appropriated monies from the incineration program into the ACWA account. Pressures mounted around this time from Congress, especially from Senators Wendell Ford (D) and Mitch McConnell (R) of Kentucky, for the army to pursue additional demonstration projects on six alternative technologies certified by the chemical weapons program. The army, however, said it only had enough funds to meet the FY 1997 defense authorization bill's mandate to test at least two alternative technologies to incineration. To do more, chemical weapons program officials claimed, would mean transferring anywhere from $3 million (for a third demonstration project) to $32 million (for six demonstration projects) from funding needed for incineration.

Not surprisingly this position generated immense opposition from grassroots ENR groups living near disposal sites. They saw it as further proof that the Pentagon was deceitful, unresponsive to community concerns, and never really serious about funding the ACWA program. A skeptical Paul Walker of Global Green USA and a member of the ACWA Dialogue Committee shot back sarcastically, "It could be done this fiscal year if the powers that be [want to] make it happen. . . . [As a former staff member for a congressional committee, I know that] [t]here is loose change in every program. There's a built-in fudge factor in every program. . . . The tightness [of the budget] is unconvincing."[60] Added another Dialogue Committee member from Alabama, David Christian, "There was suspicion that [ACWA] was just a side show," and this proves it.

Strongly demurring from that charge, Prociv gave a glimpse into the powerful inertial forces in the army when it came to accustomed standard operating procedures: "I can assure you, this has not been a side show . . . [but] . . . the generals don't understand" why they are being pushed by Congress to test more than two technologies. Normally, he continued, "the [demonstration testing] list starts with about seven competitors and ends with one company . . . but ACWA is trying to keep up to six technologies going to the end of the demonstration program."

But greening proponents in Congress had yet another card to play. The merits or demerits of funding account transfers aside, defense appropriators refused to consider the reprogramming of funds until the army was more forthcoming about its chemical weapons expenditures. This after the army was unable to track accurately what happened to millions of dollars appropriated to the $800 million chemical weapons disposal account. Nor could it certify how much remained in unobligated funds that might be suitable for reprogramming. "The problem," according to one congressional staff member, was that "we keep getting different numbers [from the army] . . . and the appropriators are upset with the lack of positive leadership coming out of the Department of Defense."

Anti-incineration members of Congress then went ballistic when the army confirmed their suspicions. Precisely at a time when service officials were claiming insufficient funds for nonincineration demonstrations, the Pentagon had reprogrammed $49 million out of the chemical demilitarization account to at least partially pay for operations in Bosnia. Events further spiraled out of control when it was learned the army had paid outside consultants to lobby members of Congress to increase funding for incineration during 1998 and 1999. An irate House Appropriations Committee retaliated by proposing to *cut* $4.5 million from the chemical weapons program.[61]

Enter the Auditors

Even this flirting with the outskirts of federal antilobbying laws, however, paled in comparison to the storm unleashed in Congress by a DoD comptroller investigation of the chemical weapons program led by Ron Garant, director of investment. Alleging in mid-1999 that the actions uncovered "were almost criminal," Garant found $416 million in unobligated funds in the program at the end of 1998.[62] Reminiscent of the financial legerdemain discovered in DERA cleanup funding (chapter 4) and in Legacy Resource Management Program funding (chapter 7), this finding was infinitely more complex and serious.

The chemical weapons disposal program stood accused of "hid[ing]" portions of its funds for chemical weapons destruction "by double obligating [i.e., twice obligating funds for the same project] or transferring money unnecessarily to contracts for which no work was being billed [e.g., at Sandia National Laboratory] so that the funds would not be labeled excess." Garant also found an additional $57 million in unexpended operations and maintenance money from FY 1997. Quipped Garant, "When it comes to the [p]rocurement funds it is like drilling for oil in Saudi Arabia."

Reacting swiftly, angry appropriators mandated cuts in all chemical weapons account budget requests and ordered reprogramming of available funding. The House Appropriations Committee justified its actions with a stinging rebuke of the army's integrity in managing the program's financing: "Not only [this] Committee, but also the Office of the Secretary of Defense Comptroller's staff, can not determine the validity of the program's prior year obligations."[63] Similarly incensed, Ted Stevens (R-AK), chairman of the Senate Appropriations Committee, joined with Senator McConnell to request an "all-out review" by the GAO of chemical demilitarization accounts from 1993 to 1999.

Nor did McConnell pull any punches: "I am concerned that the Army is pulling a bait and switch. We gave them enough money to fully study all viable alternatives and now they say they don't have it." Moreover, when the Clinton administration reacted by saying that the program would "die" if Congress persisted in these cuts, a congressional staffer charged that "they [the administration] let it founder" and allowed money to be diverted to unrelated military activities. Still, a subsequent 1999 DoD comptroller's office investigation of army malfeasance in the matter afforded ammunition to both the army's friends and foes, issuing a "report for all seasons."[64]

The investigation failed to find that the army had either abused its finances or engaged in "near criminal" activity. Yes, a "scrubbing" of the army's books did reveal some $845 million in unexpended appropriations since FY 1995, and yes, there were some "questionable budget practices." But "a lack of programmatic and technical stability" rather than conscious intent explained why the army failed to spend nearly 26 percent of appropriated funds between FY 1995 and FY 1999.[65] Significantly, a GAO preliminary report chartered by Congress came to similar conclusions. Investigators found that program delays were largely beyond the "influence and control" of the chemical weapons demilitarization program's managers (see below).[66]

But everyone knew that the army's various counteroffensives were responsible for these delays. Moreover, the comptroller found that neither OSD nor the army had tried hard enough to find monies for the testing of all six viable incineration alternatives. As one observer outside the Pentagon put it, a disturbing question begged an answer: "Why did Ted Prociv swear up and down [a year ago] . . . that there wasn't a nickel he could give to ACWA" when other chemical weapons projects were not crying out for these unexpended funds?[67] Moreover, this was especially curious given how assiduously the Pentagon scrubbed chemical weapons accounts to fund contingency military operations throughout the Clinton years.

Nor were ENR activists and congressional opponents of incineration buying into the DoD comptroller's explanation for the chemical weapons demilitarization program's laggard expenditure rates for disposal alternatives. According to the comptroller, chemical weapons demilitarization program expenditures *were* "slow and not in line with historical averages for programs in the same budget title."[68] For instance, although other programs in the same title had expended 83 percent of their FY 1997 procurement budgets by mid-1999, the chemical weapons program had expended only 9 percent of its procurement funds. The comptroller, however, attributed these discrepancies entirely to "unique factors which are not normally confronted by Defense program managers."[69] Included among these were delays in attaining state permit clearances (39 percent), in awarding contracts (11 percent), and in technical design and redesign of facilities (5 percent).[70] To which proponents of alternative technologies responded, again, that delays were due to the army's obsession with pursuing the technologically flawed and politically unpalatable incineration program. Added one congressional observer making no effort to conceal his feelings about illegality, "The reality of it is they've now had six months to clean up their books."[71]

On the Defensive

Under siege, the army unabashedly contested the comptroller's findings about its program administration, arguing that it was "using adequate program management controls, and . . . abiding by proper financial regulations."[72] Nonetheless, the DoD comptroller wrote to Senator McConnell in mid-1999 and identified funding for research and development to test all six incineration alternatives.[73] Clearly, the army had been caught in a financial sleight of hand that would come with financial consequences. In due course, congressional appropriators reduced the army's FY 2000 budget request for the chemical weapons demilitarization program by $140 million. Moreover, a year after these actions by Congress, the GAO concluded that the army still had not "consistently and systematically" tried to improve its financial management systems in the program.[74]

Thus, left again in the wake of all this was a halfway, halting, and patchworked financial management system, one characterized by Arthur Anderson consultants as so rife with "complex[ity] and confusion" by the end of the Clinton administration that it, too, was contributing to inordinate and costly program delays.[75] The army, wrote GAO investigators, "has not adequately managed program activities and tracked disbursements to ensure the timely liquidation of funds appropriated for the Chemical Demilitarization Program. This has occurred because of a lack of attention to and a fragmented organizational structure for managing program activities."[76] Quipped one Pentagon interviewee, the army "wouldn't know if they had enough money [or] didn't have enough money if it hit them right between the eyes."[77]

Discussion

"If you explain to your subordinates the end state you want and the time line you'd like to get there," says chairman of the Joints Chiefs, Gen. Peter Pace, "you can observe progress, provide resources, and know they're going to do things to get you to the goal. Maybe differently than you would do it. Often better. Sometimes worse. But inside the lines you've painted."[78] "Sometimes worse" would have to be the sobriquet applied during the Clinton years to the army's efforts to stay "within the lines painted" in preferring incineration over less environmentally threatening demilitarization alternatives. Wrought in the process of this civil–military dispute were sorely misaligned administrative, responsibility, and accounting structures for promoting anything beyond a reactive posture toward ENR protection, let alone a beyond-compliance ethic when it came to chemical weapons demilitarization.

Was There a Trajectory of Contestation?

As in the preceding chapters the overall trajectory of contestation in this policy arena began with perceptions of historical-structural mismatches, followed by offensives and counteroffensives leading to crises of authority. Left in their wake again, however, were misaligned consolidations of structures, processes, and procedures that in turn only provided the seeds for future conflict. Indeed, by the end of the Clinton years, a bruised and battered army still clung to its incineration program in most situations. Had it made compromises? Yes. Were those compromises geared toward institutionalizing a corporate sense of responsibility for greening its chemical demilitarization efforts? No. Indeed, the Cold War heroic myth of sovereignty, secrecy, and sinecure still flickered in the army's chemical weapons demilitarization program as George W. Bush became president in 2001. And once more the patterns of politics throughout this trajectory of contestation were steeped in the pursuit of the political, organizational, and personal prerogatives perceived by proponents and opponents alike.

What Motivated the Participants' Behavior?

Taking each component of this trajectory of contestation in order, first came perceptions of historical-structural mismatches spawned by the shock of the end of the Cold War, which in turn inspired minishocks related to the demilitarization of U.S. chemical weapons stockpiles. Of these shocks and minishocks, three were pivotal. First, the end of the Cold War bequeathed huge and potentially unstable chemical weapons stockpiles that by statute and treaty had to be eliminated by a certain time. Second, the army's historical approach to chemical weapons demilitarization—incineration—began drawing mounting opprobrium for being inadequate to protect public health from toxic risks. Finally, chemical weapons storage at the nine actual and proposed disposal sites began drawing unaccustomed scrutiny from elected officials in Gunbelt states for inadequate emergency planning, especially for low-income and minority citizens.

Again noticeable was how interpretations of the best approaches for redressing these mismatches involved sense making, filtered through contestants' respective interests and understandings. Moreover, they were framed and reframed accordingly to mobilize allies in efforts to (re)enact environments to their advantage. As such, one sees again how selective attention to and marshaling of "facts" (i.e., "filtering"), plus issue framing by the combatants, were crafted to advance their interests, as perceived largely through their perceptions of history, context, and contingency. For instance, these shocks were discerned and framed broadly by greening proponents originally as threats to public health and safety, and for which alternative and less-threatening disposal technologies were being ignored by an intransigent army chemical weapons disposal program. In turn, the army clung tenaciously to incineration; claimed insufficient time or resources to pursue untried alternatives because of CWC deadlines; and blamed others for its scheduling lapses, foibles, and frustrations. Nor did issue framing and reframing on these terms stop there, as the offensives of greening proponents were met by counteroffensives from the military and its allies.

As army intransigence continued apace, for example, greening proponents reframed the issues, respectively, as blatant disregard for public health and safety, as disingenuous arguments unsupported by research and budget realities, and as bordering on deliberate malfeasance. Responding to these efforts by greening proponents to impose and diffuse their preferred nonincineration alternatives on the Pentagon, the army pursued a counteroffensive that reframed nonincineration alternatives as risky because prolonged storage of M-55 rockets risked explosions. Program officials also said that alternatives were technically unfeasible within the CWC time frames, non-cost-effective, and jeopardized the international prestige of the United States because of the threat they posed to missing CWC deadlines.

As also witnessed in previous chapters, one finds ample examples in this chapter of how filtering and issue framing throughout the Clinton years were affected by, and also tried to influence, issue status. Most important again to the patterns of politics witnessed were shifts in salience, proximity, and boundary effects. In regard to shifting issue salience, the chapter chronicles how state regulatory and congressional action mounted throughout the Clinton years as the issue of incineration grew more salient to citizens living near depots. In turn, illustrative of issue proximity effects was how the army accommodated experimentation with nonincineration alternatives in Maryland (Aberdeen) and Indiana (Newport Army Ammunition Plant) as local political pressures mounted at these sites. This was a classic case of how the salience of an issue for a given organization mounts in the face of rising issue salience from nearby (in this instance, grassroots) stakeholders (i.e., as the proximity of issues arises). Relatedly, changes in its positions because of boundary effects were also noticeable after threats arose of potential litigation from the Common Ground alliance, as well as when terrorism threats related to disposal morphed into prominence. As boundary effects do, these "spilled over" into the chemical demilitarization issue, thus illustrating a more open access structure in this policy arena than the military was accustomed to in the Cold War era.

The impacts of history, context, and contingency, however, were perhaps best noted in the ways they affected the army's counteroffensives. Once again the impact of history is witnessed in the military's inherited organizational cultures, political economies, priorities, and resources. These, after all, had allowed military dominance over the substance, scope, and pace of chemical demilitarization during the Cold War and, in particular, its long-held and largely unchallenged preference for incineration. Prominent, also, was the impact of the political, social, economic, and technology contexts existing at any given time. Most important in this regard was the extent to which these waxed and waned in protecting or jeopardizing the existing structures, processes, and procedures supporting that dominance over chemical demilitarization. More conceptually, these changes helped influence shifts at any point in time in chemical weapons demilitarization decision structures (who had the formal authority to make decisions) and access structures (the ability of issues to get joined with chemical demilitarization issues), as well as in energy loads (how commensurate organizational resources were with old and new demands upon it) and energy distributions (the relative balance of power among the contestants). Finally, the impact of contingency was seen again in the vulnerability of various greening initiatives to delay or threaten the army's control over the substance, scope, or pace of chemical demilitarization.

Notable in these regards, for example, was how the army's counteroffensive again comported with its historical proclivity to define problems narrowly and technically to suit its needs while searching for a single correct answer rather than exploring alternatives. Equally illustrative were examples of the army's historic tendency to rely on its own rather than others' technical analyses unless they supported the army's position. Symptomatic, too, was its continuing embrace of the heroic myth of "holding the front" through hiding and moving funds around for chemical weapons disposal (and likely shifting some to contingency operations). Moreover, it did so despite greening proponents talking about the shifting context—especially technologically—of chemical weapons disposal. Meanwhile, greening proponents took advantage of shifting social, political, and economic circumstances in the states (especially in state legislatures and regulatory agencies) and near disposal sites in efforts to cut off army options. To these must also be added the proclivity of the Pentagon to mount campaigns to shape, prepare, and respond to these unaccustomed Gunbelt state regulatory initiatives, threatening as they were to disposal deadlines (real and contrived).

What Specifically Were They Fighting Over?

Wrought once more by this thrust-and-parry politics of contestation were crises of authority that persistently plagued and hobbled the greening of the chemical demilitarization process during the Clinton years. Moreover, in these authority crises, the targets or "fodder" for contestation again included nested battles over constitutional, collective choice, and operational rule sets. In terms of battles over constitutional rule sets, these again involved federalism issues. Illustrative in this instance was the targeting of authority rules related to the primacy or preemption of state authority and standards, rather than federal authority and standards, applicable to chemical weapons disposal. So, too, was the targeting of scoping rules dealing with functional responsibility among federal and state actors for emergency planning programs (e.g., between FEMA and the DoD) and among program offices. Also looming as background again were issues related to the unitary executive theory and the Antideficiency Act. This, as the military sought to maintain the supremacy of federal (national defense) over state decision makers when permit disputes arose.

These constitutionally and jurisprudentially important issues, in turn, helped shape and inform subsequent crises of authority over the collective choice and operational rule sets that followed. Especially noteworthy in this regard were battles over scoping and authority, information, aggregation, entry and exit, and positional rules. Among the most prominent disputes targeting scoping and authority rules was the dispute over re-delegation of funding and oversight responsibility for the chemical demilitarization program from the OSD to the army (collective choice rule sets).

Likewise notable was the targeting for contestation of such information and aggregation rules as NEPA regulations regarding how to assess and integrate the costs and benefits of alternatives to incineration (collective choice rules) and how to calculate "burn efficiency" and disposal rates at specific disposal sites (operational rules). To these, one also might add military challenges to the information and aggregation rules used in NRC and GAO studies that contradicted the army's position on the shelf life of M55 rockets. Similarly illustrative were efforts by greening proponents to stop the army from constructing disposal sites until feasibility studies for nonincineration technologies were reviewed by Congress.

Challenging enough in their own right, these crises of authority involving collective choice and operational rule sets also included the targeting of such entry and exit rules as how firm the "fence" was around both chemical weapons and military operations and maintenance funds. Fodder, too, in this regard were rules specifying what the appropriate boundaries should be for potentially affected areas when computing fatalities from toxic plumes. So, too, were contests targeting various position rules regarding who could or could not gain either a degree of transparency or direct participation in incineration disposal decisions. Included among those rules developed or targeted by the combatants, for example, was the creation by Congress of the ACWA Dialogue Committee to assist in evaluating incineration alternatives.

What Strategies and Tactics Did They Use?

Witnessed throughout these crises of authority were examples of various strategies and tactics used by the military that were reminiscent in attitude and in aim of the Cold War era. Not unlike in prior chapters, and in addition to the examples noted above, these repertoires of contestation included both issue (re)definition and ally (de)mobilization. Illustrative of the interaction of these two tactics, for example, were the army's efforts to gain allies by painting chemical weapons neutralization as creating toxic sludge that would require interstate transport to alleviate. Also illustrative were its efforts to draw boundaries in its fatality assessments to mobilize and demobilize actors (itself a boundary activation/deactivation strategy), to demobilize opposition with initial concessions at Aberdeen and Newport and later at Blue Grass, and to marshal support from foreign policy actors by touting U.S. embarrassment if CWC deadlines were not met.

Likewise present were efforts at countermobilization by greening proponents, especially as the demilitarization program tried to mobilize support for incineration in state legislatures and among state regulators. These included threats of lawsuits by grassroots groups such as the National Toxics Campaign, Greenpeace, and the CWWG if the army did not respond properly. Equally illustrative were the persistent efforts from U.S senators (e.g., Wendell Ford and Mitch McConnell), representatives (e.g., Peter DeFazio and Karen Shepard), governors (e.g., Evan Bayh), and whistle-blowers to fight incineration, publicize chemical weapons incineration problems, and further mobilize incineration opponents.

Also visible again were efforts at delegitimation, deinstitutionalization, and disinformation strategies by the military and its allies. Delegitimation repertoires were focused largely on challenging the legitimacy of studies that did not support the army's positions. In addition to the NRC studies noted above, these even included reports done by the DoD comptroller's office, as well as research by the Army Soldier, Biological, and Chemical Command and the Army Audit Agency. To these were joined such deinstitutionalization strategies as objective shifting and defunding tactics. Illustrating the former were Deputy Secretary

Hamre's efforts to devolve chemical weapons program authority to the army and to combine the PMCD and ACWA programs as mere best business practices under Secretary Cohen's DRI. Relevant, too, were congressional stop-and-start funding, the army's slow funding obligation rates, and its claims (embarrassingly discredited by Garant in the comptroller's office) that it had only enough funding to test two (rather than six) incineration alternatives. Marbled throughout the chapter were instances of both minor and egregious distortions of information designed to advance the army's arguments. These included the cooking of safety numbers, suppressing internal studies, and falsifying of data by chemical weapons disposal contractors.

What Were the Implications?

In the end, the consolidation phase of the trajectory of contestation accompanying efforts to get the army to perform chemical weapons demilitarization expeditiously while protecting public health and safety left halfway, halting, and patchworked structures, processes, and procedures in its wake. Was the chemical demilitarization program characterized by transparency, responsiveness, and resource reengagement by the end of the Clinton years? More so than during the Cold War, but nowhere near as much as needed. Indeed, during the Clinton years, the army remained stubbornly tied to its Cold War "mental models" or "schema" when it came to incineration.

Neither, however, did the army gain as much stability, predictability, and security of operations as it clearly preferred. By saying the "bastards could go no further," the army had heaped upon itself the opprobrium and lack of trust of state regulators and grassroots activists across the country. In the process, inter national chemical weapons disposal deadlines were missed. As I will illustrate in chapter 9, the travails of building a corporate sense of responsibility for pollution prevention, environmental research and development, and energy conservation in the U.S. military would come nowhere close to reaching the extent of obstinance, sleight of hand, and skullduggery witnessed in the chemical weapons demilitarization program. Yet progress there also would leave halfway, halting, and patchwork structures in its wake; send mixed signals about the priority of developing a beyond-compliance rather than a reactive green ethic in the services; and thus fail to ensure enduring progress in the post–Cold War era.

Notes

1. This vignette is summarized from James Kitfield, *Prodigal Soldiers* (New York: Simon and Schuster, 1995), 15.

2. It is important to note, however, that nearly 80 percent of the chemical weapons that have been demilitarized in the world since 1997 were destroyed in the United States. Moreover, the GAO

concluded that it would take Russia until 2027 at best to dispose of all its stockpiles. In addition, by 2006, nearly two-thirds of all U.S. chemical weapons were demilitarized.

3. "Rumsfeld Acknowledges Chem Weapon Disposal Deadline Won't Be Met," *DEA* 14, no. 8 (April 18, 2006): 8–9.

4. A chemical weapons system has four interrelated and complicated parts: (1) a delivery mechanism for the weapon, (2) munitions to disseminate the chemical agent, (3) the chemical agent and/or its activation system, and (4) the environment itself as a medium or receptor for disseminating the chemical agent to its intended targets.

5. CWWG, "Army Audit Agency Blasts Incineration Program: Managers Ignored Cost, Schedule and Environmental Compliance Rules in Thousands of Design Changes at Burn Sites," June 7, 2001; emphasis added, http://www.cwwg.org/pr_06.07.01audit.html (June 8, 2001).

6. Carl H. Builder, *The Masks of War: American Military Styles in Strategy and Analysis* (Baltimore: Johns Hopkins University Press, 1989), 106.

7. Stephen K. Scroggs, *Army Relations with Congress: Thick Armor, Dull Sword, Slow Horse* (Westport, CT: Praeger, 2000), 126.

8. "Army Pursues Alternatives to Incineration Chemical Weapons Stockpile," *DEA* 3, no. 18 (September 6, 1995): 13.

9. Seth Shulman, *The Threat at Home: Confronting the Toxic Legacy of the U.S. Military* (Boston: Beacon Press, 1992), 139. Bulk containers of chemical agent and all munitions are placed in dirt-covered igloos reinforced by concrete bunkers. See John W. Birks, "Weapons Foresworn: Chemical and Biological Weapons," in *Hidden Dangers: Environmental Consequences of Preparing for War,* ed. Anne H. Erlich and John W. Birks (San Francisco: Sierra Club Books, 1990).

10. J. D. Lloyd, 1984, "Maximum Credible Events (MCEs) and 1% Lethality Distances for DARCOM Chemical Agent Storage Sites," memorandum, Director, U.S. Army DARCOM Field Safety Activity, Charleston, Indiana, to Lt. Col. Leideritz, March 2, 1984.

11. Arthur D. Little, Incorporated, "M55 Rocket Separation Study," M55-OD-8, 1985.

12. "NRC Defends Incineration Amid Controversy Over Chemical Weapons," *DEA* 2, no. 17 (August 24, 1994): 7–8, at 8. The NRC panel argued that the data would not have changed its conclusions, whereas the army said it was merely holding on to the data to "verify the findings." But as Senator Ben Nighthorse Campbell (D-CO, later R) put it, this discovery was "one less reason to go ahead with incineration."

13. Birks, "Weapons Foresworn," 171.

14. Suzanne Marshall, "Chemical Weapons Disposal and Environmental Justice," November 1996, http://www.cwwg.org/history.html (December 11, 1996).

15. CWWG, "Chem-Weapons Disposal Chronology," July 9, 2001, http://cwwg.org/chronology .html (July 9, 2001).

16. "Army Offers Concessions in Response to Landmark Incineration Study," *DEA* 2, no. 8 (April 20, 1994): 4.

17. "Army Seeks Permit for Chemical Weapons Incinerator in Kentucky," *DEA* 3, no. 21 (October 18, 1995): 20–21. Whereas Tooele, for example, was slated to handle 42 percent of all chemical weapons disposals, Aberdeen and Newport handled only 1.5 percent of the nation's chemical weapons stockpile. The Aberdeen plant began operations in 2003; the Newport plant opened in 2004.

18. "NRC Calls Neutralization Best Option for Bulk Sites," *DEA* 4, no. 20 (October 2, 1996): 30, 27–29. Also see Sandor Schuman and John Rohrbaugh, "Four What Ifs? Evaluation of Alternative Technologies for the Destruction of Chemical Weapons," *Journal of Policy Analysis and Management* 23, no. 4 (2004): 901–8.

19. Army researchers, for example, found that neutralization produced two to three times more toxic liquid waste than the volume of the original agent.

20. For example, if alternatives to incineration were tried, Arthur Anderson consultants concluded, it would boost costs by $1 billion at Blue Grass and $2 billion at Tooele. Slowed, too, by anywhere from eighteen to fifty months would be the army's ability to gain RCRA operating permits necessary before prospective stockpile sites could begin operation.

21. "DoD Likely to Miss Chemical Weapons Destruction Deadline in Int'l Treaty," *DEA* Special Report (September 28, 1998): 1–3.

22. "Army Study Finds Auto-Ignition of Leaking M55 Rockets Unlikely," *DEA* 7, no. 21 (October 19, 1999): 7.

23. "U.S. Awards $600 Million Contract to Destroy Russian Chemical Weapons," *DEA* 5, no. 2 (January 15, 1997): 18.

24. "Despite Congressional Review, States May Decide Fate of Chem Demil Program," *DEA* 2, no. 10 (May 18, 1994): 22.

25. "Ford Amendment Forcing Alternative Destruction Program Revised," *DEA* 4, no. 13 (June 26, 1996): 12.

26. "Law Group to File Suit Over Planned Army Chemical Weapons Incinerator," *DEA* 3, no. 20 (October 4, 1995): 11. For instance, in Indiana, Kentucky, and Maryland, state regulations required incinerators to demonstrate burn efficiency rates of 0.0001 before issuing construction permits.

27. "Indiana Governor Urges Army to Slow Down on Its Path to Incineration," *DEA* 4, no. 16 (August 7, 1996): 14–15.

28. "Army Faces Many Challenges to Meeting CWC Destruction Deadline," *DEA* 7, no. 24 (November 30, 1999): 14.

29. "FDMA Launching Review of Emergency Program at Umatilla," *DEA* 8, no. 3 (February 8, 2000): 5–6. In late 1999, for example, lengthy delay-inducing investigations were started when a false alarm sounded at Umatilla, resulting in jammed telephone lines and outside loudspeakers giving conflicting instructions to citizens in English and Spanish in two different counties. Discerned from this review was that the army had no plans (or sense of responsibility for developing plans that by law were FEMA's responsibility), the County Emergency Management division lacked decontamination units, local hospitals had inadequate supplies of atropine to counter health effects from toxic accidents, and the Oregon Department of Environmental Quality had no plans for handling earthquakes (a major threat in the region).

30. "House Approves More Funding for R&D of Incineration Alternatives," *DEA* 4, no. 11 (May 29, 1996): 8.

31. "Citizens File Environmental Equity Complaint Against Pine Bluff," *DEA* 7, no. 14 (July 13, 1999): 8–9.

32. "Alabama Officials Want $70 Million for Incineration 'Impact Fees'," *DEA* 8, no. 16 (August 1, 2000): 14.

33. "Environmentalist Challenges Army's Estimate for Alternative Technologies," *DEA* 4, no. 24 (November 20, 1996): 14.

34. "Governor Advises DoD on Pueblo Destruction Technology Issues," *DEA* 7, no. 23 (November 16, 1999): 9–10.

35. The nation's "Big Ten" environmental groups are the Audubon Society, Environmental Defense, Isaac Walton League, National Parks Conservation Association, Natural Resources Defense Council, Nature Conservancy, National Wildlife Federation, Sierra Club, Wilderness Society, and the World Wildlife Fund.

36. "NRC Critiques Army Assessment Criteria for Incineration Alternatives," *DEA* 4, no. 2 (January 24, 1996): 18–19. The title of the NRC report was "Review of Acute Human-Toxicity Estimates for Selected Chemical Warfare Agents." Also see "Incineration Opponents Say Chemical Agent Exposure Levels are Flawed," *DEA* 6, no. 19 (September 22, 1998): 11–12; "GAO Says Chemical Agent Destruction Will Hit Cost Overruns," *DEA* 5, no. 5 (February 26, 1997): 11. This report was issued by the Army's Soldier, Biological, and Chemical Command. See CWWG, "Chem-Weapons Disposal Chronology."

37. Raytheon held the incineration contracts for the Johnston Atoll, Pine Bluff, and Umatilla. EG&G held the contract for Tooele.

38. "Plaintiffs Allege Witness Tampering in Tooele Whistleblower Case," *DEA* 4, no. 12 (June 12, 1996): 6–7.

39. "Accusations of Safety Deficiencies at Tooele Lead Utah to Investigate," *DEA* 4, no. 25 (December 4, 1996): 3.

40. "Whistleblower Charges Improper Waste Management at Tooele," *DEA* 5, no. 4 (July 1, 1997): 17.

41. "Whistleblower Alleges Tooele Hid Permit Violations from State," *DEA* 8, no. 1 (January 11, 2000): 4–5.

42. Nonstockpile weapons are known or suspected chemical weapons that are buried in at least 215 locations in thirty-three states. They consist largely of binary chemical weapons, recovered chemical weapons, and various other recovered weapons. In 1994, the army estimated that it would take approximately $12 billion to remediate nonstockpile weapons. See "Sierra Club Raising Alarms over Chemical Weapons Transport," *DEA* 2, no. 18 (September 7, 1994): 24; "House Approves Restriction on Chemical Weapons Transportation," *DEA* 2, no. 11 (June 1, 1994): 15–16. This action by Shepard actually supported the army's official position at the time that transportation was too dangerous, because older munitions were decaying and in fragile condition, which could set off catastrophic events.

43. "Murkowski's Chemical Weapons Amendment Dies in Conference," *DEA* 5, no. 23 (November 4, 1997): 11.

44. "Senator Pushes Mandate for Army Review of Incineration Alternative," *DEA* 2, no. 15 (July 27, 1994): 16–17.

45. "Seven Incineration Alternatives Pass First Test for Assessment," *DEA* 5, no. 22 (October 21, 1997): 20. Although seven alternatives had passed the army's threshold criteria for testing and deployment, full-scale testing for each of these seven was said to exceed available army funding. Environmentalists would push for testing of all seven.

46. Called the Assembled Chemical Weapons Assessment program when first established by Congress in 1996, its name was later changed in 2003 to the Assembled Chemical Weapons Alternatives program.

47. Ultimately, the ACWA Dialogue Committee certified that six alternative technologies should be tested further at all sites, a recommendation made by its Citizens Advisory Technical Team (CATT). The CATT was comprised of four citizens and a technical consulting firm selected by the Dialogue Committee.

48. "White House Seeks Mechanism to Delay Chemical Arms Destruction Deadline," *DEA* 5, no. 5 (February 26, 1997): 23.

49. "Hamre Orders Immediate Consolidation of Chemical Weapons Programs," *DEA* 6, no. 4 (February 24, 1998): 7–8.

50. "Reform Plan to Transfer Chemical Weapons Destruction Authority to Army," *DEA* 5, no. 24 (November 18, 1997): 5.

51. "New Head of Chem Demil Oversight Sees Cost Factors Coming Under Control," *DEA* 6, no. 7 (April 7, 1998): 22.

52. "Army Backs Off from Legislation to Merge Chem Demil Programs," *DEA* 7, no. 8 (April 20, 1999): 9.

53. "DoD Plans Complete Transfer of Chemical Demil Funding Authority in FY99," *DEA* 5, no. 26 (December 16, 1997): 4–5.

54. "DoD Watching Senate Proposal to Transfer Chem Demil to New Agency," *DEA* 6, no. 11 (June 2, 1998): 8.

55. "DoD Plans Complete Transfer of Chemical Demil Funding Authority in FY99," 4.

56. "DoD Watching Senate Proposal to Transfer Chem Demil to New Agency." The Defense Threat Reduction Agency was charged with countering the proliferation of weapons of mass destruction. The DoD's rationale for not transferring the ACWA program to this agency was that, by law, the program had to be run by an acquisition office. This obstacle, of course, could have been overcome by asking Congress to change the law. As we shall see, there was a move in Congress to do precisely this.

57. "Army Backs Off from Legislation to Merge Chem Demil Programs."

58. "Independent Assessment Calls for Chem Weapons Program Overhaul," *DEA* 6, no. 25 (December 15, 1998): 16.

59. Ibid.

60. The following quotations related to ACWA contracts are taken from "ACWA Contracts Still in Limbo as Congress Presses DoD for Answers," *DEA* 6, no. 15 (July 28, 1998): 3–4.

61. "House Severely Cuts Chem Demil Program, Denouncing DoD Practices," *DEA* 7, no. 15 (July 27, 1999): 4.

62. The following quotations related to Garant's memo are taken from "Internal Comptroller Memo Charges DoD Hid Chem Demil Funds," *DEA* 7, no. 12 (June 15, 1999): 3–14.

63. The following quotations related to House cuts are taken from: "House Severely Cuts Chem Demil Program," 4–5.

64. "Observers Say Findings Prove Money was Available for ACWA Tests," *DEA* 7, no. 16 (August 10, 1999): 7.

65. Ibid.

66. "Pentagon Nips Chem Demil Funding in Program Budget Decision," *DEA* 7, no. 25 (December 14, 1999): 5.

67. "Observers Say Findings Prove Money was Available for ACWA Tests."

68. "In About-Face, Pentagon Calls for Funding More ACWA Technology Tests," *DEA*, Special Report (July 30, 1999): 4.

69. Ibid.

70. Ibid., 3.

71. "Observers Say Findings Prove Money was Available for ACWA Tests."

72. Ibid.

73. "In About-Face, Pentagon Calls for Funding More ACWA Technology Tests."

74. "GAO Says Chem Demil Program Inadequately Managed Finances," *DEA* 8, no. 10 (May 9, 2000): 5.

75. "Internal Report Suggests Actions to Cut Cost, Delays in Chem Demil," *DEA* 8, no. 15 (July 18, 2000): 5.

76. "GAO Says Chem Demil Program Inadequately Managed Finances," 5.

77. "Pentagon Nips Chem Demil Funding in Program Budget Decision," 6.

78. Pace is quoted in Jerry Useem, "How to Make Great Decisions," *Fortune Magazine* 75 (June 27, 2005), http://jcgi.pathfinder.com/fortune/fortune75/articles/0,15114,1070964-2,00.html (May 6, 2006).

CHAPTER NINE

Pollution Prevention, Energy Conservation, and the Perils of Châteaux Generalship

During World War I commentators coined the term *châteaux generalship* to note favorably the wisdom of high commanders on the western front establishing their headquarters in châteaux located safely behind the front lines. Their expertise was too valuable to put in harm's way. In the immediate aftermath of a war in which so much blood and treasure were squandered in inconclusive trench warfare, however, châteaux generalship lost its luster. As military scholar B. H. Liddell Hart wrote in 1926, "In modern warfare, no feature has tolled more heavily against decisive results than the absence of the commander's personal observation and control."[1]

As I will illustrate in this chapter, commanders' abilities to know, see, and be observed are equally essential to creating a corporate sense of responsibility for greening the military through pollution prevention, energy conservation, and the purchase of environmentally preferred products (EPPs).[2] As in the private sector, the high short-term costs of investments in these areas can distort views of their long-term benefits in cost savings by avoiding ENR liabilities. Moreover, these costs become even more problematic when green investments are seen as threats to, rather than guarantors of, military readiness and modernization in an era of tight resources. Still, the shock of the end of the Cold War, and subsequent minishocks cascading through the national security state, buoyed the spirits of greening proponents for overcoming what Michael Barzelay and Colin Campbell call the "tyranny of distance."[3] The defense industry was undergoing massive consolidations, the production of global weaponry was rising, and the nascent ENR international standards movement to facilitate global trade was taking off.[4]

As in previous chapters, the hopes of proponents of these greening initiatives were not entirely dashed during the Clinton years. However, any progress made had to come in the wake of less politically charged but nonetheless real resistance. This resistance again tested the patience, will, and political acumen of greening proponents. As Maureen Sullivan, the DoD's director of compliance and pollution prevention, put the dilemma after seven years of pollution prevention's prominence in Sherri Wasserman Goodman's C³P² plus technology agenda, "There's [still] not a lot of acceptance all up and down the chain of command . . . so we have a long way to go."[5] Added the DoD's Bruce deGrazia, deputy assistant secretary for environmental quality, pollution prevention and energy conservation initiatives still were seen within the military services as "nice but not necessary."

Similarly, Tad McCall, an otherwise upbeat Air Force environment chief, averred in 2001 that the Pentagon still needed "to break down the wall between environmental and other programs."[6] On leaving office, Goodman noted that "it has been difficult for the military to accept changes in its business practices in order to better protect human health and the environment."[7]

Difficult indeed. By the end of the 1990s, the DoD's inspector general consistently was finding pollution prevention plans across the military services "not being finalized and program deficiencies occurring in funding, training, and awareness."[8] Likewise, on the environmental research and development front, a study by the DoD inspector general found that only twenty of sixty-three technologies developed over the previous decade actually were used at DoD sites, and only one was used at multiple sites.[9] Additionally, offensives by greening proponents persistently were met with counteroffensives by the services and their allies throughout the Clinton years. To see how and why this was the case in this arena of civil–military relations, this chapter analyzes the patterns of politics both driving and driven by three major questions. First, on whose terms would acquisition processes at DoD be revamped to reduce the purchase of products producing toxic pollutants? Second, to what extent could transparency of military operations occur to create top-line incentives for pollution prevention that would overcome bottom-line disincentives? Third, could the services be persuaded that investments in energy conservation would serve their readiness needs in cost-effective ways?

The Green Purchasing Challenge

The U.S. Army estimates that 75 percent of its operating costs for weapons systems stems from ENR cleanup requirements, whereas 20 to 25 percent of its labor costs for weapons systems is attributable to environmental compliance.[10] Likewise, a DoD study of total ownership costs for armor penetration munitions found that 10 to 20 percent of training costs was attributable to environmental compliance costs. But facts can be argued "round" or they can be argued "flat," the grist for issue framing and reframing whenever policy change or redirection is the aim of an administration. For proponents of greening the military's acquisition processes for products, parts, and chemicals, these data promised significant pollution prevention savings that could be reinvested in military readiness and modernization if "seen and known" by purchasing agents. Greening opponents, however, saw in the same data reasons to press for military exemptions from ENR requirements.

Confronting the ODC Challenge

The most immediate and visible "shock" on the pollution prevention front for the U.S. military began in 1987 when the United States signed the Montreal Protocol on Substances that Deplete the Ozone Layer. The protocol responded to an international scientific consensus that chlorine and bromine-based chemicals entering the atmosphere were depleting stratospheric ozone, thus exposing the public to cancer-causing ultraviolet radiation. Under the original terms of the protocol, chemical manufacturers were to reduce their emissions of five chloro-fluorocarbon chemicals by 50 percent (1995) and 85 percent (1997) of their 1986 levels, respectively. By 2000, they were to eliminate chlorofluorocarbon, halon, and carbon tetrachloride production and then stop producing methylchloroform by 2005. But when scientists concluded that these Class I ozone-depleting chemicals (ODCs) were depleting the ozone layer more rapidly than expected, the protocol was amended to end all chlorofluorocarbon production and "all but essential" halon production by 2000.

The rub for the Pentagon was that the U.S. military was among the world's largest consumers of ODCs.[11] Thus, after the United States signed the Montreal Protocol, the Reagan Pentagon joined the EPA and industry representatives in an ad hoc working group to identify alternative cleaning agents for chlorofluoro-carbon solvents used by the military. After the inauguration of President George H. W. Bush, Secretary of Defense Richard Cheney then directed the services to reduce their long-term dependence on chlorofluorocarbons and halons and to identify mission-critical uses of ODCs. Once identified, substitutes were to be found or exceptions granted until replacements were available.

Most troubling immediately to greening proponents was how the military approached this task, as well as the subsequent number and inconsistency of exemptions claimed. In terms of process, the George H. W. Bush administration left it to each service to determine the definition of "mission critical," issuing no clear definitional guidelines. The OSD then overwhelmingly deferred to the services' decisions.[12] With no corporate sense of responsibility coming from the E-Ring, the services categorized approximately 35 percent of their 1989 ODC purchases as mission critical and thus eligible for continued use, with definitional inconsistencies rife in these determinations.

Into this maelstrom of controversy waded the new Clinton administration. Consonant with her focus on creating a corporate sense of responsibility for pollution prevention, as well as with the administration's focus on acquisition reform generally, Goodman focused her efforts on eliminating common aspects of the acquisition process that caused the services to purchase ODCs in the first place. Present with her as a strong ally on Capitol Hill was Congressman Mike Synar (D-OK), chairman of the House Government Operations Committee. Synar, in fact, for two years had held hearings highlighting the military's poor acquisition record and pressing the Pentagon to incorporate pollution prevention into its acquisition process.

Buoyed by support from congressional allies such as Synar, Goodwin pressed ahead. Moreover, she did so buttressed by an executive order (EO) issued by Clinton during his first year in office. In trying to impose and diffuse a pollution prevention ethic throughout the federal government, Clinton's EO 12843 ordered all federal agencies to amend their procurement procedures and policies to reduce the use of ODCs "to the maximum extent practicable."[13] For the services, this meant identifying any military specifications (milspecs) and standards requiring the use of hazardous substances and toxic chemicals, and revising them accordingly. Also consonant with his NPR initiative, Clinton issued EO 12856 stipulating performance goals against which to measure pollution prevention progress.[14] By 1999, for example, the DoD was to reduce toxic chemical emissions by 50 percent from 1993 levels.

Prompted partially by these presidential initiatives and by the increasing cost impracticalities of tedious milspec review processes, Secretary of Defense William Perry and Acquisition Chief John Deutch launched the DoD's Acquisition Pollution Prevention Initiative in 1994. This initiative was designed not only to make it easier for industry and the services to validate then-untested alternatives to hazardous materials but also to identify production processes that were more environmentally benign. In the process, as Perry put it, the Pentagon would "dismantle [the milspecs] empire," which had favored particular vendors, buttressed ODC purchases, and preserved Cold War succor.[15]

Perry knew, of course, that the ongoing consolidation of the defense industry, the rise of global weaponry (i.e., of weapons manufactured with parts from a variety of nations and needing interoperability because of joint military actions with allies), and the nascent international standards movement (e.g., ISO 14000 ENR standards issued by the International Organization for Standardization to facilitate global trade) made such a move politically possible.[16] Against this background, the dominant subsystems of weapons contractors, weapons systems, and Gunbelt politicians described in chapter 3 were in flux and looking for their own version of stability, predictability, and security of operations.

Implementing Perry's charge, Deutch authorized the military to replace milspecs with various national and international standards (e.g., the National Aerospace Standard 411 [NAS 411], ISO 9000, and ISO 14000) when issuing contracts for new weapons systems.[17] Environmental activists, however, were wary. After all, the design of these standards was dominated by industry groups, dependant on self-certification, and focused on systems operations rather than on actual ENR outputs and outcomes (see below). What is more, the tendency for former military personnel to join these industries was legend and rife with the potential for mischief. Thus, to many greening proponents, this looked once again like the military trying to ensure "backdoor" self-regulation.

The Funding Games Begin

In the short term, these worries were overtaken by internecine bureaucratic warfare within the OSD, with Goodman at the heart of the imbroglio. Specifically, Goodman was disturbed that the administration's NPR efforts to deregulate the acquisition process at the Pentagon were giving short-shrift to environmental considerations. Led by Colleen Preston, deputy undersecretary of defense for acquisitions, that effort was not asking industry task forces to provide information on environmental performance. An equally distressed Synar immediately commissioned a GAO study on whether or not Preston's initiative was ignoring ENR concerns. Also strengthening Goodman's hand against Preston, Synar made sure that Get Moy, Goodman's director for pollution prevention, became the lead DoD person on the GAO probe.[18]

Temporarily on the defensive, Preston's process action team (PAT) on mil-specs and standards announced in mid-1994 that reducing toxic pollutants in weapons systems in the research and development process was to be a top priority in the Pentagon. The team then offered an integrated strategy (*Blueprint for Change*) for revising milspecs and standards to accomplish this end.[19] "The EO [12856] requires a level of effort that is comprehensive," wrote PAT members, "and therefore much greater than the ad hoc responses [taken by the Pentagon] to date to meet environmental requirements."[20] Also to help facilitate this transition, the team recommended creating a high-level toxic pollutant panel, headed by Goodman, and comprised of assistant and deputy undersecretaries implementing Secretary Perry's goals.

The PAT also warned candidly that incorporating pollution prevention into the acquisition process "may require extraordinary resources," estimating that nearly $68 million would be needed through FY 1998. They were quick to add, however, that "the long-term cost avoidance [catalyzed by doing so] will be an offset to the initial costs."[21] Again, however, the shocks and minishocks associated with the 1994 rout of the Democrats in the congressional midterm elections put Goodman on the defensive. Indeed, her ally Synar was defeated in the Democratic primary that year and would have lost the chairmanship of his committee had he won. Spawned in the aftermath of that election were persistent Congressional cuts in DoD funding for pollution prevention projects.

Still, in a series of high-visibility fora between 1994 and 1997, the DoD boasted about the services' progress in eliminating ODCs at their facilities and in their weapons systems. Especially heralded was the army's progress. Still, by 1997 the army's Acquisition Pollution Prevention Support Office painted a decidedly different picture.[22] The army chief of staff for installation management had required that Class I ODCs be eliminated at bases by the end of FY 2003. Yet 90 percent of army facilities still were dependent in 1997 on chlorofluorocarbon refrigerants, and 800,000 pounds of halon remained in fire-suppression systems. Likewise, the Acquisition Pollution Prevention Support Office reported in 2000 that 470,000 pounds of halon still remained at army installations alone. Moreover, by the final year of the Clinton administration, the Naval Audit Service labeled the service's ODC program a "material deficiency" area. Auditors noted that, despite progress, Class I ODC conversion was persistently a victim of the navy shifting its operations and maintenance funds to more pressing needs.[23]

Buttressing these assessments, auditors concluded in mid-2000 that "program managers [in both the army and navy] have not been following existing [ODC] policies."[24]

The reason, to some, was that only a "'spattering' of funding" existed for ODC acquisition reform during the mid to late 1990s.[25] Although the army, for instance, for years had defined "ODC elimination as a readiness issue, and not an environmental issue[,] . . . no central funding [from the Department of the Army was] available."[26] This meant that funding had to come out of installation operations and maintenance (O&M) budgets. But faced with an estimated $400 million in costs for developing and implementing ODC elimination plans at bases, along with the low-priority funding of ODC plans because they were not litigation- or compliance-driven, most installations were not producing these plans in a timely fashion.[27]

Granted, the military frequently acknowledged the need to invest in pollution prevention. Yet funding reductions belied this commitment, with needs related to core warfighting missions marginalizing ENR concerns in the E-Ring.[28] The army, for example, slashed funding for pollution prevention in its FY 2000 to FY 2005 program objective memorandum in order to fund training pay, an increase in contingency operation costs, and a Defense Working Capital Fund bill.[29] Most symbolically striking among these proposed cuts was the zeroing-out of funding for the M1 Abrams tank, the heralded "flagship" of the army's ODC-retrofitting program. Moreover, when Goodman's office launched an offensive to create a high-level task force within DoD to bring a corporate focus to phasing out ODCs, turf-conscious military services objected so strenuously that the proposal died aborning. Seeing this as yet another effort by Goodman to seize the services' control over the substance, scope, and pace of greening, the military framed a DoD-wide task force as superfluous, because the services already were developing ODC phase-out plans.

Muddling Through Strategically

But funding shortfalls, reprogramming of funds, litigation-driven priorities, and even turf consciousness were not the only complicating factors. To begin with, the Clinton administration's offensive regarding the acquisition program was animated by three contradictory principles. Two called for reregulating the acquisition process, whereas the third pushed for deregulating it. The three principles were (1) rewriting acquisition standards for ODCs and other pollutants to encourage the use of less environmentally destructive products, (2) moving away from writing prescriptive and procedurally based acquisition standards more generally under the NPR initiative, and (3) moving toward more process-oriented international standards such as ISO 14001 and NAS 411.

Fundamentally at odds, the ultimate "reconciliation" of these efforts was pragmatic but halfway, halting, and patchwork. Standards became merely guidance rather than how-to prescriptions, leaving friends and foes of greening with venues for challenging each other's positions.[30] As Maj. Bob Lang of the Air Force Materiel Command at Wright-Patterson Air Force Base put the dilemma in 1994, "The biggest problem we [had wasn't] the technical challenge; it [wasn't] the financial burden; it [was] the flow of communication."[31] But it did not help, said one interviewee, that the ODC review processes specified in Clinton's EO "were unplanned and unbudgeted" in the services' five-year program objective memorandum.[32] Unhelpful, too, was the de facto "procurement holiday" regarding weapons modernization that occurred during the Clinton years (see chapter 2). Not only compounding the military's zero-sum ENR budgeting mentality, the procurement holiday also extended the life of many ODC-dependent weapons beyond the Montreal Protocol's production deadlines and before replacements were available.[33]

Challenging enough in their own right, these constraints on aggressively greening the acquisition process were compounded when the services got DoD to do away with an overarching pollution prevention guidance plan. Accepting the argument that guidance from Goodman's office was redundant because the services already had issued guidance documents,[34] the Pentagon also disregarded around this time a DoD inspector general report excoriating the navy for regarding NEPA requirements as "optional" and "not applicable to its major Defense [sic] acquisition programs."[35] Mounting evidence also suggested that the military's cultural tendency to regard in-house assessments and less-complex technology as superior was making the greening of weapons acquisition unattractive to the services. Specifically, a predisposition remained to "not consider private-sector experience in the commercial market . . . an appropriate basis for considering military use of the same technology."[36] Relatedly, the military's fears about keeping complex weapons "mission capable" in battle made some queasy; green weapons might add complexity.[37]

Over the years, however, the military did progressively embrace NAS 411 and ISO 14001 approaches to acquisition, especially as milspecs reviews grew more costly and congressional funding diminished. Moreover, as Tad McCall argued in 1996, ISO 14001 was a "bridge" that the military services had to cross, because their contractors in global weaponry were doing so. Observed McCall: "Anyone who wants to do business internationally will have to get on board."[38] Related to this minishock cascading through a by then consolidating military-industrial complex, defense contractors frustrated by the tediously slow pace of milspecs reviews were demanding change. "We in industry," opined one, "can't wait seven years for these [milspecs] tests to be run to change to alternatives."[39]

Yet part of the initial attraction of standard-based systems was their apparent consonance with the military's heroic Cold War myth of sovereignty, secrecy, and sinecure. ISO 14001 standards, as envisioned, were predicated on self-assessments and self-policing by the military, whereas DoD had developed NAS 411 standards jointly with the aerospace industry. What is more, ISO 14001 did not compel polluters to disclose publicly any details of actual environmental performance, or even to be in compliance with ENR laws.[40] All the services had to do was show that an environmental management system was in operation.[41] Still, by the end of the Clinton years, the services began to rethink their flirtation with ISO 14001 standards, as ENR activists pilloried the Pentagon for not wanting independent auditors to review those systems.

The Saga of Environmentally Preferred Products

One final dimension of the greening of the military's acquisition process for products and services involves a greening offensive promoting the purchase of environmentally preferred products (or, as noted earlier in this chapter, EPPs). Products or services that are environmentally preferable have a lesser or reduced negative effect on human health and the environment when compared with competing products or services that serve the same purpose. This comparison includes more environmentally benign raw materials acquisition, production, manufacturing, packaging, distribution, reuse, operation, maintenance, and disposal of the product. In this endeavor, the aims are twofold: to protect the environment and to create guaranteed markets that might eventually make these products more price competitive with less environmentally benign products or services.

The EPP offensive began in 1993 to the applause of greening proponents with the issuance of EO 12873 (Federal Acquisition, Recycling, and Waste Prevention). Clinton subsequently tried in 1998 to build on and correct deficiencies in this EO. Specifically, he set timetables for developing short-term (2000) and long-term (2005 and 2010) plans for increasing the purchase and use of EPPs. Then, in 1999, the White House issued EO 13101 (Greening the Government Through Waste Prevention, Recycling, and Federal Acquisition) and EO 13134 (Developing and Promoting Biobased Products and Bioenergy). Both added so-called biobased products to the list of EPPs.[42]

Importantly, again, all of these initiatives were conspicuously silent about funding for meeting timetables set or consequences for failing to do so. EO 12873, for example, called only for agencies to give preference to, rather than mandate the purchase of, EPPs, a goal that went largely unfulfilled by the military as core missions claimed resources.[43] Then, when Senate Agriculture Committee Chairman Tom Harkin (D-IA) threatened legislation in 1998 to require federal agencies to use EPPs unless impossible, DoD officials countered that they already had an EPP program. They pointed specifically to their work incorporating EPP information into the Federal Logistics Information System. Unsatisfied, Harkin told acquisition officials that they had to do more than just keep a database; among other things, DoD had to mandate the purchase of EPPs in order for sufficient progress to occur.[44]

Moreover, even when progress did occur, strategy-structure mismatches continued to plague efforts to heighten "affirmative procurement" requirements for

EPPs. These were slowed sometimes by protective turf wars. For example, the environment and acquisition communities within the army quarreled over who would implement EO 13101. Senior environment and installation officials argued that acquisition officials were responsible for implementing the program, whereas the latter said the former were.[45] Likewise, although the EPA, DoD, DOE, and General Services Administration tried throughout Clinton's second term to add required "environmental attributes" to the Federal Logistics Information System for all items they purchased, this effort was still very incomplete when he left office. Then, in 2000, the Army Audit Agency reported that the service's EPP program still lacked policy to implement the program, that its roles and responsibilities remained undefined, and that key management controls and reporting systems did not exist.[46]

The Top-Line Transparency Challenge

Although the greening of the acquisition process was clearly an important aim throughout the Clinton years for addressing longer-term "bottom-line" funding issues, creating a "top line" of pollution reduction outcomes was equally important to greening proponents. Central to this greening offensive was making the true life-cycle costs of military operations more transparent. Only sensitivity to these numbers, proponents argued, could make pollution prevention a financially attractive option to the services. The rub, however, was that Goodman lacked a solid statutory basis to alter financial incentives in this fashion.

The Emergency Planning and Community Right-to-Know Act (EPCRA) of 1986 had nominal applicability to Goodman's goals for greater financial transparency. In passing EPCRA, Congress tried to ensure that those living near polluting facilities would be aware of any chemical risks they faced. Thus EPCRA required polluters releasing significant quantities of over three hundred toxic chemicals to self-report the volume and disposition of their releases in annual Toxics Release Inventory (TRI) reports. Using this "regulation by revelation" or "blame and shame" approach, Congress hoped polluters would reduce emissions voluntarily.[47] Yet EPCRA specifically had exempted the military from TRI reporting; knowledge of what chemicals the military used or how they were stored could prove dangerous in Soviet hands.

As the first administration to take office free from Cold War threats, however, the Clinton administration felt the time had arrived for ending this exclusion in the interests of environmental security. Opting for a transparency that cut to the quick of the military's Cold War ethic, President Clinton's White House offensive began with a series of EOs that were elaborated and extended during the 1990s. Clinton first directed all federal departments and agencies to comply with the reporting requirements of the TRI (in EO 12856 and later in EO 12969).[48] Meanwhile, Goodman focused at the OSD level on two transparency-related initiatives that became ample fodder for contestation during her eight years at the Pentagon. First, she tried to institutionalize environmental life-cycle cost accounting (ELCCA) in the acquisition process, framing it as in the self-interest of the armed forces.[49] "'All our studies have shown,' she argued, 'that if the program manager focuses only on what it takes to get a weapons system developed and doesn't account for . . . operation and maintenance savings [from greening], then we've missed' ways to significantly reduce logistics costs" for the services.[50] Second, Goodman worked to set up effective TRI accounting structures, processes, and procedures while working the Hill to amend EPCRA to include the military.

The ELCCA Offensive Begins

When Goodman began her campaign to mandate the use of ELCCA in the acquisition process, even some in her own office worried about a revolt of flag officers if the proposal placed "an additional workload [on the military] when resources are coming down."[51] However, it was not just the workload and budget costs of this process that worried flag officers. With competition growing among the services for different weapons platforms in an increasingly zero-sum funding environment, they feared that ELCCA could give a price advantage or disadvantage to one service's weapons systems over another's.

Unpersuaded, Goodman pressed ahead, and when Perry approved a comprehensive pollution prevention strategy for acquisition and procurement in 1994, he mandated ELCCA for *all* products purchased by the services, including weapons systems.[52] Not surprisingly, however, those advantaged by the existing acquisition process and their allies in Congress began dragging their feet on implementing the plan or pressing TRI legislation on the Hill. Confronted by this subtle and sometimes subterranean counteroffensive, Goodman and her colleagues seized on a 1995 "rolling report" of the Defense Science Board (DSB) to advance their cause in the Pentagon and in Congress.[53]

A biting attack on the military's greening efforts generally, the report noted that the military still was not adequately incorporating environmental life-cycle costs in the acquisition process.[54] Noting the "growing potential [of ENR violations] for degrad[ing] operational readiness," the "skyrocket[ing]" costs of cleanups, and the spiraling risks to base commanders of personal and financial liabilities for environmental infractions, the DSB excoriated the military for its laxity.[55] The military promptly counterattacked, impugning the integrity of both the DSB and Goodman's office. Not only were the report's conclusions uninformed by input from the military services, but they relied only on briefings and papers by officials in Goodman's office. "The bottom line?" groused one military observer at the time. "They're [Goodman and her colleagues] trying to justify all the money" that her office spends.[56]

This impugning of motives notwithstanding, the mid to late 1990s saw pockets of actors in the Pentagon actually pushing for ELCCA in areas they controlled. For example, in 1994, a joint service group was charged by the Joint Logistics Commanders with bringing a corporate perspective to reducing hazardous materials in weapons systems.[57] Known as the Joint Group on Acquisition Pollution Prevention (JG-APP), these proponents launched an initiative in 1997 to eliminate the disincentives against greening weapons systems occasioned by the military's historical focus on greening individual weapons systems.[58] Instead, members sought to identify common environmental life-cycle costs incurred by all the services across the production processes of all weapons systems and to find cost-effective alternatives to them.[59]

Nor was this transparency offensive focused solely on the services. In mid-1995, for example, the Defense Logistics Agency sought to make the environmental records of contractors a consideration in allocating contracts.[60] To these ends, it proposed evaluating firms on several ENR dimensions. These included their past environmental commitment, how green their present operations were, and what their compliance record had been over the years. Not unlike a broader initiative proposed by the Clinton administration for all federal agencies, however, industry opposition quickly scuttled this proposal.[61] Too much succor was at stake, it seems, for companies to put contracts at risk on ENR grounds, even with global weaponization under way.

Even so, much remained to correct *inside* the military before ELCCA could be meaningfully institutionalized as a Pentagon-wide ethic. The military, for example, repeatedly packaged ENR data in opaque ways that made it difficult for pollution prevention to gain as much traction as it might in acquisition processes. As noted, until the JG-APP initiative to develop a cross-weapons perspective, ELCCA was limited to single weapons systems. This meant that if a single weapons program wanted to "go green," manufacturers had to create a separate production line for it, at considerable added expense. Moreover, no set of metrics existed for determining common and significant ENR cost drivers across weapons systems (e.g., hazardous waste disposal costs). Consequently, analyses were costly, redundant, and unattractive for the individual services to conduct. Nor did it help that the military made ENR cost measures in their analyses indistinguishable from other cost components. This made it nearly impossible for program managers to see where environmental cost savings might accrue.[62]

Finally, transparency-reducing and conflict-spawning constraints on greening inured during the Clinton years in the military's persistent failure to compute its total environmental liability accurately.[63] When its first consolidated statement was issued in FY 1997, the Pentagon's estimate of $27 billion for ENR liabilities was excoriated by auditors as "wildly underestimated."[64] Particularly egregious was DoD's refusal, after repeated prodding by the GAO, to include estimates for liabilities associated with disposal of hazardous wastes and remediation of environmental contamination.[65] The services also failed to offer estimates of liabilities for major weapons systems (such as aircraft, missiles, ships, and submarines) and for ammunition. Claiming that it had neither the resources nor the time to provide this information in its FY 1997 estimates, DoD promised more accurate and complete accounting in subsequent years.

Even then, however, private sector firms bridled at what they saw as a double standard: The military estimated its liabilities on the basis of cleanup remedies and shortcuts that government regulators would never allow corporate polluters to take. To be sure, the Pentagon included a broader swath of weapons systems in subsequent reports, with projections of ENR liabilities spiraling to nearly $80 billion and over $63 billion in FY 1999 and FY 2000, respectively. Yet the DoD inspector general still criticized both reports as "unreliable and likely to be materially understated." In the FY 1999 report, for example, the services still failed to estimate ENR liabilities for Nimitz-class nuclear aircraft carriers, Black Hawk helicopters, F-15 Strike Eagles, and the C/KC-135 Stratotanker. Worrisome, too, were still-rampant "deficiencies in internal controls and accounting systems."[66]

Thus a decade after ENR liability reports were first required by Congress and three years after Secretary of Defense Cohen's DRI began, a stunning "lack of adequate financial management and feeder systems for compiling accurate and reliable financial data" remained.[67] Moreover, liabilities that *were* reported remained unverifiable "because of insufficient controls and inadequate audit trails" during both the FY 1999 and FY 2000 cycles.[68] Nor were these problems limited to any one of the military services. The inspector general found, for instance, that each service's FY 2000 liability estimates lacked "supporting documentation" and were premised on "procedures and controls" so inadequate that reported values lacked credibility.[69] Nor, until the late 1990s, did DoD afford installations guidance about what constituted "environmental costs" when assessing liabilities. Then, nine months after Clinton left office, the Pentagon's inspector general again scolded DoD for lacking a standardized ELCCA system for weapons purchases.[70]

The Travails of TRI

With ELCCA progress halfway, halting, and patchwork amid these complications, TRI reporting *was* done during the Clinton years. Indeed, in several instances, the services themselves took the initiative. What Goodman was not able to do, however, was get permanent statutory authorization mandating TRI reporting for the military. Arguably, the sources of these seemingly contradictory results (i.e., low resistance to TRI reporting and fighting statutory amendments to require it in EPCRA) were threefold. First, toxic reductions were quite easy to obtain as bases closed and realigned across the country in the post–Cold War era.[71] Second, reporting these reductions helped diffuse congressional interest in stronger transparency requirements. Third, as subsequent rounds of realignment and closures at bases were delayed during the Clinton years, easy, less costly, and less mission-irrelevant reductions in toxic pollutants were not as readily available to trumpet.

Thus when Senator Paul Coverdale (R-GA) tried legislatively to apply TRI reporting requirements to all federal facilities, the services worked through their congressional allies on key House and Senate oversight committees to squash the effort.[72] Neither, however, did greening proponents in the Pentagon, the Congress, or the White House retreat from their efforts to enhance the transparency of the military's operations. By late 1998, for instance, Goodman mounted an offensive amid service opposition to declare "as DoD policy" that military training ranges were "facilities" and thus had to meet TRI reporting requirements.

In addition, on the heels of Coverdale's failure came Clinton's EO 13148 (Greening the Government Through Leadership in Environmental Management). Dubbed as being "as forward-thinking an executive order as we've [ENR military personnel] had in a while," Clinton's initiative required the services to reduce their annual use of "at least fifteen 'priority'" TRI chemicals by 40 percent between 2001 and 2005.[73] Yet once again the aims of the EO were compromised by not affording new resources and by allowing the *military* to perform regulatory compliance audits. Self-regulation remained the coin of the Pentagon's realm.

The Bottom-Line Energy Conservation Challenge

Similarly challenging for Goodman and her associates was her offensive to institutionalize a corporate sense of responsibility for energy conservation within the U.S. military. Consider the situation she faced in this regard upon her appointment in 2001. An EO issued by President George H. W. Bush in 1991 and the enactment in 1992 of the Energy Policy Act were designed to push energy (and water) conservation to the forefront within private *and* public organizations. Under the Energy Policy Act, consumers like the military were to reduce petroleum fuel use by 10 percent and 30 percent by 2000 and 2010, respectively. They also were tasked by the year 2000 with reducing energy consumption in their buildings and other operations (e.g., flight simulators) by 20 percent. Yet as one DoD official observed in 1994, conservation was only "looked upon as an irritant" within the military during the first Bush presidency.[74]

All this was but a prologue to the early Clinton years, however. Again, Clinton hit the ground running by issuing a series of EOs that pushed conservation expectations progressively higher for the military services. In 1994, for example, EO 12902 (Energy Efficiency and Water Conservation at Federal Facilities) charged the Pentagon with finding ways to reduce energy consumption 30 percent by the year 2005. However, the agency-forcing aspects of this initiative were watered down not only by a deferred deadline, but with the words "to the extent that these measures are cost-effective." Reasonable, yes, but wiggle room for opponents nonetheless. Moreover, even as the DSB called for additional research on more fuel efficient jet fuel (a major component of DoD's fuel consumption), Congress cut funding in 1999, in part to save money for military operations abroad.[75]

Left wanting early on, too, were budget and accounting systems that worked against energy conservation. Conservation projects still were not formally integrated into DoD's budgeting processes by the mid-1990s. Thus they were pitted against immediate readiness priorities in the O&M budgets of base commanders. Moreover, as one service member observed, the DoD comptroller will put any cost savings realized from energy conservation into "things that fight" (i.e., weapons and readiness) rather than into additional conservation on military installations.[76]

What Clinton appointees did try to address were the initial capital costs incurred by the services for energy conservation. Consistent with Cohen's DRI, for instance, the Pentagon launched a program to leverage the services' resources for energy conservation by negotiating Energy Savings Performance Contracts (ESPCs) with private utilities. In this program, private utility contractors were to invest upfront in the upgrading of military facilities (e.g., upgrading old heating systems) and await payment from the monies saved by these conservation investments.[77]

Yet this initiative, too, quickly ran into financial and conceptual problems. By 1999, the House authorized only enough funding for 20 percent of ESPCs scheduled in the FY 2000 construction cycle. This was a devastating outcome that the Senate could only partially correct in conference.[78] Moreover, this incident made clear to private utilities precisely how volatile funding for ESPCs could be in the years ahead, an unattractive prospect because stable funding is essential in these types of projects. Consequently, the Pentagon watched a significant bidder drop-off in bidders for contracts during the remainder of the Clinton administration. Hindered in the process was a program originally expected to produce a fourfold return on investment in energy conservation, savings the military wanted to reprogram for readiness needs.[79]

While these perverse incentives and funding cutbacks transpired on the public utility front, President Clinton issued yet another conservation-related EO (13031) in 1996.[80] This time he pressed the military to pursue more aggressively the purchase of alternative fuel vehicles to save energy and reduce greenhouse gas emissions. Moreover, he hoped these purchases would foster a larger market for alternative fuel vehicles (AFVs) and thus provide incentives for building a nationwide AFV refueling and maintenance infrastructure. Once more, however, congressional defunding and operational problems quickly emerged. These forced the services to announce late in 1998 that they would fail by 9 percentage points to meet Clinton's goal of increasing the percentage of AFVs to 33 percent of their fleet, a still not insignificant achievement.[81]

Nor did the White House's efforts end here, although they continued to proceed without commensurate funding increases, credible accounting structures, or meaningful consequences for noncompliance. For example, Clinton's EO 13123 raised energy conservation targets, requiring the military to reduce energy consumption 30 percent from 1985 levels by 2005 and 35 percent by 2010.[82] But as fast as the White House issued these EOs, the military was just as fast in asking for waivers from them. In 1998, for example, the Pentagon got exempted from meeting energy efficiency standards for military support, training, and combat vehicles. Congress, the services correctly argued, was unlikely to fund the retrofitting of these vehicles adequately.[83]

Also in an ironic twist, the pace of the military's conservation efforts was slowed by a 1998 Clinton White House decision to link energy conservation directly to greenhouse gas reduction under the proposed Kyoto Protocol. Although certainly not debilitating, this spillover effect complicated acquisition and energy conservation reforms appreciably, because they came amid a rancorous House and Senate debate over Kyoto. House appropriators who opposed Kyoto feared that Clinton would try to implement the protocol administratively. Consequently, they put language in the FY 1999 budget prohibiting all federal agencies from implementing Kyoto requirements.[84] Then, months later, Senate opponents of Kyoto put language into the FY 2000 budget to block implementation of Clinton's EO 13123 on energy efficiency and water conservation. After Clinton threatened a veto that they did not have the votes to override, opponents stripped this language from the bill, replacing it with language that curtailed the EO.[85]

Nor did implementation woes end there when it came to greenhouse gas reductions, their linkage to Kyoto, and mounting costs for contingency operations. For example, Congress cut $98 million from DoD's portion of the Federal Energy Management Program in the FY 1998 Defense Appropriations Act.[86] It did so by shifting money from the program's accounts into the services' O&M and readiness accounts, a move defended as integrating energy efficiency projects more fully into current programs and programmatic thinking. Yet the short-term results of this action were also clear and consonant with the aims of opponents of the Kyoto Protocol: A variety of energy-efficiency projects were delayed indefinitely.

Discussion

During the Punic War, the Roman historian Polybius saw in Scipio Africanus the epitome of heroic leadership: "He could both see what was going on, and being seen by all his men, he inspired the combatants with great spirit."[07] Similarly, greening proponents in this chapter believed that "seeing" total ENR costs, potential toxic threats, and dollar savings was critical to their efforts to advance greening in the U.S. military. Yet despite a less intensely antagonistic posture toward pollution prevention, energy conservation, and EPPs because of the potential long-term savings promised, a familiar pattern of politics quickly prevailed. In the process these politics constrained the progress made in greening the acquisitions process, made the costs of ignoring ENR impacts less visible, and complicated improved energy conservation. Yes, progress was again made in this area of civil–military relations. But not without resistance, and not on a scale or with a level of institutionalization necessary to advance a corporate sense of responsibility for a beyond-compliance ethic during the Clinton years.

Was There a Trajectory of Contestation?

As in the preceding chapters, the overall trajectory of contestation in this hybrid policy arena began with perceptions of historical-structural mismatches, followed quickly by offensives (in this case, largely led by Goodman's initiatives and Clinton's EOs) and counteroffensives by opponents. These again produced crises of authority from which misaligned consolidations of structures, processes, and procedures resulted after bargaining among the contestants, all of whom made accommodations to realpolitik. These in turn not only planted the seeds for future reform efforts, but guaranteed a role for the combatants in those battles. Once more, too, the patterns of politics witnessed throughout this trajectory of contestation over pollution prevention, energy conservation, and the purchase of EPPs were steeped in the pursuit of the political, organizational, and personal prerogatives perceived by the combatants.

What Motivated the Participants' Behavior?

Taking each component of this trajectory of contestation in order, first came perceptions of historical–structural mismatches spawned by the shock of the end of the Cold War, which in turn inspired minishocks related to acquisition reform, pollution prevention, and energy conservation. Greening proponents saw Cold War milspec systems as too often mandating the purchase of toxic and greenhouse gas-emitting products now banned or targeted for reduction by U.S. or international laws (e.g., the Montreal Protocol and EPCRA). They also saw Cold War pollution prevention structures, processes, and procedures as out of step with post–Cold War operational and tactical doctrines requiring global weaponry, as well as with the global consolidation of the defense weapons industry and the greening of the international standards movement (e.g., ISO 14001). Moreover, in an era of significant military drawdowns in force size, falling or stunted budget growth, and heightened operational tempo, many perceived that energy conservation (along with pollution prevention) could save money that might be reallocated to military readiness and weapons modernization needs.

Evidence in this chapter also shows again how disagreements by greening proponents and opponents were intensely fueled by and filtered through perceptions of principle, self-interest, and realpolitik, and they were framed (and reframed over time) as issues in ways calculated to advance these interests. Moreover, one again sees how this sense making, filtering, and subsequent issue framing were affected by perceptions of history (i.e., organizational culture, inherited resources, structural arrangements, and constellations of power); context (i.e., the social, economic, political, and technological situation they find themselves in at the time); and contingency (i.e., how delays incurred by greening initiatives would affect core military missions). In turn, these were susceptible to shifts in issue valence (i.e., positive or negative connotations) and boundary effects (i.e., spillover effects from other issues).

In launching their offensives, for example, greening proponents framed reform issues in light of a variety of ongoing changes in economic, political, and legal contexts, as well as contingency factors related to the impact of delay on core military missions. These included post–Cold War consolidation of the weapons industry, the need for joint military operations with other nations (e.g., in the North Atlantic Treaty Organization) who embraced international green standards, and more aggressive enforcement of ENR laws in the post–Cold War era. These laws, they argued, required milspecs reform, greater transparency and appreciation for ENR life-cycle costs of purchases, and energy conservation. Conceding that these were extensive and costly short-term behavioral changes, proponents nevertheless touted their long-term savings for reinvestment in the military's core mission.

In response, the military and its allies initially launched their counteroffensive by framing the issues as ones of impracticality, inordinate costs, and threats to core military missions. Respectively, replacements for ODCs were not available, nor was the infrastructure for AFVs; inventorying ODCs and retrofitting fleets were too costly in the short term given other funding constraints; and acquisition delays, product shortages, and weapons malfunctions could threaten core military missions. Moreover, once congressional opponents of the Kyoto Treaty linked Clinton's EOs for energy conservation to Kyoto (i.e., once issue boundary effects occurred), energy conservation orders were framed negatively (i.e., they took on a negative valence).

More precisely, greening opponents emphasized the threats to national security that transparency, international standards, and Kyoto Treaty emission reductions could afford, as well as the inconsistencies between Clinton's NPR, milspecs reduction, and greening. To these problems, they also linked (and, hence, framed) the acquisition targets for EPPs and AFVs as impractical because of poor information, product shortages, and lack of AFV infrastructure. Indeed, not until the costs of oil surged into the seventy-dollars-per-barrel range during President George W. Bush's second term did a rationally self-interested military begin focusing heavily on carbon fuel replacements. To be sure, although the military and its allies positively framed greening initiatives like environmental management systems, ISO 14001, and ESPCs, they also saw virtue in the regulatory relief they could offer. These included self-certification; a focus on process rather than results; load-shedding of controversial ENR responsibilities to private utilities; and avoidance of costly, lengthy, and mission-threatening milspec reviews.

Granted, framing these issues in this fashion was in no way inaccurate. But more fundamentally at stake for the services were three other threats related to history, context, and contingency. The first was the threat the military perceived to such cultural icons and path-dependent processes as service-driven weapons purchases and the Pentagon's focus on purchasing individual weapons systems (i.e., organizational history). For example, the JG-APP threatened the military's historic focus on individual weapons systems. Illustrative, too, was how opponents initially brandished cultural taboos from the Cold War era about threats to service members from complex and uncertain green weaponry.

The second threat perceived was to the military's historical ability to control the substance, pace, and scope of greening in general, and in particular to existing decision structures, processes, and procedures supporting that dominance. Some of these involved changes prompted by shifts in the aforementioned political, economic, and social context, such as the push for milspec reforms, TRI and ELCCA, and Kyoto. These brought new actors with greening interests into existing acquisition decision structures; placed responsibilities (e.g., milspec reviews and energy conservation audits) incommensurate with existing resources in those systems (i.e., created imbalanced energy loads); and linked to acquisition processes green values related to interoperability, the globalization of weaponry, and the international standards movement (i.e., opened up decision and access structures).

The third threat perceived involved the contingency relationship between time delays and the military's warfighting mission. More precisely, the services worried about their ability to acquire the weapons they wanted to complete their missions as they defined them. Ostensibly, and accurately, the services feared that their war-fighting mission could be compromised through delays, product shortages, or weapons malfunctions. Less nobly, however, they also worried that ELCCA threatened existing and future allocations of weapons succor within and across the services because of its potential to tip the costs of weapons systems. Put more directly, the military worried that the logrolling decision rules historically characterizing weapons acquisition (e.g., the informal agreement to "live and let live" by not challenging each others' requests) were jeopardized. In the process, enhanced civilian control of acquisition processes might occur, the historical bête noire of the services since the tenure of Defense Secretary Robert McNamara in the 1960s. Indirectly threatened, after all, were the services' "information asymmetry" and thus their power advantage over the OSD when it came to specifying weapons needs.

What Specifically Were They Fighting Over?

Wrought once more by this thrust-and-parry politics of contestation were crises of authority that persistently plagued and hobbled the pollution prevention, energy conservation, and EPP processes during the Clinton years. Moreover, in these authority crises, the targets or "fodder" for contestation again included nested battles over constitutional, collective choice, and operational rule sets. In terms of battles over constitutional rule sets, the primary battles were more tangential than in previous chapters but nonetheless real. Most notable was where one draws the line between citizens' constitutional rights to know what the government is doing and the potential national security impacts of that information being of use to actual or potential adversaries (e.g., TRI reporting requirements). More implicitly, issues related to U.S. sovereignty versus international treaty commitments also were involved (e.g., regarding the Kyoto Protocol).

Important also in this chapter was the targeting for conflict of various nested collective choice and operational rule sets. Especially noteworthy in this regard, and consistent with the patterns of politics described in previous chapters, were battles over entry and exit, scoping, authority, information, and aggregation rules. Targeted, for example, were entry and exit rules applicable at both the service and military base levels. These included rules defining what constituted mission-critical ODCs, EPPs, and the kinds of military vehicles falling under Clinton's executive orders on energy conservation. Controversy also swirled over scoping and authority rules regarding whether the OSD or the individual services would define "mission critical" for ODCs. Fodder as well were operational rule sets determining if, how much, and when ELCCA should be a consideration in weapons purchases (i.e., over information and aggregation rules). Moreover, payoff rules were in play throughout this initiative, including rules related to installation O&M carrying the burden of costs related to ODC elimination studies and the potential of ELCCA to shift the distribution of weapons purchases.

What Strategies and Tactics Did They Use?

While more narrowly tailored and applied on a less intense scale in this chapter, strategies and tactics again animated these battles that were reminiscent in attitude and aim of those pursued during the Cold War era. Not unlike in prior chapters, and in addition to the issue-framing strategies noted above, one finds evidence of ally (de)mobilization, deinstitutionalization, delegitimation, and (dis)information strategies in this chapter. Taking mobilization strategies first, most notable were the Pentagon's efforts to get congressional allies to stop legislative initiatives mandating TRI reporting and assessing defense contractors on the basis of their ENR records. Illustrative, too, were the military's initial efforts to gain legislation excluding the services from environmental liability reporting and then to calculate liabilities differently from private polluters. Also related were the military's claims that private sector experience was not applicable to weapons purchases. Meanwhile, on the demobilization front, the Pentagon tried to load-shed energy conservation responsibilities to private utilities under the ESPC program in order partially to shift the ENR controversies related to them to the private sector.

Ally mobilization and demobilization strategies like these by the military, of course, were met again by countermobilization strategies by greening proponents. These included the aforementioned efforts on the acquisitions reform front by Congressman Synar (and urged on by Goodman) to get Colleen Preston's process action team to consider environmental impacts when doing milspecs reform. They also included continuing efforts by Senator Harkin to get more faithful DoD implementation of the EPP program, as well as initiatives by greening proponents in Congress to push for TRI and ELCCA legislation. Goodman also again pressed repeatedly and sometimes successfully to get her pollution prevention initiatives imposed and diffused by Clinton (through his EOs), in Congress (e.g., when Synar assigned her director, Get Moy, to lead the GAO probe of the process action team on milspecs), and through her supervisors in the OSD (e.g., Perry and Deutch when it came to launching their Acquisition Pollution Prevention Initiative).

Likewise, albeit not as prevalent or severe as in prior chapters, among the most significant delegitimation tactics observed was the military impugning the integrity of the DSB as becoming Goodman's lapdog when its rolling report criticized greening progress in the military. Simultaneously, corporate deinstitutionalization strategies included defunding, diversion, information, and devolution tactics. Respectively, these included "starts and stops" in congressional and Pentagon funding, diversion of funds by the military to contingency operations, poor Pentagon guidance for EPP and TRI information technology systems, and devolving ODC "mission critical" evaluations to the services absent clear and consistent guidance. What is more, when these were not formidable enough obstacles to full and continuing progress in countering greening initiatives, disinformation tactics further complicated pollution prevention and energy conservation efforts. Most notable in this regard was the military's repeated failure to afford complete and accurate costs of environmental liabilities during the Clinton years.

What Were the Implications?

In the end, the consolidation phase of efforts to green the acquisitions process, advance pollution prevention, and gain greater amounts of energy conservation left halfway, halting, and patchwork structures, processes, and procedures in its wake. Combined with the mixed signals sent by these patterns of politics about greening priorities, all this once more left the military woefully shy of the accountability, transparency, and resource reengagement necessary to institutionalize a beyond-compliance ethic in the U.S. military. Thus, as in previous chapters, bequeathed to the post-Clinton years was a still formidable strategy-structure misalignment, one that worked against institutionalizing the mental models and schema that such an ethic required. Moreover, this misalignment also had remnants of Cold War châteaux generalship in it, remnants sorely compromising the "seeing and knowing" of the true ENR costs so vital to building a beyond-compliance ethic in the post–Cold War era. What the Bush administration did with this and other aspects of Clinton's greening legacy during the new president's first six years in office is the subject of chapter 10.

Notes

1. B. H. Liddell Hart, *Scipio Africanus* (1926; reprint, Cambridge, MA: Da Capo Press, 1994), 33.

2. Environmentally preferred products or services have a lesser or reduced effect on human health and the environment when compared with competing products or services that serve the same purpose. This comparison considers raw materials acquisition, production, manufacturing, packaging, distribution, reuse, operation, maintenance, or disposal of the product or service.

3. Michael Barzelay and Colin Campbell, *Preparing for the Future: Strategic Planning in the U.S. Air Force* (Washington, DC: Brookings Institution Press, 2003), 137.

4. Global weaponry is manufactured with parts from a variety of nations and needed interoperability of parts because of joint military actions with allies.

5. "DoD Official Cites Resistance by Military to Apply P2 to Achieve Compliance," *DEA* 6, no. 25 (December 15, 1998): 9.

6. "DoD Revamping Pollution Prevention Strategy, Pushes Funding," *DEA* 7, no. 25 (December 14, 1999): 3.

7. "Weapons Acquisition, UXO Key Areas for Environmental Technology," *DEA* 8, no. 25 (December 5, 2000): 4.

8. "IG Finds Funding, Training Deficient in Pollution Prevention Programs," *DEA* 5, no. 22 (October 21, 1997): 6.

9. "IG Says Tech Center Should Better Disseminate P2 Technologies," *DEA* 9, no. 10 (May 8, 2001): 5–6.

10. "Army Exploring Ways to Improve Integration of Environment in Acquisition," *DEA* 7, no. 9 (May 4, 1999): 4.

11. In 1991, the services found that fifteen chlorofluorocarbons and three halons used in military operations were regulated under the protocol and U.S. law, as were thirty-four hydrochlorofluorocarbons of varying impact to the military.

12. Initially, the OSD defined three very broad categories of use. *Mission critical uses* are those with direct impact on combat mission capabilities. Generally, these consist of chemicals used to cool electronics and weapons systems, as well as fire- or explosion-suppression systems on board military vehicles (e.g., on aircraft or ships). In contrast, *essential uses* have indirect effects on combat missions. These include cooling and fire or explosion suppressing processes for area protection of electronics. *Nonessential uses* include all remaining chemicals used.

13. EO 12843 was formally titled Procurement Requirements and Policies for Federal Agencies for Ozone-Depleting Substances.

14. EO 12856, Federal Compliance with Right-to-Know Laws and Pollution Prevention Requirements.

15. "Pollution Prevention to Get Boost from Pentagon Acquisition Chief," *DEA* 2, no. 4 (February 23, 1994): 26. The initial review of 32,000 milspecs, for example, found 173,000-plus references to toxic chemicals and hazardous substances in acquisition rules.

16. The ISO 14000 series specifies a framework for environmental management for organizations, with ISO 14001 the cornerstone of the series. The latter offers the criteria by which environmental management systems can be certified by third parties.

17. NAS 411 was an aerospace industry design for reducing, eliminating, or controlling hazardous substances in weapons systems.

18. "Congress Probing DoD Efforts to Cut Pollution in Acquisition," *DEA* 1, no. 3 (November 17, 1993): 4. Mr. Moy's official title was assistant deputy under secretary for pollution prevention.

19. "DoD Says Pollution Prevention Must Be Top Priority in Acquisition," *DEA* 2, no. 11 (June 1, 1994): 1, 3, 5–10.

20. Ibid., 5. The only exception to this rule was if milspecs and standards were approved by the acquisition executive in any service.

21. "PAT on Mil Specs Reform Projects High Initial Costs, Then a Leveling Off," *DEA* 2, no. 11 (June 1, 1994): 3.

22. "Army Reevaluating ODC Elimination Program to Decide Funding Scenario," *DEA* 5, no. 22 (October 21, 1997): 5.

23. "Audit Questions Whether Navy Will Meet ODC Phaseout Requirement," *DEA* 8, no. 1 (January 11, 2000): 16.

24. "Army Pilot Project Aims to Recover ODC Halon from Installations," *DEA* 8, no. 7 (April 4, 2000): 19.

25. "Army Reevaluating ODC Elimination Program to Decide Funding Scenario," 5.

26. Ibid.

27. Ibid.

28. "Senate Bill Shifts $24 Million from Cleanup to Pollution Prevention," *DEA* 6, no. 10 (May 19, 1998): 8–13.

29. "Army's FY00-05 Fiscal Projections Cut Environmental Programs," *DEA* 6, no. 13 (June 30, 1998): 3–4.

30. "Guidance Offers Steps for Merging Pollution Prevention, Acquisition Reform," *DEA* 4, no. 17 (August 21, 1996): 14–15.

31. "Integration of Pollution Prevention Efforts Critical to Success, Officials Say," *DEA* 2, no. 18 (September 7, 1994): 13.

32. "DoD Plan to Cut Use of Toxics Could Be Stalled by Lack of Funds," *DEA* 2, no. 24 (November 30, 1994): 3.

33. "Army Pilot Project Aims to Recover ODC Halon from Installations," 18–19; "Interim Armored Vehicle Must Be Free of ODCs, Army Says," *DEA* 8, no. 11 (May 23, 2000): 33–34.

34. "DoD Bows to Service Pressure to Scrap Pollution Prevention Guide," *DEA* 2, no. 14 (July 13, 1994): 19–20.

35. "Navy Defends Position on Environmental Assessments Against IG Attacks," *DEA* 2, no. 8 (April 20, 1994): 18.

36. "Air Force Official Outlines Challenges in Revising Milspecs for Pollution Prevention," *DEA* 2, no. 3 (February 9, 1994): 21. "In support of this view, it has been argued that military equipment is used in more harsh environments [and] that the military needs better reliability" (21).

37. Chris C. Demchak, *Military Organizations, Complex Machines: Modernization in the U.S. Armed Forces* (Ithaca, NY: Cornell University Press, 1991). The technologically sophisticated Apache helicopter, Abrams M-1 main battle tank, and M2/3 Bradley fighting vehicles were notorious for problems.

38. "Air Force to Develop Military Strategy and NATO Guide for ISO 14000," *DEA* 4, no. 7 (April 3, 1996): 15.

39. "Industry, Military Leaders Gauge Progress in 'Greening' Acquisition Process," *DEA* 4, no. 3 (February 7, 1996): 12.

40. This discussion of ISO 14001 relies on Jan Mazurek, 2004, "Third-Party Auditing of Environmental Management Systems," in *Environmental Governance Reconsidered: Challenges, Choices, and Opportunities*, 455–81, ed. Robert F. Durant, Daniel J. Fiorino, and Rosemary O'Leary (Cambridge, MA: MIT Press, 2004).

41. Organizations with an EMS typically adopt a written environmental policy; identify aspects of their activities, products, and services that affect the environment; set objectives and targets for improved performance; assign responsibility for implementing the EMS (such as training); and evaluate and refine the EMS in an effort to improve the system and its results.

42. As defined in EO 13101, a bio-based product is "a commercial or industrial product (other than food or feed) that utilizes biological products or renewable domestic agricultural (plant, animal and marine) or forestry materials."

43. "Iowa Senator Urges DoD to Adopt Greater Purchases of Bio-Based Products," *DEA* 6, no. 9 (May 5, 1998): 10–11.

44. Ibid. The Federal Logistics Information System is a component of the Defense Logistics Information Service, whose mission is to "create, obtain, manage and *integrate logistics data* from a variety of sources for dissemination as *user-friendly information* . . . to the warfighter" (David Ray Tompkins, "Federal Logistics Information System (FLIS)," http://www.dtic.mil/ndia/2001systems/tompkins.pdf (November 4, 2006). Included among the information collected are data on environmental properties, products, and services purchased by the Defense Logistics Agency.

45. "Auditors Assign Acquisition Office Lead on Affirmative Procurement," *DEA* 8, no. 12 (June 6, 2000): 6–7.

46. Ibid.

47. The Pollution Prevention Control Act of 1990 also instructed EPA to develop, expand, and maintain such a database on toxic chemicals.

48. EO 12969, Federal Acquisition and Community Right-to-Know.

49. *Life-cycle cost* means the amortized annual cost of a product, including capital costs, installation costs, operating costs, maintenance costs, and disposal costs discounted over a product's lifetime.

50. "Weapons Acquisition, UXO Key Areas for Environmental Technology," 4.

51. "Draft Memo Signals Major Acquisition Reforms for Pollution Prevention," *DEA* 2, no. 3 (February 9, 1994): 3.

52. "Perry: DoD Must 'Embrace' Pollution Prevention in Acquisition," *DEA* 2, no. 18 (September 7, 1994): 28.

53. A *rolling* report is jargon for a document that remains a work in progress as further information is collated and analyzed.

54. Formally, this report was known as the *Draft Report of the Defense Science Board Task Force on Environmental Security*. See "Science Board Launches Probe into Environmental Security Programs," *DEA* 2, no. 23 (November 16, 1994): 5–6.

55. "Defense Science Board Panel Says Regulations Threaten Readiness," *DEA* 3, no. 5 (March 8, 1995): 3, 7.

56. Ibid., 7.

57. The Joint Logistics Commanders is comprised of top-level flag officers who serve as the senior logistics officials in each service.

58. "JG-APP Preparing to Develop Environmental Lifecycle Cost Analysis," *DEA* 5, no. 3 (January 29, 1997): 14.

59. For example, waste stream generation, hazardous waste disposal, and protective equipment for personnel.

60. "Defense Industry Attacks DCMC Move as Overreach, Waste of Resources," *DEA* 3, no. 1 (January 11, 1995): 3–4.

61. "Logistics Commanders Agree to Furthering Pollution Prevention Measures," *DEA* 5, no. 7 (March 26, 1997): 22.

62. "JG-APP Preparing to Develop Environmental Lifecycle Cost Analysis."

63. "In First Comprehensive Accounting, DoD Estimates $27 Billion in Cleanup Liability," *DEA* 6, no. 8 (April 21, 1998): 14–15. Under the Chief Financial Officers Act of 1990 and the Federal Management Reform Act of 1994, each agency of the federal government has to annually report its total assets and liabilities to the Treasury Department. Collated figures are then published in a consolidated financial statement for the entire federal government.

64. Ibid., 14.

65. Ibid.

66. "IG Finds Flaws in DoD's $80 Billion Bill for Environmental Liabilities," *DEA* 8, no. 5 (March 7, 2000): 4.

67. Ibid.

68. Ibid. Also see "DoD IG Cites Deficient Environmental Liability Statements for FY00," *DEA* 9, no. 6 (March 13, 2001): 5–8.

69. Ibid., 5.

70. "DoD Needs Life-Cycle Cost Accounting for Weapon Systems, IG Says," *DEA* 9, no. 18 (August 28, 2001): 16.

71. As the military argues, however, BRACs were not the sole reasons for TRI progress. Progress was also attributable to pollution prevention efforts and to improved reporting and more accurate accounting of materials.

72. "Legislation Would Codify Federal Facilities' EPCRA Reporting," *DEA* 7, no. 9 (May 4, 1999): 8.

73. "Draft Order Would Require Drastic Cuts in Highly Toxic Chemical Use," *DEA* 7, no. 19 (September 21, 1999): 3.

74. "President Ups Government Conservation Requirement by 10%," *DEA* 2, no. 6 (March 23, 1994): 19.

75. "Defense Science Board Assessing Fuel-Efficient Technologies," *DEA* 7, no. 23 (November 16, 1999): 10.

76. "DoD Seeks Greater Base Participation in Utility Conservation Programs," *DEA* 2, no. 3 (February 9, 1994): 19.

77. "First USAF Conservation Pact Offers Expedited Contracting Model," *DEA* 2, no. 6 (March 23, 1994): 17–18; also see "DoD Details Greenhouse Gas Reduction Plan for Facilities," *DEA* 5, no. 24 (November 18, 1997): 3–4.

78. "DoD Seeks Changes in Defense Bill to Avert Adverse Effects," *DEA* 7, no. 15 (July 27, 1999): 8–12; "Executive Order Sets Greenhouse Gas Cuts, New Energy Efficiency Goals," *DEA* 7, no. 12 (June 15, 1999): 20, 19.

79. "Excerpts: Department of Defense Appeals on FY 2000 Defense Authorization Bill," *DEA* 7, no. 15 (July 27, 1999): 11.

80. EO 13031, Federal Alternative Fueled Vehicle Leadership.

81. "DoD Misses Mark on Purchases of Alternative Fueled Vehicles," *DEA* 6, no. 16 (August 11, 1998): 3–5.

82. "DoD Appeals Cuts to Chemical Weapons Destruction Program," *DEA* 8, no. 16 (August 1, 2000): 8–9. EO 13123 (Greening the Government through Efficient Energy Management) superceded EO 12902 (Energy Efficiency and Water Conservation at Federal Facilities).

83. "New Draft Executive Order Specifies DoD Energy Efficiency Exemption," *DEA* 6, no. 25 (December 15, 1998): 20.

84. "DoD Reviewing Energy Cutback Measures for Possible Executive Order," *DEA* 6, no. 14 (July 14, 1998): 14, 13.

85. "Chemical Disclosure Bill Passes Congress, Moves to White House," *DEA* 7, no. 16 (August 10, 1999): 21.

86. "DoD Says Energy Program Cut Could Impede Greenhouse Gas Reduction Plans," *DEA* 5, no. 25 (December 2, 1997): 8–9.

87. Hart, *Scipio Africanus*, 33.

CHAPTER TEN

Avoiding the Harder Right in the Post-Clinton Era?

The Cadet Prayer at West Point is well known, principled, and inspiring: "Encourage us in our endeavor to live above the common level of life. Make us to choose the harder right instead of the easier wrong, and never be content with a half truth when the whole can be won." Arguably, the Clinton years witnessed the most concentrated, sustained, and potent effort in the modern military era to take what presidents since Truman saw as the "harder right": ensuring United States military readiness while minimizing or avoiding risks to public health, safety, and the environment. To this end, multiple offensives were waged during the Clinton years to institutionalize a common sense of purpose for greening the services with a beyond-compliance ethic without jeopardizing U.S. national security.

What kind of civil–military legacy did these efforts bequeath to the post-Clinton years? As the preceding chapters illustrate, critics claiming that the Clinton years did not witness a positive change in the U.S. military's behavior when it came to ENR issues miss the pockets of significant progress that were made. As Pentagon observer Peter Eisler writes, after lagging behind the private sector at the end of the Cold War, the military was "generally doing as well as private industry in making current activities comply with environmental laws."[1] This hardly constitutes the beyond-compliance ethic sought by greening proponents, and begs the question dealt with later in this book about whether parity is sufficient for public organizations.

Still, the progress made should not be gainsaid. Indeed, critics claiming no progress are as misguided as those in the military who argue that an epiphany occurred to institutionalize greening in the U.S. armed forces during those years. The military may have been on the road to Damascus by the time Clinton left office, but that road was pitted with potholes, detours, speed bumps, and even U turns. Left, as recounted, was a halting, halfway, and patchwork set of misaligned structures, processes, and procedures that rendered prior and future progress vulnerable to changing patterns of politics.

Hence, greening proponents awaited with trepidation the swearing in of George W. Bush as president in 2001, putting control of the White House and the House of Representatives initially in the hands of an unenvironmentally predisposed national leadership. Appreciating Cicero's encomium that "the sinews of war are infinite money,"[2] candidate George W. Bush pledged that "help was on the way" for the military after the alleged neglect of the Clinton years. Nor did that promise look farfetched when Bush took his oath of office. The Congressional Budget Office estimated a ten-year budget surplus of $5.6 trillion. Yet only two years later, tax cuts combined with spending growth, a recession, the economic shock of September 11, and stock market woes in the aftermath of the dot-com meltdown reduced official surplus projections to $1 trillion. Moreover, by the time Bush campaigned for reelection in 2004, the war in Iraq, operations in Afghanistan, an urgent homeland security agenda, a major and costly effort by Secretary of Defense Donald Rumsfeld at military transformation, and enactment of a costly prescription drug benefit for Medicare recipients prompted the Congressional Budget Office to project a ten-year deficit of well over $4 trillion. Thus, continued framing of a zero-sum contest among readiness, weapons modernization, and environmental protection by greening opponents returned with a vengeance.

Nor did greening proponents have long to wait for the military's greening counteroffensive to spiral. Invited by greening opponents on Capitol Hill to testify on the need for ENR regulatory relief months before Clinton left office, the services launched an ENR counteroffensive following the 2000 elections, one that spiraled after the shocks of September 11. As one FWS official recalls, "my telephone calls [to the military] didn't get returned anywhere near as fast as they did before the election."[3] Moreover, by the end of Bush's first term, Christopher Jones, president of the Environmental Council of the States, observed that "there's a frustration that the Defense Department has gotten tougher to deal with." Added Daniel Miller, assistant attorney general for Colorado, more bitingly, the services had "become the most recalcitrant entities we deal with on cleanups. They think they're beyond accountability." Perhaps best encapsulating the Bush Pentagon's attitude was a comment by Sherri Wasserman Goodman's successor, Raymond DuBois, in 2004. Opined DuBois, "Some of these regulators are doing wrongheaded things based on poor scientific evidence. . . . Shouldn't we, as stewards of the taxpayers' money, decide how we're going to clean up [contaminated sites]?"[4]

With their opponents on the march to regain as much sovereignty, secrecy, and sinecure as possible for the services, greening proponents now had to fight a rearguard action to preserve as much as possible the progress they had made during the Clinton years. In this chapter I offer a postscript to convey a general substantive and conceptual sense of how, why, and with what consequences resistance to greening the U.S. military spiraled and was parried during the first six years of the George W. Bush administration. Revealed again in necessarily broad strokes given the chapter's breadth of topical coverage are the same patterns of politics identified during the Clinton years, albeit with greening proponents now on the defensive.

For Thee to Fight?

Anticipating a decidedly less ENR- and more defense-friendly Bush administration, the military wasted little time ramping up a broad-based offensive for regulatory relief. The services did so, as noted, by "invitation" from several key House and Senate members who historically had opposed greening as nondefense-related spending.[5] Quick to respond in terms of issue framing, some military witnesses offered conspiratorial interpretations of ENR reformers' motives. Vice Adm. James Amerault, for example, warned in Cold War–reminiscent words that environmental laws "provid[e] a powerful weapon for those who oppose the military." Others, such as Maj. Gen. Edward Hanlon Jr. of the Marine Corps, were decidedly less conspiratorial in asking for exemptions. But they, too, revived familiar (and negative issue–valenced) Cold War language by asking members of Congress to "consider the unique nature of military activities when . . . reauthorizing these laws."[6] But would they?

The Encroachment Relief Challenge Redux

In short order, the Bush administration took a step long sought by green reformers: Goodman's Environmental Security Office was reorganized to put ENR and installation responsibilities under one roof. In the process, her former position, deputy under secretary of defense for environmental security, was retitled deputy undersecretary of defense for installations and environment. Yet not only did the reorganization signal the demise of environmental security as a central component of national defense policy, it also failed to put a fence around ENR funds, thus leaving them susceptible to budget raids for core military responsibilities on installations. Moreover, the reorganization also created two separate units under the new deputy under secretary, putting the onus of faithful integration on the person heading it.[7] Thus when Bush appointed Raymond DuBois, a former deputy undersecretary of the army to the position, pessimism soared among greening proponents. They saw this move as an effort to deinstitutionalize the office's former zeal.

Nor, as expected, did the new administration waste any time before trying to lessen ENR regulatory pressures on the military in the pre–September 11th era. Sought unsuccessfully, for example, was a delegitimating and deinstitutionalizing rider to the FY 2002 appropriations bill preventing the FWS from using funds to comply with future court orders to designate critical habitat.[8] Then, in a proposal designed to have a chilling effect on regulators, the Pentagon unsuccessfully asked Congress to require a "national security impact statement" anytime the military had to do an environmental impact statement under NEPA.[9] And as this effort at amending aggregation, payoff, and authority rules took place, members of Congress such as James Gibbons (R-NV) remained contemptuous of ENR laws in their issue framing: "We owe our service members and their [families] at least the same consideration and protection we give to the Fairy Shrimp, Tidewater Goby, or any other creature."[10]

Amid this offensive, however, greening proponents in Congress tried to reframe this issue by portraying the services' claims as only the latest wrinkle in a decades-long effort to comply with ENR laws on the military's terms. Others portrayed an even more nefarious agenda afoot, rekindling the idea that opponents of the ESA were using military encroachment issues to skewer a law they were trying more broadly to eviscerate.[11] But after the September 11 terrorist attacks, the military and its congressional allies kicked their anti-encroachment offensive into even higher gear. Most significantly, the Pentagon circulated for comment a draft of the Sustainable Defense Readiness and Environmental Protection Act (later renamed the Readiness and Range Preservation Initiative, or RRPI).

Again trying to delegitimize less sympathetic ENR committees by end-running them, the Pentagon attached this rider to the defense appropriations bill. But an equally swift and predictable reaction came from state regulators and ENR activists.[12] They portrayed the military as using the War on Terror to win legislatively what had eluded the services during the Clinton years, or to roll back structures, processes, and procedures that had advanced green goals historically. Riling greening proponents most was exit and entry rule language in the draft bill giving blanket exemptions from major ENR laws for military training and readiness activities.

A by then familiar litany of rule changes were sought. These included exempting the military from the Clean Air Act (CAA) for five years; exempting munitions, explosives, and other equipment from classification as pollutants or "dredge or fill material" under the Clean Water Act, excluding munitions and other DoD equipment from classification as solid wastes under the RCRA; allowing the president to declare any military action exempt from the Coastal Zone Management Act; and exempting the military from the Marine Mammal Protection Act (MMPA) and the Migratory Bird Treaty Act.

After the FWS and EPA filed strong protests, the Pentagon modified its original draft, but the new draft still called for significant exemptions from the regulatory processes and procedures of each of these six ENR laws.[13] The military, for example, sought a narrower definition of harassment of marine mammals under the MMPA, arguing that the current definition was so broad that permits had to be obtained for training involving "relatively benign operations."[14] Sought, too, were a three-year delay on compliance with CAA standards and exclusions for munitions and related pollutants as hazardous wastes under Superfund and RCRA.

Ultimately legislators allowed only temporary exemptions in 2002 to the military for incidental killing of migratory birds during training, and placed restrictions on how much land the military had to set aside for critical habitat designations. Congress also rejected the military's requests for a three-year delay in complying with CAA standards and excluding munitions-related pollutants from Superfund and RCRA. Also disappointing to the military was language requiring the Interior Department to develop regulations limiting the incidental taking of migratory birds during training.

Everyone understood, however, that these results might not hold in future years. The late start the bill got in Congress made major hearings and changes infeasible. Potent as well was the determined opposition of a coalition of congressional Democrats, a handful of Republicans, environmental activists, and state regulators. But, most significantly, Democrats still held a majority in the Senate. Senate Armed Services Committee chairman Carl Levin (D-MI), for example, refused to consider several major provisions, stating that ENR laws did not fall within the original jurisdiction of his committee. Further infuriating Levin was the Pentagon's familiar deinstitutionalizing and delegitimating tactic of submitting ENR proposals to his committee only days before markup began, in this case on the 2003 defense authorization bill. So frustrating, in turn, were Levin's actions to the Pentagon and its congressional allies that they floated incendiary language for the FY 2003 defense authorization bill. Ultimately unsuccessful, that language would have stripped (i.e., delegitimated) the authority of congressional ENR committees to review defense-related bills involving encroachment issues.

All this changed swiftly, however, after the 2002 midterm elections. Duncan Hunter (R-CA), a member rarely opposing the military, became chair of the House Armed Services Committee. Likewise, implacable eco-cynic James Inhofe (R-OK) became chair of the Senate Environment and Public Works Committee (EPWC) while serving on the Senate Armed Services Committee. This after Republicans regained the Senate majority and the EPWC chairmanship they had lost when James Jeffords (R-VT) became an Independent in 2001. As one environmentalist lamented in the election's aftermath, "I see DoD salivating over what they [the military] got" politically as a result of the midterm elections.[15]

Fully understanding the uphill battle they now faced, greening proponents seized upon a 2004 GAO report in hopes of stemming the tide. The report found that the services had not sufficiently documented that encroachment had compromised the quality of their training or increased their costs.[16] This, despite the military's pleas for altering the ENR regulatory structures, processes, and procedures applicable to them because they did so. Yes, the GAO found that the military had documented that land available for training *had* decreased because of encroachment. Yet the services still lacked compelling data proving that this had actually decreased military readiness.

Characteristically uncowed and optimistic, the military launched into a revitalized congressional offensive to attach its unaccepted RRPI proposals to the FY 2004 defense authorization bill. Reprised, too, were the services' efforts to delegitimize ENR committees by circumventing them in both chambers. Nor was procedural legerdemain the final military card played in this offensive. With the 2005 round of BRACs looming, the Pentagon did not discourage rumors that military bases with ENR encroachment problems might be shut down or realigned. In a virtuoso act of political jujitsu, the Pentagon's silence on the possibility of revamped aggregation rules related to BRAC prompted several states like Texas to require *communities* near military bases to "lower the impact of planning decisions *on military readiness*."[17] The onus, it seemed, would be largely on civilians and not the military to reduce encroachment threats, a trend that by 2006 found DoD and four southeastern states working collaboratively either to zone out development near bases or to create partnerships to purchase lands near them for buffer zones.[18]

Meanwhile, an imbroglio ensued over the true breadth of the Pentagon's call for process and procedural exemptions from ENR statutes in the FY 2004 bill. This happened after the services tried reframing the exemptions they sought as "narrowly focused clarifications." Irate, critics countered by trying to mobilize opposition from traditional greening allies in the states. Postponing for three years the military's conformance with CAA state implementation plans, they argued, ignored the military's contribution to ozone, particulate matter, and carbon monoxide violations. As such, public health would be compromised appreciably and cleanup costs in nonattainment areas shifted to private industry. Overly broad as well, said critics, were national security exemptions to the MMPA: The military's "narrow" request actually applied "to *any* requirement of the [MMPA] for *any* action taken by the military on the grounds of national defense."[19] Indeed, by 2006, justifications on these and other grounds related to the U.S. Navy's plans for major coastal zone projects off the Virginia and California coasts, and for an undersea training range on the East Coast, ran pell-mell into state challenges. Regulators charged the navy with filing takings claims for mammals that were "unacceptability high" and premised on inadequate scientific grounds as well as making inappropriate claims of exemptions from federal waste regulations.[20]

Still, the most potent arrows in the quivers of RRPI opponents were, first, that regulators had never used the laws the military sought exemptions from (namely, the CAA and RCRA) to limit military activities and, second, the services' still-inadequate statistical support for their encroachment military-readiness claims.[21] When the DoD forwarded its encroachment report to Congress in March 2004, for example, GAO criticized the military for using "invalidated cost assumptions" and "inconsistent methodologies" in computing encroachment costs (i.e., for using faulty information and aggregation rules).[22] Added state regulators, "DoD's proposal would create a blanket exemption for military readiness activities . . . irrespective of the need for the exemption or the impact on air quality and public health."[23]

Absent more compelling evidence to inform this crisis of authority, Congress again disallowed blanket exit and entry rule exemptions to the military for RCRA, the CAA, and CERCLA. They did, however, again accommodate the military on the natural resources front, making it more difficult for regulators to claim low-frequency sonar or other harassment of sea life during training exercises under the MMPA.[24] Critters, it seemed, were expendable, but people were not. Moreover, the FY 2005 defense authorization bill granted in legislation what the military had acquired only administratively from the FWS (see chapter 7): any base with an existing integrated natural resources management plan automatically satisfied critical habitat designation requirements for environmental impact statements.[25]

Still insatiated, however, the Pentagon announced in 2005 that it would mount yet another counteroffensive to gain exemptions from RCRA and CERCLA rule sets for, among other things, UXO contaminants.[26] Bridled perennial DoD critic Rep. John Dingell (D-MI) as he sought to reframe the issue, the "Department of Defense has no idea what contamination is present on their operational ranges and has no intention of finding out. Our military families deserve a Defense Department that protects drinking water supplies, not a Defense Department that protects its sorry record." Scoffed others in noting the crises of authority their actions provoked, the military "won't budge unless they're forced."[27]

Nor were fears like these mollified in mid-2004 by the leak of a series of internal communications from the army's installation management director, Maj. Gen. Anders Aadland, to installation commanders. Aadland mandated a freeze on environmental expenditures in light of budget constraints. He attributed these constraints to "fighting a war [on terrorism] on several fronts, maintaining combat readiness on others, and transforming our warfighting force." Aadland then instructed installation commanders to cut ENR expenditures "immediately to do our part to get through this challenging year." Later rescinded, the disclosure prompted Jeff Ruch of Public Employees for Environmental Responsibility to frame this incident as "an order to base commanders authorizing pollution of American soil when it saves money."[28]

Meanwhile, congressional work on the RRPI continued into 2005 with the Pentagon's regulatory relief proposals appended to the FY 2006 defense authorization bill. But the Pentagon added a new wrinkle to its mobilization strategy. This time it tried to gain state allies by raising the threat of cuts in highway fund projects if three-year environmental exemptions for the CAA were not granted. Also dusting off its penchant for committee shopping, Senate EPWC chairman Inhofe declined original jurisdiction over the RRPI, stating unabashedly that it had "a better chance of approval in the armed services committee."[29] In the end, however, the military lost this round, too. Moreover, by 2006, the House Armed Services Readiness Subcommittee refused to include the Pentagon's "limited push" to gain further RRPI regulatory relief in the FY 2007 version of the RRPI.[30] But the message was clear: countering still-formidable tendencies among greening opponents to return to the military's heroic myth of sovereignty, secrecy, and sinecure required strong countervailing political headwinds. These came when Democrats retook control of Congress in the 2006 midterm election.

The Range Rule

As noted in chapter 5, still prompting a crisis of authority when the Pentagon withdrew its range rule in November 2000 was the question of what constituted an adequate risk-ranking methodology for prioritizing UXO dangers at closed, transferred, and transferring ranges. Handicapping progress in determining these information and aggregation rules were the military's resistance to meaningful and timely stakeholder participation in the development of that methodology, its insistence on applying army rather than federal and state ENR standards, and its efforts to retain final dispute resolution authority within the Pentagon.

At loggerheads over these rule sets, DoD officials agreed early in the first term of the George W. Bush administration to a scoping meeting with state regulators to discern how to get closure on a range rule. By that time, too, Congress was so disturbed over the pace of progress on UXO cleanups that the FY 2002 Defense Authorization Act required the DoD to inventory and prioritize *all* its UXO sites immediately. Released in early 2003, the Pentagon's data gap–addled inventory identified 1,691 UXO sites at FUDS, 542 UXO sites at active bases, and 74 UXO sites at closing bases. Conceding that it still was not sure where or to what extent UXO problems existed on FUDS, the Pentagon projected cleanup costs of roughly $11.5 billion.[31]

Then, as congressional pressures mounted, the Pentagon announced in late August a three-pronged range rule approach to prioritizing cleanups. Drawing on three sets of risk modules (explosive, chemical, and health and environmental risks), the DoD proposed that UXO sites be ranked in priority for cleanup action based on the highest ranking attained in *any* of the three risk modules. Moreover, in a minor sop to critics of purely quantified rankings, the proposal also allowed some deviation from the absolute ranking given. For example, commitments expressed in federal facility agreements, stakeholder concerns, or cultural, social, and economic factors could push a site into a higher-priority category.

After nearly two months of study, however, state regulators dismissed the Pentagon's proposal as "just the range rule risk methodology 'in camouflage'."[32] Most distressing, according to ASTSWMO, was that the scoring method inaccurately portrayed public health hazards. Disconcerting as well was the failure to document the logic underpinning the posited relationships among the risk values.[33] Nor was ASTSWMO sanguine about the military using census data and indicators like "numbers of inhabited structures" to calculate exposure to dangers. Despite millions of visitors each year, for example, national parks would get a low-priority cleanup ranking.

Thus, as voters went to the polls in 2004 ultimately to reelect George W. Bush, the hope for agreement on a range rule resided largely in the work of an EPA-led working group of federal, state, and tribal officials.[34] Known as the Technical Working Group on Hazard Assessment, participants aimed for a document by December 2005 that would give consistent guidance to the military for assessing and prioritizing UXO explosivity. Left unaddressed by the group, however, was a methodology for assessing and prioritizing the toxic risks of explosives. Still absent after a decade of negotiations was an agreed-upon chemical risk assessment model for the range rule. Moreover, by 2006 DoD was fighting the application of statutory deadlines for UXO cleanup schedules as well as the application of the munitions rule to cleaning up ordnance on closed testing and training ranges.[35]

What *was* clear by 2006, however, was that the military's assumptions regarding aggregation rules assessing explosivity dangers on UXO sites were inaccurate. Contrary to DoD's sampling assumption that UXO was spaced evenly at sites, researchers found that hazards clustered. As the military's regulators had long claimed, defining sites as clean on the basis of random sampling was simply too dangerous.[36]

Cleanups, Institutional Controls, and Range Conservation

Recall from chapters 4 to 6 that one of the major points of contention regarding cleanups during the Clinton years was who had final authority when disputes arose between and among regulators and the military. Most contentious among a host of subissues were the meaning of DoD's designation as the lead agency in Superfund law and whether the EPA and the states were merely consulted on site characterizations, remedy selections, and NPL deletions. To be sure, disputes over the military's use of chemicals like perchlorates did not help the situation during George W. Bush's first term.[37] Still, what Mike Gearheard of EPA's Region X cleanup office terms dysfunctional "king of the hill disputes" remained the single most important factor in this crisis of authority as backlogs in remedial determinations, remedy completions, and NPL deletions grew.[38] By the end of Bush's first term, for example, the military had delayed signing federal facility agreements and interagency agreements at over seventy cleanup sites, holding out successfully to remove language prohibiting future construction on still-contaminated sites.[39]

Moreover, growing especially pronounced were crises of authority over the military's burgeoning choice of institutional controls over permanent cleanup remedies. As EPA's Federal Facilities Restoration and Reuse Office complained in 2003, over ninety military cleanups and nearly twenty federal facility agreements were left hanging until these disputes were resolved.[40] In addition, what seemed to be progress in compliance rates was at least partially a consequence of broad constraints on the EPA administrator's authority to take actions when EPA-DoD disagreements over site characterizations and remedy selections arose.[41]

By the same token, even when real progress on these kinds of authority and scoping rules occurred, the Pentagon sometimes worked purposely to leave a patchwork system in place. Consider the army and navy's agreement with EPA on institutional controls. Developing a standard federal facility agreement that included legally binding commitments to local land use plans was a longstanding aim of the EPA and state regulators. Yet even when these were signed at several army and navy bases, some at the highest levels of the Pentagon fought extending the use of these ad hoc agreements service-wide as legally binding documents. In response, George W. Bush's EPA still planned only to require annual reviews of sites and legally nonbinding standards to hold them accountable. Then, when the agency announced in late 2004 that it was thinking of relaxing institutional controls at Superfund sites to encourage redevelopment, greening proponents worried that these diminished scoping, authority, information, and aggregation rule sets were "eroding the integrity" of the program.[42] Thus, by 2006, both the GAO and EPA were recommending full life-cycle cost accounting for institutional controls before they were consummated.[43]

Similarly, recall how debates over the participation of state, local, and tribal governments in developing integrated natural resource management plans during the Clinton years created crises of authority between the military and regulators. The George W. Bush administration first tried to address these authority and position rule set issues indirectly in late 2001. The president issued a controversial executive order allowing "cooperative conservation" initiatives involving the DoD and the Interior, Agriculture, and Commerce departments.[44] This effort ultimately derailed, however, when the Pentagon joined the U.S. Chamber of Commerce and the Business Roundtable in expressing fears that a patchwork of inconsistent state ENR regulations would ensue.[45] Not until late in the 2004 presidential campaign would the Bush administration tackle these issues again.[46] But the president's proposal protected the military from patchwork regulations and gave the Pentagon final authority when disputes arose. This left the services well positioned structurally to control the substance, pace, and scope of range conservation efforts.

Moreover, even when clear and positive range conservation initiatives *were* launched by the OSD in the Bush Pentagon, resistance from the services and their allies remained. For instance, the Army Audit Agency reported that the army pursued deinstitutionalizing strategy by failing to budget for these programs until the FY 2005 cycle. Even then, the service failed to afford effective management controls, raising old fears about raids on the funds for core readiness missions. Also, despite the Pentagon issuing range conservation initiatives in 1999, the army "did not instruct its commands and installations to implement them and did not provide implementing guidance until 2003."[47]

Finally, by the end of the sixth year of George W. Bush's presidency, seasoned observers noted how the military was "using the White House to come from the top [on these range and cleanup issues]. Rather than having the same standing as states, communities, industry groups or anyone else, they're above everybody."[48] Nor were things any better on the land transfer front. State and local governments and developers remained wary over recent changes in laws allowing the military to sell still-contaminated properties "as is" while remaining liable for cleanup costs. Meanwhile, the average number of EPA inspections at military bases was down 26 percent from the last three years of the Clinton administration. Yes, the services remained liable for new costs, which seemed to rise "every time you turn a spade of dirt," but the military "moved pathetically slowly" once they did not own the land.[49] Until they did move, developers and state reuse authorities were left footing the bill as the services haggled over reimbursement costs that the Pentagon argued were excessive. Moreover, in 2006 the Pentagon played its resource dependency card by, first, denying EPA funding for oversee-ing cleanups at BRAC V bases.[50] It then conditioned receipt of DSMOA funds for state oversight on the regulators waiving enforcement actions until a dispute resolution process occurred.[51] Consequently, nearly two decades after the first round of BRAC, ENR cleanup issues over exit and entry, authority, scoping, in-formation, aggregation, position, and payoff rules had delayed the transfer of nearly 80 percent of these properties for development.

Pollution Prevention, Energy Conservation, and Privatization

Barely three months after the September 11th terrorist attacks, DuBois took a page from Goodman's book and began linking various aspects of his office's re-sponsibilities to military readiness issues, in this case to the administration's War on Terror. Also like Goodman, and to the accolades of some environmentalists, DuBois argued that pollution prevention was the cornerstone of the military's environmental quality program. Following on the heels of Dubois's comments, John Paul Woodley Jr., assistant deputy under secretary of defense for environ-ment, safety, and occupational health, stated that expanding the Clinton admin-istration's initiatives on environmental management systems was the key to pollution prevention, sustainable range, and encroachment issues. Noting that the DoD's "industrial partners" (i.e., their contractors) were using environmen-tal management systems predicated on, among other approaches, ISO 14001 processes, Woodley argued it was critical to establish environmental manage-ment systems where applicable by the end of 2005.[52]

Not unlike during the Clinton years, of course, environmental management systems remained attractive to the Pentagon. They were voluntary and did not focus explicitly on ENR outcomes, two features that many state regulators and ENR activists insisted would advance the military's quest for self-regulation. Soon, however, perennial patterns of politics kicked into gear repertoires of de-institutionalization tactics. To be sure, by September 2004 two-thirds of the 649 U.S. Air Force, Army, Defense Logistics Agency, Marine Corps, and U.S. Navy installations deemed appropriate for environmental management systems had completed policy documents and assessments to launch these efforts. Yet only twenty-seven had environmental management systems in operation because of inadequate funding and skill sets for doing so. These shortcomings put in jeop-ardy the faithful realization of Clinton's original goal of full implementation by the end of 2005. Moreover, none of the services individually had more than 50 percent of their EMS guidance documents issued, and the Defense Logistics Agency had policies in place at only 10 percent of its installations.[53] Even were they all in place, determination of what constituted a successful EMS was left to the military rather than co-determined with EPA and the states.

At the same time, many of the structural problems afflicting pollution preven-tion efforts during the Clinton years continued unabated. Consider, for instance, the continued opaqueness of the Pentagon's accounting systems. These foiled, for example, the transparency so necessary for information and aggregation rule sets related to environmental life-cycle cost accounting to advance a beyond-compliance corporate ethic. Likewise, by mid-2004, the army's inspector general (with the support of DoD comptroller Dov Zakheim) was excoriating the services's BRAC office for underreporting environmental liabilities by $382 million. The culprit? The BRAC office had set a cap on liabilities reported, thus either "encourag[ing] installations to revise estimates using a more optimistic approach or arbitrarily chang[ing] site estimates."[54] This was so egregious that the DoD inspector general told the army to institute ethics training throughout the service!

Indeed, culturally imbued norms of "creative" or "hold-the-fort" accounting, reinforced by perverse institutional incentives, would not die easily within the army or the other services during Bush's first term. For example, when the Pentagon issued its environmental liability statements for FY 2002 and FY 2003, the DoD's inspector general noted improvement. But once again he called them unreliable estimates. In yet another version of an all-too-familiar refrain from the Clinton years, the inspector general noted that "problems with environmental liabilities continued to exist related to guidance, audit trails, the use of estimating models, and inventories of sites."[55]

Around this time, Comptroller Zakheim accurately noted that the military had made progress in several management areas related to greening (including financial management), and that the Pentagon planned to address other short-comings with a department-wide information technology financial management architecture.[56] Moreover, subsequent GAO reports cited progress on this front. For example, analysts noted better site characterization and estimation of costs based on more valid assumptions when the services reported $64.4 billion in ENR liabilities for FY 2004. Yet, GAO also noted that a litany of familiar shortcomings remained unaddressed: insufficient guidance and audit trails; incomplete inventories of ranges, landfills, and open burning pits; and eleven agency-wide material weaknesses in financial statements.[57] Nor were the services following up sufficiently on inspector general recommendations for correcting deficiencies in prior environmental liability statements, even when instructed to do so by the OSD. In the process, not only was nearly $83 million allocated to sites with overstated compliance requirements and away from those with under-stated compliance requirements, but the true costs of cleanup versus pollution prevention efforts were distorted.[58] In light of these revelations, DoD promised in 2006 to have its ENR liability problems straightened out by 2010, over a decade and a half after first required to do so.

Importantly, the DoD still was the first federal agency to finalize a "green pro-curement" policy and strategy for purchasing recycled products, EPPs, alternative fuel vehicles, and bio-based products as per Clinton-era statutes and executive orders. No minor accomplishment, significant structural obstacles nonetheless remained to inculcate an enduring pollution prevention ethic in the military. In announcing the DoD's green procurement policy, in fact, John Coho of the department's Office of Environment, Safety, and Occupational Health noted that "strong and unambiguous" support for green procurement had to be improved in the services.[59] Also lacking were information collection and aggregation-related rules advancing automated databases and processes for monitoring the progress and effectiveness of pollution prevention policies Pentagon-wide.

Meanwhile, on the energy conservation front, the first year of the George W. Bush administration brought calls from the Defense Science Board for the military to focus on increasing fuel efficiency in weapons acquisition as a means for freeing up funds for readiness, a position adopted by the Bush administration in 2006 as energy costs soared.[60] Shortly thereafter the Senate, in its version of the 2002 defense authorization bill, pushed for expansion of the acceptable types of alternative fuel vehicles by FY 2005. Going beyond the requirements of the Energy Policy Act, the Senate version required the military to purchase only hybrid electric vehicles for its light-duty trucks after FY 2005. It also upped the percentages of vehicles designated by the act to be alternative fuel vehicles.[61]

But in opposing this provision, the military argued that it already was having trouble meeting existing requirements; supplies of alternative fuel vehicles in these categories were limited, and the refueling infrastructures for alternative fuel vehicles were largely nonexistent. Conferees, nonetheless, included the stepped-up requirements in the 2002 authorization bill, modifying the final version only by allowing all types of hybrid engines and not just hybrid electronic vehicles. Moreover, in the wake of skyrocketing energy prices in 2006, Pentagon officials themselves began to pressure the services to improve fuel efficiency and seek alternative fuels for cost-cutting and national security reasons. The rub for the military, however, was that the search for alternative fuels in the United States also increased its encroachment problems.[62] This as "energy corridors" in the West and off-shore drilling threatened to interfere with military training exercises.

Not surprisingly, ENR load-shedding and demand-management efforts begun during the Clinton administration gained momentum during George W. Bush's first six years. Recall how the Clinton Pentagon had begun a concerted effort under the rubric of Defense Secretary William Cohen's Defense Reform Initiative to privatize such traditional responsibilities as utility provision and cleanups. In terms of utility privatization, Bush's Pentagon pushed immediately for reauthorization of Energy Savings Performance Contracts. Extremely popular among federal agencies by the end of Bush's first term (with the military employing nearly 70 percent of them), the program ran into reauthorization troubles in 2003 that further limited its expansion.[63] Also, despite the efforts of sympathetic members of the House and Senate, reauthorization stalled for the remainder of Bush's first term, bogged down in debate over the larger energy bill.

Finally, performance-based contracts for cleanups ran into similar funding problems. Although pronouncing general support for these contracts throughout the first six years of the Bush presidency, ASTSWMO's Base Closure Focus Group also argued that "the contracts can carry a number of drawbacks, such as a significant increase in state regulatory oversight, major changes to cleanup work plans and funding states receive from DoD for oversight work they do, confusion over how to resolve disputes, and changes to public input into cleanup decisions." In particular, state regulators were "concerned that [they would] have little or no input into [contractors'] work efforts until too late in the [cleanup] process to have significant impact on the project."[64] ENR activists worried, too, that even if sufficient resources and staffing could be generated by DSMOAs, the same resource-dependency situation discussed in earlier chapters held the potential for mischief. Hardly insolvable, debates like these four years after Clinton left office and eight years after privatization was first proposed afforded a distressing sense of déjà vu. The military would budge, but it would budge most readily and profoundly only when the Pentagon perceived that delay in taking greening actions directly threatened its warfighting mission.

Chemical Demilitarization

Upon taking office, Secretary Rumsfeld immediately was confronted by long-time critics of the army's chemical demilitarization program: Senator Mitch McConnell (R-KY) and Senator Richard Shelby (R-AL). They implored Rumsfeld to include the program in what he said would be a comprehensive review of DoD operations. In urging him to pay special attention to safety, management, and public outreach flaws in the program, they were joined by Senator Ted Stevens (R-AK). As chairman of both the Senate Appropriations Committee and its Defense Appropriations Subcommittee, Stevens threatened to shut off funding for the program until these concerns were addressed to the senators' satisfaction.[65]

Were this not enough to get Rumsfeld's attention, a leaked internal army report about the program in early 2001 projected that it would "likely be years off" its target for destroying U.S. chemical weapons.[66] Feeling vindicated, grassroots populists such as the CWWG ramped up their longstanding complaint that the army had disingenuously used the 2004 statutory and 2007 CWC deadlines as ruses to eliminate nonincinerator options. Thus, with calls increasing for more oversight and restructuring of the chemical weapons disposal program from senators such as Shelby and McConnell, Secretary of the Army Thomas White acted preemptively by shifting oversight responsibilities within the service. As during the Clinton years, White's reorganization left the PMCD responsible for the program's day-to-day operations. But rather than have oversight responsibilities split between the army's assistant secretary for installations and environment and its assistant secretary for acquisitions, logistics, and technology, the army consolidated this responsibility within the former.[67]

Lauded by many environmentalists, White's reorganization was overturned in 2003 amid congressional pressure for reform.[68] In this instance, oversight responsibilities were shifted to acquisitions, logistics, and technology. This happened after a leaked memo indicated that the army's assistant secretary for installations and environment at the time, Mario Fiori, planned to blame local and state officials for shoddy emergency preparedness plans if any emergencies developed at the nine disposal sites.[69] As Craig Williams of the CWWG explained, "We thought putting de-mil in the Army Environmental Office made sense at the time, but we didn't count on a management style based on covert operations and the total exclusion of public participation."[70]

In the end, the reorganization provoked by these crises over authority, scoping, and position rule sets left in its wake the kind of halting, halfway, and patchwork consolidation of structures, processes, and procedures that typified greening efforts throughout the post–Cold War era. The army reassigned oversight of all policy matters relating to the chemical weapons disposal program to the assistant secretary of the army for acquisitions, logistics, and technology, plus responsibility for the emergency management components of chemical demilitarization. The secretary of the army then ordered this assistant secretary and the commanding general of the Army Materiel Command to create the Chemical Materials Agency (CMA). The CMA, in turn, was given responsibility for handling storage and disposal of the chemical weapons stockpile. The CMA then redesignated the old PMCD position as the program manager for the elimination of chemical weapons. The person holding this position became responsible for sites under construction. Meanwhile, the CMA director of operations had responsibility for managing three sites (Newport, Pine Bluff, and Umatilla) from operation to closure, whereas the Assembled Chemical Weapons Alternatives program retained oversight for Aberdeen, Anniston, Johnston Atoll, and Tooele. The fabled Rube Goldberg could not have fashioned a more fractionated system.

For Congressman Marty Meehan (D-MA), ranking member of the terrorism subcommittee, the reasons for doing all this fit neatly into a longstanding pattern:

> I feel compelled to mention that politics, indecisive management, and a lack of true commitment to funding has led to the current state within which we find ourselves. I am frustrated that "other DoD priorities" have repeatedly won out in the resource game. I am frustrated that the Army has transferred program management from one office to the next. And I am frustrated with political opportunism—both within the Pentagon and throughout our nation's communities.[71]

Moreover, the more things changed structurally, the more the army continued to fight old battles with by now familiar justifications. For instance, despite at last certifying in 2003 that neutralization-biotreatment *was* a cost-effective alternative to incineration at Pueblo and Blue Grass, no additional sites were approved for neutralization. In addition, the Pentagon once more threatened to scale back Assembled Chemical Weapons Alternatives funding at both sites because of cost overruns, argued for accelerating incineration because of terrorism threats, and again asked Congress to allow transportation of wastes to disposal sites in other states.

An incredulous Senator McConnell, expressing the frustration of many of his colleagues at this series of déjà vu–inspiring events involving deinstitutionalization, de-skilling, defunding, and issue reframing, pulled no punches:

> The department [DoD] claims ACWA [Assembled Chemical Weapons Alternatives] sites must be downgraded to caretaker status because they are over budget due to cost overruns. Yet the department's own schizophrenic decisionmaking is what led to these costs. The department has repeatedly stopped or slowed down design work and then restarted, adding unnecessary startup and stop-work costs. They stingily parcel out appropriated monies in such small quantities that it is impossible to spend it efficiently. Thus, it is the department's own bureaucratic mismanagement that has created the cost problems.[72]

Conclusion

Certainly, nothing has changed since 1989, when then-Secretary of Defense Richard Cheney argued that to "choose between [defense and ENR protection] is impossible in this real world of serious defense threats and genuine environmental concerns."[73] Indeed, sixteen years after Cheney's charge to the military, President George W. Bush's new assistant deputy under secretary of defense for environment, safety, and occupational health, Alex Beehler, still was pushing with some success (see chapter 1) for what he called "environmental improvement" across the DoD. But in this contentious arena of civil–military relations, Beehler's otherwise laudatory assessment of the military's compliance with ENR laws in 2005 noted that he was still jousting with many of the same windmills Cheney's reform efforts sought to eliminate. Moving "beyond compliance," said Beehler, meant "the military . . . dealing with past stovepipes, where all too often [people said] 'that's an environmental issue, [push it] over there, [and] let the environmental experts deal with it.'"[74] Clearly, taking the "harder right" of reconciling national security with public health, safety, and environmental values in the post–September 11 era has not, and will not ever be, a task for the meek, the impatient, or the political unastute.

Notes

1. Peter Eisler, "Pollution Cleanups Pit Pentagon Against Regulators," *USA Today*, October 14, 2004, www.usatoday.com/news/nation, 1 (April 21, 2006).

2. William Grimes, "How a Struggling Colony Became an Economic Colossus," *New York Times*, December 3, 2004, www.nytimes.com/2004/12/03/books/03book.html (April 25, 2006).

3. Thomas Baca, Regional Office, U.S. Fish and Wildlife Service, Albuquerque, NM, interview with author, Crofton, MD, March 2002.

4. Eisler, "Pollution Cleanups Pit Pentagon Against Regulators," 5. It is important to note that individual service efforts like the army's vaunted "Strategy for the Environment: Sustain the

Mission—Secure the Future" continued throughout the Bush years as they sought to garner as much stability, predictability, and security of operations as they could.

5. "Military Asks Senators to Clarify Environmental Requirements," *DEA* 9, no. 7 (March 27, 2001): 3–4.

6. Ibid., 3.

7. "Impact of DoD Environment Changes Still Unknown, Sources Say," *DEA* 9, no. 11 (May 22, 2001): 7.

8. "Endangered Species Rider Dropped from House Appropriations Bill," *DEA* 9, no. 13 (June 19, 2001): 9–10.

9. "House Committee Passes National Security Impact Analysis Provision," *DEA* 9, no. 17 (August 14, 2001): 6.

10. "Weldon Calls for 'Common Sense' Approach to Environmental Laws," *DEA* 9, no. 12 (June 5, 2001): 4–5.

11. "Lawmakers Seek to Address Military Concerns in ESA Reforms," *DEA* 9, no. 11 (May 22, 2001): 3–5.

12. "New Pentagon Group to Coordinate All Encroachment Issues," *DEA* 9, no. 26 (December 18, 2001): 4; "Navy Internally Discussing Exemption Provision for Wartime Actions," *DEA* 10, no. 1 (January 1, 2002): 3.

13. "Environmentalists Urge Opposition to DoD Fast-Track Legislation," *DEA* 10, no. 12 (June 4, 2002): 7–8; "Pentagon Asks Congress for Environmental Regulatory Relief," *DEA* 10, no. 9 (April 23, 2002): 3–4, 25.

14. "DoD Agrees to Examine Administrative Solutions to Encroachment," *DEA* 11, no. 3 (February 11, 2003): 3.

15. "Pentagon Discussing Next Legislative Environmental Proposal," *DEA* 10, no. 24 (November 19, 2002): 3.

16. "GAO Study on DoD Cleanup Costs May Hinder Military Exemptions," *DEA* 12, no. 14 (July 13, 2004): 20.

17. "Texas Bill to Fortify Bases Against Closure, Urban Sprawl," *DEA* 11, no. 4 (February 25, 2003): 7; emphasis added.

18. "DoD, Southeast States Eye Land Pact to Preserve Training Uses," *DEA* 14, no. 9 (May 2, 2006): 7–8.

19. "Defense Department Ponders Tightening Potential Loopholes in Bill," *DEA* 11, no. 6 (March 25, 2003): 8; emphasis added.

20. "Federal Regulators Call Navy Sonar Plan Unscientific, Urge Changes," *DEA* 14, no. 4 (February 21, 2006): 3–4. Also see "Government, Activist Attack on EIS May Slow Navy Undersea Range Plan," *DEA* 14, no. 3 (February 7, 2006): 3–4.

21. EPA had used the Safe Drinking Water Act, rather than RCRA or CERCLA, at the Massachusetts Military Reservation to halt training activities.

22. "GAO Cites Deficiencies in DoD Report on Training Range Constraints," *DEA* 12, no. 12 (June 15, 2004), 6–7.

23. "Revised DoD Environment Bill Offers Air Quality Concessions to States," *DEA* 13, no. 5 (March 8, 2005): 3.

24. "Regulators Investigating Odd Whale Behavior Near Navy Exercises," *DEA* 12, no. 14 (July 13, 2004): 17.

25. "Senate Bows to House on DoD-Favored Environment Provisions," *DEA* 11, no. 23 (November 18, 2003): 8–10.

26. "GAO Study on DoD Cleanup Costs May Hinder Military Exemptions"; see "Revised DoD Environment Bill Offers Air Quality Concessions to States."

27. "GAO Study on DoD Cleanup Costs May Hinder Military Exemptions."

28. "Army Won't Tap Environmental Funding for War Expenses," *DEA* 12, no. 11 (June 1, 2004): 4.

29. "Senate Panel Faces Showdown over DoD Push for Environmental Waivers," *DEA* 13, no. 9 (May 3, 2005): 3.

30. "Despite Limited Push, DoD Likely to Continue Introducing Exemptions Bill," *DEA* 14, no. 9 (May 2, 2006): 4.

31. "Pentagon Proposes Three-Pronged Approach to UXO Cleanups," *DEA* 11, no. 17 (August 26, 2003): 4.

32. "States Say Munitions Prioritization Protocol Has 'Fatal Flaws'," *DEA* 11, no. 24 (December 2, 2003): 3.

33. Ibid.

34. "Federal-State Group Adopts Outline for Assessing Explosive Hazards," *DEA* 12, no. 23 (November 16, 2004): 18.

35. "Illinois Cleanup Dispute May Determine Regulatory Status of UXO," *DEA* 14, no. 9 (May 2, 2006): 3–4.

36. "New Study Backs EPA on UXO Detection, Distribution at Military Sites," *DEA* 14, no. 2 (January 24, 2006): 9–10.

37. See, for example, "DoD Objects to Stringent Colorado Standards for TCE," *DEA* 12, no. 18 (September 7, 2004): 3; "Colorado Sets First-Time Water Standard for 1,4-Dioxane," *DEA* 12, no. 19 (September 21, 2004): 3; "New Mexico Agency Sets Residential Cleanup Levels at Fort Wingate," *DEA* 12, no. 19 (September 21, 2004): 9–10.

38. "Regulator-DoD Authority Disputes Overshadow Successes," *DEA* 11, no. 17 (August 26, 2003): 3.

39. Eisler, "Pollution Cleanups Pit Pentagon Against Regulators," 3.

40. "Regulator-DoD Authority Disputes Overshadow Successes."

41. Military facilities without federal facility agreements in place within six months of a Record of Decision signing, after all, were categorized as in noncompliance with the law.

42. "EPA to Revisit Land Use Controls in New Superfund Development Plan," *DEA* 12, no. 24 (November 30, 2004): 9.

43. "EPA Guide on Land-Use Control Costs May Spark Backlash," *DEA* 14, no. 17 (August 22, 2006): 7.

44. "Bush Order May Boost States' Role in Crafting Environmental Rules," *DEA* 9, no. 18 (August 28, 2001): 20–21; "Bush Order on Federalism Stalls Amid State, Industry Dispute," *DEA* 9, no. 22 (October 23, 2001): 16.

45. "Bush Order on Federalism Stalls Amid State, Industry Dispute."

46. "New Executive Order Calls for 'Cooperative Conservation'," *DEA* 12, no. 18 (September 7, 2004): 11.

47. "Audit Finds Army Slow to Implement Range Sustainment Actions," *DEA* 11, no. 23 (November 18, 2003): 24.

48. "Peter Eisler, "Sides Armed with Science, Studies in Conflict Over Health Risks," *USA Today*, October 13, 2004, www.usatoday.com/news/nation, 1 (April 20, 2006).

49. Peter Eisler, "Cleanup Fights Stall New Uses for Old Bases," *USA Today*, October 14, 2004, 1, 3, www.usatoday.com/news/nation (April 21, 2006).

50. "Pentagon Denies EPA Oversight Funds for BRAC Round V," *DEA* 14, no. 15 (July 25, 2006): 3–4.

51. "Despite State Concerns, DoD Wins New State Oversight Funding Plan," *DEA* 14, no. 12 (June 13, 2006): 3–5.

52. "Implementing Environmental Management Systems is Top Priority," *DEA* 9, no. 26 (December 18, 2001): 11.

53. "DoD Continuing to Move Toward Goal of EMS in Place by End of 2005," *DEA* 12, no. 18 (September 7, 2004): 9–10.

54. "Pentagon, Army Dispute BRAC Environmental Liabilities," *DEA* 12, no. 11 (June 1, 2004): 4. The army challenged these findings, but the Army Audit Agency stuck by its charges.

55. "DoD Reports $59 Billion in Environmental Liabilities in FY02 Statement," *DEA* 11, no. 5 (March 11, 2003): 9.

56. Ibid.

57. "DoD Environmental Liabilities Increase to $64.4 Billion in FY04," *DEA* 12, no. 25 (December 14, 2004): 20–21.

58. "Audit: Air Force Environmental Liability Reporting Remains Deficient," *DEA* 11, no. 5 (March 11, 2003): 12–13.

59. "Defense Department Developing New Green Procurement Policy," *DEA* 12, no. 17 (August 24, 2004): 4.

60. "DoD Broadening Energy Efficiency Focus to Include Weapons Systems," *DEA* 14, no. 8 (April 18, 2006): 4–5.

61. "Senate Legislation Calls for Detailed UXO Cleanup Cost," *DEA* 9, no. 20 (September 25, 2001): 6–8.

62. "Military Faces Energy-Related Encroachment on Readiness Activities," *DEA* 14, no. 5 (March 7, 2006): 5–7.

63. "Proponents Seek to Revive Energy Savings Contracts Program," *DEA* 12, no. 9 (May 4, 2004): 5–6. Also see "Administration Moves to Halt Expansion of Energy Savings Contracts," *DEA* 12, no. 11 (June 1, 2004): 8–9.

64. "States Raise Concerns Over DoD Push for Performance Contracts," *DEA* 12, no. 23 (November 16, 2004): 3.

65. "Senators Advocate Rumsfeld Intervention in Chemical Weapons Program," *DEA* 9, no. 10 (May 8, 2001): 6–8.

66. "Citizens, Army Battle It Out Over Chemical Demilitarization 2007 Deadline," *DEA* 9, no. 10 (May 8, 2001): 8.

67. "Army Reorganizes Oversight of Chemical Demilitarization Program," *DEA* 9, no. 26 (December 18, 2001): 13–14.

68. "Senators Question Management Shifts in Chem Demil Program," *DEA* 10, no. 12 (June 4, 2002): 9.

69. "Fiori Resigns as Army Installations and Environment Top Official," *DEA* 11, no. 24 (December 2, 2003): 11–12.

70. "Activists Hail White's Action to Revamp Chemical Demil Program," *DEA* 11, no. 2 (January 28, 2003): 4.

71. "Military Claims Some Gains in Streamlining Chem Demil Program," *DEA* 11, no. 22 (November 4, 2003): 4.

72. "Top GOP Senator Faces DoD Resistance on Chem Weapons Disposal," *DEA* 13, no. 8 (April 19, 2005): 3.

73. Seth Shulman, *The Threat at Home: Confronting the Toxic Legacy of the U.S. Military* (Boston: Beacon Press, 1992), 115.

74. "Beehler Pushes for 'Environmental Improvement' Across DoD," *DEA* 13, no. 5 (March 8, 2005): 11.

CHAPTER ELEVEN

Lessons for Theory and Practice

The Roman general Gaius Marius once threatened the Greek potentate Mithridates before joining battle, "King, either try to be stronger than the Romans, or else, keep quiet and do what you are told."[1] Those trying to green the U.S. military during the Cold War can identify with Mithridates. With the dawning of the post–Cold War era and especially the election of Bill Clinton, the planets seemed aligned to protect any greening gains made during the Cold War and to advance a beyond-compliance green ethic in the U.S. military. Doing so required sustained and persistent assaults on the military's heroic Cold War myth of sovereignty, secrecy, and sinecure, offensives aimed at creating a post–Cold War ethic of accountability, transparency, and reengagement of resources.

This aim soon gave way under repeated counteroffensives by the military and its allies to shape, prepare, and respond the greening battlefield to their liking. Honed, instead, was a military ethic of gaining as much stability, predictability, and security of operations as the services could extract from a decidedly less hospitable task environment in the post–Cold War era. In the process, these dynamics not only sent mixed signals from the Pentagon and from military leaders to their subordinates about the priority of greening efforts. They also wrought a not insignificant yet still halting, halfway, and patchwork record of progress in protecting prior gains and institutionalizing a green ethic in the U.S. military in the post–Cold War era.

This occurred not for want of trying by Sherri Wasserman Goodman and her team, the White House, congressional allies, state regulators, and environmental activists. Of the eight lessons for success that Sergio Fernandez and Hal Rainey draw from the massive scholarly literature on large-scale organizational change reviewed in chapter 1, efforts were mounted on all fronts.[2] However, they waxed and waned over the years in light of realpolitik. Specifically, recall how persistent efforts were made to "ensure the need" for change, to provide a comprehensive plan, to build both top-management and external support, to acquire and provide resources, to overcome internal resistance, and to institutionalize change. But recall, too, how these efforts were routinely trumped or diluted by other factors, including shifting Clinton administration priorities, electoral changes on Capitol Hill, and internal bureaucratic turf wars.

Still, by the end of the Clinton presidency, even some of the military's staunchest critics conceded that the services were more accountable, transparent, and engaged than ever before with ENR issues. Moreover, although the "pact" so widely reported between the White House and the Pentagon ("Don't push us and we won't push you") on general matters of civil–military affairs may have been real (as noted in chapter 1), the Clinton administration left office able to claim progress made in spite of strong military counterpressures to marginalize greater environmental sensitivity. However, as the constant leitmotif against which the administration's greening efforts at the Pentagon were sometimes hedged, this pact inevitably left uneven progress in its wake.

Also clear by the time Clinton left office was that misaligned structures, processes, and procedures left in the wake of coaxing progress from the U.S. military did not so much resolve conflict as plant the seeds for future crises of authority. Chronicled has been a tale of large-scale organizational change being less about the power of ideas than about the protection and pursuit of the political, organizational, and personal prerogatives perceived by the combatants. And one way to advance these prerogatives was for the contestants to protect or create administrative, responsibility, and accounting structures that institutionalized roles for themselves, thus ensuring future access and influence for all involved.

In the process of doing so, however, the structural compromises bequeathed to Clinton's successors new constraints on greening if the political, economic, or international context shifted to advantage greening opponents. Nor did it take long for this to happen. First came the election of George W. Bush as president, followed by September 11, the War on Terror, the U.S. invasions of Afghanistan and Iraq, and the Iraqi insurgency. In short order, a counteroffensive by the military began to gain broad-based exemptions from U.S. ENR laws. The law did not fall silent in time of war, but not for lack of effort by elements in the White House, the military, the Pentagon, and their congressional allies.

With this as background, this final chapter returns to the implications of these dynamics for theory and practice. Integrated *across* the cases are the substance, logic, and empirical grounding for the consistent trajectory, motives, issues, tactics, and implications of contestation witnessed for theory building and practice. Not only are these the empirical "answers" to the research questions posed throughout this book, but they comprise the interrelated conceptual elements of the polity-centered perspective on large-scale organizational change discerned from the analyses.

The Trajectory Question Revisited

Perhaps most striking across the chapters in this book has been a clear, persistent, and enduring trajectory of contestation accompanying efforts to green the U.S. military in the post–Cold War era. As noted in chapter 1, this arc is akin to, but not isomorphic with, the pattern of politics that Stephen Skowronek describes in his classic work on American political development, *Building a New American*

State.[3] Notable in the patterns of politics witnessed are historical-structural impasses, offensives, counteroffensives, crises of authority, and consolidations.

Historical–Structural Impasses

Confronting the actors involved in organizational change in each of the chapters were major shocks to the system. These included, for example, the end of the Cold War, the rise of asymmetric threats, massive budget deficit projections, and the expansion of urban development near military training bases. Indeed, as historical institutionalists might say, these shocks collectively reflect the impact of a conjoint set of factors that propelled efforts to create a corporate sense of responsibility for building a beyond-compliance ENR ethic within the military.

As rational adaptive theories of organizational change predict, perceptions that existing administrative, responsibility, and accounting structures were not up to the task of dealing with these shocks (i.e., that historical-structural impasses existed) stimulated what Thomas Barnett calls horizontal, reflexive, and minishocks throughout the regulatory, national security, and military communities.[4] These included the revamping of strategic, tactical, and operational doctrines; downsizing the U.S. military and closing military bases; building faster, more mobile, and more lethal weapons systems that required greater land and airspace to train the way the military fought; and disposing of chemical weapons.

These shocks in turn cascaded (1) downward (e.g., intergovernmentally, within and across federal and state regulatory agencies, affected communities, Native American tribes, private contractors, and interest groups), (2) outward (e.g., internationally, in terms of the CWC and the interoperability of weapons systems for joint military operations with the North Atlantic Treaty Organization and other allies), and (3) upward (e.g., judicially, from the legal actions of grassroots environmental activists). As sociological institutionalists might say, the field of affected government regulators, regulatees, interests, and ideas was faced with a series of policy and structural choices that were typically multiway, recursive, and reflexive.

The cases also show, however, that the meanings of these shocks are not objective "givens" and are just as hotly contested as predicted by the proactive set of change theories in chapter 1 (especially dialectical-conflict theories). Indeed, battles over meaning (i.e., sense making) sometimes changed over time with shifting perceptions of advantage, a constant theme of recent scholarship on civil–military relations. At all times, however, information about the meanings and implications of these shocks, minishocks, and proposed reforms was filtered through the institutional, professional, program, and personal agendas of affected actors. Greening contestants within and across all levels of government then sought to enact and negotiate the environment in their respective interests, paving the way to diffusing and imposing their perceptions of problems and solutions upon other actors.

Consider the continuing struggles over the meaning of shocks and minishocks among defense intellectuals, Pentagon planners, the military, and environmentalists prior to and after September 11. Contested, for example, was the relative priority that environmental security merited (e.g., expanding national security to include ENR issues), what effective strategic doctrine might be, and how best to restructure forces. Likewise, contests occurred among the White House, the OMB, federal and state regulators, and environmental activists over how aggressively to hold the military accountable to ENR laws in the aftermath of the Cold War. Moreover, position shifts as circumstances changed were illustrated in, among other ways, the military's evolving stance on DERA fencing, the EPA's fencepost-to-fencepost policy, and questions of the applicability of the RCRA versus CERCLA at clean-up sites.

Offensives, Counteroffensives, and Crises of Authority

Next, and as dialectical and conflict theories of organizational change posit, proponents of greening launched multifaceted offensives during the Clinton years to enhance the prospects of creating a beyond-compliance ENR ethic within the U.S. military. With greening proponents at times unified on prescriptions (e.g., against incineration-based methods of chemical weapons disposal) and at other times split (e.g., federal versus state regulators over state consultation requirements), they seized upon these shocks and minishocks to pursue their goals. Some aims were old but unrealized. These included limiting sovereign immunity claims by the military, opposing open burning/open detonation of munitions, and completing cleanups at FUDS. Others were new, including adopting INRM planning, employing ELCCA, and purchasing environmentally preferred products.

Importantly, as Skowronek and theorists in the dialectical-conflict, civil–military, and policy diffusion perspectives posit, offensives frequently were tempered (i.e., diluted) by the cost-benefit tradeoffs inherent in portfolio management. Indeed, even the strongest greening supporters in the Clinton administration had to decide how far, fast, and aggressively to push for changes in the military's behavior. In some cases, for example, the White House and Goodman tamped down their initial aspirations in light of such things as pressure to transfer base properties more quickly for economic development, resource needs related to mounting numbers of military deployments, and the Republican takeover of Congress after 1994.

In turn, and as Skowronek describes, counteroffensives by opponents of greening on anything but the military's terms soon followed in the Clinton years. In the process, the greening of the military also offers support for the modified path dependency posited by historical institutionalists, as well as the calculative claims of rational choice institutionalism and dialectical-conflict perspectives regarding organizational change. One repeatedly sees, for instance, how the fate of initiatives to alter existing structures, processes, and procedures definitely favored the status quo. Thus, deviations from that path were advanced but hardly

guaranteed by systemic shocks and minishocks and their accompanying offensives. Also, part and parcel of this dynamic, one sees the constraints on perceptions of the "need to change" imposed by the size, age, and relative power of
participants. Here, power and resource differentials among the DoD, EPA, and
FWS were illustrative. Moreover, perceptions of advantage or disadvantage were
filtered through organizational cultures and subcultures, impacts on existing political economies, and calculations of personal or professional advantage.

Consider, for example, the overall impact of the services' heroic myth of sovereignty, secrecy, and sinecure whenever greening initiatives arose to threaten
that myth. Illustrative are the greater transparency threatened by INRM planning, by state involvement at UXO sites, by the incorporation of qualitative values in relative risk ranking of sites, and by mandates to compute ENR liabilities.
Similarly illustrative is the internecine turf warfare unleashed within the OSD
by several of Goodman's initiatives (e.g., on ENR research and development programs), as well as the services' fears that ELCCA might jeopardize preferred
weapons acquisitions or cost casualties on the battlefield. As such, and as Skowronek accurately posits, any organizational change that occurred was extracted
from the ancien regime, often on its terms and in ways protecting the stability,
predictability, and security of military operations.

Together, this thrust-and-parry politics produced a series of prolonged crises
of authority in each of the policy areas covered, crises followed by extended
and occasionally heated negotiations and bargaining among the actors. Sometimes these contests were propelled by disputes over statutory application (e.g.,
RCRA versus CERCLA during cleanups or the use of the Safe Drinking Water
Act rather than RCRA or CERCLA at the Massachusetts Military Reservation;
see chapter 10, note 21). At other times, they involved crises over whose methodologies, statistics, or assessments were authoritative. Consider, for example,
crises of authority over the military's relative risk-ranking methodologies, over
milspecs versus NPR reforms, and over the effects of low-frequency sonar on
whales. Illustrative, also, were conflicts over potential volatility and fatality rates
of stored chemical weapons.

At still other times, crises were provoked by internal bureaucratic turf wars
over authority. Recall, for example, the imbroglios that resulted from Goodman's
initiatives to advance civilian control over the military services, including her
effort to create regional authorities in which her office would coordinate cross-
service ENR activities. Moreover, at all times, conflicts surfaced over who had
final authority when disputes arose among the parties, with the military insistent
on protecting its authority. Relevant here, for example, were the services' positions when it came to the content and oversight of INRM plans, remedy selection at Superfund and RCRA sites, ISO 14001 self-certification, and institutional
controls at former sites.

What is more, and unlike rational choice assumptions (with the exception of
Elinor Ostrom's), it was not just Washington-centered actors who occupied the

field and provoked challenges, counteroffensives, or crises of authority. Throughout most of the chapters, subnational actors with their own independent sources of leverage worked to (re)define issues and ensure their power, access, and influence in future organizational decisions. They did so by crafting bureaucratic structures, processes, and procedures to advance their causes through organizational change. Consequently, Washington-based actors like the Pentagon, members of Congress, and federal regulators often were forced to joust with these subnational actors over structures, processes, and procedures that eventually looked decidedly different from what they preferred.

Consider the impact that state resistance from Indiana, Kentucky, and Maryland had on preferences for incineration and interstate transport of chemical weapons for demilitarization. Recall, as well, that no matter how hard the military, the White House, the OMB, the Congressional Budget Office, and the Pentagon tried to move away from a litigate-first to a risk-based, priority-ranking regime for cleanups, these subnational actors stymied such efforts. They preferred, in most instances, a court-driven and less quantitative priority-setting procedure than Pentagon models offered. Nor were governors, state regulators, and professional associations such as NAAG and ASTSWMO silent partners when it came to processes and procedures. Consider their role in designating bases as Superfund sites (first embracing and then fighting designations), the munitions rule, UXO cleanup and priority-setting procedures, and interstate shipping of chemical wastes from incinerators. Also illustrative of this phenomenon are the key roles of state regulators and state legislatures in setting and applying applicable or relevant and appropriate requirements, in oversight, in adopting institutional controls, in approving any munitions rule promulgated, and in working with federal officials on emergency preparedness plans.

To be sure, the Pentagon and its congressional allies tried to influence these decisions indirectly. They did so, for example, by not disputing rumors that environmental costs might lead to base closures in subsequent rounds of BRACs, by cutting back on state oversight assistance in DSMOA funding requests, and by providing key information at the last minute when deadlines required timely state action (e.g., on the munitions rule and its relative risk-ranking mechanisms). But in many cases the states only balked, rallied state regulatory associations to fight the efforts, appealed (sometimes successfully) to EPA or the White House, and either waited for, or went public to prod, litigious interest groups into action.

Thus these crises of authority did *not* metaphorically constitute one-way streets of influence (as most rational choice theorists posit in the U.S. context), with Washington-centered political principals the dominant actors. Rather, they were frequently more like two-way streets of influence (with career military acting as strategic and proactive players in shaping change agendas) and even more often like busy New England "rotaries."[5] In terms of two-way streets, the Pentagon and the services worked extensively (as recent scholarship on civil–military relations posits) with Congress to resist certain initiatives (e.g., legislation to make the military do TRI reporting) and to launch initiatives of their own. The latter included eliminating the DERA fence and the EPA's fence post-to-fence post policy, and pressing for the RRPI during the George W. Bush presidency. In terms of the New England rotary metaphor, actors from all levels of government and spanning all sectors influenced organizational change. Also, not unlike on New England rotaries, they did so by merging from all directions (legislative, executive, and judicial), with some fighting to enter and others to exit, and with some knowing and playing by the rules and others making them up as they went along.

Moreover, unlike the predictions of many rational choice institutionalists, the dominant players during the Clinton years in this hybrid policy arena where ENR and defense policy intersect were neither Congress and interest groups *nor* presidents and the bureaucracy. Rather, Congress and the bureaucracy (especially the career military), dominated, with state regulators and the courts offering constraints on their actions. All of which suggests that hybrid policy arenas are different from those of pure domestic or international policy realms, a hypothesis worthy of future research. Also useful would be studies of civil–military relations that go beyond the top-down principal–agent models to incorporate the more bottom-up dynamics of hybrid policy domains.

Consolidations

Appropriate metaphor aside, the bargaining produced by these crises of authority spawned a series of structural, procedural, or process consolidations (or compromises). Moreover, much like Skowronek, various rational choice institutionalists, and dialectical-conflict theorists predict, these were halfway, halting, and patchwork entities of dubious effectiveness because of their misalignment with ENR goals. Consider, for example, how parallel structures created by Goodman and her staff to advance a beyond-compliance ethic were left ambiguous after prolonged negotiations. Illustrative, too, were the misaligned structures that resulted from negotiations over authority-related disputes over pollution prevention, ENR career tracking, ELCCA, chemical weapons disposal, and the greening of weapons systems (e.g., the JG-APP). Likewise, guidance documents involving the INRM initiative, pollution control, and UXO removal came years after each of these initiatives were launched, thus leaving affected actors to work out how (or how not) to proceed. Produced, as a result, were variations in responses to greening initiatives throughout the military services.

Indeed, portfolio management again reigned supreme as military bases faced with ambiguity and misaligned structures responded to more localized bureau-political pressures. Sometimes greening efforts simply did not occur as fast as hoped across all military bases because of factors beyond the services' control. Recall, for instance, the obstacles to adoption of Energy Savings Performance Contracts at bases. At other times, structural variations resulting from cross-service cultural differences produced the dysfunctional "taken-for-granted" behavior predicted by sociological institutionalists.[6] Illustrative are the army's "creative accounting" scandals and resistance to considering alternatives to in- cineration, the air force's technical hubris when it came to NEPA environmental assessments and EISs; and the navy's resistance to limitations on low- and medium- frequency radar during training exercises.

At yet other times, variations in implementation were attributable to the tardy, ambiguous, or underresourced (budget and staff) nature of Pentagon and service guidance to base commanders. Recall, for example, the implementa- tion variations attributable to guidance ambiguity over such things as classifying ODCs as mission critical, over what constituted major federal actions under the ESA, and over computing environmental liabilities. For example, it was not until the George W. Bush administration that the Pentagon enunciated two supple- mental guidance documents, in 2002 and 2004, for implementing the five-year reviews of INRM plans required under the 1997 Sikes Act amendments and for defining what constituted environmental costs.

Likewise, despite uncertainties due to the conflict between the NPR's procure- ment reforms and the military's need to green the procurement and acquisitions process by adding or modifying milspecs, only conflicting or incomplete guid- ance documents were issued for many years. Equally infuriating to proponents of greening was the five years the Pentagon took to issue biodiversity manage- ment guidelines to ensure consistency of approach in natural resources manage- ment. But similarly, variation-inducing was unclear guidance from the services themselves to base commanders even after clear guidance from the Pentagon. Consider how this happened when it came to determining how much regulatory agency and public involvement was required in developing the Relative Risk Site Evaluation Framework, in the operation of RABs, and in the design, operations, and emergency planning of chemical demilitarization sites.

The Motivational Question Revisited

Analysis of efforts to green the U.S. military in the post–Cold War era also sug- gests that the patterns of politics driving the actors' behaviors throughout this trajectory of contestation are themselves conditioned partially by three sets of factors: history (time), context (timing), and contingency (time sensitivity). The interaction of the three appear to weigh directly into the calculi of greening proponents and opponents, affecting their perceptions of (1) shocks and mini- shocks; (2) how, when, and why to launch offensives and counteroffensives and to frame issues to advance their causes in the wake of them; (3) how intensely and prolonged they should press crises of authority; and (4) what consolidations of structures, processes, and procedures should ultimately look like to protect their interests. Moreover, these factors were affected by changes in the political, social, economic, and technological contexts that greening proponents and opponents faced at any given time. And among these considerations at all times, selective attention to and marshaling of "facts" (i.e., "filtering") and issue framing by the combatants were crafted to advance their interests.

History (Time)

Beginning with history (i.e., time), this book is rife with examples of how choices made in the past (often long in the past) confronted the present as actors involved weighed their pursuit of and reaction to greening offensives. Consider how the original politics of establishment for many of the military's regulators placed them on a path-dependent arc of incapacity when it came to holding the department accountable to the nation's ENR laws (e.g., burying and underfunding FWS in a prodevelopment DOI). These placed them clearly on the defensive, forced concessions that might not have otherwise been made, and made external pressures on the military critical for offsetting the Pentagon's advantages.

Likewise indicative of the impact on contestants' calculations is the military's Cold War heroic myth of sovereignty, secrecy, and sinecure, as well as the political economy that nourished and protected that myth over the decades. Indicative of what historical institutionalists call the sequencing of history, the dynamics reported in this book suggest that progress toward a post–Cold War ethic of accountability, transparency, and reengagement of resources did occur. However, any progress made was bounded or limited by changing perceptions of self-interest among members of the military's Cold War political economy or by changing perceptions of the relative advantages of traditional tactics as post–Cold War events transpired. Examples of the former included contractors becoming more willing to accept greening in the wake of globalized weaponry sales and becoming more or less receptive to energy conservation initiatives as energy costs waxed and waned. Illustrations of the latter included revised calculations of the relative advantages of RCRA versus CERCLA regulation and the fencing of DERA funds in light of shifting political, economic, and mission demands on the military.

Additional conditioning factors associated with the DoD's history involved lackluster management systems so critical to greening the U.S. military (e.g., financial and information management systems). Deficiencies in these areas had made perennial appearances on the GAO's high-risk lists and were deeply rooted in and protected by the Pentagon's political economy.[7] Similarly, the interaction of historical disadvantage and spiraling workloads placed regulatory agencies at a severe disadvantage relative to the U.S. military. Indeed, these regulatory agencies have coevolved in ways rendering them vulnerable to counteroffensives, resource dependency on the military, and load shedding of their own. In this vein, one thinks of the patterns of politics associated with DSMOA grants, critical habitat designations, and privatization of cleanup and enforcement responsibilities.

So without belaboring points already made, there is no question that history mattered in the decision calculi of the military and its regulators in the post–Cold War era. Witnessed throughout this book has been a historical process of stubbornly self-amplifying positive feedback loops that have constrained progress made in greening the U.S. military and that must be addressed if a beyond-compliance ethic is to take root on anything but the military's terms. The book also suggests, however, that history was not dispositive in the decision calculi of the contestants involved; choices to fight, flee, or flail were affected by shifting contexts as well.

Context (Timing)

In terms of context, the patterns of politics witnessed in prior chapters suggest that components of Michael Cohen, James March, and Johan Olsen's original "garbage can" model informed the decision calculi of the contestants.[8] Moreover, changes in these at any point in time often led to changes in actors' perceptions, strategies, and tactics. More precisely, Cohen, March, and Olsen identify several factors critical in organizational choice making, four of which seem equally potent in contestants' decision calculi during the greening of the military in the post–Cold War era. These included entry times, access structures, energy loads, and energy distributions. These in turn shifted with changes in the political, economic, sociological, or technological contexts that lead to changes in issue images.

As noted in previous chapters, *entry times* refer to the pace at which problems and decision opportunities regarding changes in rule sets confronted actors in the field at any given time. For instance, the impact of the conjunction of entry times in the cleanup arena is readily apparent. Recall how the military's hopes for priority setting for cleanups were helped by the release of the Rivlin–McGinty report, by Congress pressing for faster cleanups through CERFA, by Clinton's Fast-Track initiative, and by budget deficits. Less positively for greening, these same pressures led to protean, powerful, and effective downward pressures on cleanup standards for contaminated sites, pressures that the White House, EPA, and state regulators incorporated into their decision making.

In turn, *access structures* refer to how readily other problems and decision opportunities are or get linked by the combatants at any point in time to the offensives and counteroffensives targeting organizational change. These are important because they can expand or narrow the audience paying attention to the fight at any given time, thus either altering or protecting historical balances of forces supporting and opposing organizational change. In the process, actors' perceptions of the costs and benefits of organizational change can vary accordingly. Recall, for instance, how the military had to alter its tactics and strategies regarding priority setting with the entry of concerns about environmental justice, BRAC, and transferring properties for redevelopment. Similar changes in decision calculi affected by expanded access structures were the ways in which terrorism issues morphed into greening ones, Kyoto got linked to pollution prevention, and the military relied on larger battles over property rights to advance its perspectives on the ESA. As such, access structures also are especially vulnerable to changes in issue images, including salience (the importance of issues to key stakeholders), proximity (whether these stakeholders are affected directly or indirectly), valence (positive or negative perceptions of actors involved in the issue), and boundary (whether other issues morph or become part of an issue) effects.

Relatedly, *energy loads* refer to the nature and ratio of agency resources to agency responsibilities at any given time, whereas *energy distributions* refer to who has the resources, predisposition, and comparative strength to advance organizational change. These were all factors advancing, constraining, or reversing the decision calculi of contestants. Consider, for example, how recession concerns, budget deficits, and cuts in resources by Congress led to serious strains on energy loads relative to ENR tasks, strains that pushed the White House into less aggressive regulatory postures. These in turn resulted in cleanup delays for many years, strained the abilities of state regulators to perform oversight functions, and occasionally led to budget shenanigans like those chronicled in the army's chemical demilitarization and FUDs programs.

In turn, inadequate EPA and FWS funding at any given time, as well as misallocation of funds, affected the military's decisions regarding the extent of organizational change the services needed to pursue. For example, NPR cuts in funding alone left only 18 percent of the EPA's workforce in the regions as the Clinton administration pushed for accelerated risk evaluations under its Fast-Track Cleanup Program. Faster timetables, combined with fewer resources to do or oversee them at the EPA and in the states, eased the regulatory pressure on base commanders accordingly. Meanwhile, whistle-blowers at Utah's Tooele talked repeatedly of inadequate oversight and persistent flaws in design and operation, inadequacies leading contractors to conclude that safety perhaps was not a priority.

Implicit in all this, of course, were the ebb and flow of differences in energy distributions at any given time between the military services and their regulators. These were disparities that further altered the decision calculi of all concerned (including grassroots groups). Included among the altered calculations wrought by these disparities in resources were the military's victories on de minimis standards for early transfers of contaminated properties, in getting localities to pony up additional resources for buffer zones, and in obtaining less rigorous state oversight of clean ups. This is not to suggest, however, that the services won all these battles. They often had to cut deals with regulators in order to avoid even worse outcomes from their perspective. And when they had to cut deals, they were especially conscious of not creating precedents (e.g., at Fort Ord on UXO). It is to suggest, however, that power asymmetries favoring opponents of greening the military were important contextual forces in altering contestants' decision calculi.

Contingency (Time Sensitivity)

The final factor conditioning the decision calculi of contestants during efforts to green the U.S. military in the post–Cold War era involved the impact of delays on organizational missions, interests, and values. In this regard, considerations of political, administrative, and technical time played important roles in the decision calculi of greening opponents. On the one hand, these included the military delaying action to await election results, holding back information until deadlines for administrative actions approached (e.g., on reviews of DoD documentation and rules), and strategically using statutory and CWC treaty deadlines to justify incineration.

On the other hand, considerations of the impact of delays on organizational missions, interests, and values also sometimes constrained the military beyond what historical or contextual factors would predict. Recall how environmental activists used the delays inherent in threatened court suits to gain concessions from the services that they otherwise would not have made (e.g., when the Military Toxics Project threatened to sue the EPA and DoD over delays in issuing the munitions rule). At the same time, the extent of behavioral change that various greening initiatives required of the military interacted with the delays these might impose on carrying out the services' core warfighting mission to both animate and constrain the military's behavior. Consider, for example, the political ferocity and still precarious fate involved in shifting the army away from its preferred incineration strategy. Such a green policy change represented a significant shift from a fairly well-understood, albeit environmentally controversial, incineration technique to a then-nascent and untested neutralization strategy.

To counteract this predisposition, greening proponents often tried to link their initiatives to more core mission-related ones. Illustrative, for example, was how Goodman repeatedly tried to link her C^3P^2 plus technology agenda to major core mission events like the NPR, the DRI, and Joint Vision 2010. In the end, however, stalling by the services and their congressional allies eventually complicated or even stymied these initiatives, as intervening events occurred that became more salient and pressing. The latter included contingency operations, claims of encroachment, financial or contracting scandals, resignations of or shifts in personnel, and the release of independent reports.

Meanwhile, more incremental changes that did not pose mission-threatening delays were less opposed and more readily accommodated by the U.S. military. These included, among many others, the adoption of various cleanup techniques at contaminated sites, some pollution prevention techniques related to waste minimization like recycling, and some aspects of institutional controls such as deed stipulations. In these instances, the scope of the conflict typically was limited to the creation of informal settlement processes and parallel decision structures (e.g., within the military or among the military, regulators, and other stakeholders).

The Issues Question Revisited

Having reprised the overall trajectory of contestation and the decision calculi used by actors within it as these related to the greening of the U.S. military in the post–Cold War era, the next question with theoretical and practical import is recounting how patterns existed in the types of issues they fought over. Analysis revealed that an adaptation of Elinor Ostrom's institutional analysis and development framework hikes to a more conceptual level the fodder for contestation witnessed in the chapters. More precisely, the greening experiences chronicled indicate a persistent targeting of various types of rule sets as key components of these battles over large-scale organizational change. Ostrom defines *rules* as "shared understandings among those involved that refer to enforced prescriptions about what actions (or states of the world) are required, prohibited, or permitted."[9] Relating adaptations of her concepts to the dynamics witnessed in this book, three general types of nested rule sets were the typical fodder for battles among the contestants: constitutional, collective choice, and operational.

As developed and applied in previous chapters, constitutional rule sets are foundational rules and norms, in this case related to such things as separation of powers, checks and balances, and federalism, and the constraints they impose on organizational change. These afford a generic foundational context that shapes subsequent decisions over collective choice and operational rule sets. In turn, collective choice rule sets are rules and norms, in this case, concerning policymaking, management, adjudication, and monitoring (i.e., accounting) processes. They determine who is eligible to participate in decision making during implementation and the "specific rules to be used in changing [subsequent] operational rules."[10] They are of two types: (1) those made formally by Congress or state legislatures, regulatory agencies, the OSD, leaders in the three services (including the Joint Chiefs and service chiefs when issuing guidance documents for implementers), and the courts; and (2) those made informally by (or expected by) interest groups, associations, and other stakeholders (e.g., contractors, private citizens, and cities located near military bases, waste sites, or groundwater supplies). In turn, these rules, along with what sociological institutionalists call "rules in use" (i.e., informal understandings, norms, expectations, and taken-for-granted behavior), affect subsequent operational-level rules and actions. Lastly, operational rule sets are rules (e.g., subsequent interpretations of guidance documents to and by EPA regions and military base commanders) that affect day-to-day operational decisions in specific instances regarding policy, management, adjudication, and monitoring or accounting processes.

Importantly, adaptations of seven types of rules that Ostrom identifies within each of these three nested rule sets figured prominently in contests over the greening of the U.S. military. A partial list of illustrations for each of the seven types is provided in table 11.1. Illustrative of what she calls entry and exit rules (or boundary rules), for example, were perennial battles over constitutional rules identifying the extent to which facilities qualified as regulatory targets, and whether the national security status of military facilities qualified them for being treated differently from private polluters (e.g., over TRI reporting). So, too, were collective choice and operational rule battles over when ODCs qualified as mission critical, and when facilities entered and exited noncompliance status. Likewise illustrative were collective choice and operational conflicts over the EPA's fence post-to-fence post rule regarding Superfund site listings, over when products qualified as environmentally preferred, and over when base properties could exit public ownership for private development.

In turn, one repeatedly finds across the chapters contests regarding nested constitutional, collective choice, and operational rule sets reminiscent of what Ostrom calls battles over authority, scoping, and position rules. These refer, respectively, to allocations of decision-making power, functional responsibilities, and official status to participate. As noted, constitutional-level debates over rule sets relating to sovereign immunity, the unitary executive theory, and the Antideficiency Act were at the heart of perceptions, tactical calculations, and debates over greening. Moreover, these authority rules had cascading effects at other levels.

Examples included conflicts over collective choice and operational rules determining who had final say when disputes arose over INRM plans and UXO cleanups as well as over scoping and position rules affecting membership on RABs at BRAC cleanup sites. Similarly illustrative were scoping battles over what RAB roles were relative to local reuse authorities and BRAC cleanup teams, over devolving responsibilities and functions to the army, and over leaving final authority with the DoD in the Southwest and California Desert Protection Act collaborative initiatives (authority rules). Illustrative, too, were conflicts targeted at such authority and scoping rule issues as whether cleanups should be state led or federal led (i.e., CERCLA versus RCRA), over who had responsibility for monitoring institutional controls at transferred contaminated sites (the military or the states), and over the relationship between the JG-APP and the individual services in weapons system acquisition.

Rife with implications for greening the U.S. military, as well, were conflicts targeting information rule sets. As noted repeatedly across the cases, statutes like NEPA and the ESA, as well as INRM planning, mandating TRI, and ENR liabilities, provoked counteroffensives by the military because of the wider stakeholder participation they threatened. Challenged directly by these kinds of information rules, after all, was the services' view that they were the experts to whom others should defer and whose information was sufficient for decision making. This predisposition surfaced, for example, whenever the services tried to make their own risk-ranking models and studies dispositive (e.g., regarding the threats posed by leaching of chemicals into groundwater and in modeling of plumes from chemical weapons explosions and burns).

The final two types of collective choice and operational rules adapted from Ostrom's work that were repeatedly targeted in bitterly fought battles were aggregation rules and payoff rules. The former, as noted, refer to rules for making decisions, whereas the latter involve rules for determining the allocation of benefits and costs for required, permitted, or prohibited activities. Examples of contests targeting aggregation rules were disputes over rules requiring military acquisition officers to consider ENR impacts when buying new or retrofitting old weapons. Contentious, too, were rules regarding how much the military had to consider the ENR record of contractors before letting contracts, whether statistical sampling was sufficient at UXO-contaminated FUDS, whether de minimis standards for transferring properties were sufficiently protective of public health and safety, and what constituted appropriate mission-critical use of ODCs. Likewise indicative was the military's finessing of NEPA rules regarding the segmenting (i.e., limiting or tactically altering the scope) of environmental assessments and EISs to mask the cumulative ENR impacts of overflights and training (e.g., at MHAFB in South Dakota).

In turn, payoff rules—and the ability to monitor and enforce them—were repeatedly targeted for contestation during efforts to green the U.S. military, with the cases highlighting the nested and reflexive effects among constitutional, collective choice, and operational rule sets. Greening proponents, for instance, were able to alter rules regarding the personal liability of service personnel for egregious violations of hazardous waste dumping laws (albeit these were not targeted at military brass), to make good ENR stewardship (or at least no major stewardship embarrassments) a promotional condition for base commanders, and to prevent the shifting of ENR protection costs to taxpayers and private companies by preventing broad exemptions for the military from RCRA, the Clean Water Act, and the Clean Air Act in the post–September 11 era. They were less successful, however, when it came to preventing the shifting of payoff costs to localities that had to change zoning rules to help the military address its encroachment problems.

As Ostrom also posits, the more that greening depended on operational rule changes that in turn depended on changes in collective choice rules, the more difficult greening became. Recall, for example, the toll taken on greening by battles over rules related to how much and in what ways resources were allocated by Congress, within the Pentagon, and to and across the states. Also important in constraining large-scale organizational change were evolving strategic, operational, and tactical military doctrines, as well as changes in who made the collective choice rules associated with them. The latter included the impact following shifts in party control and committee chairmanships in the Congress subsequent to the 1994 midterm elections, as well as after the 2000 presidential election. Moreover, as Ostrom also predicts, the most difficult challenges to greening came whenever it was dependent on changes in collective choice rules that in turn depended on changes in constitutional rules. The latter included the obstacles to greening afforded by such constitutional rules as the unitary executive theory, the doctrine of sovereign immunity, and the Antideficiency Act.

Table 11.1. Rules and Illustrations

Rules	Related to
Entry and exit	When bases were "clean" and/or clean enough for transfer
	Whether Congress waived sovereign immunity for federal facilities
	What qualified as a RCRA solid waste when it came to munitions
	Which sites qualified for nonincineration technology (all or just some)
	What qualified as mission-critical ODCs
	What constituted a Superfund site
	What qualified as an EPP
	What statute applied in any cleanup situation
	What qualified as adequate effort by the military to obtain cleanup funds
	Whether the DERA fence should come down
Authority, scoping, and position	Who had final authority when disputes arose between the military and regulators across various statutes
	Whether cleanups should be state or federal led
	Whether OSD or the services should determine the allocation of DSMOA funding
	Who had responsibility (OMB or DOJ) under the unitary executive theory
	Who had responsibility in the case of emergencies at chemical waste disposal sites (FEMA or the state)
	Who should determine mission-critical ODC usage (OSD or the services)
	Who had final authority and responsibility, and for what, after contaminated properties were transferred for private development
	Who had authority for ENR personnel decisions (Goodman's office or the individual services)
	Whether the services should act independently in DoD regions or whether Goodman's office should coordinate
	What the roles of RABs were at cleanup sites
	How much LRAs should participate in decisions at cleanups
	Who has legal standing to sue DoD for environmental contamination, misfeasance, or malfeasance
Information and aggregation	Whose risk-ranking models and studies would be determinative (internal DoD models/studies or independent studies)
	The scoping of environmental assessments and EISs
	What were appropriate geographical boundaries
	How adequate was the science
	When were programmatic environmental assessments and EISs appropriate
	How much guidance the services should be given
	How accurate was the environmental liability reporting done by DoD

Table 11.1. (continued)

Rules	Related to
	Whether the military had to comply with TRI reporting requirements
	Whether acquisition officers have to consider ENR impacts when buying/retrofitting weapons
	How much of a role international organizations or businesses should play in setting milspecs
	Whether businesses with poor environmental records should be able to bid for DoD contracts
	Whether shipment of demilitarized chemical weapons across state lines was an appropriate disposal option
	How many nonincineration options the army had to consider
Payoff	What was the personal liability of service personnel for hazardous waste dumping
	Should good ENR stewardship be a condition for promoting base commanders
	Whether RCRA or CERCLA standards applied to cleanups (RCRA with stricter state standards)
	Whether ELCCA had to be applied to weapons acquisition and retrofitting (potentially shifting the distribution of weapons purchases by the services)
	Who pays for cleanups after land is transferred to private parties for development
	Should ENR positions, cleanups, and energy conservation be privatized
	When the Antideficiency Act was applicable

The Tactics Question Revisited

With the trajectory, motivational bases, and fodder of contestation for greening the U.S. military now summarized conceptually, still needed is a review of the tactics employed consistently by the contestants when fighting over these rule sets. For the reader's convenience, table 11.2 summarizes and illlustrates the five analytically distinct repertoires of contestation discerned consistently across the cases.

Definition/Redefinition

One of the most sustained, persistent, and effective aspects of the military's counteroffensives witnessed in prior chapters involved issue framing and reframing throughout the post–Cold War era (partially as a means to mobilize allies and demobilize opponents). As noted, the leitmotif against which all other issue (re)framing took place was the consistent ability of the armed forces and their congressional allies to portray greening on anything but the military's terms as a

Table 11.2. Tactics of Contestation

Repertoires	Examples
(Re)Definition	1. ENR secondary to military mission (nondefense-related expenditures)
	2. Zero-sum tradeoff among ENR-military readiness-weapons modernization
	3. Compromises "training the way we fight"
	4. BRAC threats (implied and actual)
	5. BRAC-proofing economic impact
	6. Can't meet CWC without incineration
	7. UXO cleanup as a matter of explosives expertise, not public health and safety related to toxics
	8. Peace dividend threats
	9. Environmental security counterarguments
	10. Linking Kyoto to conservation (boundary effects)
(De)Mobilization	1. Boundary activation/deactivation
	"Piecemealing" environmental assessments and EISs
	Base expansions
	Affected population data for explosives related to chemical weapons demilitarization
	Native American tribes (settling first because of unique legal status)
	2. Statute shopping
	RCRA versus CERCLA and Safe Drinking Water Act versus RCRA
	3. Constituency shopping
	Internal (Pentagon)
	External (courts, GAO, local nongovernmental organizations, confederated associations, Keystone group, NRC, etc.)
	4. Public-private arguments (same as above but to gain allies or distance the services from other initiatives applicable to private polluters)
	5. Threats on BRAC closures
	6. Private property rights movement
	7. Appeals to sovereigns
	8. "Surfing" political tides and rhythms
	9. "Load shedding," "boundary management," or "demand management"
	Privatizing cleanups
	Leasing before cleanups completed
	Institutional controls
	ESPCs program for energy conservation
(De)Legitimation (claims)	1. Sovereign immunity claims
	"Treat us like privates" or "We're not the same as privates"
	2. Financial Integrity Act to fight fees and fines
	3. Comply with substance of laws but not state procedures

Table 11.2. (continued)

Repertoires	Examples

	4. Appeals to sovereigns
	    Committee shopping (e.g., end runs of ENR committees)
	    Going through Armed Services Committees
	    Using defense authorization bills rather than ENR legislation
	    Appeals to OMB to reverse EPA regulations
	    Going around White House and submitting their own
	        regulations
	    Use of omnibus bills to go directly to floor
	    Appeals to fixers
	5. Avoiding precedent setting
	    On use of statistical sampling for UXO scoping on FUDS
	    Land transfers at Ft. Ord before UXO cleanup
	6. Challenging DSB, NRC, and Army Audit Agency studies

(De)Institution-alization	1. De-skilling (e.g., Goodman's "civilian control" initiatives)
	2. Defunding
	    Cutting back on DSMOA grants
	    Congressional funding cuts and "starts and stops"
	    Army defunding Legacy Resource Management Program
	    ATSDR cuts
	    FWS backlogs on critical habitat designations
	3. Diversion ("objective shifting"), downsizing, and devolution
	    Clinton's NPR
	    Cohen's DRI
	    Best business practices
	    Examples:
	        DERA devolvement to services
	        Devolvement of the Technical Assistance for Public
	            Participation program to army
	        Downsizing ESO office
	        Devolving chemical weapons authority to army
	        Privatization (of cleanups, ENR personnel)
	4. Dependency creation (resource/skills)
	    DSMOA grants with states for oversight of cleanups
	    DESB (for the munitions rule)
	    Full-time equivalency swaps with EPA
	    Training of EPA officials regarding munitions explosives
	5. Deadlines (leveraging them)
	    On the CWC
	    Withholding proposed range rule from states until last minute
	6. Delaying (information)
	    Poor, ambiguous, contradictory, or nonexistent guidance
	        documents for implementation of ENR initiatives by EPA,
	        DoD, or the military services

Table 11.2. (continued)

Repertoires	Examples
	7. "Load shedding," "boundary management," or "demand management"
	Privatizing cleanups
	Leasing before cleanups completed
	Institutional controls
	ESPCs program for energy conservation
(Dis)Information	1. Oversights due to:
	Lack of clear guidance
	Faulty financial management or IT systems
	Historically poor data collection on sites
	Dangers of collecting data (e.g., chemical exposure, UXO)
	2. Historically acceptable "cooking" of numbers
	Army "moving the decimal to the right" while "holding the fort"
	Army's "single-answer" mentality
	Air force's deference to internal expertise
	Navy's "beyond the horizon" mentality
	3. Deliberate distortion of the numbers (e.g., in computing
	Effects of plumes from groundwater contamination at the Massachusetts Military Reservation
	Explosion ranges for chemical demilitarization igloo explosions
	Noise levels and exposures for marine mammals of low-frequency sonar and effects of noise levels on pronghorn sheep and other creatures
	4. Deliberate unresponsiveness on, for example,
	Computing environmental liabilities
	Environmental life-cycle cost accounting
	Statistical sampling of UXO on FUDS
	5. Illegalities; for example:
	Hiding chemical demilitarization funds from Congress so as not to pursue six alternative technologies to incineration
	Contractors falsifying health and safety dangers at Tooele Incinerator

zero-sum tradeoff among ENR protection, military readiness, and weapons modernization. With budget deficits mounting, with ENR funding a component of operations and maintenance budgets for base operations, with contingency operations increasing over the years, and with the downsizing of the military in the post–Cold War era, opponents frequently framed greening operations as nondefense-related expenditures.

Fearing partially that domestic agencies were trying to raid the Pentagon's budget for a "peace dividend" after the dissolution of the Soviet empire, the armed forces and their allies were especially wary of the implications of using these funds for greening rather than for the military's warfighting mission. Moreover, these arguments were nested within the services' ability during the Clinton years to keep the debate inside the parameters of the 1-4-2-1–inspired "Cold War lite" doctrine of strategic pluralism for force structuring. Such an issue-framing device met the bureaucratic needs of the services, as well as those of members of Congress from Gunbelt states, for continuing legacy weapons production with only minor deviations.

In the wake of this issue-framing onslaught, proponents of greening the U.S. military were left with little room to maneuver. To be sure, and as noted previously, they pushed back with issue framing of their own: Only ENR expenditures for cleanup, compliance, conservation, pollution prevention, and technology (Goodman's C^3P^2 plus technology agenda) could ensure military readiness. Likewise, and as noted above, Goodman tried repeatedly (and with some success) to frame ENR initiatives as key components of evolving national security doctrines, Quadrennial Defense Reviews, and strategic vision documents. At the same time, she tried to frame ENR initiatives with appeals to the services' self-interests. As Goodman put it, "DoD does not have enough shovels" for the military to dig its way out of this quagmire without a sustained commitment to pollution prevention.[11] But the services and their congressional allies responded that workarounds of ENR laws were compromising the ability of service members to train the way they fight, and that ENR cleanups at BRAC bases were reducing the savings available for the military's warfighting mission.

Likewise, at different points in time, the military argued (and proponents of greening contested) that EPA's fencepost-to-fencepost policy was distorting the priority setting for cleanups that the White House wanted and that the fences around the DERA and Legacy Resource Management Program funds had to be removed or breached, respectively, due to contingency operation costs. Similarly, the army argued that the military's baseline incineration technology had to proceed because it was an issue of safety (i.e., weapons in igloos were unstable and could explode); because international obligations would otherwise be broken (i.e., only incineration would allow the United States to meet deadlines under the CWC); and because arms control in the former Soviet Union would be jeopardized.

Likewise, on the munitions rule, on greening the acquisitions process, and on base encroachment, the services argued that the issue was not ENR protection, but rather issues of expertise, bad science, and priority setting. Taking these in order, the military and its supporters argued variously that explosion was more of a threat than toxicity, and the DoD was the expert on explosivity, that complex green weaponry could harm or kill servicemen and women in battle, that the science on low-frequency radar was not good enough to abandon incidental takings of ocean mammals, and that it was more important to protect the lives of soldiers in combat than those of prairie toads.

Finally, it bears (re)emphasizing that prior chapters reveal persistent efforts to craft or take advantage of issue imaging. Efforts at making greening issues more salient, proximate (i.e., perceived as directly affecting potential supporters), and positively valenced included the military's silence on ENR-related rumors regarding BRACs (proximity and salience); the use of the mantra "training the way we fight" to portray ENR laws negatively as threats to service members on the battlefield (valence); and implicitly portraying state regulators as too unschooled in national security matters to participate in decision making regarding the munitions and range rules (valence).

Indicative of helping to craft or benefit from boundary effects were the ways that greening opponents in Congress negatively linked the military's energy conservation and greenhouse gas emission initiatives to fears that the Clinton White House would implement the Kyoto Protocol administratively. Also indicative was the linking of ENR laws to delays in BRAC transfers, to undersea training missions on the east and west coasts, and to weapons modernization. So too, of course, did greening proponents use boundary effects to advance their cause, most consistently in Goodman's aforementioned efforts to link greening as central to shifts in national security doctrines (e.g., the Pentagon's "shape, prepare, and respond" doctrine). Also illustrative were their efforts to portray opponents as willing to jeopardize public health and safety in, for example, the UXO, chemical weapons demilitarization, and FUDS cases.

Demobilization/Mobilization

A second set of related repertoires persistently animating the thrust-and-parry politics of creating a corporate sense of responsibility for greening the U.S. military involved efforts to either demobilize opposition to or mobilize support for the military's preferred rule sets. Occasionally, as with arguments related to the ESA, the services had only to await or build on the efforts of private opponents of ENR laws to defend or pursue their preferred positions. On other occasions, "goal creep" broadened the audience paying attention to the fight in ways either advancing or threatening the military's aims. Likewise, greening proponents could sometimes merely await the rallying to their cause of affronted state associations (e.g., ASTSWMO), ENR professional groups (e.g., the National Military Fish and Wildlife Association), national ENR groups (e.g., the Sierra Club), and grassroots groups (e.g., the Military Toxics Project and Common Ground).

Consider, for example, how the military's initial preference for "worst-first" technical priority-setting cleanup models (at CERCLA and RCRA sites) were foiled partially by goal creep. This occurred as subsequent political concerns about such things as FUDS cleanups, environmental justice, and local reuse and development of BRAC bases shifted priorities. Wrenched from these pressures was movement from a "worst-first" to a "best-to-develop-and-reuse-first" to a "most-ready-for-reuse-first" priority-setting scheme. On still other occasions, and as referenced earlier, the military services took advantage of new constellations of political forces that buttressed their positions. These included the Republican takeover of Congress, the 2000 presidential election, September 11, and the War on Terror.

Mostly, however, the services and their allies proactively tried to mobilize or demobilize actors. They used, for example, their shifts on public-private distinctions to either activate support for or deactivate opposition to their positions on rule sets. They did so notably by claiming *no difference* when it came to cleanup standards in order to get support from privates in their quest for regulatory relief or, alternatively, by claiming *differences* on such things as TRI reporting and UXO toxic standards. Recall also how the military tried to use CWC deadlines to build coalitions of support for incineration among national security experts, international organizations, state regulators and legislatures, and within the White House.

Likewise, and as alluded to earlier, opponents of greening on anything but the services' terms did little to tamp down rumors that applying more rigorous and costly cleanup standards to bases might make them vulnerable to closure and realignment in future BRAC rounds. The rumors, it was hoped, might gain the military reductions in the stringency of cleanup standards; prompt threatened cities to zone development away from training bases (e.g., as was done in California, Texas, and other states); and coax locals into cofinancing "buffer zones" around those bases. Pertinent too is how the services tried to use the aforementioned piecemealing of environmental assessments and EISs, as well as their own technical studies, to activate and deactivate potential support and opposition to their plans at places like the MHAFB, the Goldwater Air Force Range, and Fort Irwin.

Also effective in this regard was working with members of Congress to try to BRAC-proof bases in their districts for major investments and missions. Nor should one ignore the services' tendency to "deactivate" Native American concerns by settling first with tribes whenever conflicts arose. They did so because of the tribes' unique status as sovereign nations with legal privileges not enjoyed by the states, and also because of the image problems that not doing so could create for the Pentagon due to the military's sullied history with Native Americans (e.g., the army's involvement in the Cherokee Trail of Tears). In addition, although technological factors informed the army's decision to allow neutralization alternatives to incineration in Indiana, Kentucky, and Maryland, these were hotbeds of opposition to incineration that the army sought with these concessions to hive off from anti-incineration coalitions.

Meanwhile, statute and administrative order "shopping" and "amendment" by both the military and greening proponents were rampant as (de)mobilization tactics in many of the chapters. Recall, for example, the aforementioned battles over RCRA versus CERCLA application and over amending the Sikes Act to allow INRM plans. Also illustrative were disputes over the use of these plans to satisfy NEPA requirements and over the use of the Safe Drinking Water Act (rather than CERCLA or RCRA) to shut down training at the Massachusetts Military Reservation. Each of these statutes came tailored with its own set of stakeholders, so actors from all sides of each issue wanted to ensure that their interests were maintained by applying the "correct" statute in any given situation. Likewise, on the statutory amendment front, consider the tit-for-tat competing appeals to elected officials by greening opponents and proponents to specify sovereign immunity more clearly, to allow interstate shipment of chemical weapons wastes, to have OMB speed approval of the range rule, and to speed up state incineration permits.

If statute shopping was not enough to advance any participant's cause, the "losers" readily turned to external sources to expand or contract alliances. For example, the report of Clinton's FFPG (i.e., the Rivlin-McGinty group) was touted by the military services as justifying their priority-setting models. Meanwhile, groups favoring qualitative and less statistically grounded risk-ranking methods used reports by the Federal Facilities Environmental Restoration Dialogue Committee (i.e., the Keystone Dialogue Group) to insist on a broader range of values in the models and to expand representation on RABs to address environmental justice concerns. Likewise, consider Goodman's use of the DSB report on the link between environmental security and national security in her battles for SERDP, ENR training, and regional defense offices. In kind, her opponents used to their advantage the DoD comptroller's report alleging Goodman's mismanagement of ENR programs.

Finally, the military also tried to demobilize opposition by engaging in what scholars variously call "load shedding," "boundary management," or "demand management." As noted in prior chapters, they define these as occurring whenever organizations performing controversial or conflict-producing tasks try to shift them to other actors. Moreover, this is done typically on objective-sounding grounds like best business practices (see below for a discussion of "objective shifting").[12] Such was partially the Pentagon's aim in its NPR- and DRI-justified efforts to privatize cleanups, move toward institutional controls, cut ENR civilian positions in the military, adopt ISO 14001 standards, and move toward Energy Savings Performance Contracts.

Delegitimation

A third set of repertoires of contestation consistently animating the thrust-and-parry politics witnessed in the chapters involved preemptive *and* retaliatory strikes by the military and their allies on the alleged illegitimacy of efforts by greening proponents. On the preemptive side, the penultimate tactic was a familiar constitutional and legal one used during the Cold War and highlighted earlier in this chapter: The military posited sovereign immunity claims whenever it could, fought fines and other levies as violations of the Antideficiency Act, and pressed to keep disputes within the DOJ-OMB framework afforded by the unitary executive theory. Nor, as noted, did the military and its allies feel compelled to be consistent in making these claims. Rather, tactical advantage was the operant principle.

For example, state regulators and environmental activists were vocal in challenging the military's repeated claim that public-private differences justified allowing the services to self-certify compliance. On similar grounds, the military sought regulatory relief from complying with Department of Transportation storage, transportation, and disposal requirements under RCRA, with "drop-dead" deadlines for BRAC cleanups, and with ENR liability rules that were not available to private polluters. Conversely, the services argued that they should be treated the same as private polluters when, for example, it came to institutional controls and to transferring properties before cleanups were fully completed. Similar arguments informed their efforts to view NEPA requirements as "optional" and "not applicable to its major Defense [*sic*] acquisition programs," as well as when it came to using incineration technologies.[13]

Also illustrative of delegitimation efforts by the military services and their allies were their aforementioned appeals through the Pentagon to elected officials to be their "fixers" (sometimes on the invitation of congressional allies).[14] These were efforts not only to demobilize opposition (as noted above), but to delegitimate otherwise powerful opponents. These appeals included the military end-running the White House and EPA on the range rule, the army end-running OMB clearance by going directly to supporters on the Hill for legislation on base expansion issues, and DoD attaching leasing proposals to 1997 defense appropriations bills over the objections of ENR committees.[15]

Relatedly, and complementing the statute shopping noted above under (de)mobilization strategies, was consistent forum shopping and sequencing among congressional committees. These were clear efforts to delegitimate the right of more adversarial environmental committees to make decisions affecting military operations. Recall how the services and their congressional allies repeatedly tried to take advantage of or work around congressional rules on committee referrals. They did so by routing their ENR proposals through friendlier defense authorization committees or by taking them directly to the floor of both chambers. In the process, they used defense authorization and appropriation acts to stymie vetoes by Clinton, and used the House Rules Committee to shut down floor debates on concessions to the military. The height of these tactics occurred during the George W. Bush years as the military pressed for broad-based (and later more selective) exemptions from ENR laws in the RRPI. However, committee shopping had a robust heritage from the Clinton years.

Finally, were these delegitimation tactics not enough, challenging the legitimacy of research that did not support the military's positions was de rigueur. Moreover, this was true even when these studies were done in-house. Challenged, for example, were the bona fides of the DSB when it supported Goodman's greening efforts; the quality, completeness, or timeliness of the data used in various state, NRC, or Congressional Budget Office studies; and the accuracy of data submitted by the states for DSMOA reimbursements. Similarly excoriated at various times by the services as redundant, precarious, or unrelated to their activities (and, hence, illegitimate for decision making) were data related to critical habitats, animal migratory patterns, and the effects of various pollutants (e.g., dioxins and perchlorate).

Deinstitutionalization

A fourth set of tactics in the repertoire of contestation for the military and its allies involved promoting or taking advantage of the diminished capacity of ENR staff and regulators to perform their roles. In this regard, several types of interrelated tactics helped complicate the greening of the U.S. military in the post–Cold War era. These included de-skilling, defunding, diversion, devolution, divesting, downsizing, and dependency creation. De-skilling and defunding often interacted to make greening difficult. This happened as cuts in funding also diminished the in-house expertise necessary to keep up with ENR demands on the armed forces.

As each of the chapters chronicles, on-and-off-again funding repeatedly sent mixed messages about the corporate priority to be given to greening. Illustrative is the army zeroing-out ITAM funding after years of growth, later partially reversing it, and then partly rescinding it again. This pattern had many sources, including the miscues of the services, claims on resources from military operations, Cold War–lite force structuring, portfolio management, administrative reform efforts by the Clinton administration, and conservative Republican dominance of Congress during the Clinton and Bush years.

Rationale aside, however, it is important to note that these de-skilling and defunding woes occurred inside the Pentagon and military services, among regulators, and within other organizations in the implementation structure required for greening the armed forces. Recall, for example, the fate of Goodman's civilian control initiatives within the Pentagon. In the end, Goodman's office was given responsibility for many of the training and development tasks she thought the services were not providing or rewarding adequately. Yet the responsibility structures for implementing key aspects of these tasks were left fragmented, complex, and assigned partially to units not known for supporting such efforts.

Moreover, even when given sufficient training, ENR professionals still were fighting strong headwinds when it came to defunding operations in the DoD, the military, and regulatory agencies. Indeed, a survey of service ENR professionals in the late 1990s found anywhere from one-third to two-thirds of respondents reporting insufficient funding, inadequate staffing, poor implementation of natural resource plans, lack of career consequences for base commanders for resource violations, and pressures from commanders to overlook or circumvent ENR laws.[16]

Nor was much done to offset severe funding and capacity liabilities among federal and state regulators that reduced the credibility of their enforcement tools. Illustrative of these dilemmas were delays in risk analyses for various pollutants due to funding and staffing shortfalls at the Agency for Toxic Substances and Disease Registry. So, too, were the services cutting back resources for DSMOA grants to the states for overseeing cleanups, as well as personnel shortfalls and backlogs at the FWS. As noted, for instance, listing backlogs at the FWS combined with court suits (actual and potential) to prod that agency into supporting the military's proposal to use INRM plans as equivalent to EISs for critical habitat designations.

In turn, diversion of resources often worked hand-in-glove with devolution of responsibilities and defunding to deinstitutionalize commitments to greening and to render progress halfway, halting, and patchwork. For example, the dynamics in several greening offensives led to counteroffensives masked (either intentionally or unintentionally) as best business practices management reforms (Clinton's NPR, his Fast-Track initiative, and Secretary of Defense Cohen's DRI). Curiously, however, the best business practices initiatives launched under the rubric of NPR and DRI repeatedly diminished the oversight capabilities of Goodman's office (and sometimes the OSD in general).

Recall, for example, her office's share of the Pentagon's downsizing of the OSD. These were positions dedicated to the advocacy of environmental restoration, conservation management, environmental research and development, environmental technology, and conventional weapons demilitarization. Referred to by researchers as "objective shifting," shifts in responsibility structures like these that are justified on technical management grounds (e.g., best business practices) have real policy aims. Intentionally or inadvertently, they sorely complicated the building of an enduring corporate sense of responsibility for a beyond-compliance ethic in the U.S. military by deinstitutionalizing OSD's control of these tasks.

Similarly justified was the movement of the ITAM program out of the army environment office and into the office of the deputy chief of staff for operations and plans. Although offered in terms of best business practices as a location better suited to integrate conservation with base installation management, the operations and plans office was a less hospitable location for ENR activities. Illustrative, too, was the downgrading of the pollution prevention program in position and funding after this move, despite its centrality to the C^3P^2 plus technology effort. Nor in this regard can one forget how the DRI was used to justify moving environmental functions from the OSD to the U.S. Army, how privatizing or competitive-sourcing occurred for functions previously carried out or overseen by civilian ENR workers in the services (e.g., BRAC and other cleanups), and how aggressively the services pushed for privatizing water, wastewater, natural gas, and electric utility provisions at U.S. military bases.

With regard to resource dependency, some organization theorists contend that behavior is a function of whoever controls the resources, with agencies responsive to those elements in their environments that afford them succor (primarily economic). Illustrative of how resource dependency can deinstitutionalize greening capacity was the leverage the military gained relative to state regulators by devolving DSMOA funding to the services. But so, too, was the leverage gained by greening proponents from the globalization of weaponry, joint war-fighting needs, and the international ENR standardization movement. These developments were the justification, after all, for many of John Deutch's, William Perry's, and Goodman's efforts in the pollution prevention area.

Disinformation

A final set of repertoires of contestation affecting all rule sets and witnessed repeatedly in prior chapters involved sleight of hand with data, resources, reports, and guidance documents. Most illustrative are the army's "creative accounting" propensities stemming from its "hold the fort" mentality. Recall also the military's shoddy record on reporting environmental liabilities, and the army withholding several years of its own internal evaluations of the explosivity of M55 rockets that would have made nonincineration options more attractive. Likewise illustrative was the army withholding information from the states regarding UXO contamination on FUDS.

Also notable was the tendency not to consider key aspects of training in EISs, including initially leaving out of environmental assessments the impacts of chaffing and noise on the ecology and on Native Americans. Likewise, consider the military's defiance as it ignored requests over a considerable period of time for data collection at FUDS, as well as its adherence to its problematic and widely criticized statistical sampling and windshield surveys of UXO-contaminated sites. From these, one moves on to instances of consciously distorting what the services knew and did. Disconcerting were instances of the army insisting that incineration was needed to meet 2007 CWC deadlines, when internal memos showed they knew meeting that deadline was impossible.

Illustrative, too, was the army claiming not to have resources sufficient to test six incineration alternatives, a claim debunked by the comptroller's office in an embarrassing audit. Even more broadly, however, a February 2001 Army Audit Agency report issued after Clinton left office chronicled how the service's incineration sites had made thousands of design changes that "ignored cost, schedule and *environmental impacts* and violated rules both inside and outside the military in order to keep the program going."[17]

The Theoretical Implications Question Revisited

As the preceding discussion suggests, what Sergio Fernandez and Hal Rainey call dialectical-conflict and policy diffusion models of organizational change culled largely from studies of private corporations powerfully capture the dynamics witnessed in this book. The chapters also show, however, that these perspectives will be wanting in explanatory power if they fail to incorporate aspects of other theoretical perspectives to understand large-scale organizational change in public organizations. To this end, the chapters suggest the utility of integrating insights from the work of public policy, organizational change, political science, public management, and comparative state-building scholars to build a more robust and empirically grounded polity-centered perspective on change in public organizations.

To be sure, the caveats associated with generalizing from case studies are well known and well founded. Moreover, some might view the military as unique, in the sense that the hierarchical nature of either civilian control of the military or service professionalism lacks counterparts in other public agencies. Leading scholars today, however, view civil–military control as in tatters during the Clinton years and under siege today as the Iraq insurgency continues.[18] Moreover, given the nascent state of theory building on large-scale organizational change in the public sector and on change in hybrid policy arenas like this one (with ENR and national security policy intersecting), a focus on large-scale change in any public organization should advance understanding.

The specifics of the polity-centered framework derived from this focus may only be appropriate for advancing midrange theory building on organizational change involving the military in the ENR policy arena. By hiking the specifics of the cases to conceptual levels, however, the framework also might serve as a general heuristic for studying organizational change in public organizations more broadly. As such, this framework is offered hoping that others will test, elaborate, and refine it in the national security and other policy domains.

For the reader's convenience, figure 11.1 extracts from the preceding analysis and presents visually the key concepts, transactional relationships, and logic of the polity-centered framework. In examining the figure and following the framework's logic below, keep several things in mind. First, the major components in the figure correspond to the specifics of the trajectory of contestation. Thus the "environment" / "environmental perturbation" box on the extreme left captures the concept of structural-historical mismatches, whereas the "outcomes" box on the far right captures the results of the contests over organizational change. The former summarizes the kinds of shocks that are associated with claims of mismatches, whereas the nature of the structural "consolidations" and change outcomes that result from the contests are summarized in the latter. Second, and in between, the "nested rule sets and repertoires of contestation" portray the elements (i.e., the targets and tactics) of the offensive, counteroffensive, and crisis of authority components of the trajectory of contestation. Third, the rules and repertoires listed in the boxes are not matched pairs; any repertoire can be used to contest any rule type. For example, disinformation tactics can be used to try to alter any type of rule to one's advantage.

Fourth, the elliptical dotted line surrounding the nested rule sets indicates that the decision calculi of the actors contesting rule sets can be informed by the interaction of three sets of factors related to organizational history, context, and contingency. Fifth, battles over rules, though nested and evoked in the name of structural-historical mismatches, do not always have to involve all three types of rule sets. Constitutional rule sets, for instance, need not always be contested, or operational rule sets may be the only contests involved. Sixth, neither perceptions of structural-historical mismatches nor crises of authority need originate at the highest levels of government; both can start, for example, with perceptions at the operational or collective choice levels.

Keeping this in mind, researchers should hypothesize that any large-scale change offensives launched in public agencies are likely to witness a consistent pattern of politics, one best appreciated as a trajectory or arc of contestation. Witnessed initially will be disagreement over what the implications of environmental shocks and minishocks are likely to be (i.e., perceptions of historical–structural mismatches), followed by reform offensives and counteroffensives which produce crises of authority that are resolvable only through bargaining and negotiation. These processes, however, are likely to leave consolidations of structures, processes, and procedures that are halfway, halting, and patchwork and that produce similarly uneven change results. In the process, these consolidations are less likely to resolve disputes as to institutionalize them in structures, thus setting the stage for the next round of reforms.

Within this general trajectory of contestation, researchers should hypothesize that in launching and pursuing their offensives, proponents are likely to rely on enacting, filtering, imposition, diffusion, and negotiation techniques. Importantly, opponents are also likely to use similar techniques in waging their counteroffensives to shape, prepare, and respond to these change offensives. In contemplating and pursuing these offensives and counteroffensives, the contestants also are likely to try making sense not only of the implications of the shocks and minishocks unleashed, but also of what to do about them.

In all this, and throughout the subsequent crises of authority produced and consolidations rendered, researchers should hypothesize that the decision calculi of all the contestants will be animated by considerations of history (or "time"), context (or "timing"), and contingency (or "time sensitivity"). Weighed from these will be the relative concerns, advantages, and disadvantages bequeathed to them, as well as to their opponents. Importantly, these calculations are likely to shift over time. This occurs as the actors weigh their relative strengths and weaknesses partially in terms of the issue status and constellation of power extant at any point in time. They then will calibrate whether and how aggressively to pursue, modify, or oppose change initiatives or to trade them off for other values (i.e., to engage in portfolio management).

Researchers should also hypothesize that these actions will produce crises of authority (as uncertainties over whose position is dispositive remains unclear).

These battles that will take place among proponents and opponents over particular rule sets that are levers for organizational change. More precisely, these contests are likely to be fought over three nested rule sets: constitutional, collective choice, and operational. In particular, researchers should hypothesize that these battles will focus on constitutional, legal, or statutory grounds for including or exempting them from activities related to change efforts (i.e., on entry and exit rules). Expected, too, should be contests over allocations of decision-making power, functional responsibilities, and official status to participate (i.e., over authority, scoping, and position rules in change decisions). No less contested, researchers should expect, will be information rules identifying information needed to inform or pursue change, who provides it, and who judges its accuracy and applicability; aggregation rules dealing with how decisions related to organizational change will be made; and payoff rules sorting out what benefits and costs will be incurred by whom for required, permitted, or prohibited activities related to the change effort.

In turn, researchers should hypothesize that the contestants—largely legislative, bureaucratic, interest group, and judicial actors—will use a host of political, organizational, and legal tactics (i.e., various repertoires of contestation) to either promote or resist changes in these rule sets. Opponents, for example, are likely to pursue strategies aimed at challenging and reducing the legitimacy or bona fides of change agents (i.e., to use delegitimation strategies). Included among such tactics are invoking sovereign immunity claims, end-running unsympathetic executive and congressional sovereigns, and avoiding precedent-setting change decisions that might limit their options or otherwise disadvantage them in the future. Also hypothesized should be strategies designed to advance opponents' positions by framing change issues to their advantage (i.e., by pursuing issue definition or reframing tactics) and by expanding or contracting the type, content, and scope of information available for making change-fostering decisions (i.e., by pursuing information or disinformation strategies). The latter strategy includes shoddy guidance on change-related implementation actions, deliberate manipulation of information, funding sleights of hand, and unresponsiveness to calls for data.

Researchers should also hypothesize that these strategies will be complemented by others designed to mobilize or demobilize support or opposition for aspects of the large-scale change being pursued (i.e., by mobilization of allies and demobilization of opponents). These tactics are likely to include contesting which of a variety of statutes might affect the change effort positively or negatively (i.e., by statute or committee shopping); altering the assumptions and appropriate metes and bounds of studies to add or reduce opposition to change (i.e., by boundary [de]activation); pursuing or taking advantage of shifts in issue salience, valence, boundary effects, and timing constraints that can affect change; and seeking to privatize controversial activities that change opponents wish to avoid (i.e., by using load-shedding tactics).

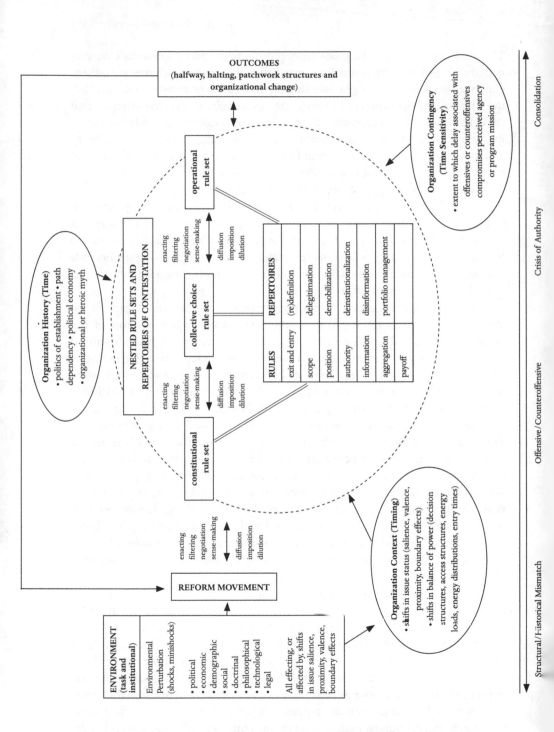

Figure 11.1 A Polity-Centered Conceptual Framework

Finally, researchers should hypothesize that opponents of large-scale organizational change will pursue a persistent strategy to reduce the institutional capacity of change proponents to advance their agenda (i.e., to employ deinstitutionalization strategies). Among the tactics pursued in using this strategy will be seizing upon resource shortages to increase dependence on opponents (i.e., to create resource dependency). Likely prominent, too, will be tactics to downsize and cut resources from those pursuing organizational change (i.e., to de-skill, downsize, and defund them); to use broader administrative reform initiatives to thwart changes (i.e., to engage in objective shifting and devolution tactics); and to leverage statutory or administrative deadlines by withholding information needed to advance or operationalize large-scale organizational change (i.e., to pursue delaying tactics).

Researchers should also hypothesize that all this is likely to bring, first, confusion over what rules are dispositive (i.e., to create crises of authority), and then, bargaining over what ultimately will become compromises over structures, processes, and procedures critical to the change effort. They also should expect that the bargaining processes involved are likely to be circular (i.e., resolutions become the fodder for future contestation that begins almost immediately) and pursued in a variety of arenas (legislative, executive, and judicial) within and across the Madisonian system. And again, bargaining postures are likely to shift with changes in issue valence, salience, proximity, and boundary effects and their impacts on decision structures, access structures, energy loads, and energy distributions.

Ultimately, researchers should expect bargaining to produce a consolidation of administrative, responsibility, and accounting structures that satisfies none of the combatants. More precisely, crises of authority are likely to leave fragmented structures, processes, and procedures in their wake—entities open to interpretation, future exploitation by change opponents within and outside the organization, and future conflict. All this in turn is likely to mean that although progress typically will be made toward large-scale change, it is likely to be uneven, staggered, and iterative. Moreover, future progress is likely to remain vulnerable to changes in the political environment, because large-scale change has not been sufficiently internalized in the minds of organizational leaders or institutionalized in administrative structures, policies, and procedures.

The Practical and Normative Implications Questions Revisited

What do the patterns of politics witnessed in this book suggest about how well institutionalized a beyond-compliance ENR corporate ethic has become in the armed forces? The progress, strategies, and tactics exhibited by the military and its allies offer mixed support for the expectations offered by James Q. Wilson and Patricia Rachal in their seminal work nearly three decades ago. In contrast to their thesis, significant progress in greening the U.S. military has been made in the post–Cold War era. This is the case at least in regard to comparable performance levels with the private sector in all areas except cleanups. But consistent with Wilson and Rachal's thesis, that progress has been uneven, largely reactive to external pressures, and fraught with resistance to greening on anything but the military's terms.

Like any organization, the military services have tried to buffer their core operations from environmental turbulence and to preserve as much relative autonomy as possible for themselves throughout the post–Cold War era. Lost in the process is a sufficient alignment of structures with strategy, alignment that is central to any hope of institutionalizing a beyond-compliance ethic in any organization. Gained, as a consequence, have been halting and patchwork structures and outcomes that serve as continuing platforms for challenging rather than institutionalizing greening. As Dan Henk also noted recently:

> The U.S. military has little comprehensive or sustained environmental focus. It tends to defer substantive concern for environmental issues to a handful of civilian experts and to its engineers, preeminently the US Army Corps of Engineers. . . . The environmental content in the education of most military officers is very limited—so limited that it does not exert much influence on the organizational culture. None of the staff colleges or war colleges offers substantial instruction examining the connections between the environment and security. . . . [Meanwhile] the Office of the Deputy Under Secretary of Defense for Installations and Environment [has a] lack of numbers and obscure placement . . . [and its] environmentalists [are] capable and committed, but [do] not appear in 2005 to have much visibility or impact among the senior officials in the department [of defense].[19]

As a consequence, strong, persistent, external pressures from green proponents on Capitol Hill, in state regulatory agencies, and among national and grassroots ENR groups will continue to be necessary. Otherwise, "taken for granted" mental models or schema that view a beyond-compliance ethic as central to protecting national security will be elusive.

This is not to suggest that inevitable challenges by the Pentagon and the military are necessarily flawed in their substance. But it does beg the question of whether "comparable performance" and patterns of contestation mimicking private sector polluters are sufficient for a public sector organization. The answer to this question is hardly as straightforward as it seems. Witnessed throughout this book, for example, are the virtues some associate with battles over intragovernmental regulation.[20] First, the challenges of federal agencies—because they are so controversial and noteworthy—can bring the sustained attention of elected officials to bear on the unanticipated consequences of public policies. Second, challenges can provide elected, not just appointed, officials and an aroused public an opportunity to adjust, and perhaps even to reconcile, conflicting policy goals in light of implementation experience. Finally, because no one bureaucracy has a monopoly on virtue or wisdom, challenges can correct any technical, legal, or judgmental errors made by implementers in applying policies to target populations. Moreover, given a legislative process ill-suited to a priori consideration of policy interaction, they are sometimes essential.[21]

Weigh how apt this claim is in terms of the plight of base commanders facing, as noted in chapter 2, nearly twenty federal and international environmental statutes, with approximately ten thousand pages of regulations, and with each spawning pages of state and/or local regulations that are oftentimes inconsistent. Navigating these legal minefields, discerning how to reconcile their competing premises, and integrating on the ground their diverse means and ends in ways never contemplated by lawmakers suggest that no one actor or set of actors has an automatic lock on the truth in ENR regulatory disputes.

Thus simplistic assumptions that resistance to particular greening initiatives is inherently bad or good are inappropriate criteria for evaluation. More appropriate and useful in assessing initiatives like the ones in this book are *process* criteria. That is, absent clear-cut, willful, and substantial violations of ENR laws or indifference to redressing them (some of which have been chronicled in this book), the key criterion in this regard is *the extent to which the actors involved exhibit behavior that either advances or hinders a full, transparent, probative, participatory, data-driven, and results-based deliberative process regarding the issues involved.*[22] Thus when Goodman's successor, Raymond DuBois, asks (see chapter 10), "Shouldn't we [the Pentagon and the military], as stewards of the taxpayers' money, decide how we're going to clean up [contaminated sites]?" the legal and process answers to that question are a resounding "no."[23]

Only federal and state ENR regulatory agencies have the authority to make these final decisions, with or without input from regulatory targets. On this basis, the persistent pattern of the military's attitudes, strategies, and tactics in the post–Cold War era indicates that a fully institutionalized commitment to these deliberative values is nowhere near as strong as citizens expect from representatives of their government. In a democratic republic, the military's behavior must at a minimum be better on the process values noted above, because public health, safety, and environmental protection can hang in the balance. Moreover, to the extent that the capacity of the services to pursue these values suffers from political forces beyond the military's control (as they do, for example, when billions of dollars in congressional earmarks for nondefense purposes take money away from readiness concerns), opprobrium goes beyond the services to Congress and the White House.

Be this as it may, the patterns of politics chronicled in this book also suggest that proponents of furthering a corporate sense of responsibility for ENR protection that encompasses these values have their work cut out for them. This will be the case even when presidents and congresses are sympathetic to greening and budget surpluses loom. The power of ideas *do* matter. However, the specifics of those ideas will always be filtered through the lenses of the political, organizational, and personal prerogatives of those affected by them. Constraints on budgets during the War on Terror will proceed apace, as will the military's cultural predilection for strategic pluralism. Undiminished also will be the appetites of members of Congress to protect existing succor in their districts, as well as the predisposition of the military to engage in zero-sum issue framing and to control the substance, scope, and pace of whatever greening does take place. Consequently, greening proponents must assume that they will have to labor tirelessly, strategically, and astutely for years to come amid the trajectory, motivations, strategies, tactics, and contingencies of contestation identified in this book.

As They Were?

All of which leads back to where this book began: Red Square in Moscow. Fourteen years after Mathias Rust flew his Cessna airplane into Red Square, and ten years after the end of communist rule, only a sparsely attended rally of approximately one hundred people "celebrated" the anniversary of the fall of the Soviet empire. Almost surreally, an absent President Vladimir Putin issued a statement congratulating President Bill Clinton on his birthday but said nothing about the tenth anniversary of freedom from communist rule. "One type of non-freedom was replaced by another type of non-freedom," sighed Joseph Laskavy, a pathologist present that day in Red Square. "This is not the freedom I dreamed of," said Laskavy. "Our tragedy is that we don't choose between good and bad. We always have to take the least stinking of all the goats."[24] Such a stark choice is certainly not the case when it comes to national defense and ENR protection in the United States. Large-scale multinational corporations *have* learned from their past and have moved toward a profitable, stable, and predictable future that mitigates or eliminates old ways and incorporates greener ones. So, too, can the U.S. military, as its uneven progress to date suggests. But even if it wanted to, the military no longer can live "a world apart" from ENR laws and still protect national security. "Keeping thine honor bright" in the post–Cold War era will require no less of the U.S. military. Neither, however, can ENR regulators and environmental activists live "a world apart" from defense needs, lest national security be put at risk in the process. Ours cannot be a world of civil–military relations in which the choice is between ENR regulatory truculence or military intransigence; neither is it a prudent option in the post–September 11 era. Precisely how far, fast, and functionally this alignment of ENR and national security goals can occur is unclear, fraught with peril for national defense and environmental protection, and worthy of monitoring if not engagement by all concerned.

Notes

1. Rex Warner, trans., *Plutarch: Fall of the Roman Republic* (New York: Penguin Classics, 1972), 45.

2. Sergio Fernandez and Hal G. Rainey, "Managing Successful Organizational Change in the Public Sector: An Agenda for Research and Practice," *Public Administration Review* 66, no. 2 (2006): 168–76.

3. Stephen Skowronek, *Building a New American State: The Expansion of National Administrative Capacities, 1877–1920* (Cambridge: Cambridge University Press, 1982).

4. Thomas P.M. Barnett, *The Pentagon's New Map: War and Peace in the Twenty-First Century* (New York: G. P. Putnam's Sons, 2004).

5. George A. Krause, *A Two-Way Street: The Institutional Dynamics of the Modern Administrative State* (Pittsburgh: University of Pittsburgh Press, 1999); George A. Krause and Kenneth J. Meier, *Politics, Policy, and Organizations: Frontiers in the Scientific Study of Bureaucracy* (Ann Arbor: University of Michigan Press, 2003). For a more in-depth treatment of this finding and its implications for rational choice institutionalism, see Robert F. Durant, "Agency Evolution, New Institutionalism, and 'Hybrid' Policy Domains: Lessons from the "Greening" of the U.S. Military," *Policy Studies Journal* 34, no. 4 (2006): 469–90.

6. Andrew H. Van de Ven and Marshall S. Poole, "Explaining Development and Change in Organizations," *Academy of Management Review* 20 (1995): 510–40.

7. GAO, *High-Risk Series: An Update*, GAO-05-207, January 1 (Washington, DC: GAO, 2005), 2.

8. Michael D. Cohen, James G. March, and Johan P. Olsen, "A Garbage Can Model of Organizational Choice," *Administrative Science Quarterly* 17 (1972): 1–25.

9. Elinor Ostrom, "Institutional Rational Choice: An Assessment of the Institutional Analysis and Development Framework," in *Theories of the Policy Process*, ed. Paul A. Sabatier (Boulder, CO: Westview Press, 1999), 50.

10. Ibid., 59.

11. "Environmental Concerns at Heart of Acquisition Reform, DoD Says," *DEA* 2, no. 9 (May 4, 1994): 8.

12. See, for instance, John Clarke and Janet Newman, *The Managerial State: Power, Politics and Ideology in the Remaking of Social Welfare* (Thousand Oaks, CA: Sage, 1997).

13. "Navy Defends Position on Environmental Assessments Against IG Attacks," *DEA* 2, no. 8 (April 20, 1994): 18.

14. Eugene Bardach, *The Implementation Game* (Cambridge, MA: MIT Press, 1977).

15. Michael A. West, "Editor's Corner," *Federal Facilities Environmental Journal* 7, no. 3 (1996): 2. No fewer than twenty-eight federal facility provisions relating to the environment were incorporated in the National Defense Authorization Act of 1997 alone. Of these, eleven of the thirteen provisions proposed by the services in their "omnibus legislative package" found their way into that legislation, ten without any significant modifications. Moreover, twelve of the twenty-eight provisions changed laws that were in the primary jurisdiction of congressional committees other than defense oversight committee allies.

16. Public Employees for Environmental Responsibility, "Survey of Refuge Managers of the National Wildlife Refuge System, 1999, http://www.peer.org/pubs/surveys/1999_nwr_refugemgr.pdf (June 11, 2000).

17. CWWG, "Army Audit Agency Blasts Incineration Program: Managers Ignored Cost, Schedule and Environmental Compliance Rules in Thousands of Design Changes at Burn Sites," http://www.cwwg.org/pr_06.07.01audit.html (June 7, 2001); emphasis added.

18. Peter D. Feaver, *Armed Servants: Agency, Oversight, and Civil-Military Relations* (Cambridge: Harvard University Press, 2003), 2.

19. Dan Henk, "The Environment, the US Military, and Southern Africa," *Parameters: U.S. Army War College Quarterly* (Summer 2006): 102.

20. Robert F. Durant, *When Government Regulates Itself: EPA, TVA, and Pollution Control in the 1970s* (Knoxville: University of Tennessee Press, 1985), 144–45.

21. Ibid.

22. By substantial violations, I exclude technical violations (e.g., incomplete or late reporting) that are not threatening to public health, safety, or life.

23. Peter Eisler, "Pollution Cleanups Pit Pentagon Against Regulators," *USA Today*, October 14, 2004, www.usatoday.com/news/nation, 5 (April 22, 2006).

24. Peter Baker and Susan B. Glasser, "Little Cheer on Russian Anniversary: Quiet Remembrance of Communism's Collapse Underscores Changed Climate," *Washington Post*, August 20, 2001, p. A10.

Index